Contents

Le Chevalier d'Eon, Volume 4....1

Translation Notes....192

Preview of *Le Chevalier d'Eon*, Volume 5....196

Le Chevalier d'Eon

Volume 4

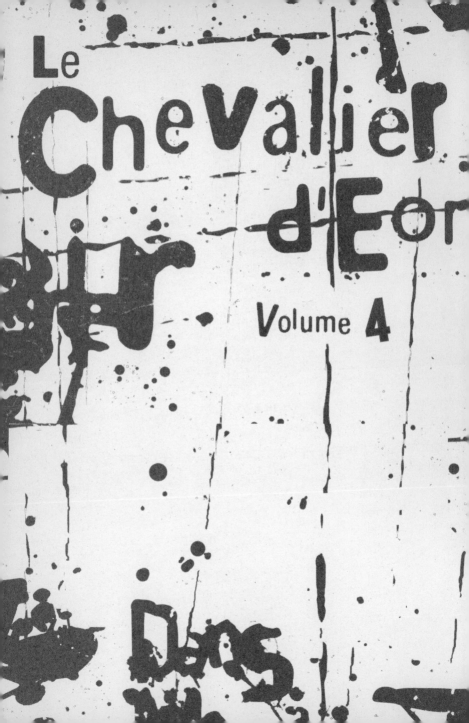

TABLE DES MATIÈRES
TABLE OF CONTENTS

CHAPTER 18
THE CIRCULAR POEMS
4

CHAPTER 19
THE DISCLOSED PATH
43

CHAPTER 20
THE BROKEN CIRCLE
73

CHAPTER 21
LAMEMAL
115

CHAPTER 22
TWITTER
145

CHAPTER 23
ELEANOR
175

Le Chevalier D'Eon

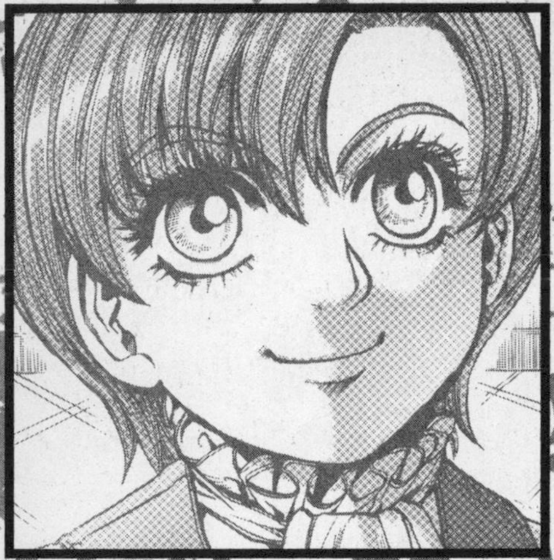

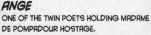

SUMMARY OF VOLUME 3

AT HER WIT'S END REGARDING SOPHIE'S CONDITION, MADAME DE POMPADOUR INVITES THE INFAMOUS ALCHEMIST COMTE SAINT-GERMAIN TO VERSAILLES. WANTING TO SEE THE COMTE AS SOON AS POSSIBLE, MADAME TRAVELS TO PARIS, ONLY TO BE KIDNAPPED BY TWIN POETS, EMMA AND ANGE. MADAME DE POMPADOUR IS BEING HELD HOSTAGE AT THE LOUVRE PALACE WHILE THE TWINS DEMAND SOPHIE IN EXCHANGE FOR HER MOTHER. D'EON RECEIVED AN ORDER FROM KING LOUIS TO RESCUE MADAME BEFORE SUNRISE...

Introduction of Characters

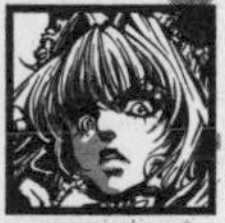

SPHINX (LIA)

WHEN LIA DESCENDS INTO HER BROTHER'S BODY, SHE BECOMES THE CHEVALIER, HUNTER OF MURDEROUS POETS.

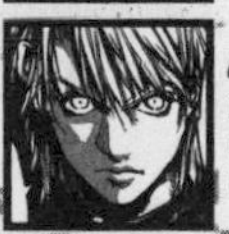

D'EON

HE'S A MEMBER OF KING LOUIS'S SECRET POLICE (KNOWN AS LE SECRET DU ROI) AND AN OFFICER FOR THE PARIS POLICE.

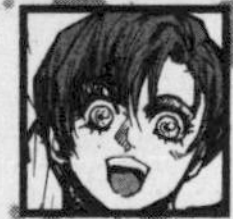

ROBIN

D'EON'S LOYAL ATTENDANT, ROBIN'S VERY BLUNT AND SHOWERS HIS MASTER WITH TOUGH LOVE AND SARCASM.

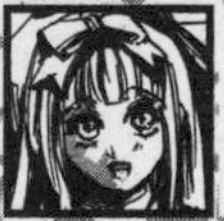

SOPHIE

SHE'S THE DAUGHTER OF KING LOUIS XV. THE VERSES OF THE PSALMS MYSTERIOUSLY APPEAR ON HER BODY, AND HER VOCABULARY HAS BEEN REDUCED TO A SINGLE WORD, "PALM."

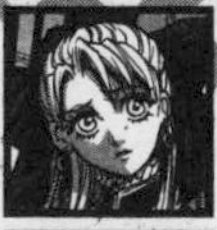

MADAME DE POMPADOUR

LOUIS XV'S PARAMOUR AND SOPHIE'S MOTHER. SHE'S AN INFLUENTIAL POLITICAL FIGURE.

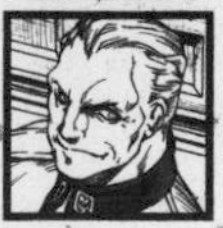

DOUGLAS

MEMBER OF THE SECRET POLICE. HE BATTLES THE POETS WITH A HOLY LANCE BLESSED BY THE POPE. HOWEVER, HE'S NOT A POET.

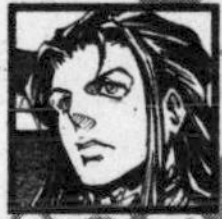

LOUIS XV

GRANDSON OF LOUIS XIV, ALSO KNOWN AS THE SUN KING. HE BELIEVES IN ABSOLUTE MONARCHY AND RULES ACCORDINGLY DURING HIS REIGN.

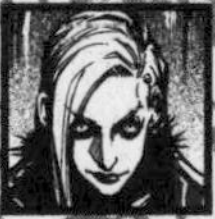

JEAN LE ROND D'ALEMBERT

A SECRET POLICE OFFICER, ALSO KNOWN AS NOSTRADAMUS III.

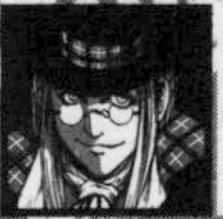

COMTE SAINT-GERMAIN

A MYSTERIOUS FIGURE WITH MUCH INFORMATION ABOUT THE DEADLY POETS. CLAIMS TO BE AN ALCHEMIST WHO HAS LIVED FOR A THOUSAND YEARS.

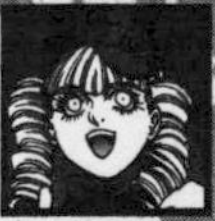

EMMA

ONE OF THE TWIN POETS HOLDING MADAME DE POMPADOUR HOSTAGE.

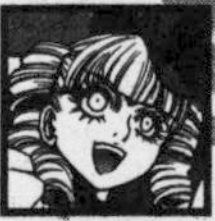

ANGE

ONE OF THE TWIN POETS HOLDING MADAME DE POMPADOUR HOSTAGE.

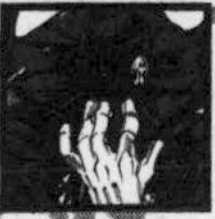

ROBLE

A MYSTERIOUS FIGURE WHO SERVES AS THE SHADOW AND MENTOR OF POETS.

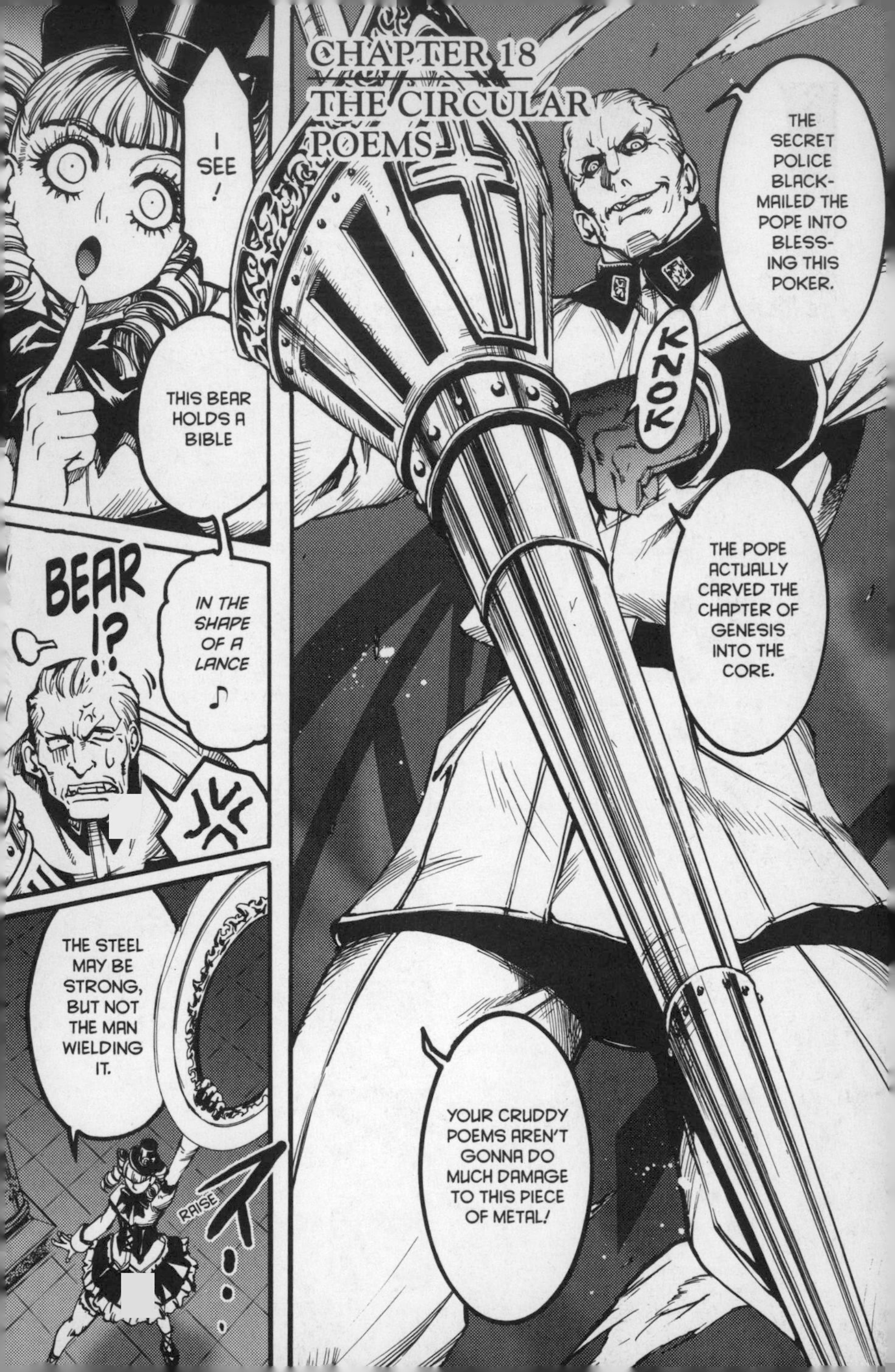
CHAPTER 18
THE CIRCULAR POEMS
THE SECRET POLICE BLACK-MAILED THE POPE INTO BLESS-ING THIS POKER.
KNOK
THE POPE ACTUALLY CARVED THE CHAPTER OF GENESIS INTO THE CORE.
YOUR CRUDDY POEMS AREN'T GONNA DO MUCH DAMAGE TO THIS PIECE OF METAL!
I SEE!
THIS BEAR HOLDS A BIBLE
IN THE SHAPE OF A LANCE ♪
BEAR!?
THE STEEL MAY BE STRONG, BUT NOT THE MAN WIELDING IT.
RAISE
...

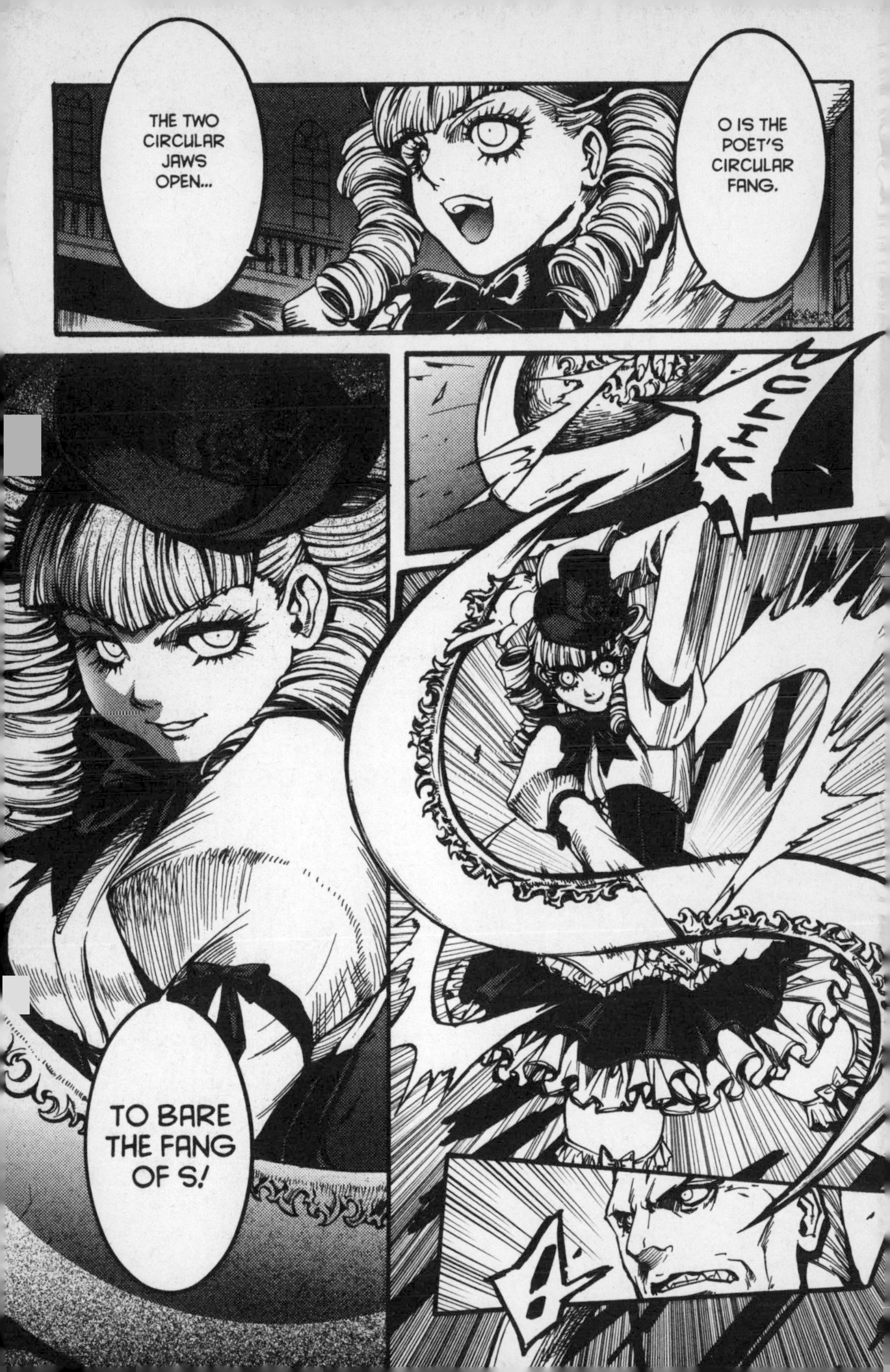

O IS THE POET'S CIRCULAR FANG.
THE TWO CIRCULAR JAWS OPEN...
SCLIK
!
TO BARE THE FANG OF S!

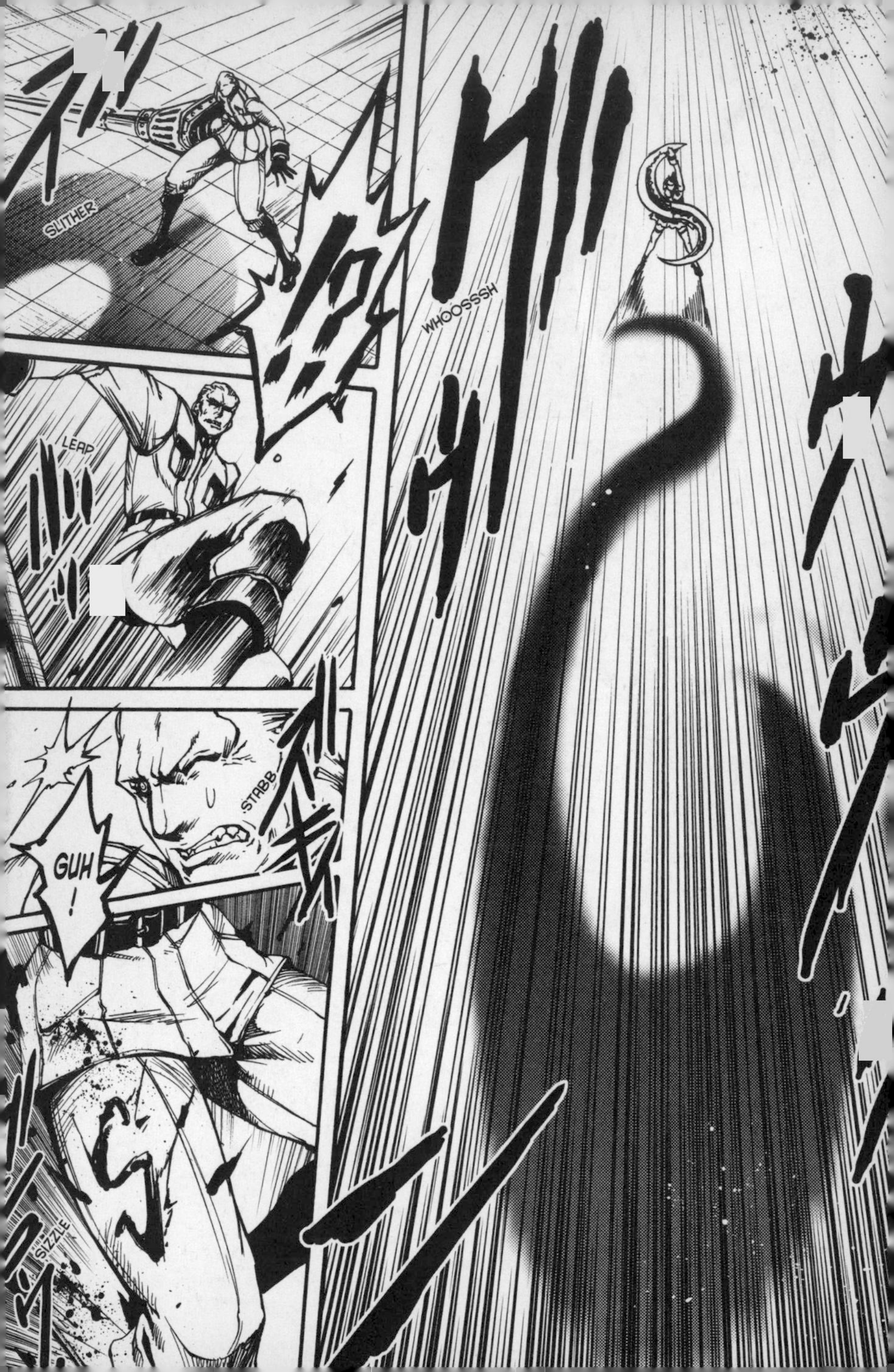
WHOOSSSH
SLITHER
LEAP
STABB
GUH!
SIZZLE

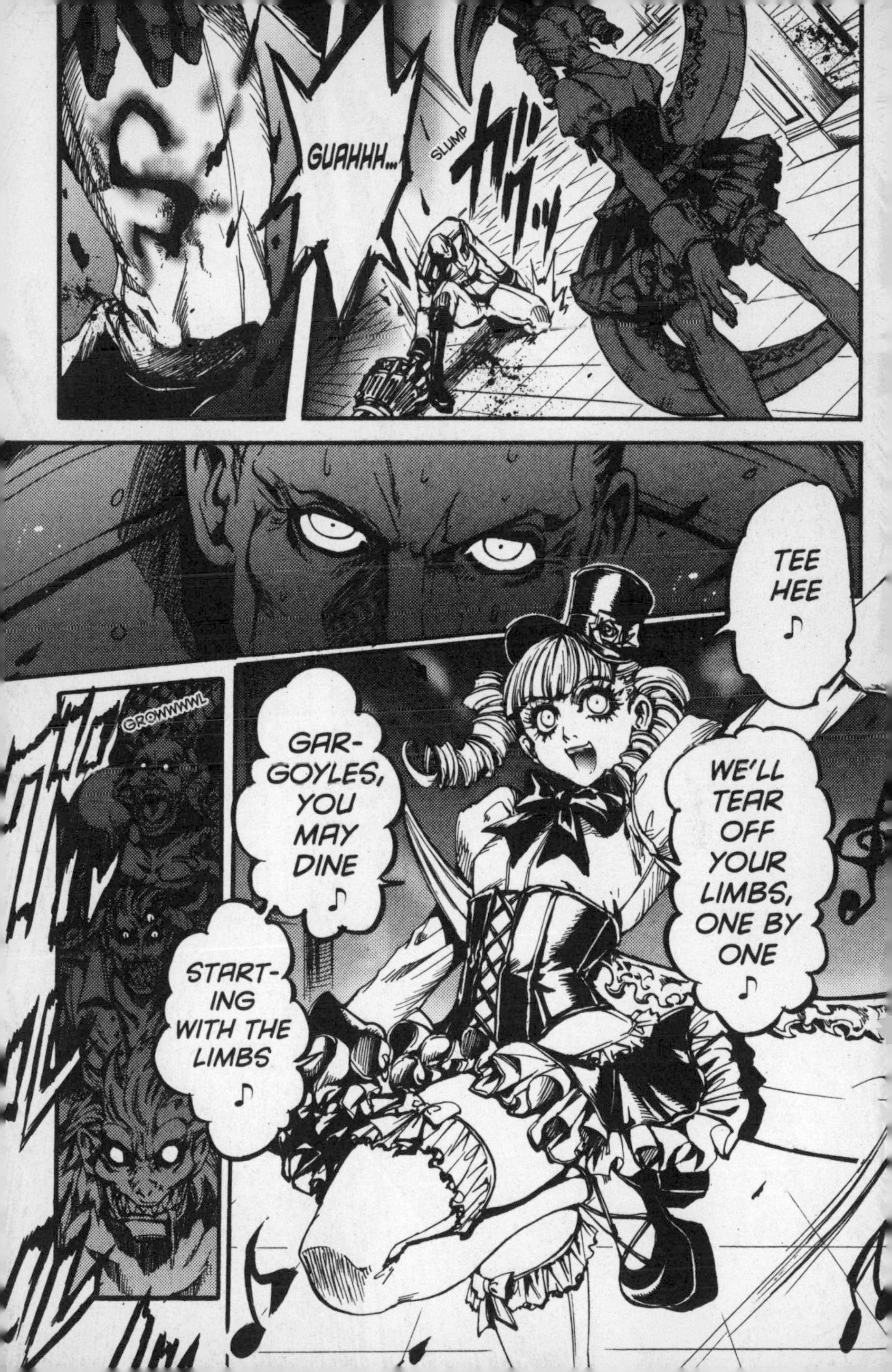
SLUMP
GUAHHH...
TEE HEE ♪
WE'LL TEAR OFF YOUR LIMBS, ONE BY ONE ♪
GAR-GOYLES, YOU MAY DINE ♪
START-ING WITH THE LIMBS ♪
GROWWWWL

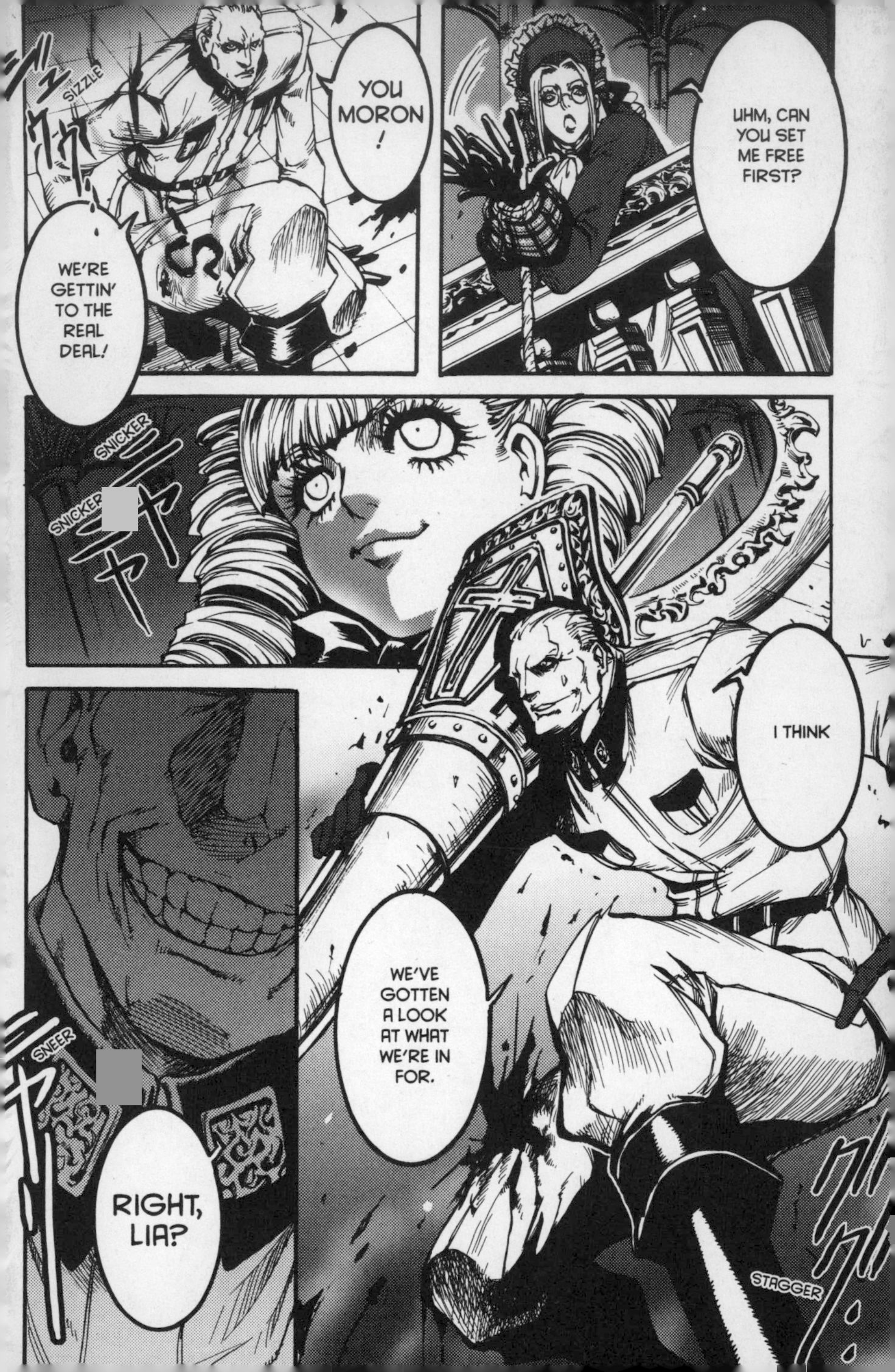
UHM, CAN YOU SET ME FREE FIRST?
SIZZLE
YOU MORON!
WE'RE GETTIN' TO THE REAL DEAL!
SNICKER
SNICKER
I THINK
WE'VE GOTTEN A LOOK AT WHAT WE'RE IN FOR.
STAGGER
SNEER
RIGHT, LIA?

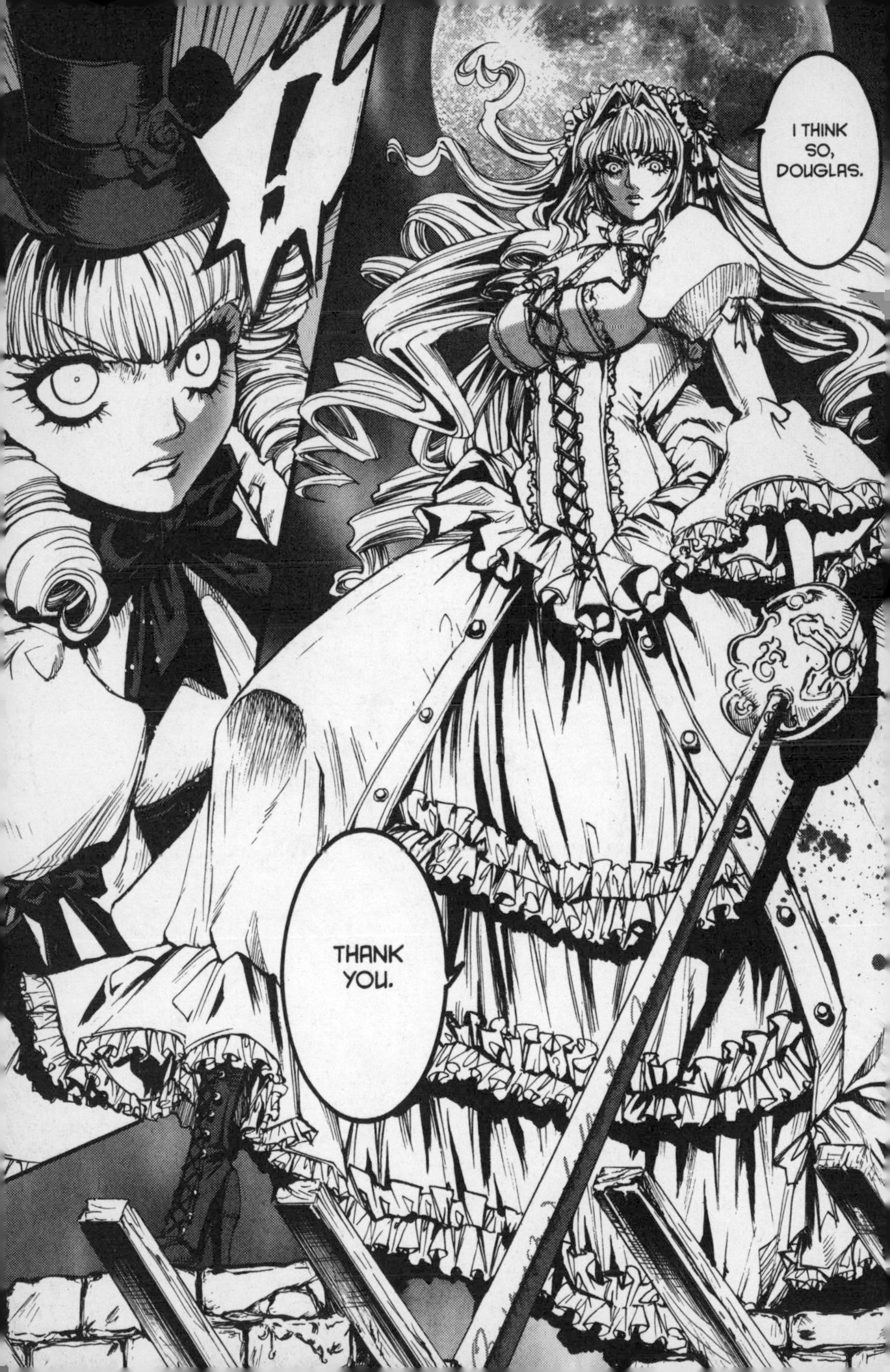
I THINK SO, DOUGLAS.
!
THANK YOU.

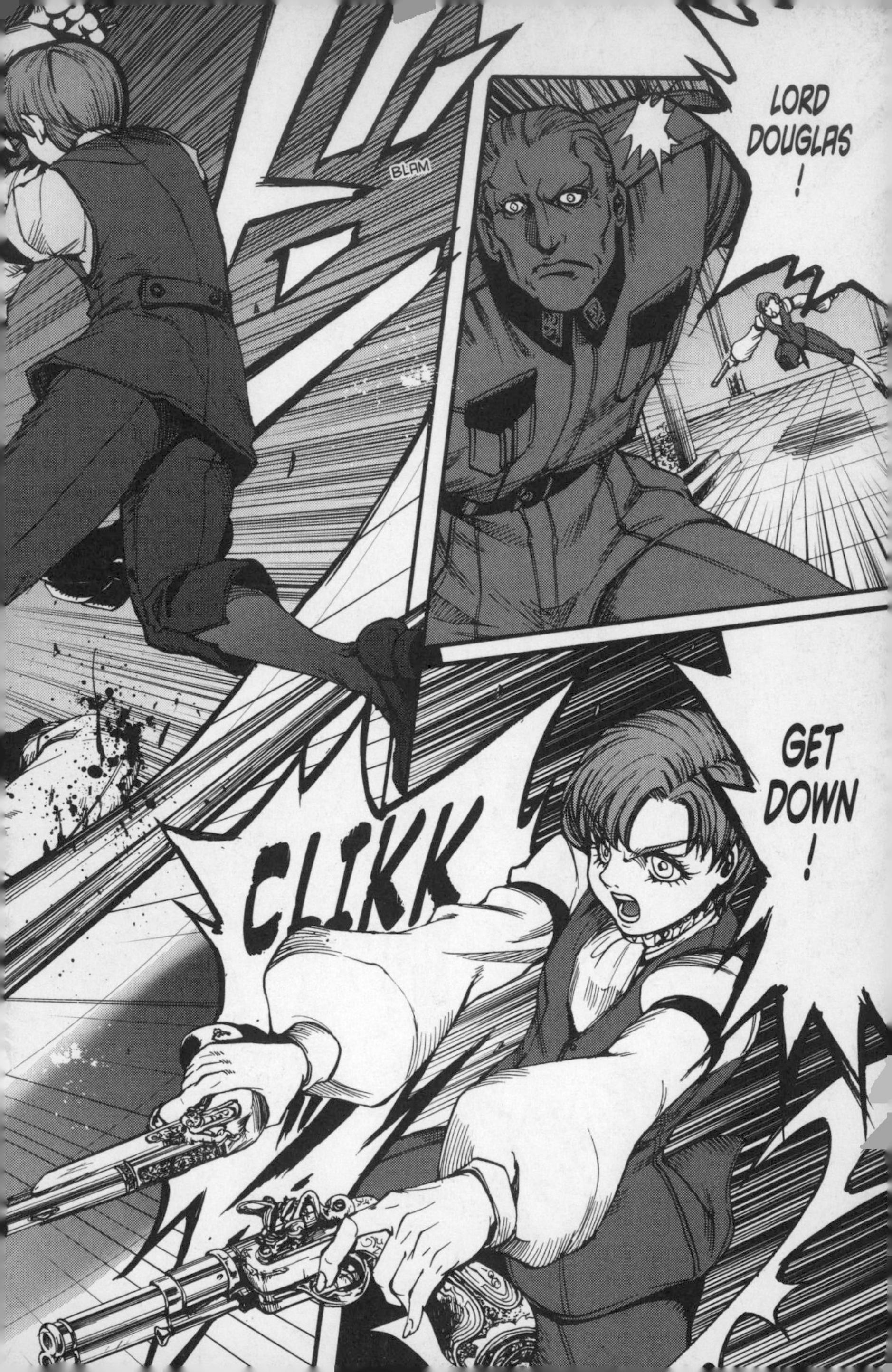
LORD DOUGLAS !
BLAM
GET DOWN !
CLIKK

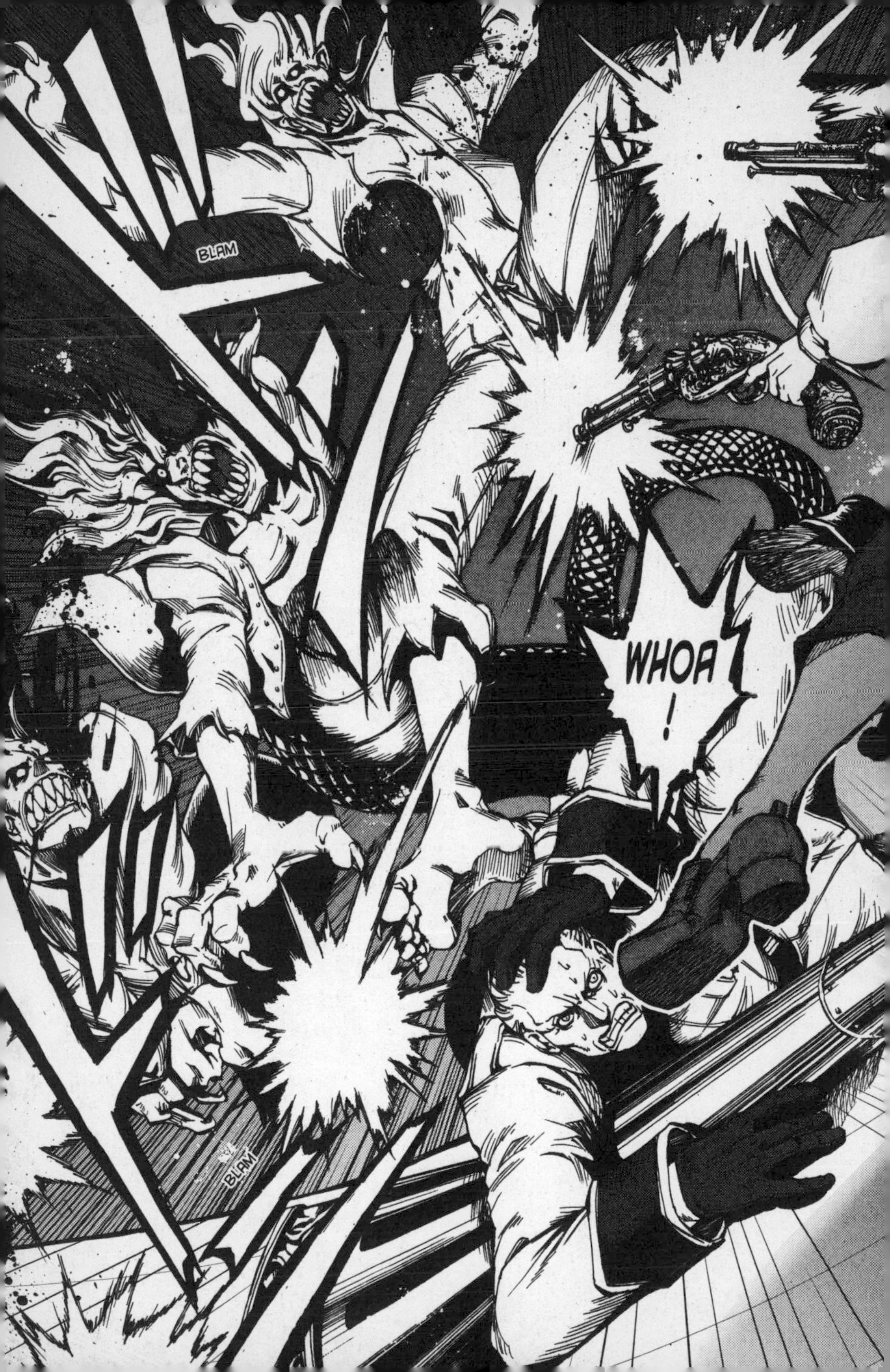
BLAM
WHOA !
BLAM

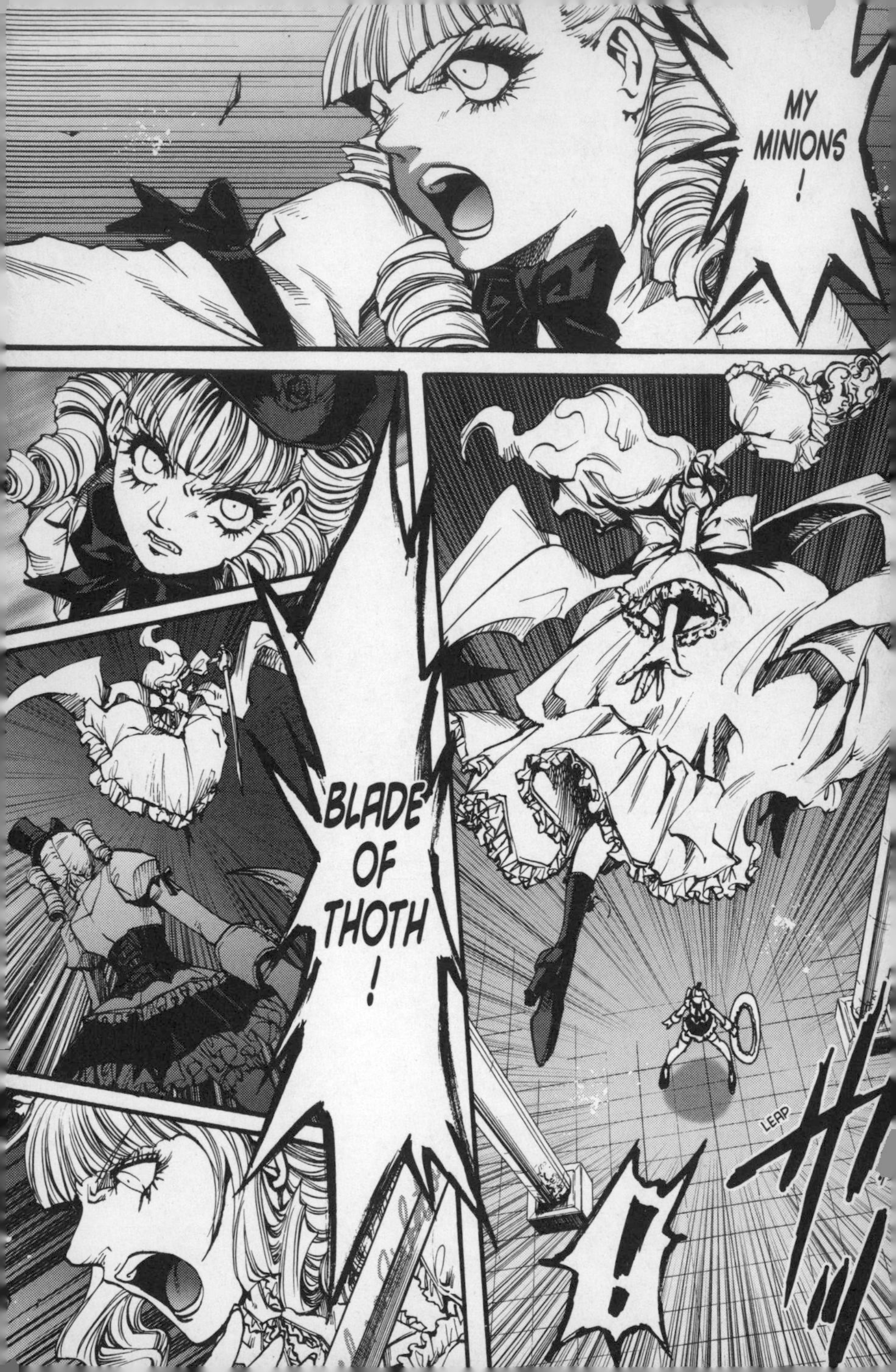
MY MINIONS!
BLADE OF THOTH!
LEAP
!

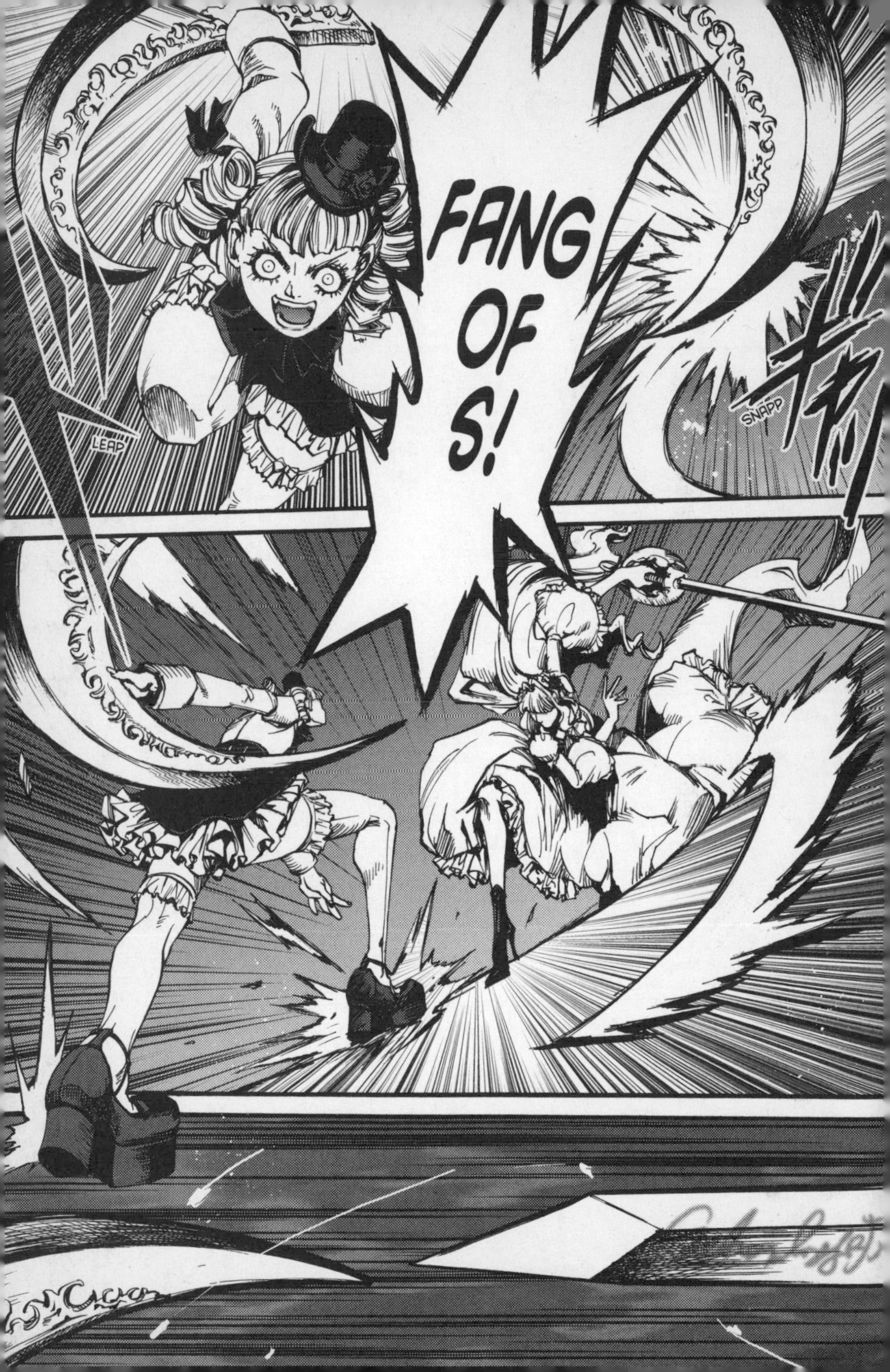
FANG OF S!
SNAPP
LEAP

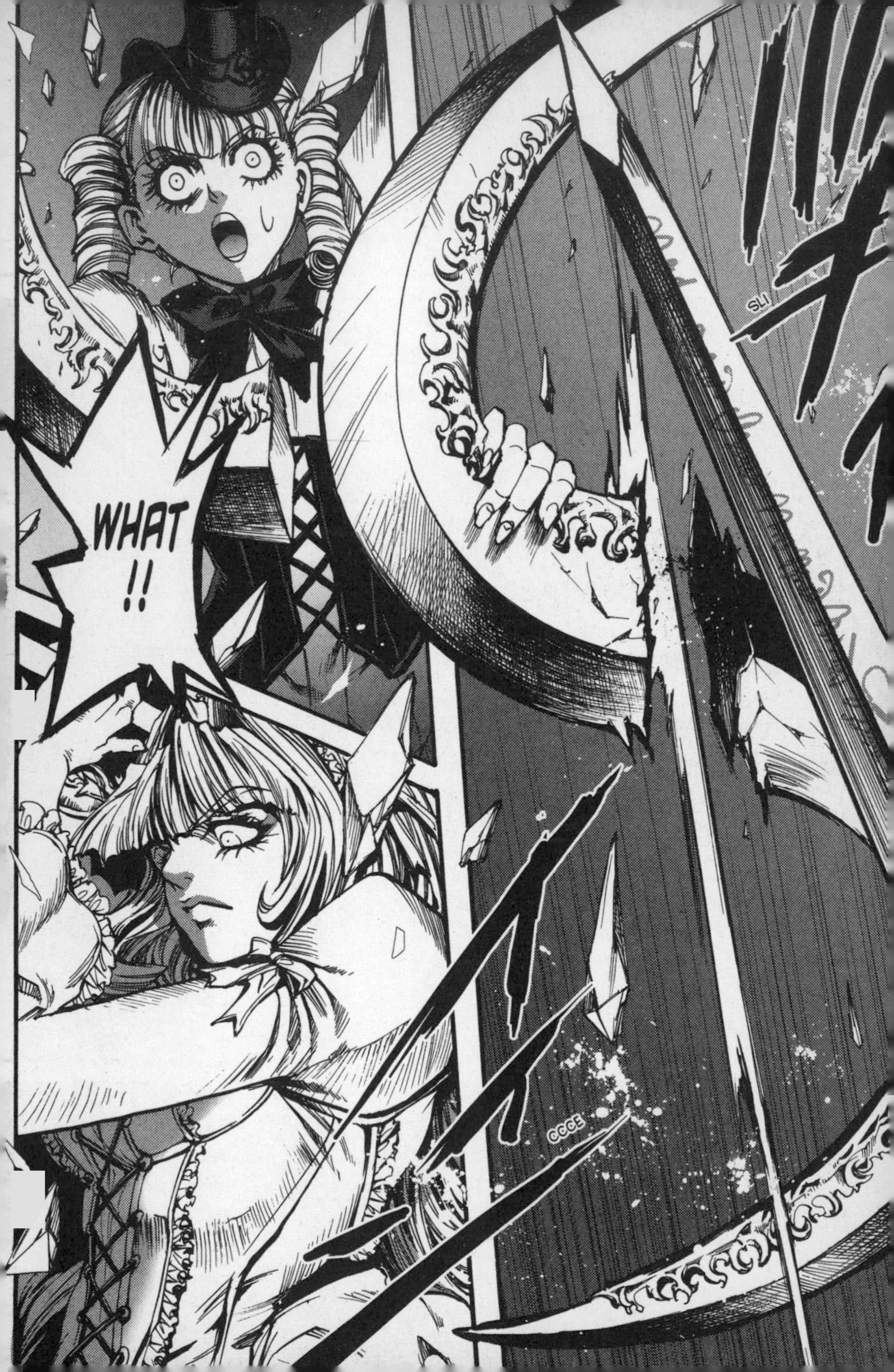
SLI
WHAT !!
CCCE

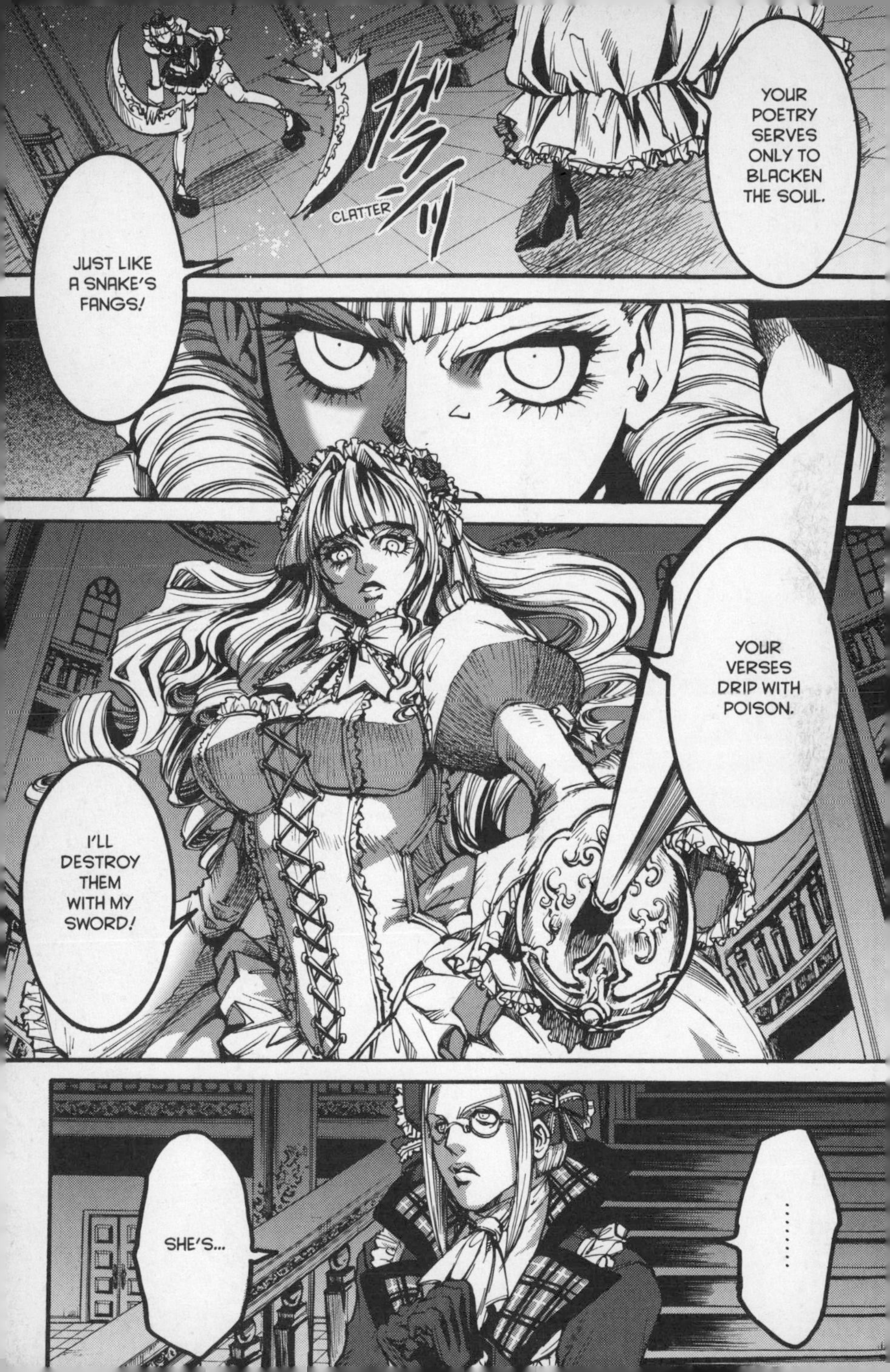
YOUR POETRY SERVES ONLY TO BLACKEN THE SOUL.
CLATTER
JUST LIKE A SNAKE'S FANGS!
YOUR VERSES DRIP WITH POISON.
I'LL DESTROY THEM WITH MY SWORD!
......
SHE'S...

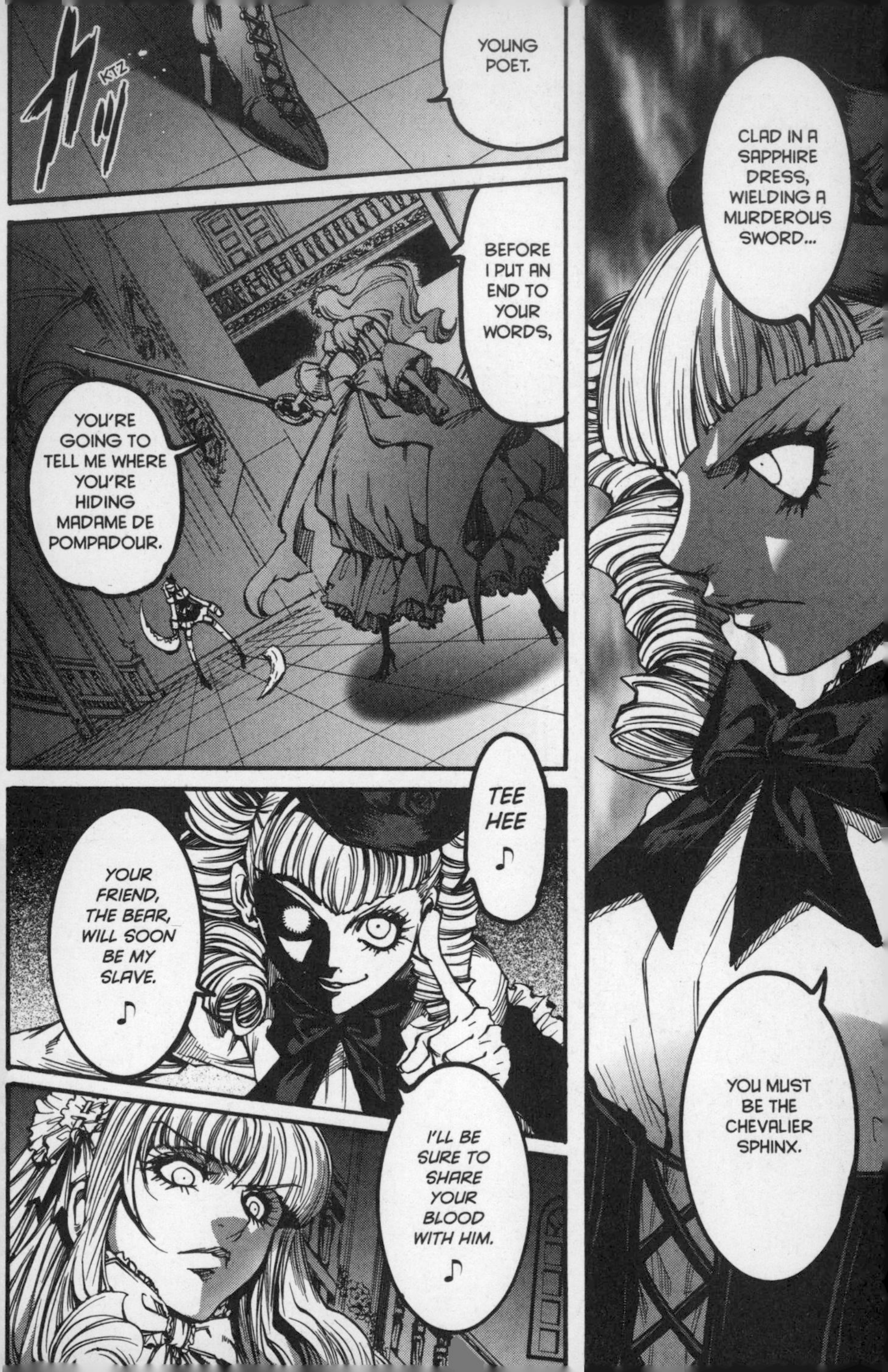

CLAD IN A SAPPHIRE DRESS, WIELDING A MURDEROUS SWORD...
YOU MUST BE THE CHEVALIER SPHINX.
KTZ
YOUNG POET.
BEFORE I PUT AN END TO YOUR WORDS,
YOU'RE GOING TO TELL ME WHERE YOU'RE HIDING MADAME DE POMPADOUR.
TEE HEE ♪
YOUR FRIEND, THE BEAR, WILL SOON BE MY SLAVE. ♪
I'LL BE SURE TO SHARE YOUR BLOOD WITH HIM. ♪

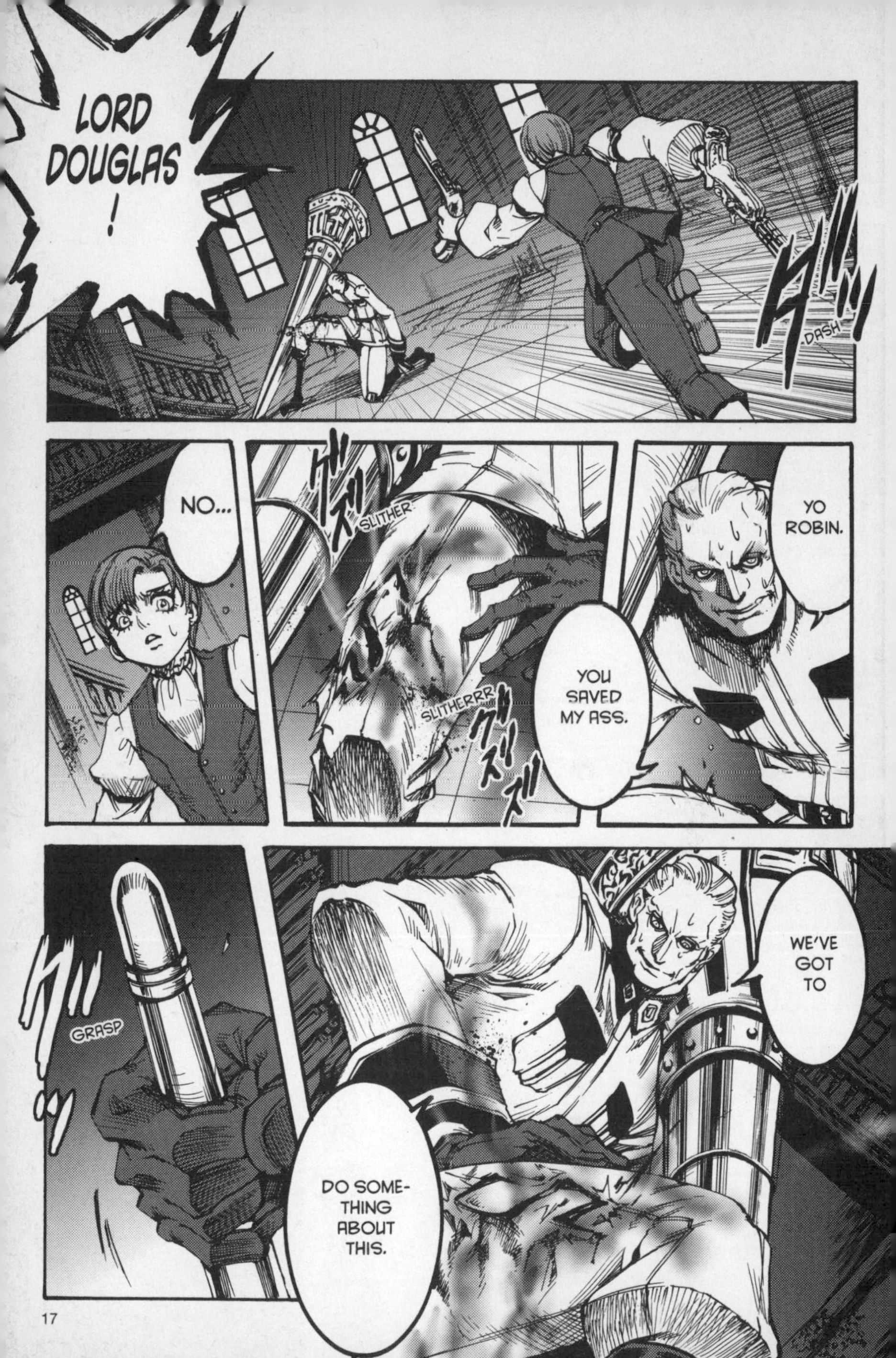
DASH
LORD DOUGLAS !
YO ROBIN.
YOU SAVED MY ASS.
SLITHER
SLITHERRR
NO...
WE'VE GOT TO
DO SOME-THING ABOUT THIS.
GRASP

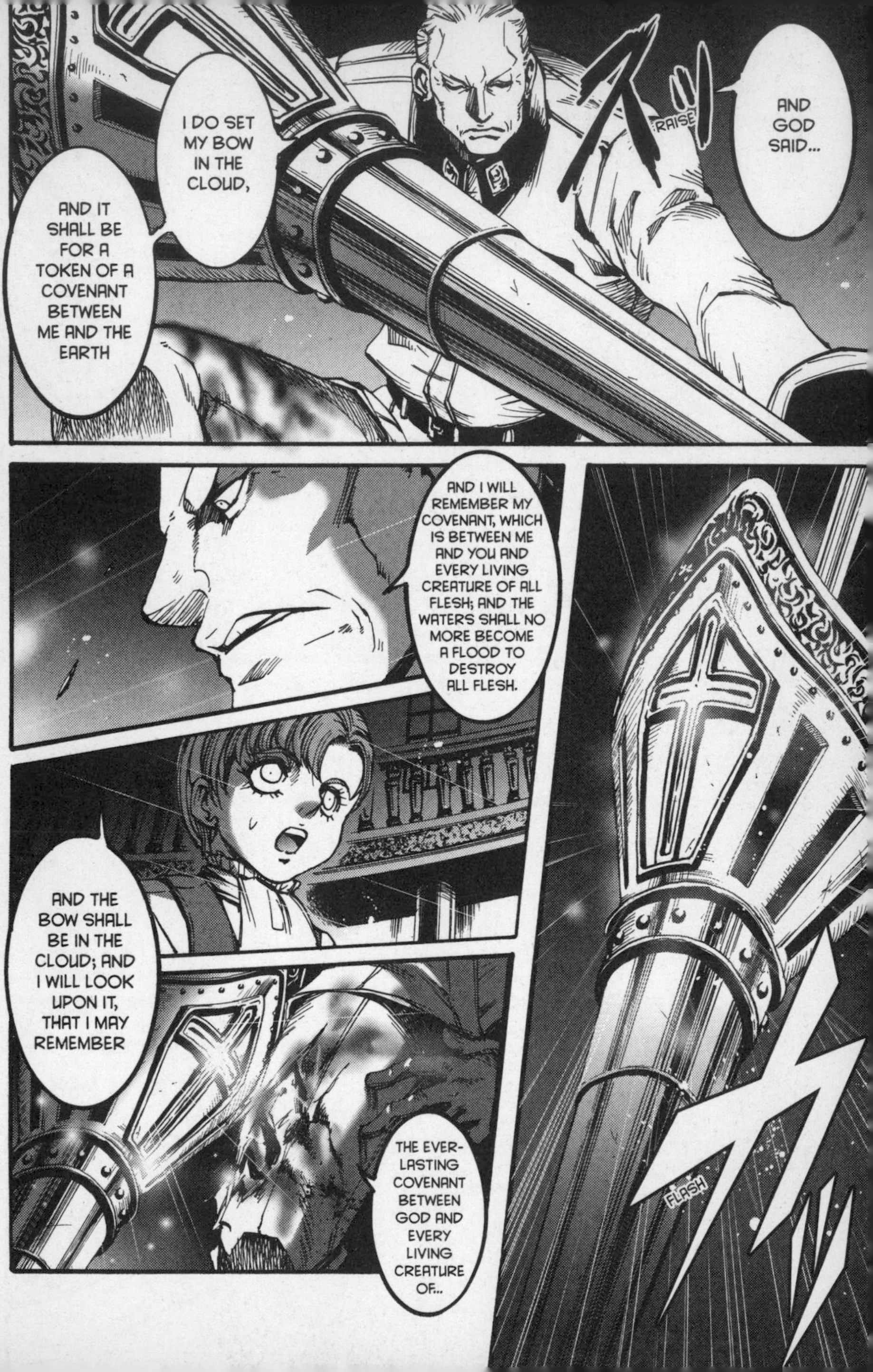
AND GOD SAID...
RAISE
I DO SET MY BOW IN THE CLOUD,
AND IT SHALL BE FOR A TOKEN OF A COVENANT BETWEEN ME AND THE EARTH
FLASH
AND I WILL REMEMBER MY COVENANT, WHICH IS BETWEEN ME AND YOU AND EVERY LIVING CREATURE OF ALL FLESH; AND THE WATERS SHALL NO MORE BECOME A FLOOD TO DESTROY ALL FLESH.
AND THE BOW SHALL BE IN THE CLOUD; AND I WILL LOOK UPON IT, THAT I MAY REMEMBER
THE EVER-LASTING COVENANT BETWEEN GOD AND EVERY LIVING CREATURE OF...

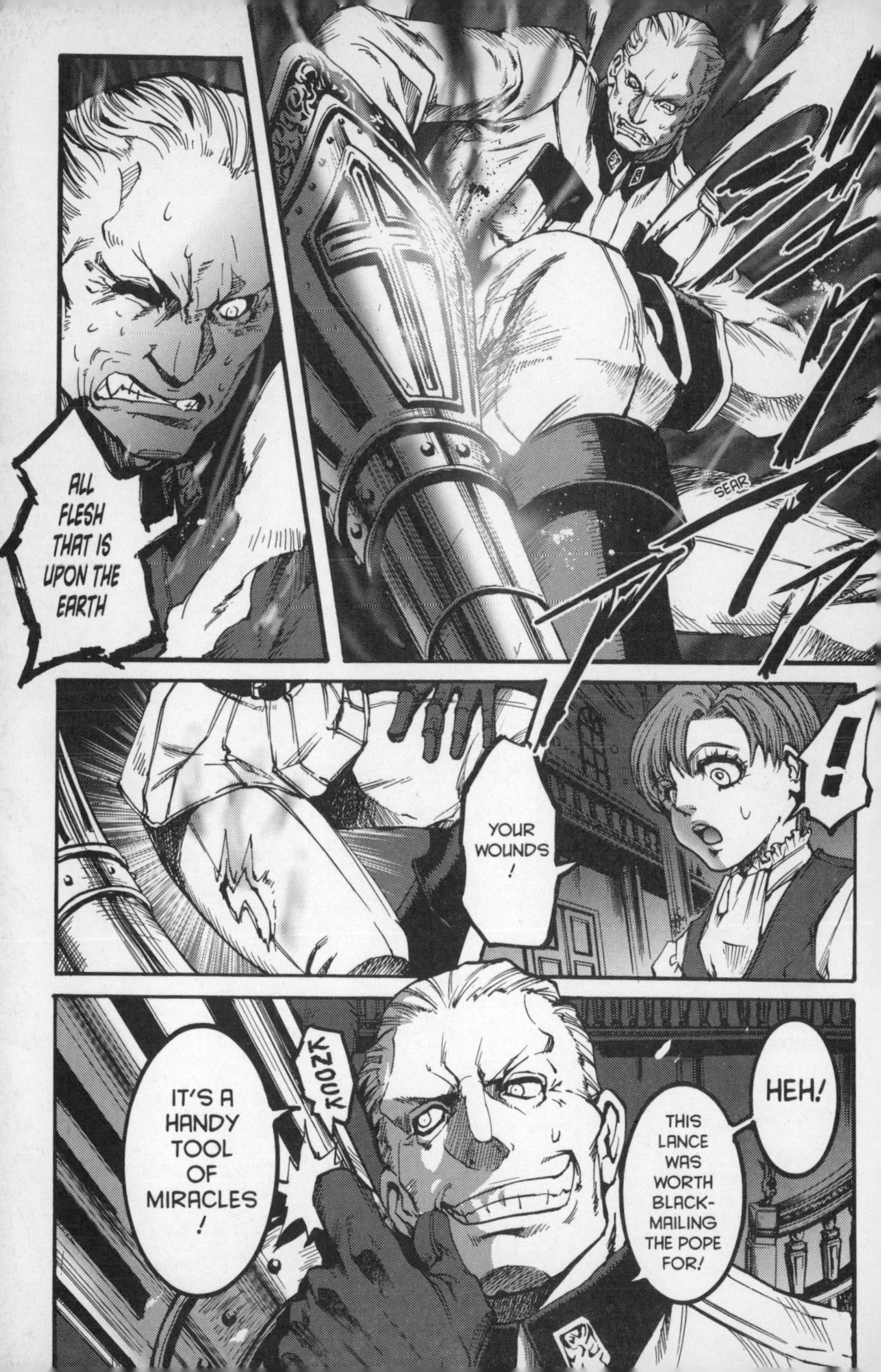
SEAR
ALL FLESH THAT IS UPON THE EARTH
!
YOUR WOUNDS !
HEH!
THIS LANCE WAS WORTH BLACK-MAILING THE POPE FOR!
KNOCK
IT'S A HANDY TOOL OF MIRACLES !

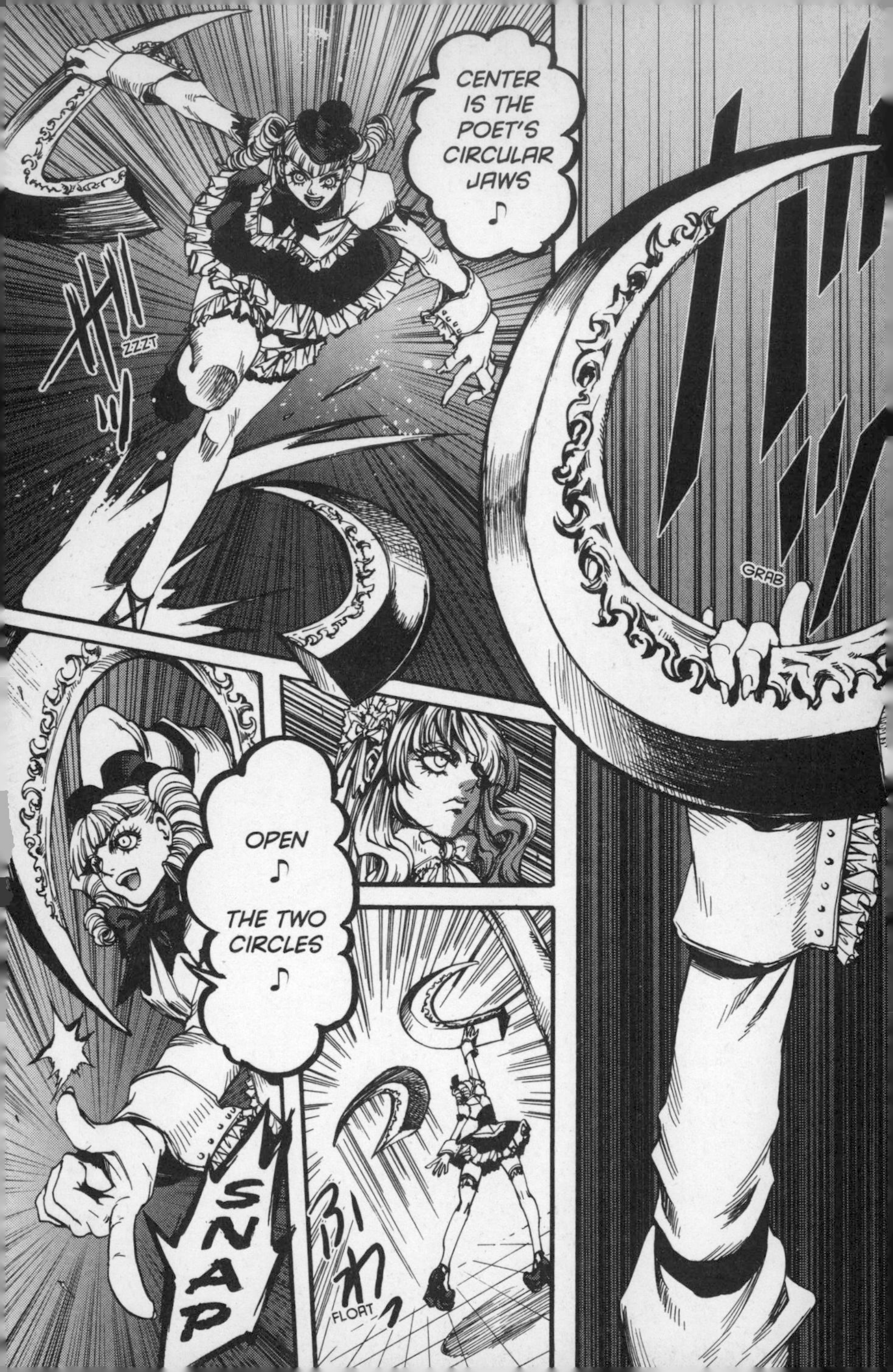
GRAB
CENTER IS THE POET'S CIRCULAR JAWS ♪
ZZZT
FLOAT
OPEN ♪ THE TWO CIRCLES ♪
SNAP

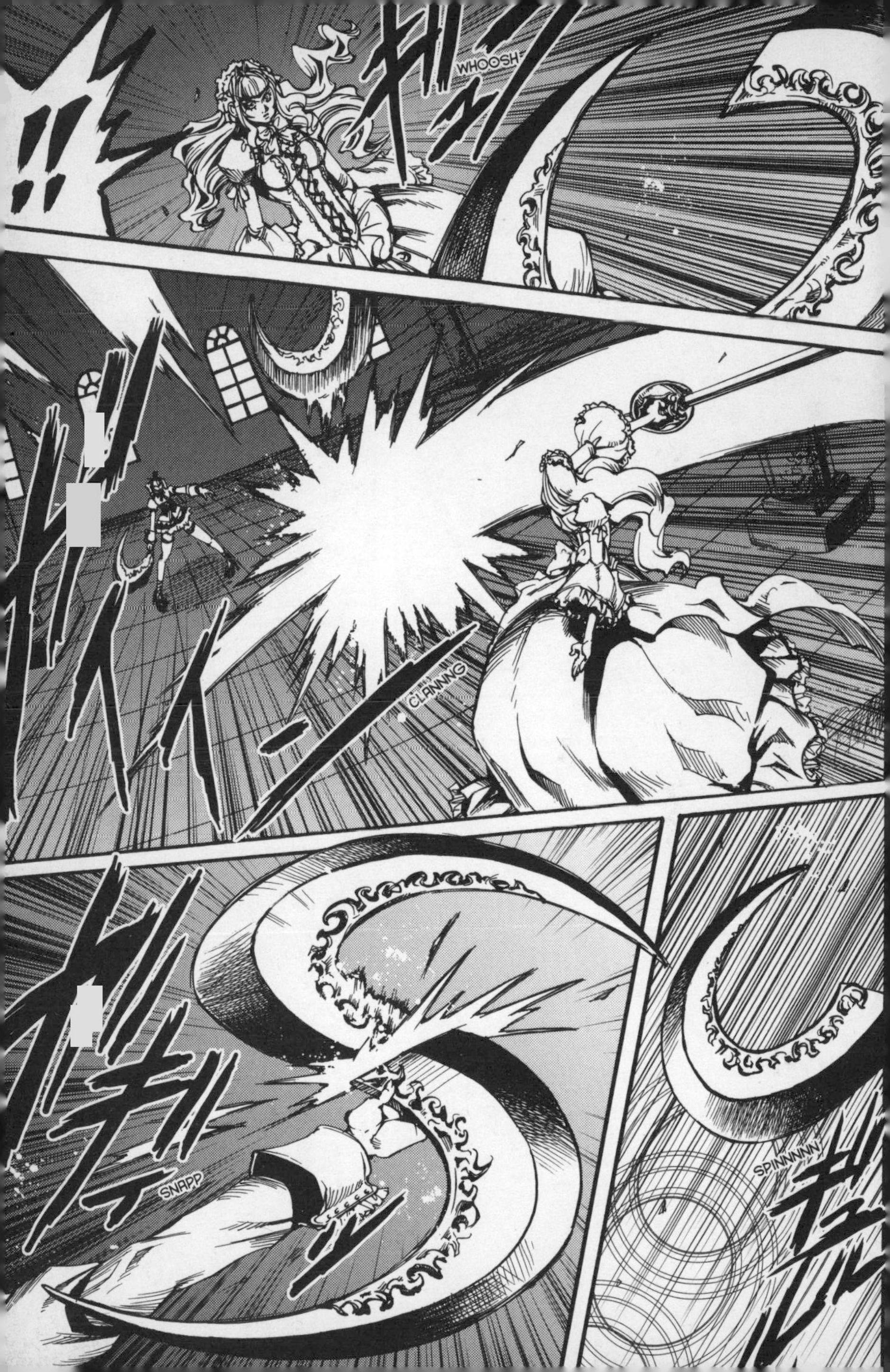
WHOOSH
!!
CLANNNG
SPINNNNN
SNAPP

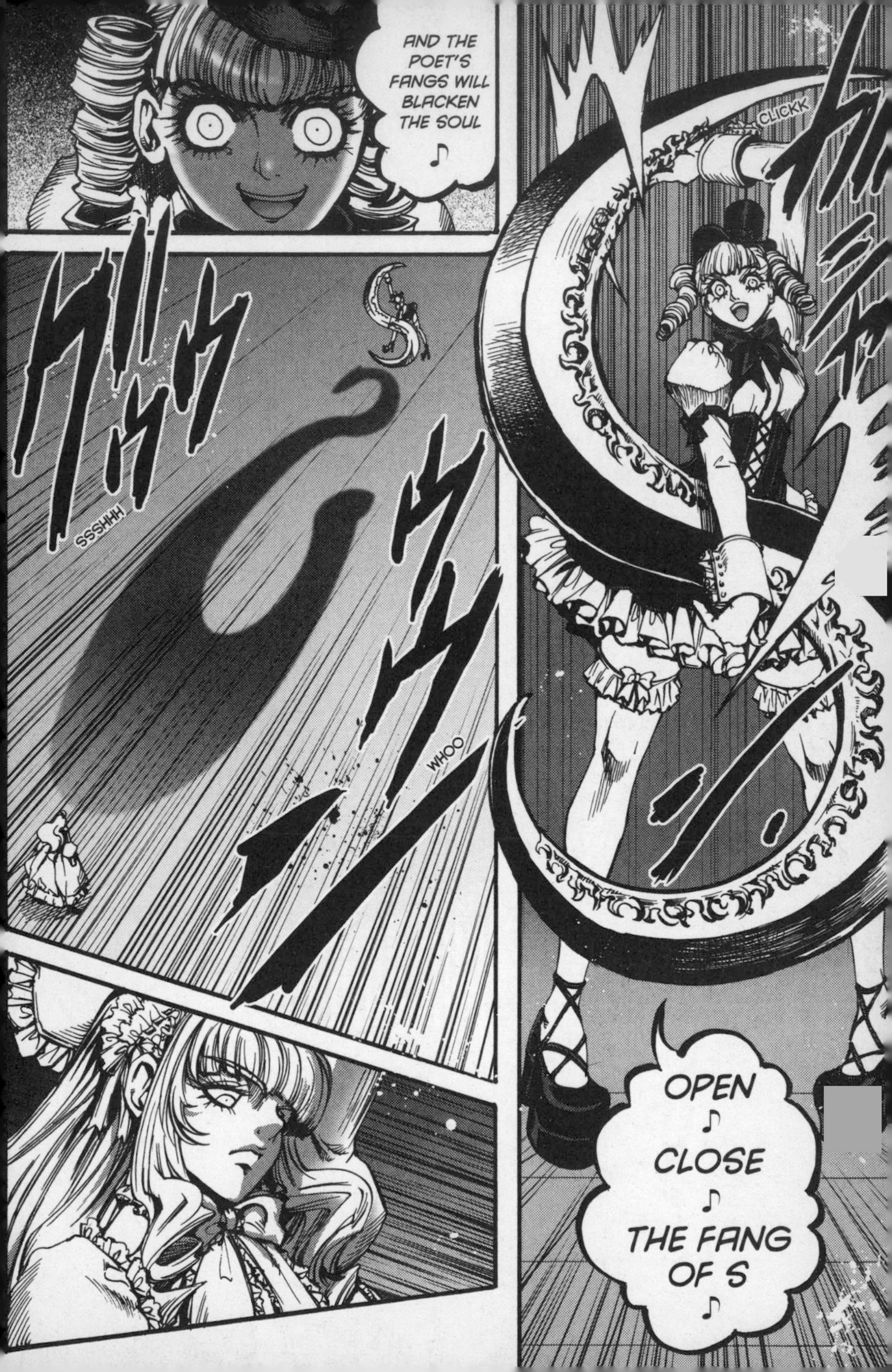
CLICKK
OPEN ♪ CLOSE ♪ THE FANG OF S ♪
AND THE POET'S FANGS WILL BLACKEN THE SOUL ♪
SSSHHH
WHOO

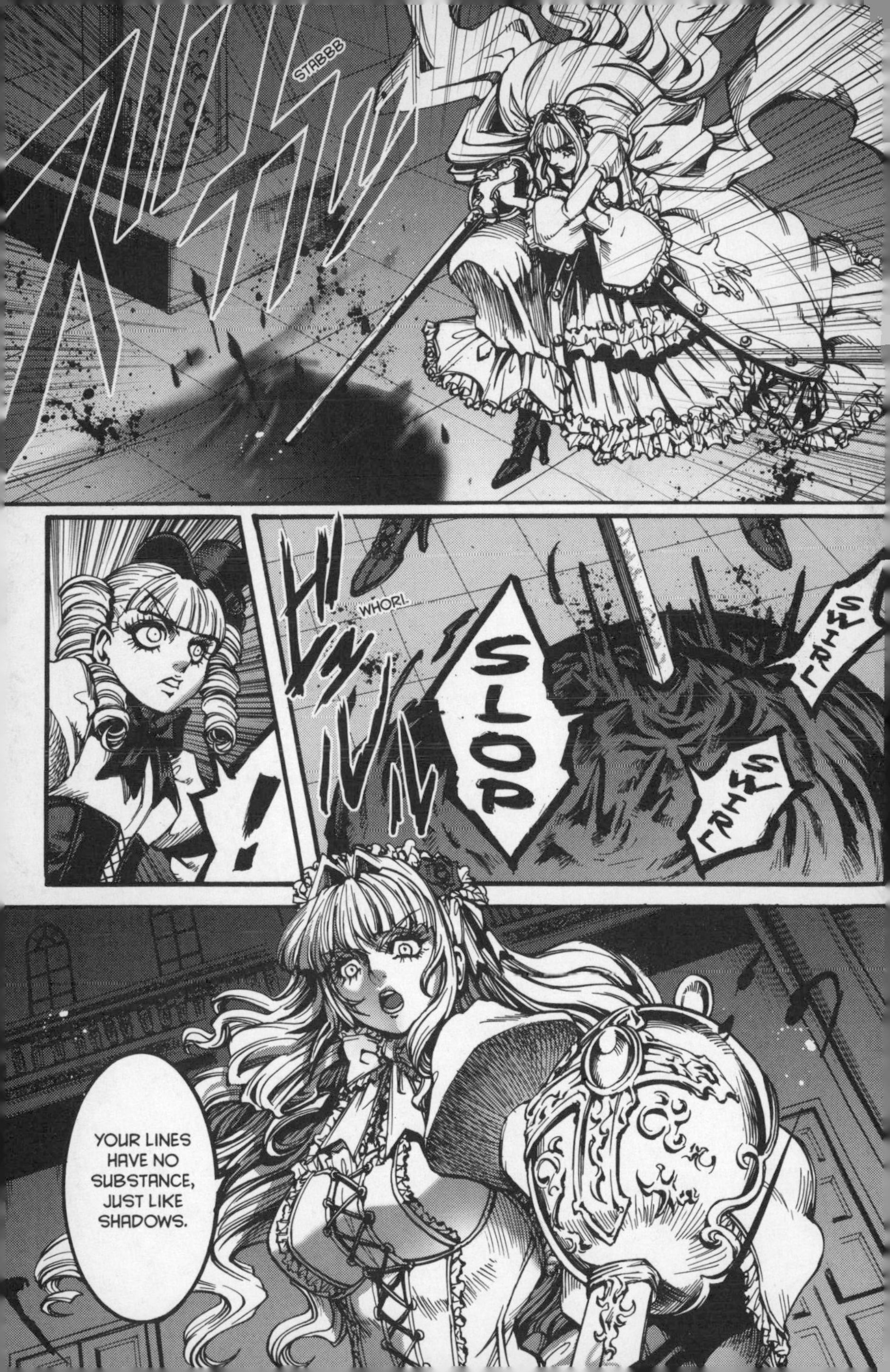
STABBB
SWIRL
SWIRL
SLOP
WHORL
!
YOUR LINES HAVE NO SUBSTANCE, JUST LIKE SHADOWS.

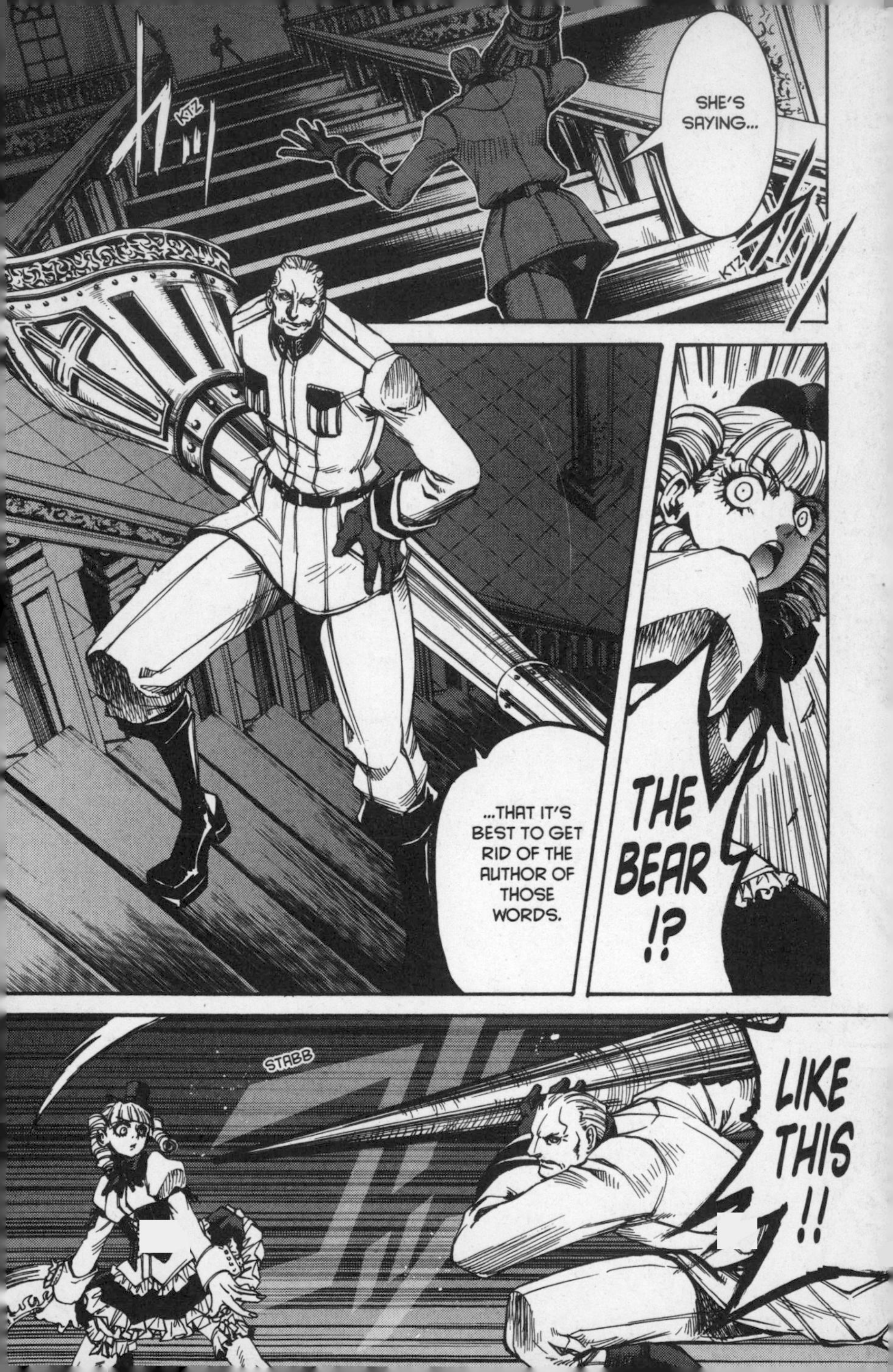
SHE'S SAYING...
KTZ
KTZ
THE BEAR !?
...THAT IT'S BEST TO GET RID OF THE AUTHOR OF THOSE WORDS.
LIKE THIS !!
STABB

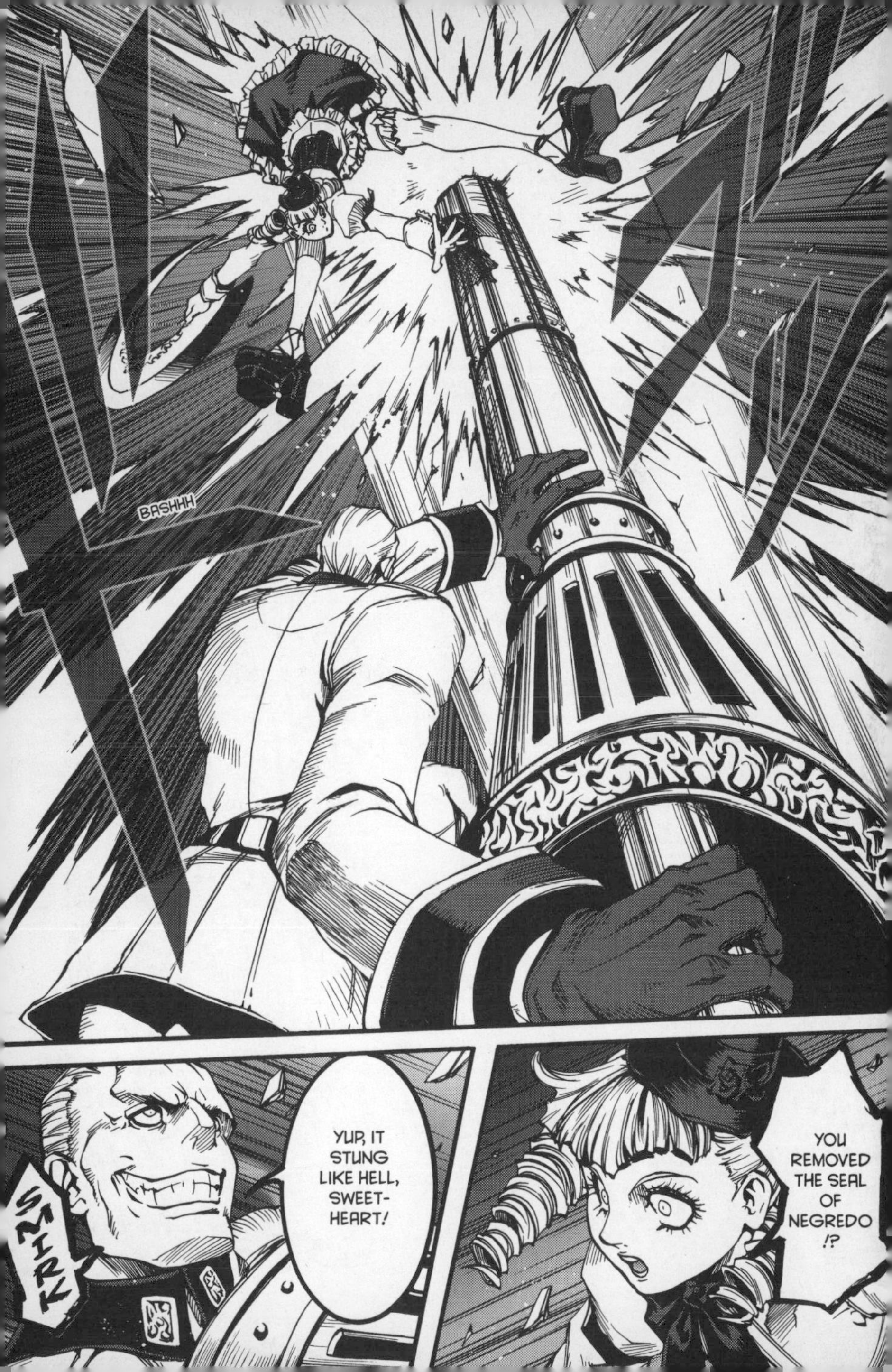
BASHHH
YOU REMOVED THE SEAL OF NEGREDO !?
YUP, IT STUNG LIKE HELL, SWEET-HEART!
SMIRK

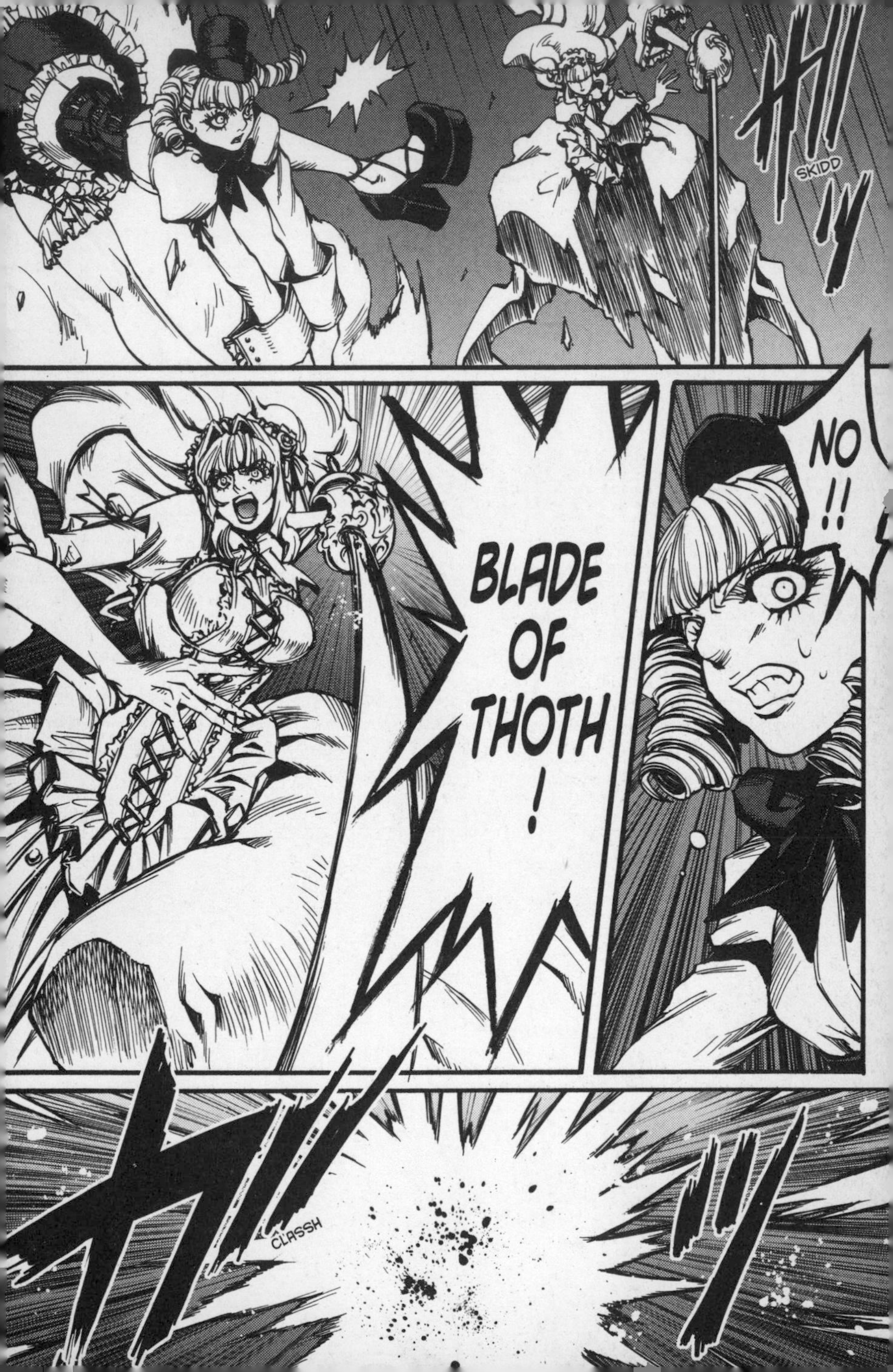
SKIDD
NO !!
BLADE OF THOTH !
CLASSH

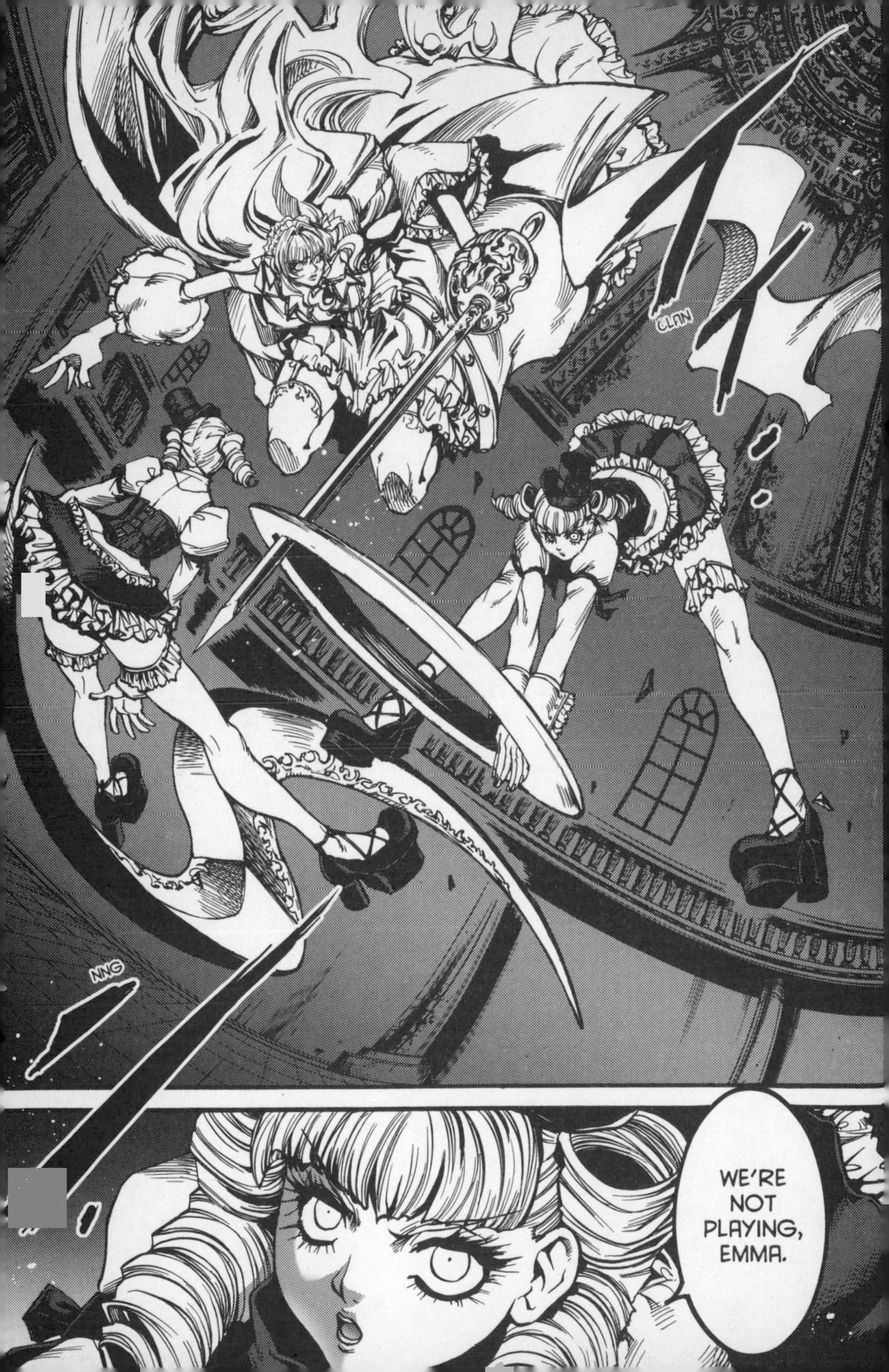
CLAN
NNG
WE'RE NOT PLAYING, EMMA.

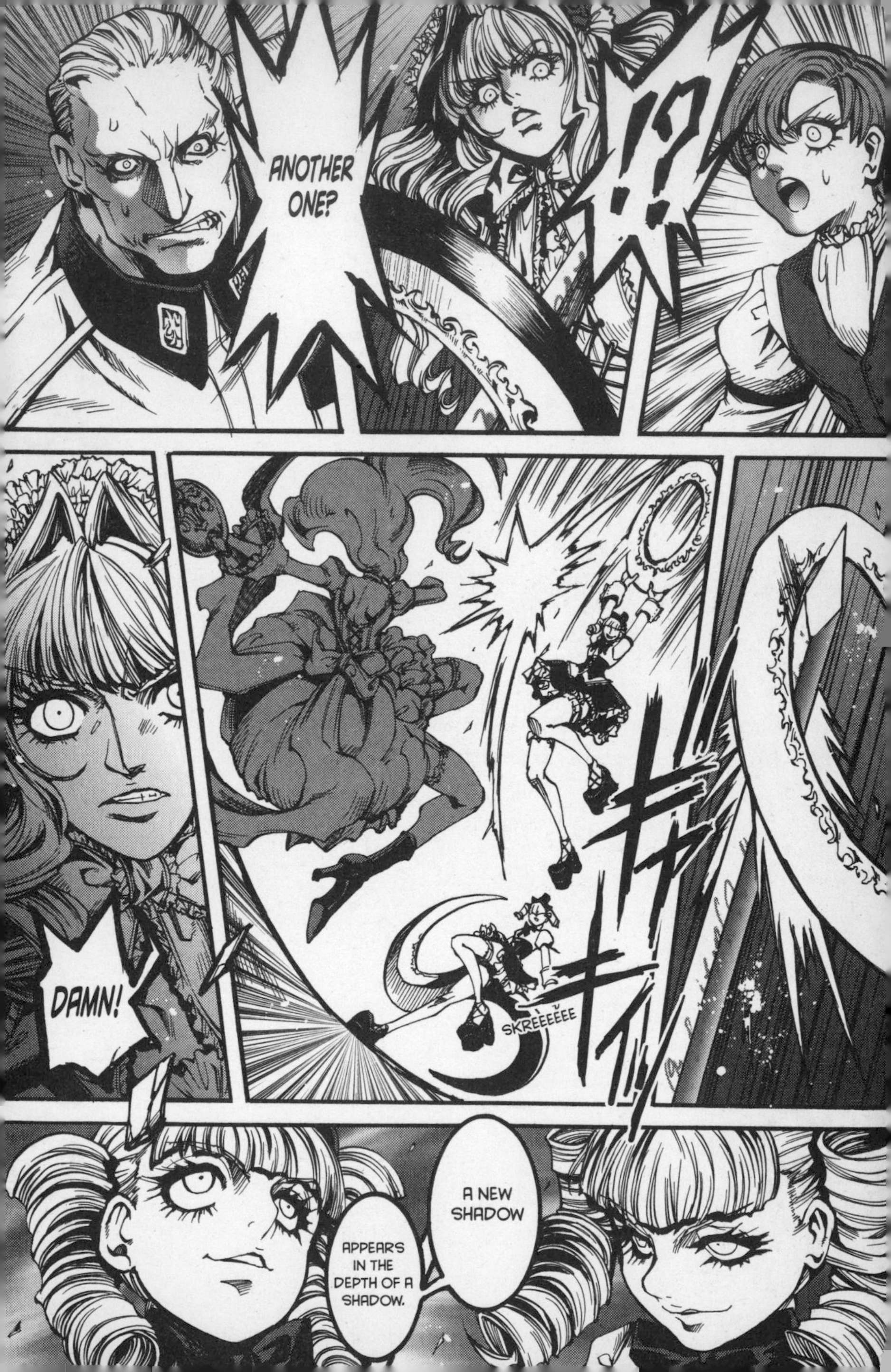
!?
ANOTHER ONE?
SKREEEEEEE
DAMN!
A NEW SHADOW
APPEARS IN THE DEPTH OF A SHADOW.

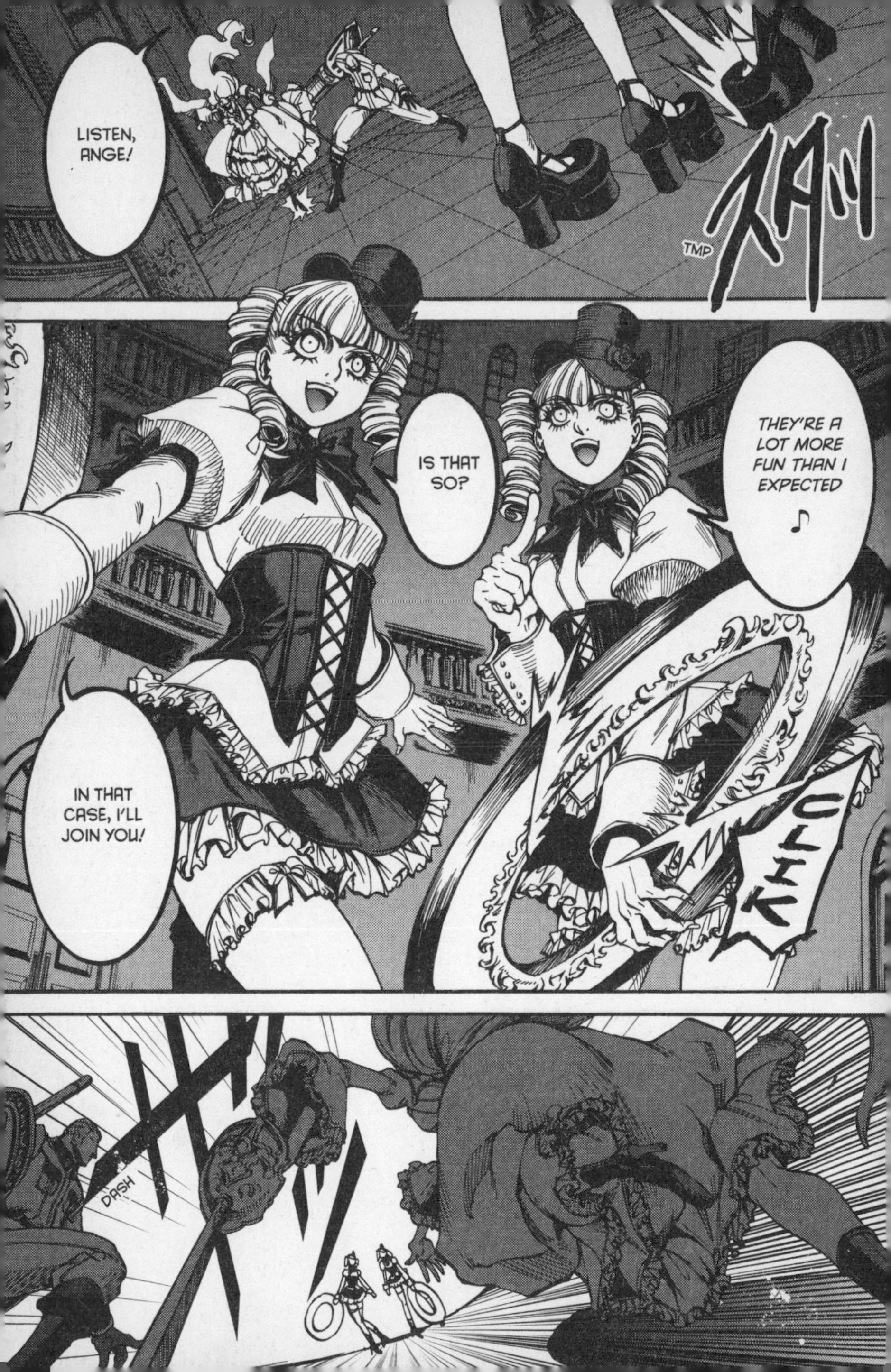

TMP
LISTEN, ANGE!
THEY'RE A LOT MORE FUN THAN I EXPECTED ♪
IS THAT SO?
CLIK
IN THAT CASE, I'LL JOIN YOU!
DASH

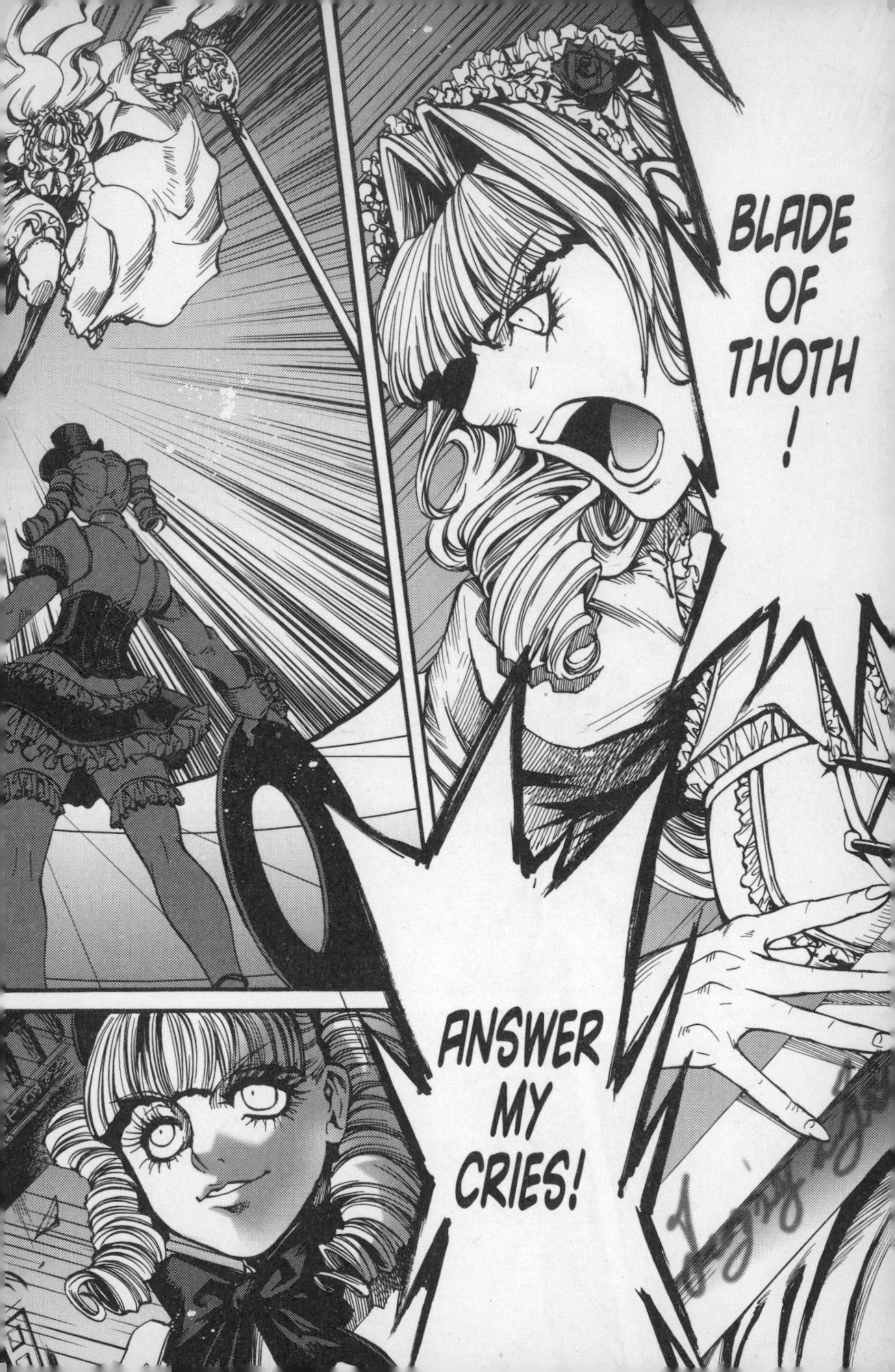
BLADE OF THOTH!
ANSWER MY CRIES!

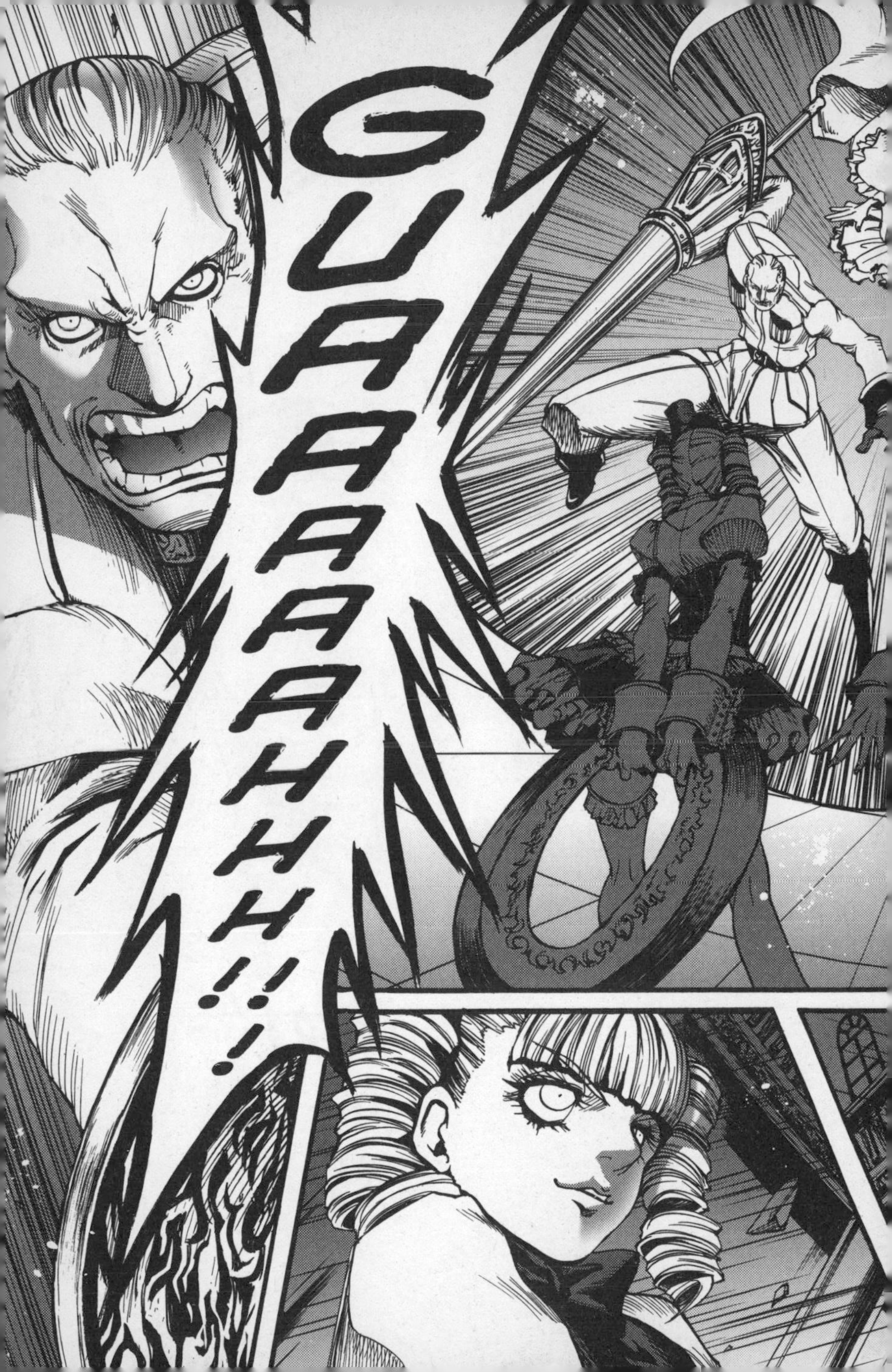
GUAAAAAAAHHH!!!

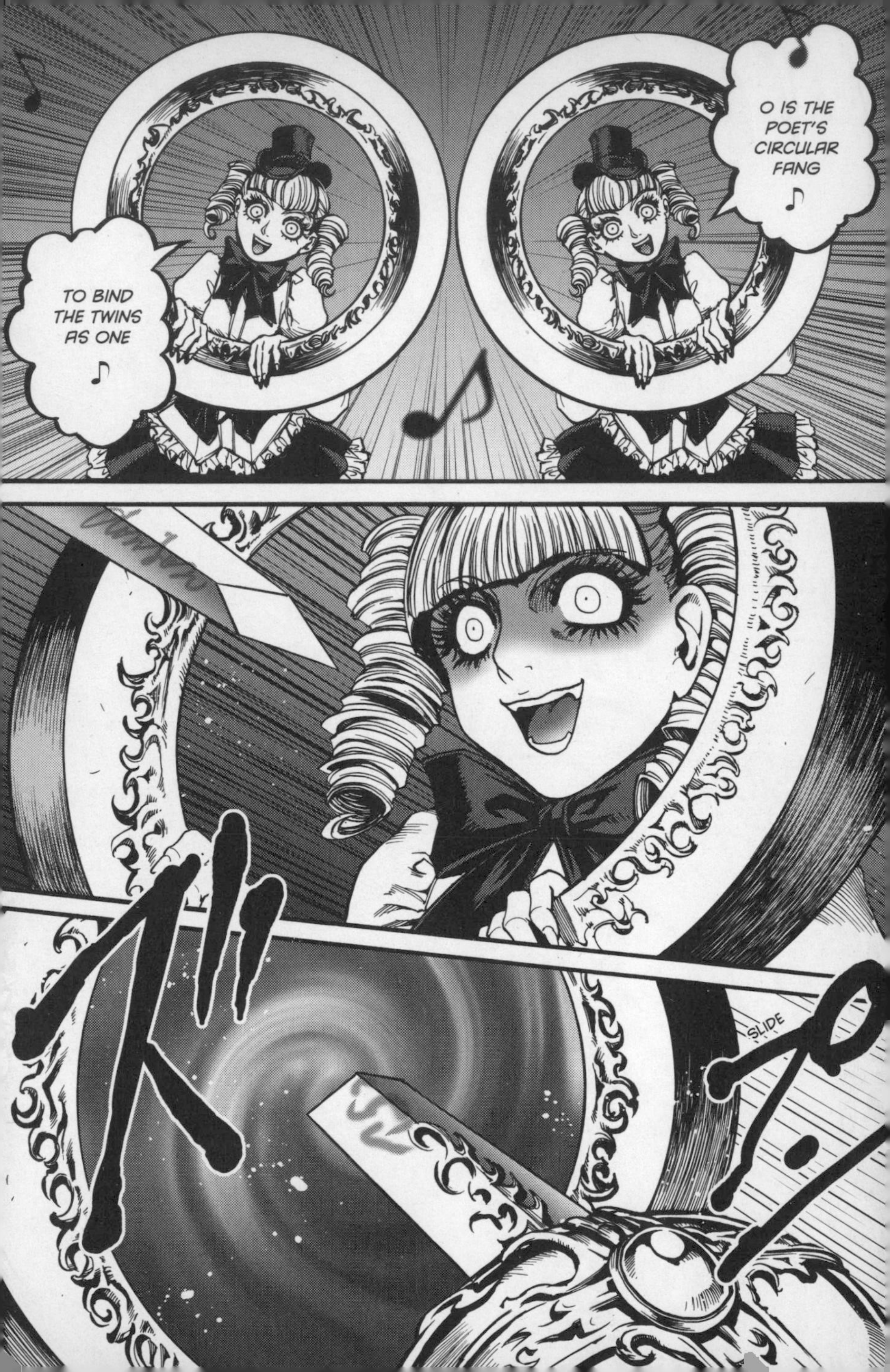
O IS THE POET'S CIRCULAR FANG ♪
TO BIND THE TWINS AS ONE ♪
SLIDE

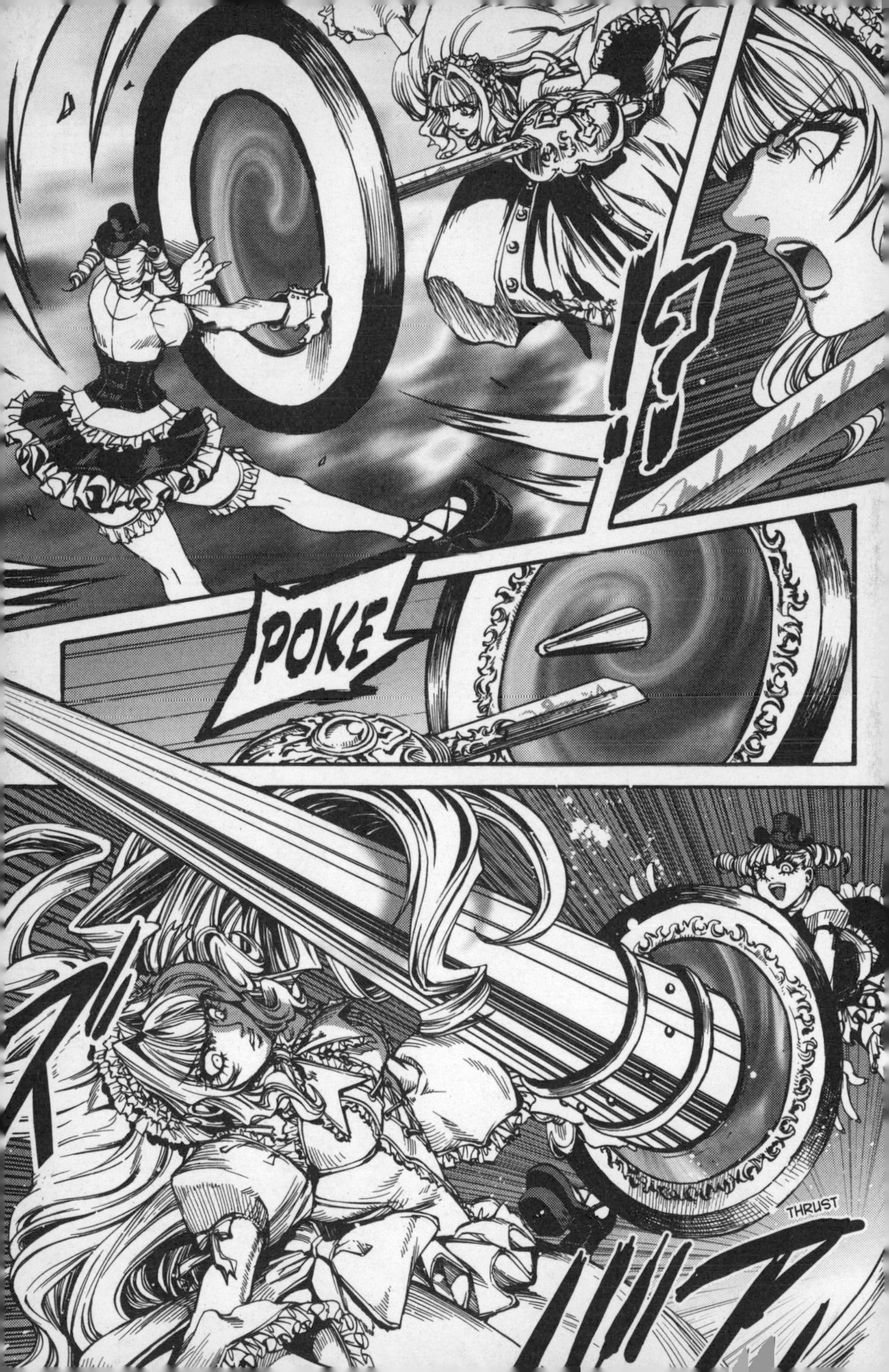
!?
POKE
THRUST

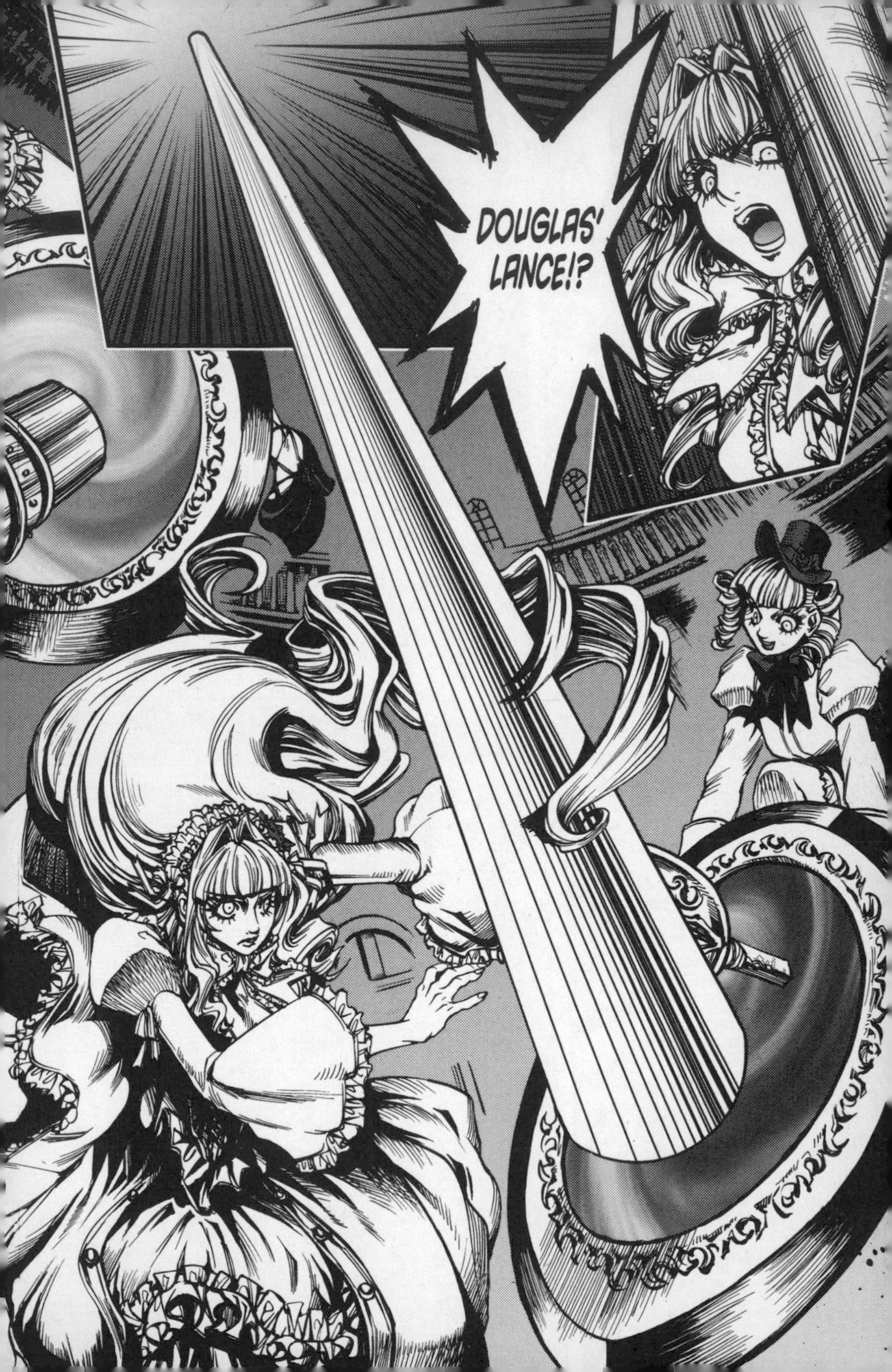
DOUGLAS' LANCE!?

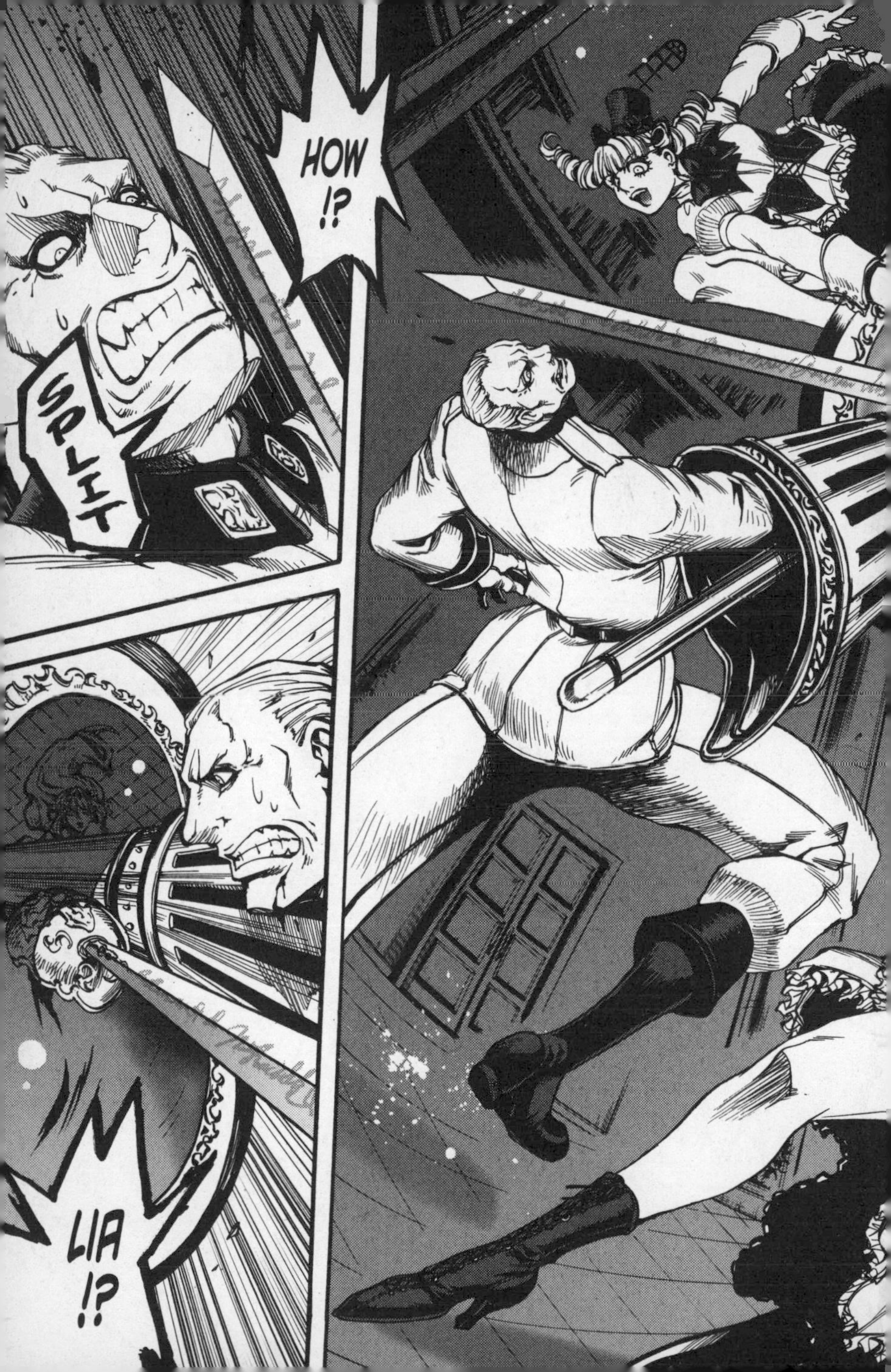
HOW !?
SPLIT
LIA !?

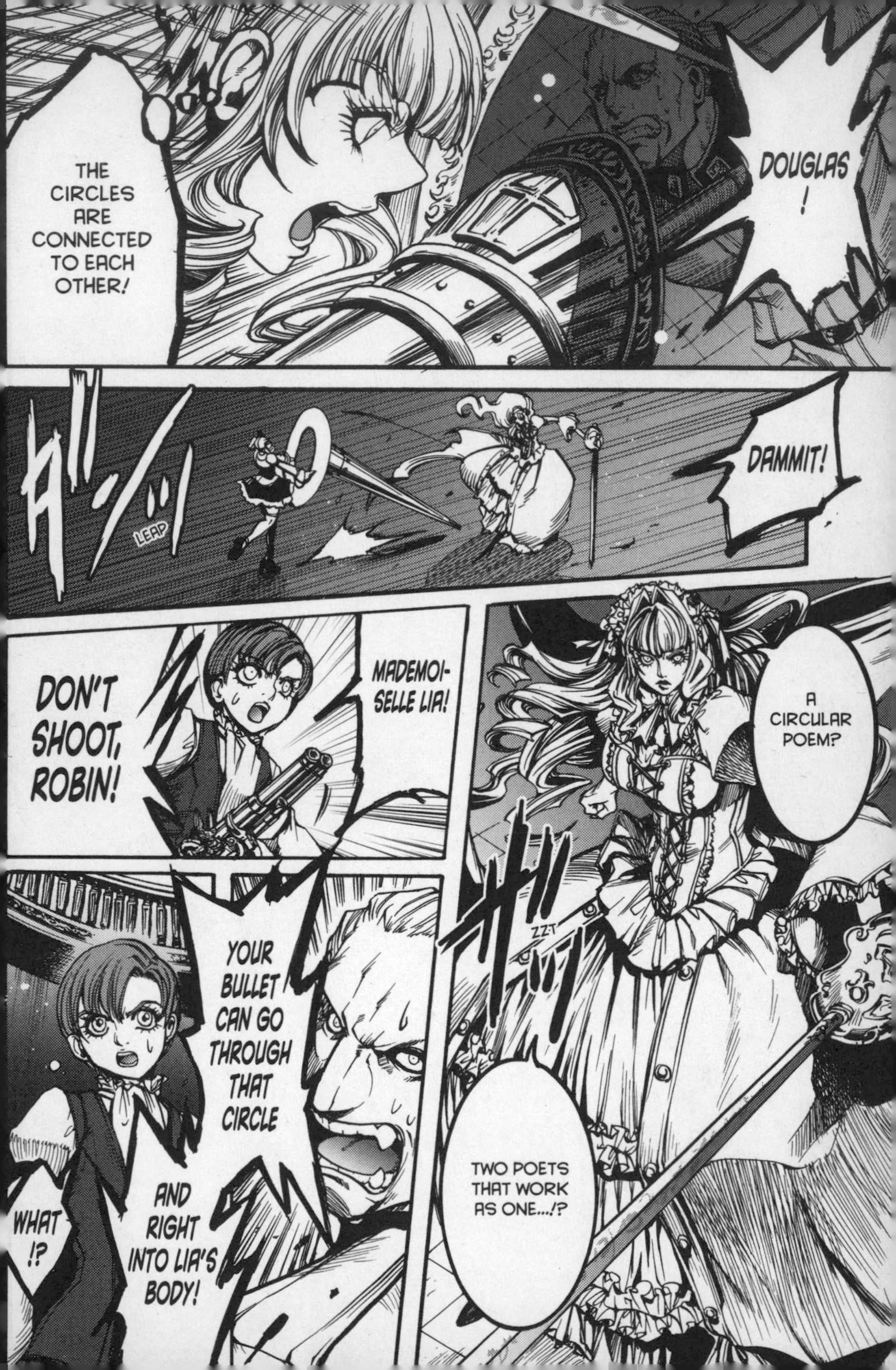
DOUGLAS!
THE CIRCLES ARE CONNECTED TO EACH OTHER!
DAMMIT!
LEAP
A CIRCULAR POEM?
ZZT
TWO POETS THAT WORK AS ONE...!?
MADEMOI-SELLE LIA!
DON'T SHOOT, ROBIN!
YOUR BULLET CAN GO THROUGH THAT CIRCLE
AND RIGHT INTO LIA'S BODY!
WHAT!?

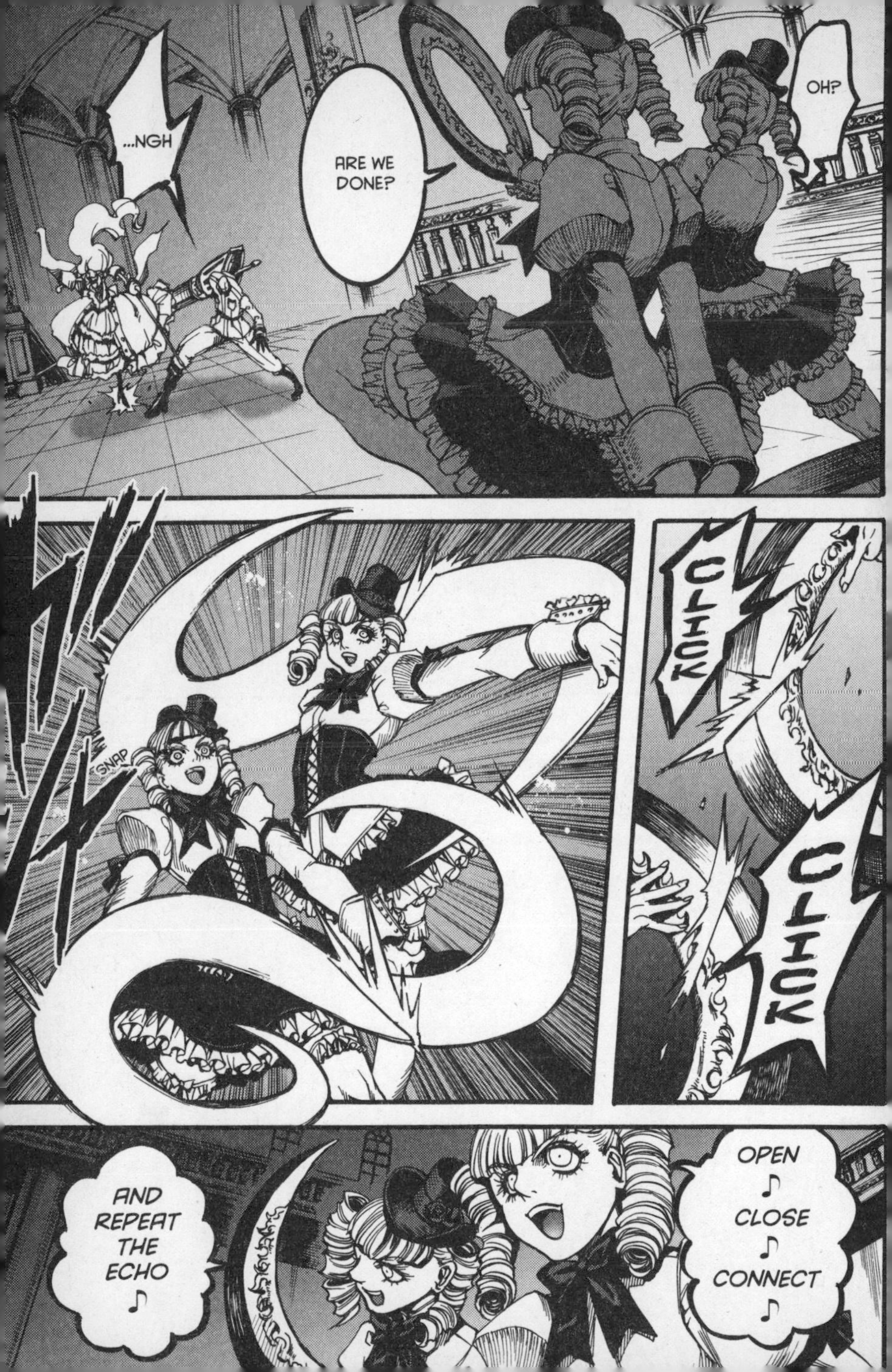
OH?
ARE WE DONE?
...NGH
CLICK
CLICK
SNAP
OPEN ♪ CLOSE ♪ CONNECT ♪
AND REPEAT THE ECHO ♪

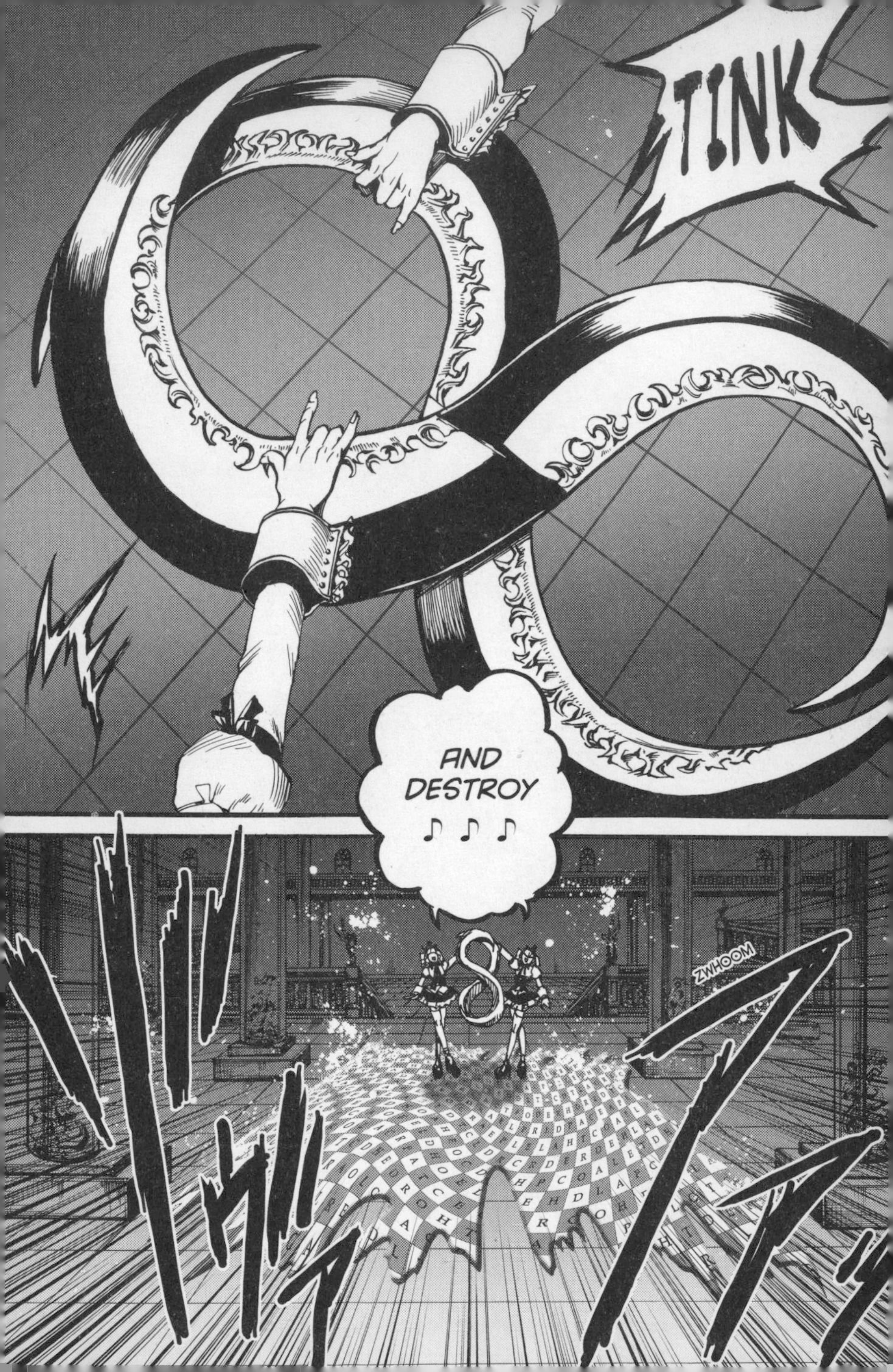
TINK
AND DESTROY ♪ ♪ ♪
ZWHOOM

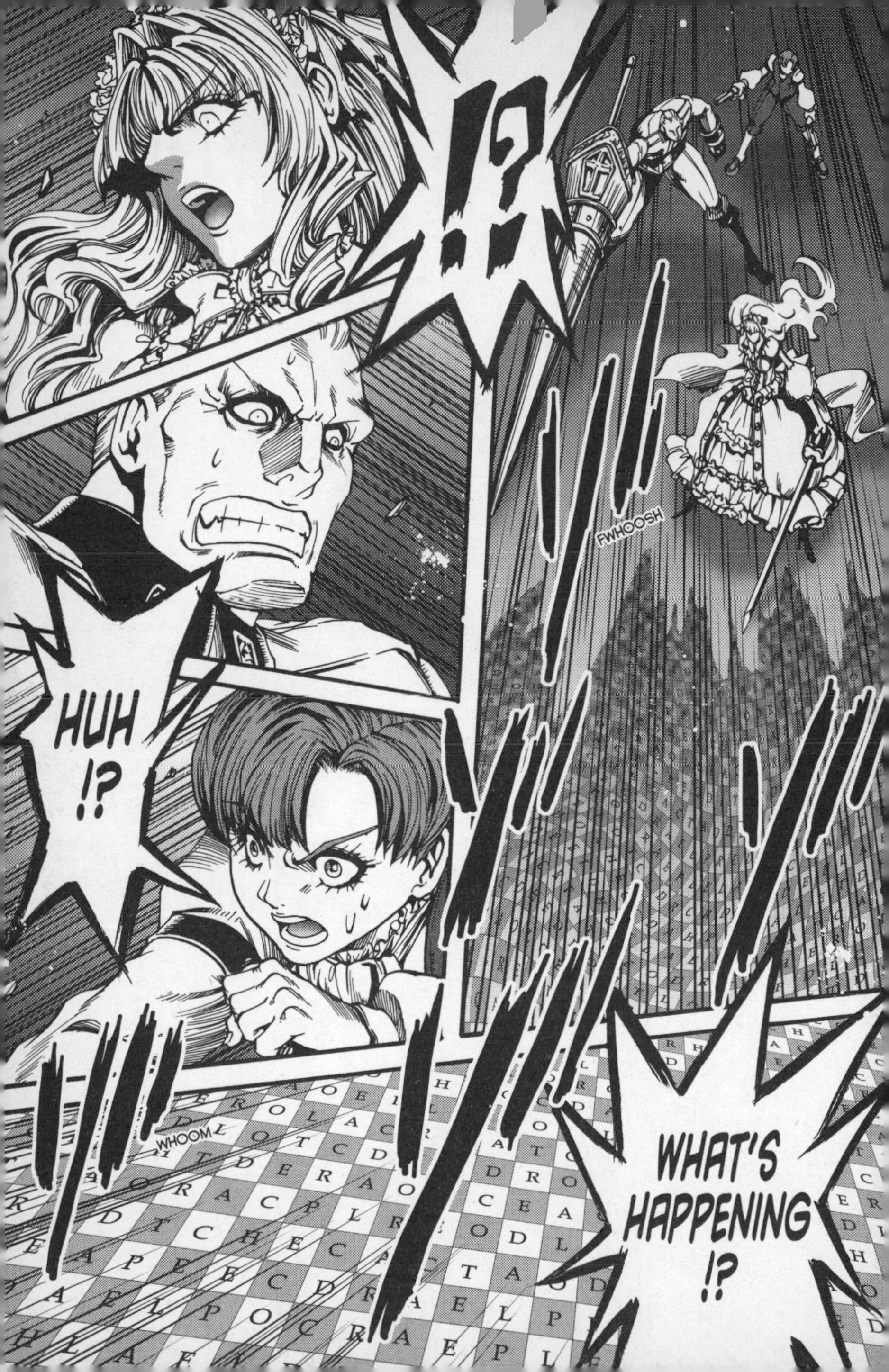
FWHOOSH
!?
HUH !?
WHAT'S HAPPENING !?
WHOOM

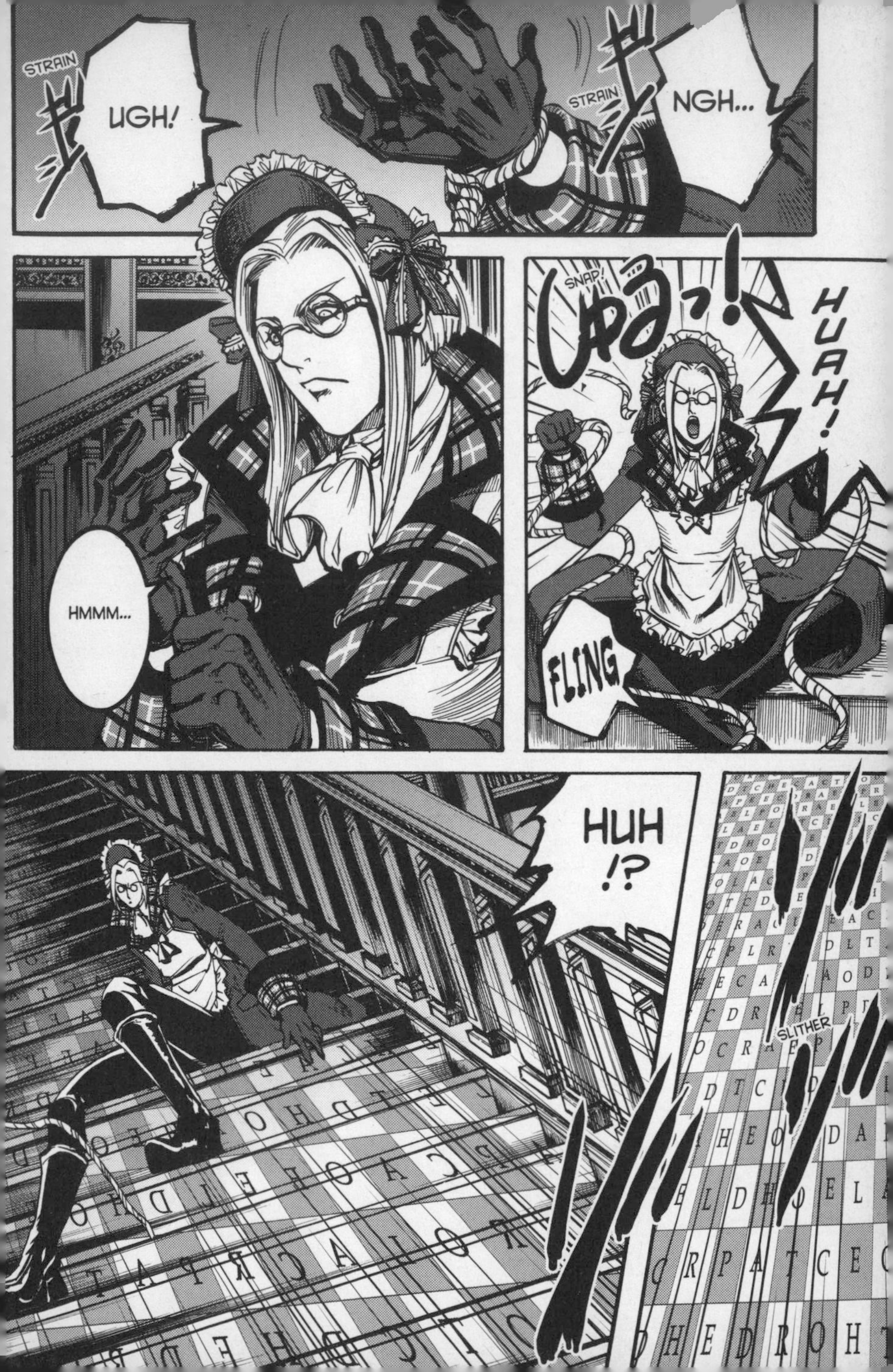
STRAIN
NGH...
STRAIN
UGH!
SNAP!
HUAH!
FLING
HMMM...
SLITHER
HUH !?

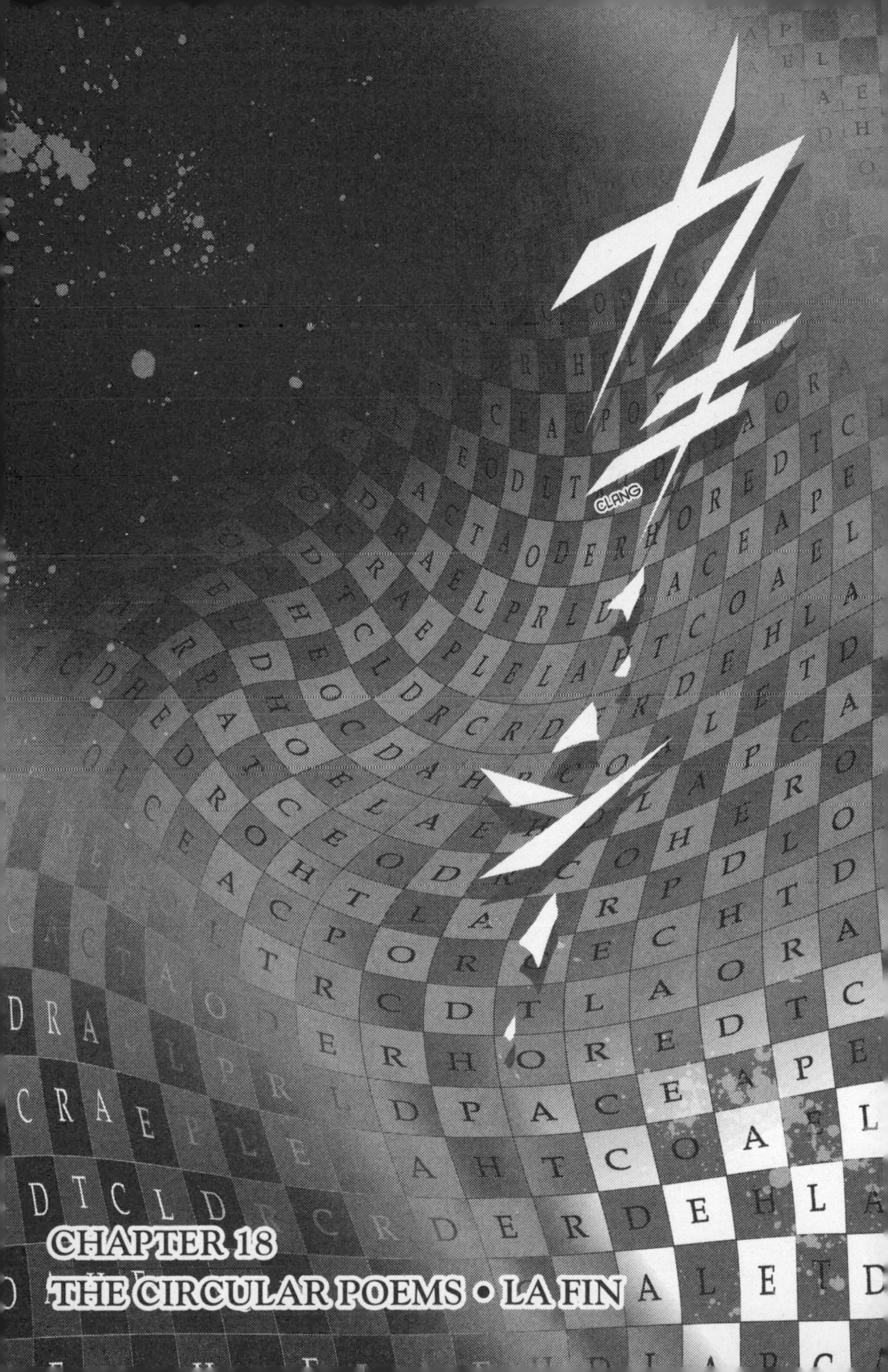
CLANG
CHAPTER 18
THE CIRCULAR POEMS • LA FIN

CHEVALIER

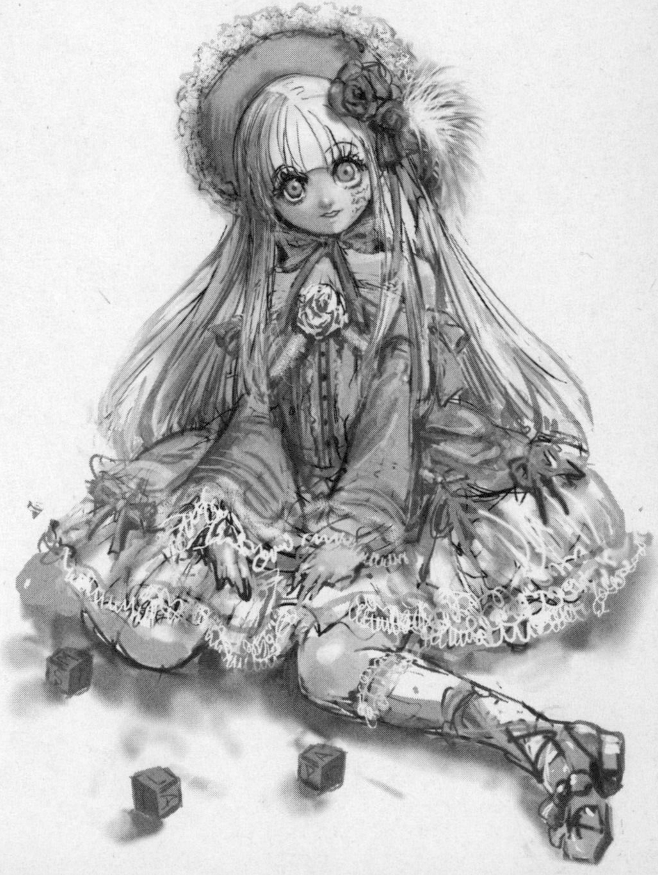

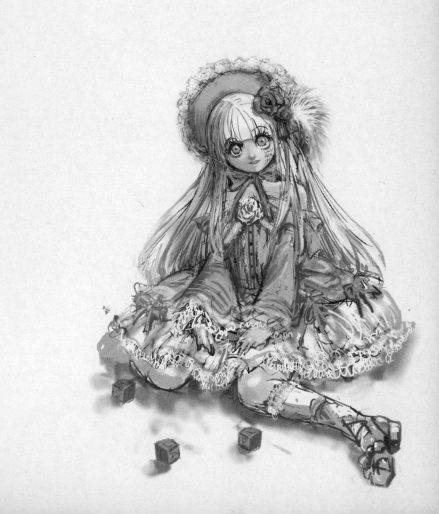

CHAPTER 19
THE DISCLOSED PATH

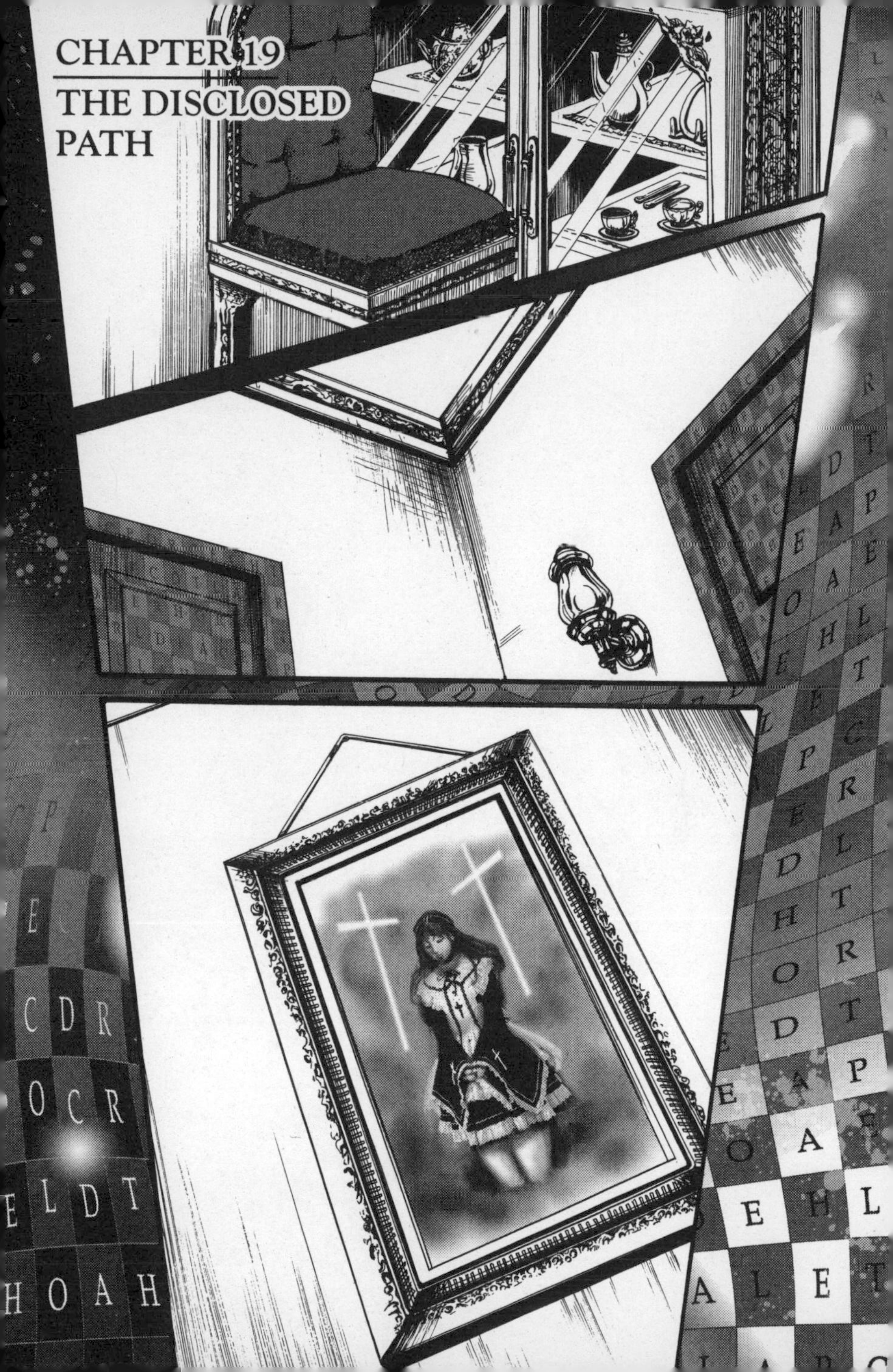

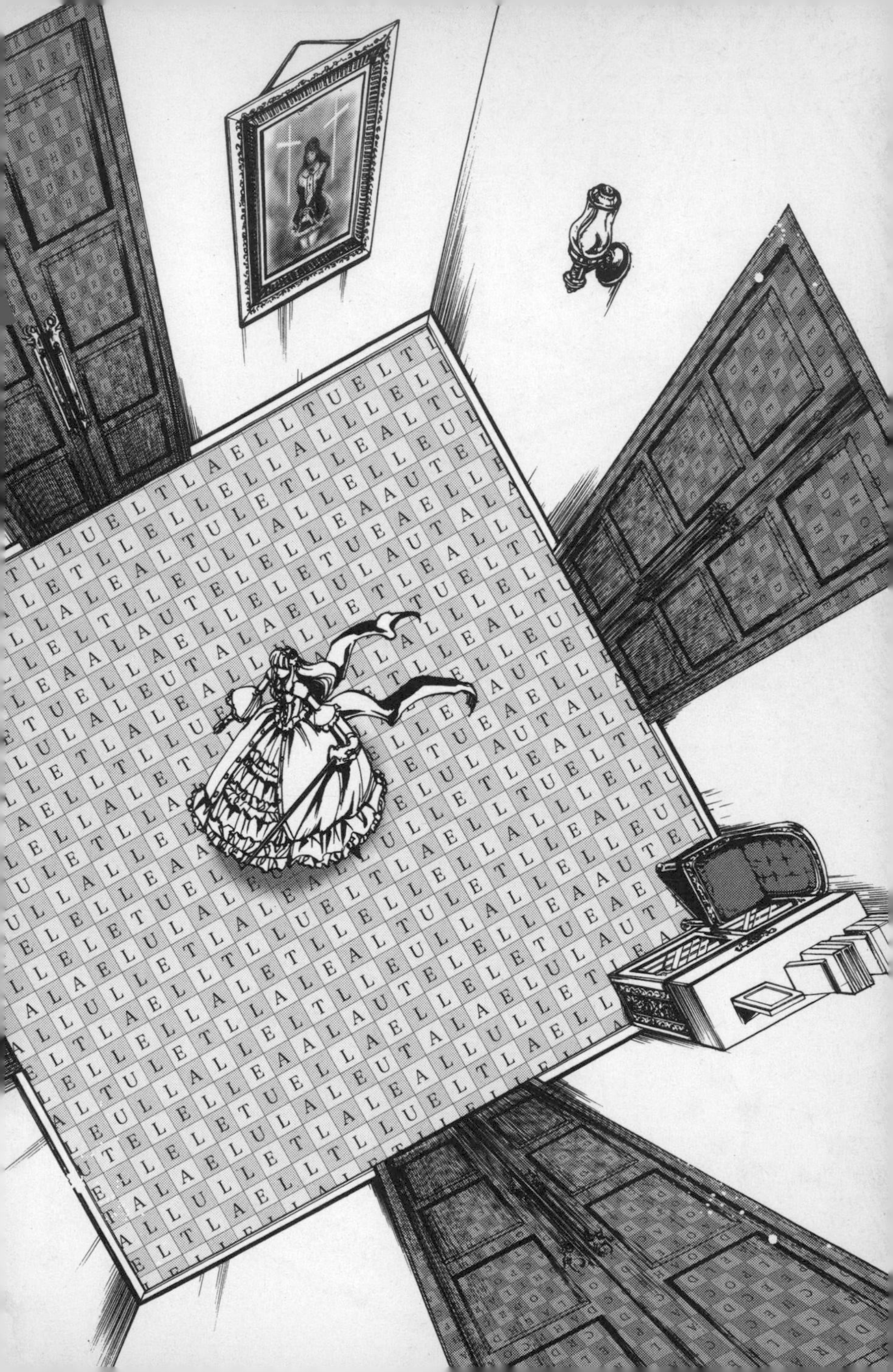

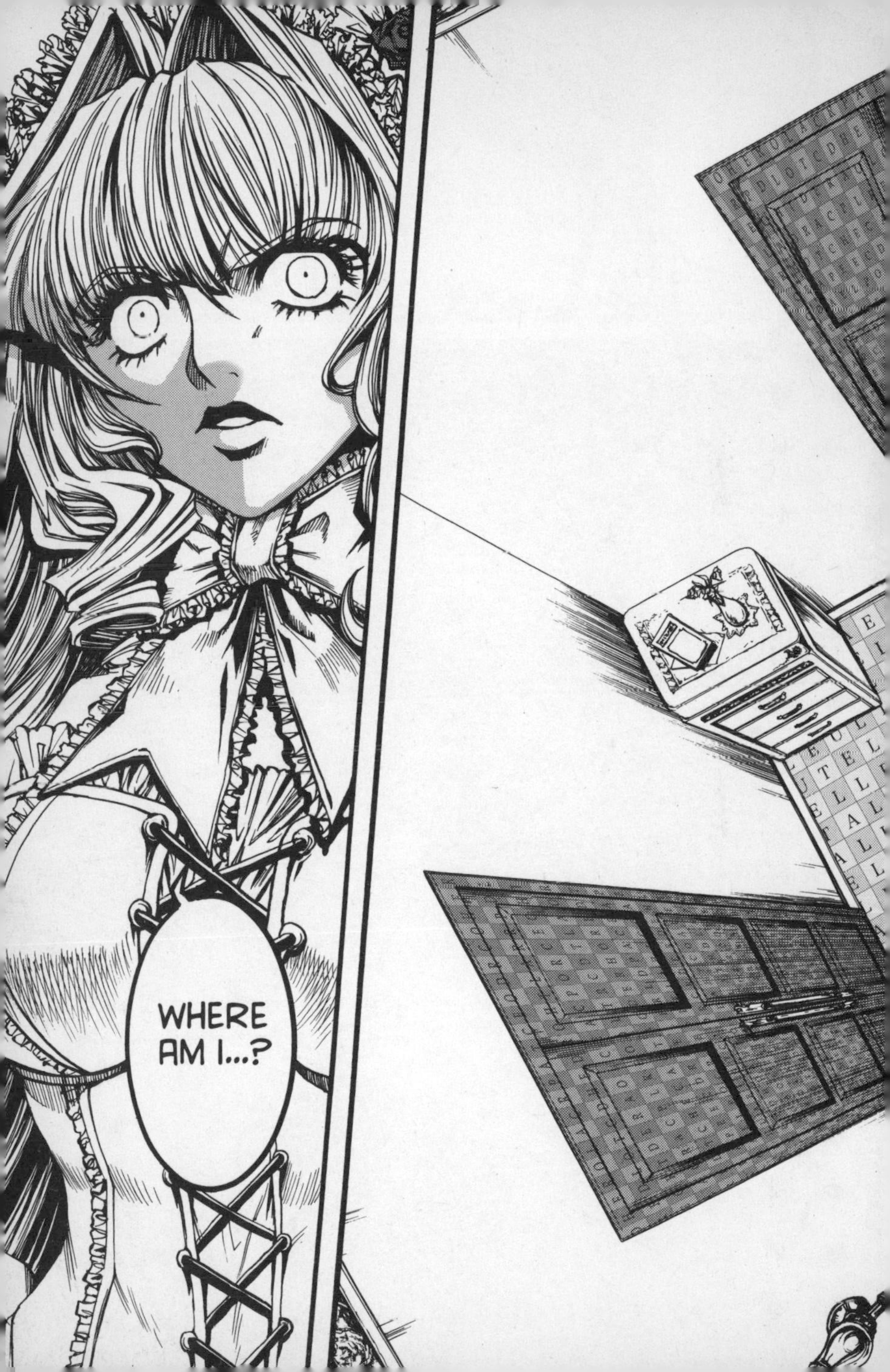
WHERE AM I...?

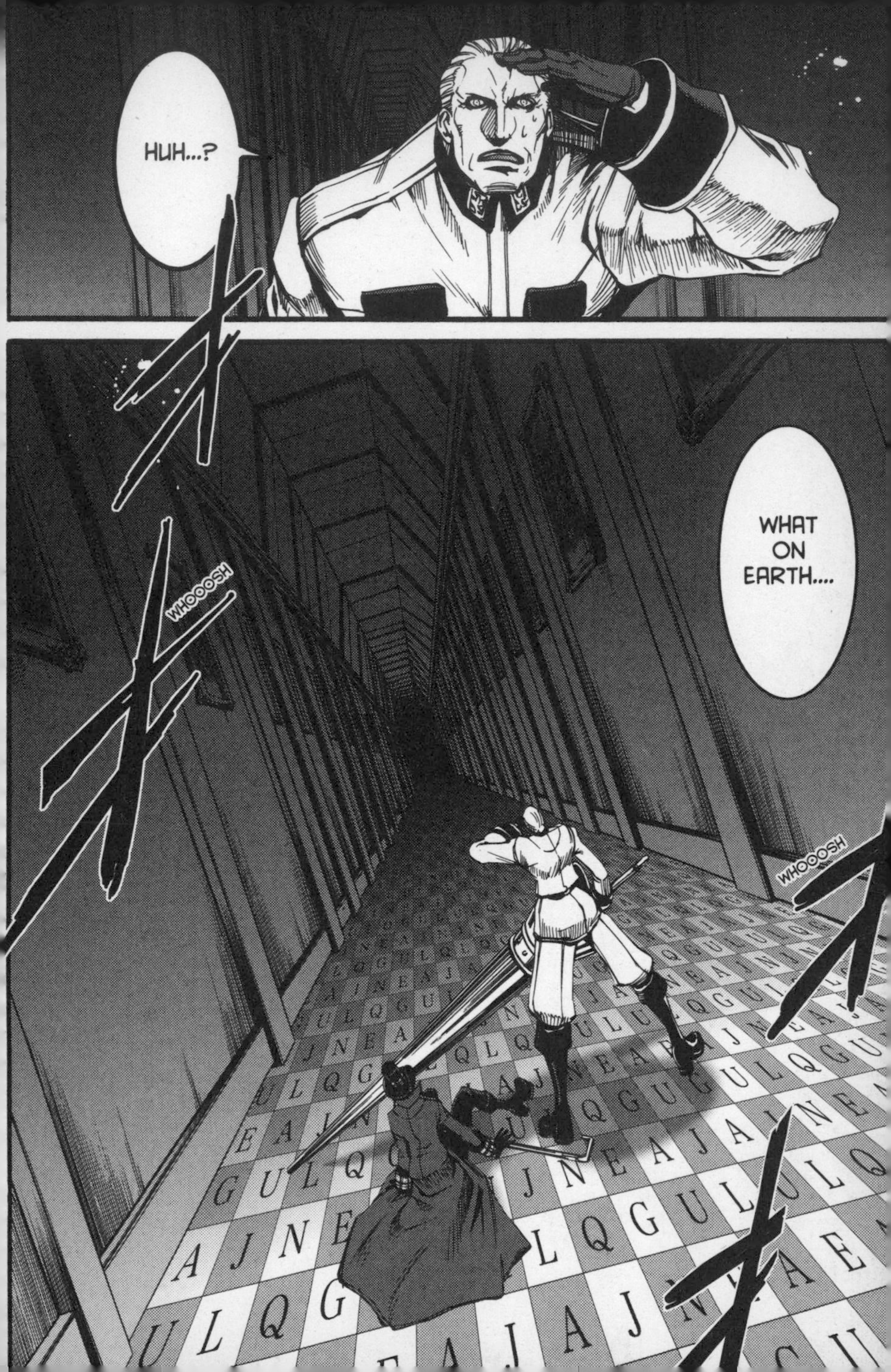
HUH...?
WHAT ON EARTH....
WHOOOSH
WHOOOSH

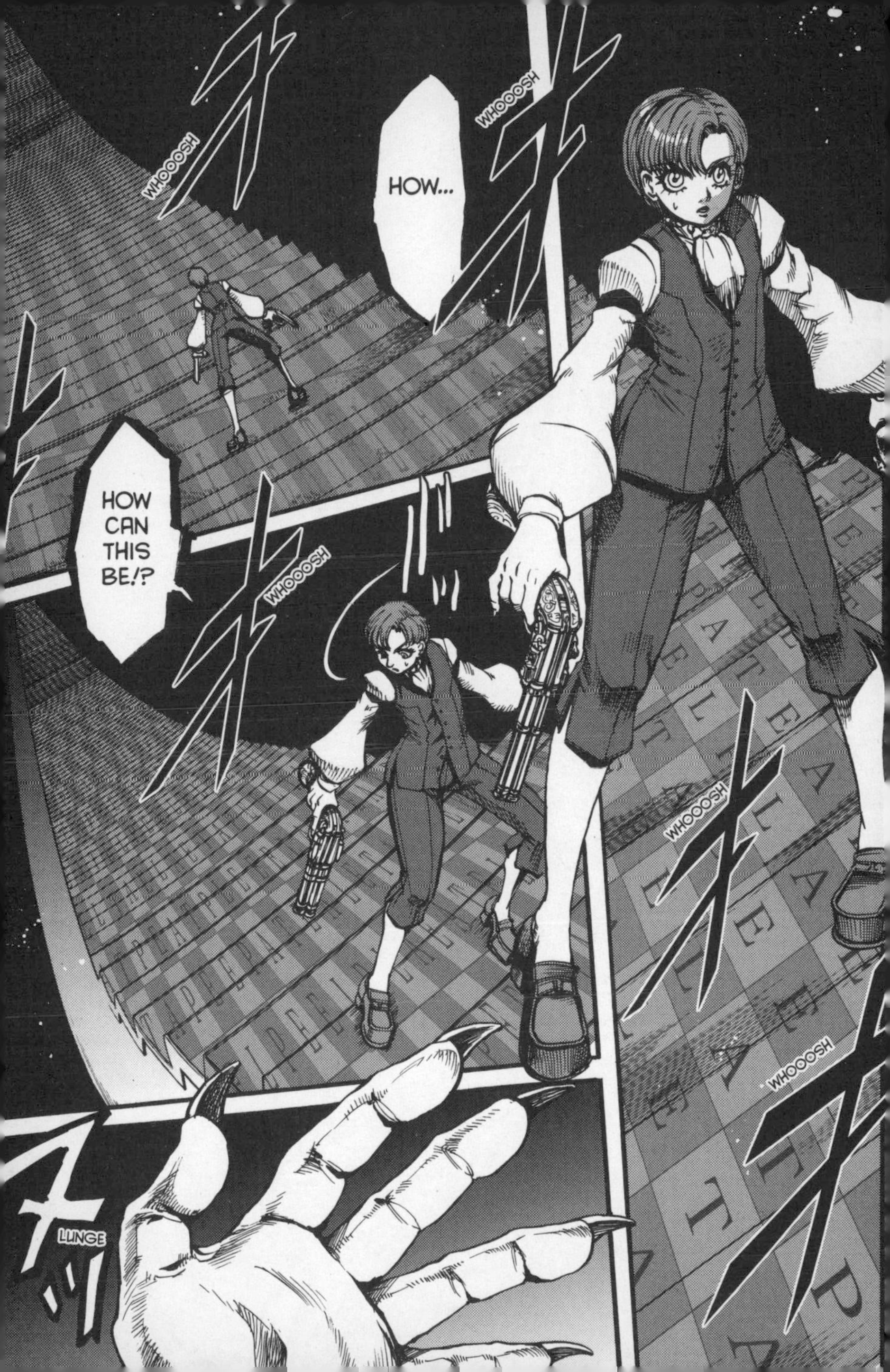
WHOOOSH
WHOOOSH
WHOOOSH
HOW...
WHOOOSH
WHOOOSH
HOW CAN THIS BE!?
LUNGE

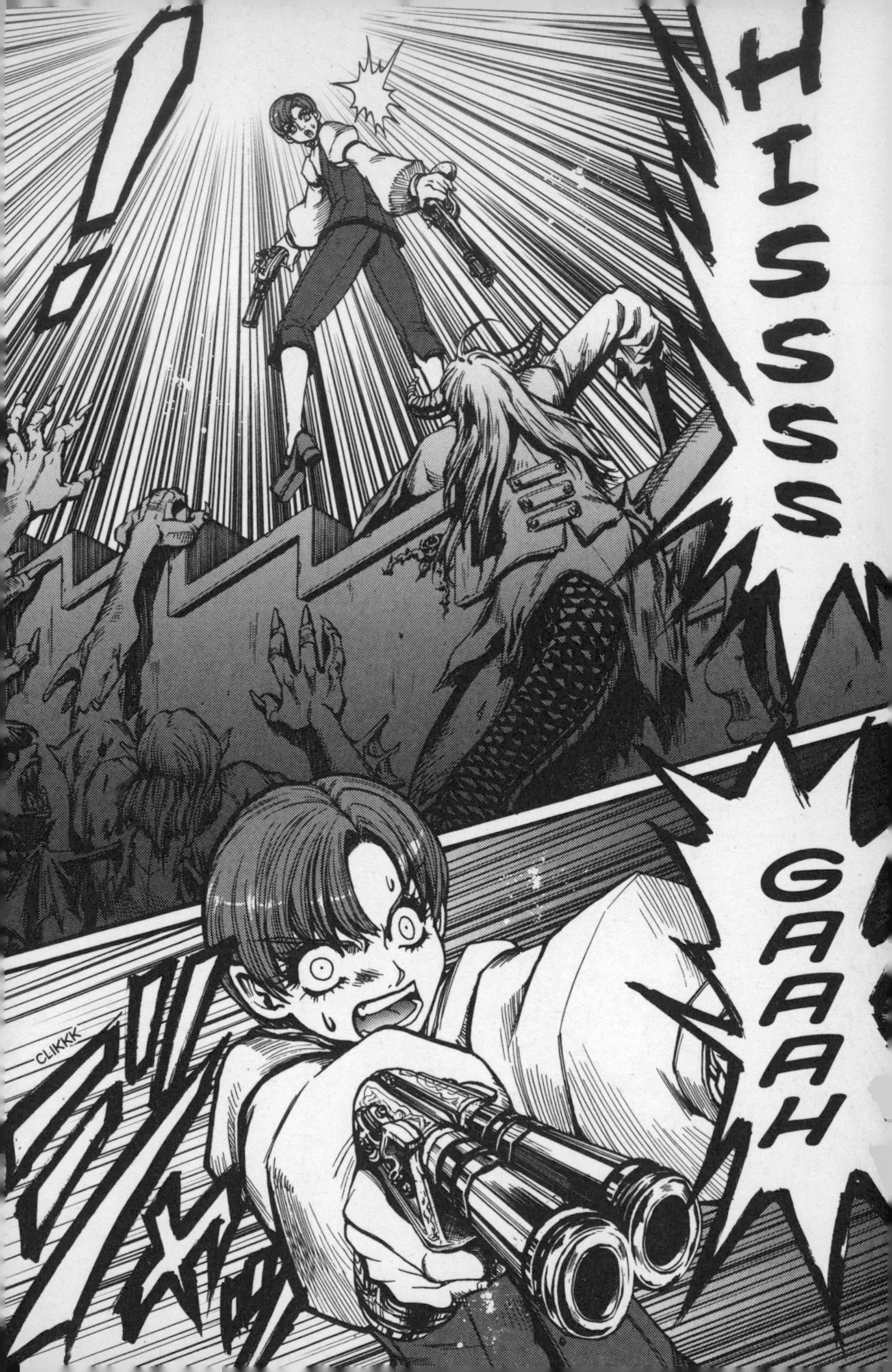
HISSSS
!
GAAAH
CLIKKK

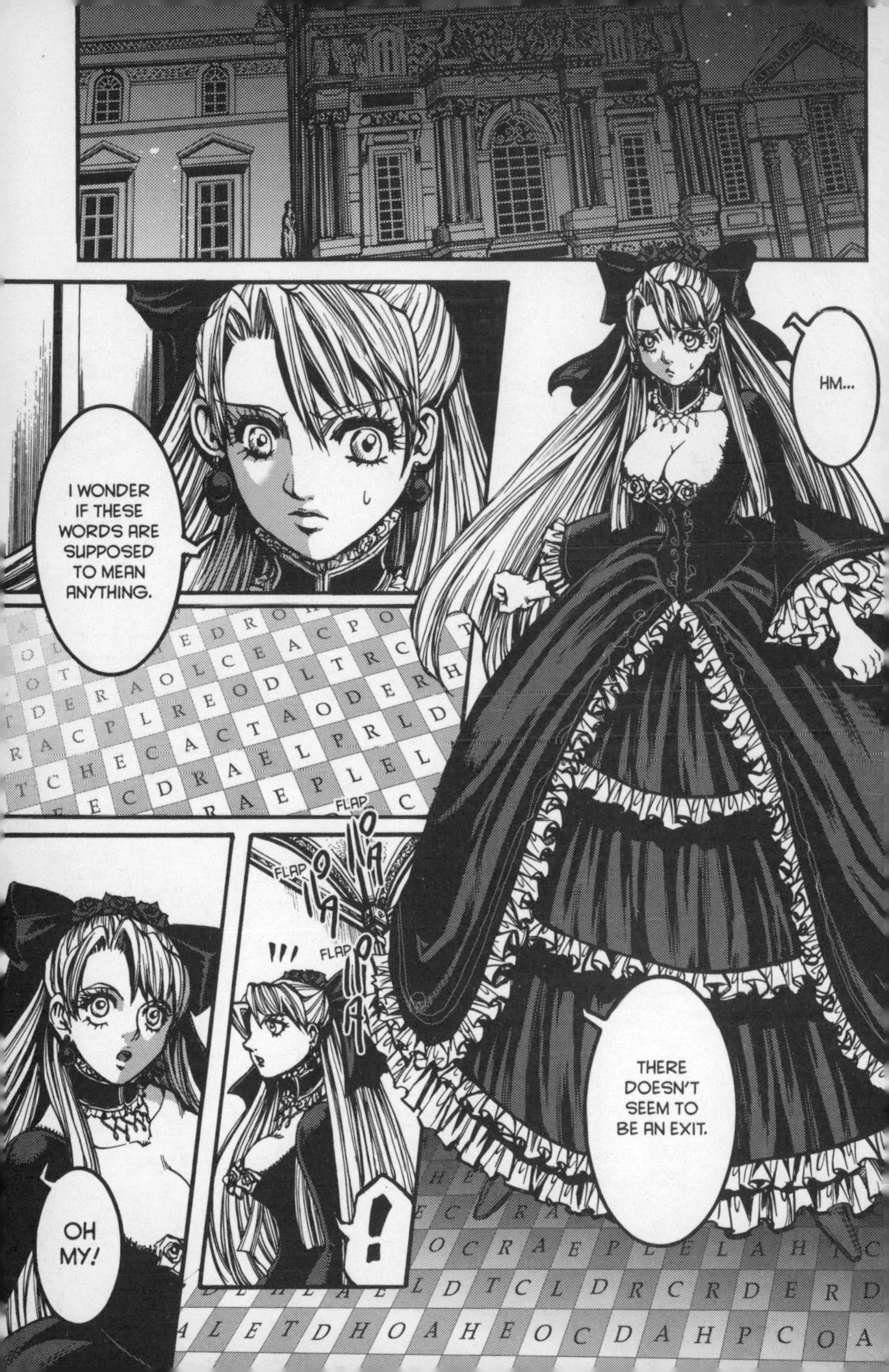
HM...
THERE DOESN'T SEEM TO BE AN EXIT.
I WONDER IF THESE WORDS ARE SUPPOSED TO MEAN ANYTHING.
FLAP
FLAP
FLAP
OH MY!

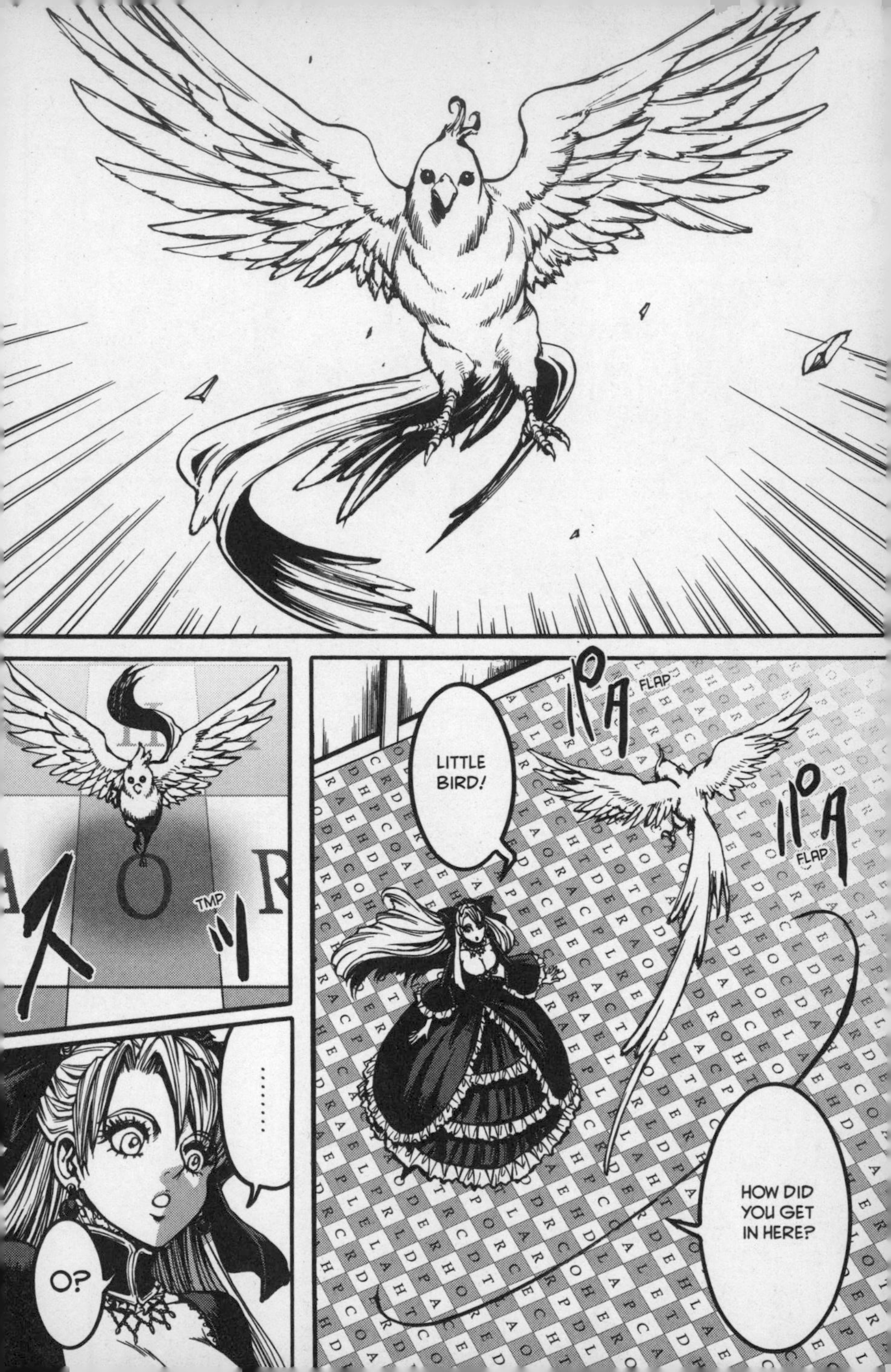
FLAP
LITTLE BIRD!
FLAP
HOW DID YOU GET IN HERE?
TMP
......
O?

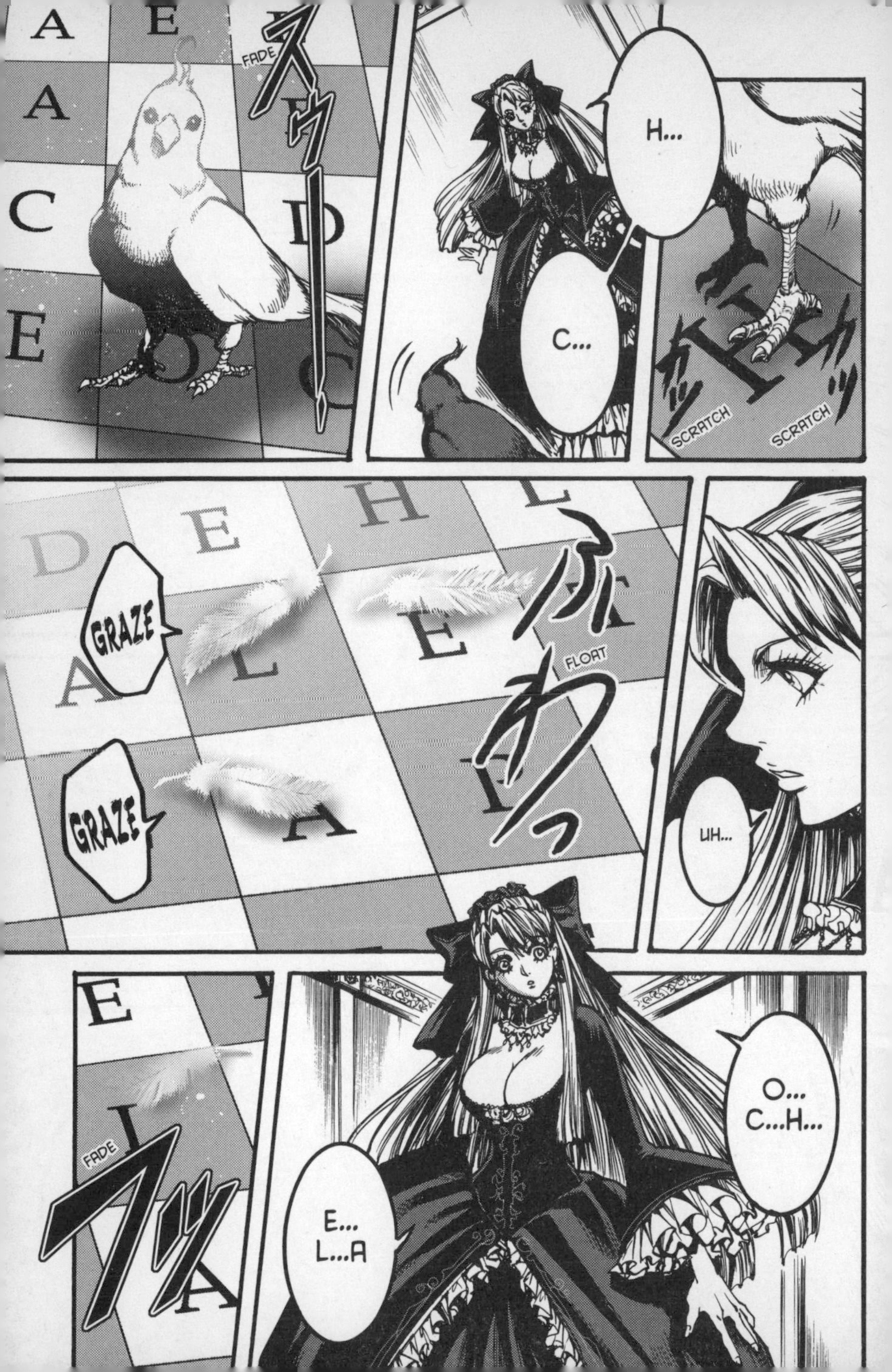
SCRATCH
SCRATCH
H...
C...
FADE
UH...
FLOAT
GRAZE
GRAZE
O... C...H...
E... L...A
FADE

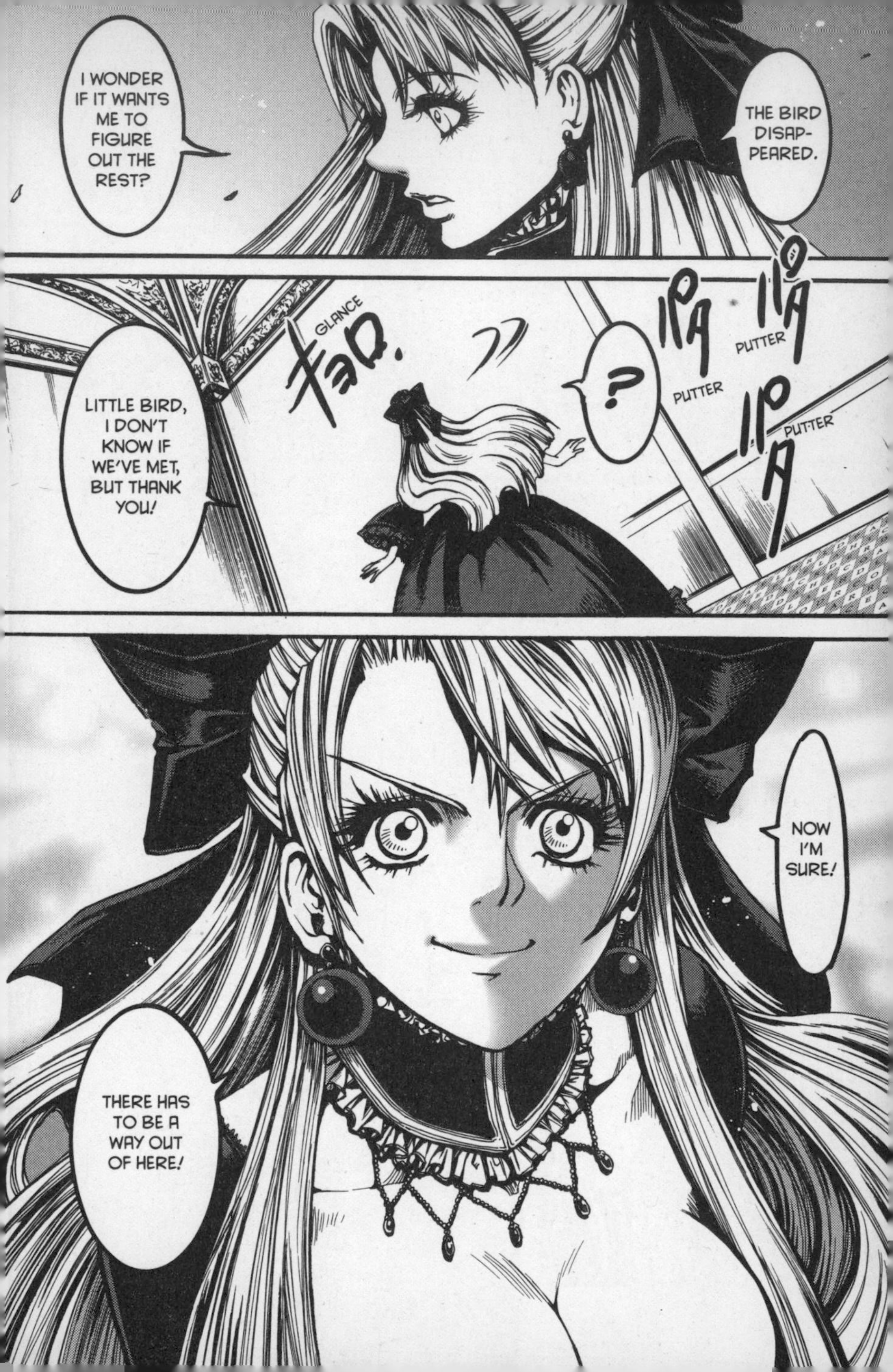
THE BIRD DISAP-PEARED.
I WONDER IF IT WANTS ME TO FIGURE OUT THE REST?
PUTTER
PUTTER
PUTTER
?
GLANCE
LITTLE BIRD, I DON'T KNOW IF WE'VE MET, BUT THANK YOU!
NOW I'M SURE!
THERE HAS TO BE A WAY OUT OF HERE!

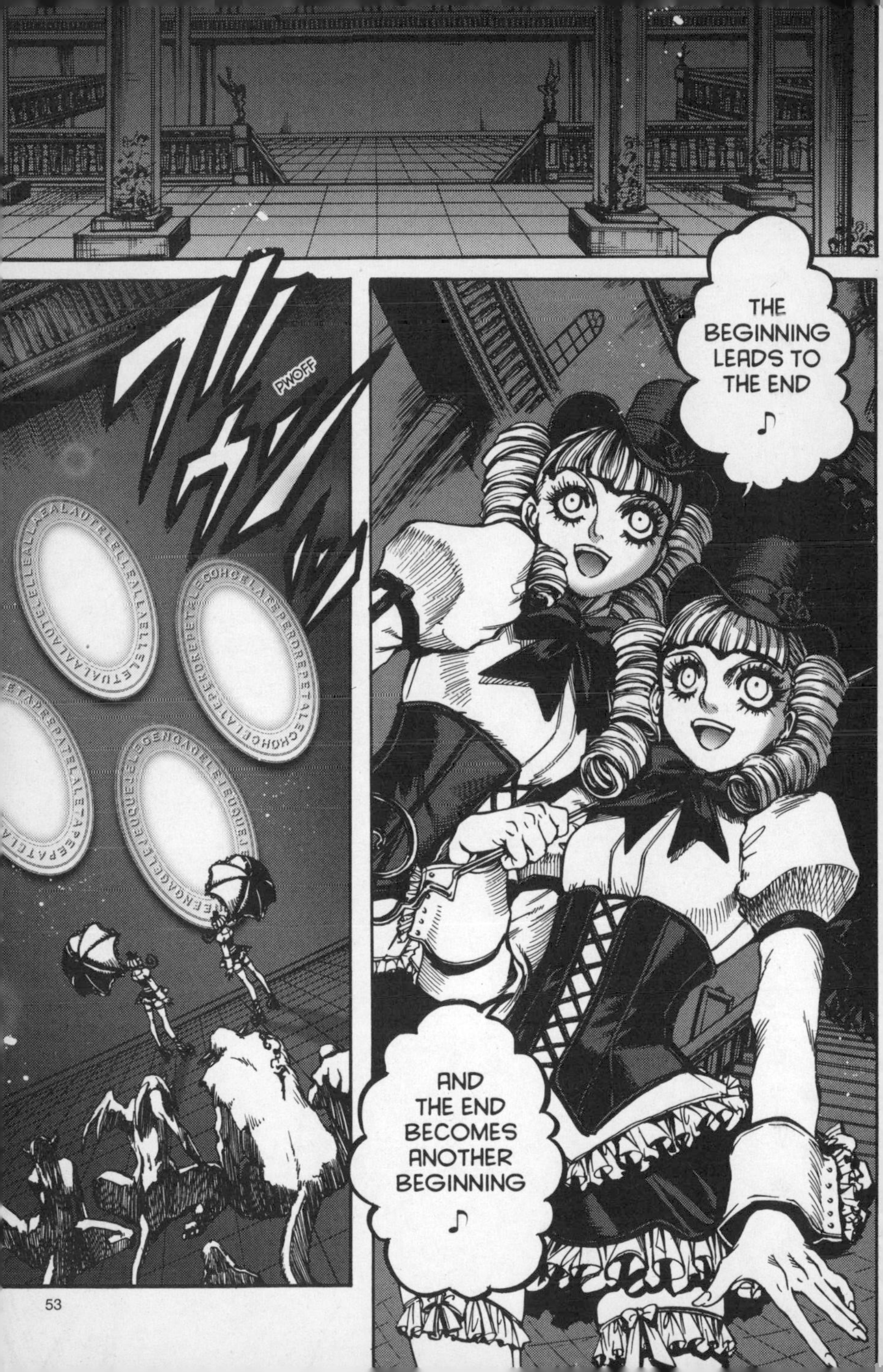
THE BEGINNING LEADS TO THE END ♪
AND THE END BECOMES ANOTHER BEGINNING ♪
PWOFF

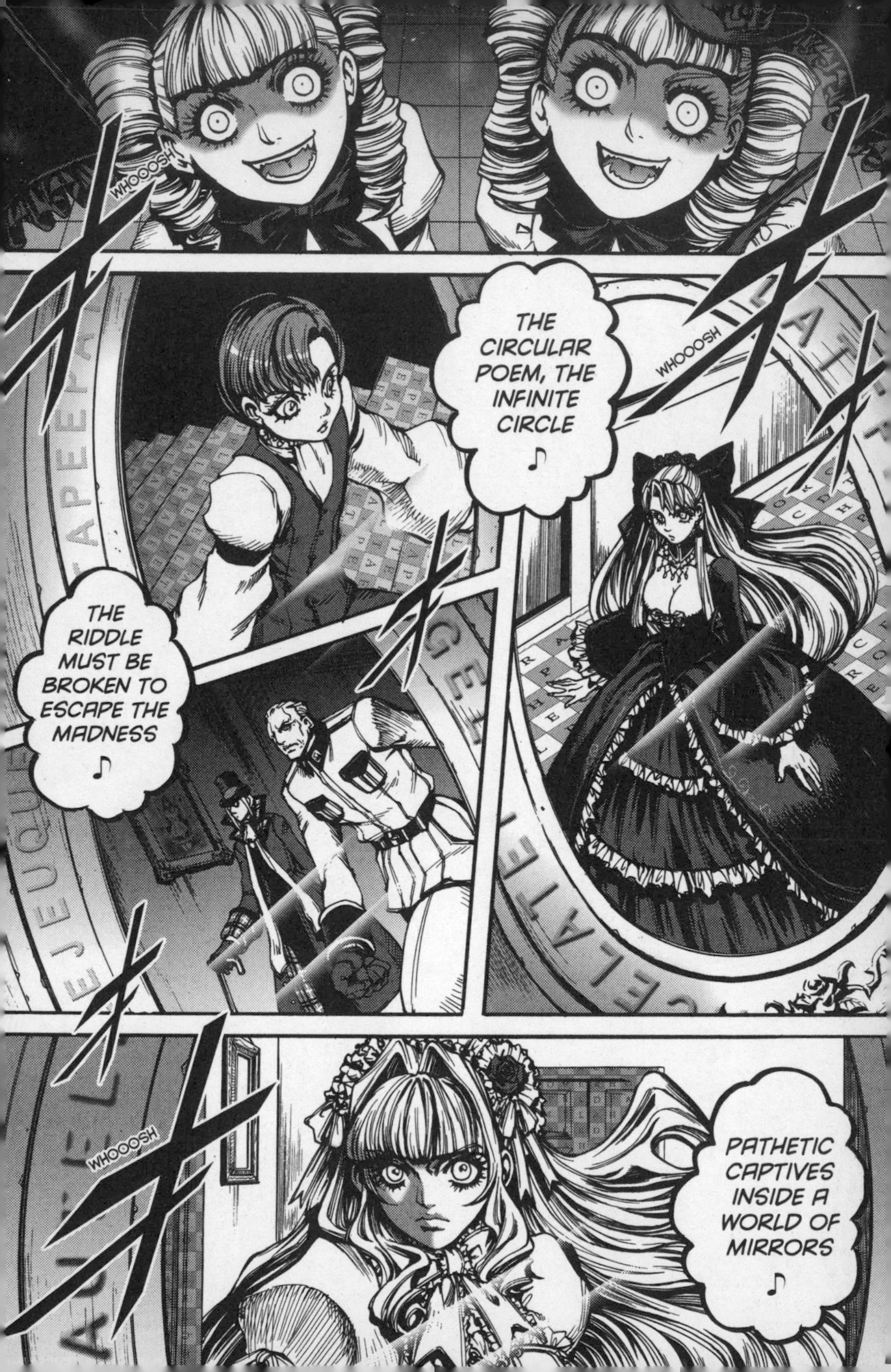
WHOOOSH
WHOOOSH
THE CIRCULAR POEM, THE INFINITE CIRCLE ♪
THE RIDDLE MUST BE BROKEN TO ESCAPE THE MADNESS ♪
PATHETIC CAPTIVES INSIDE A WORLD OF MIRRORS ♪
WHOOOSH

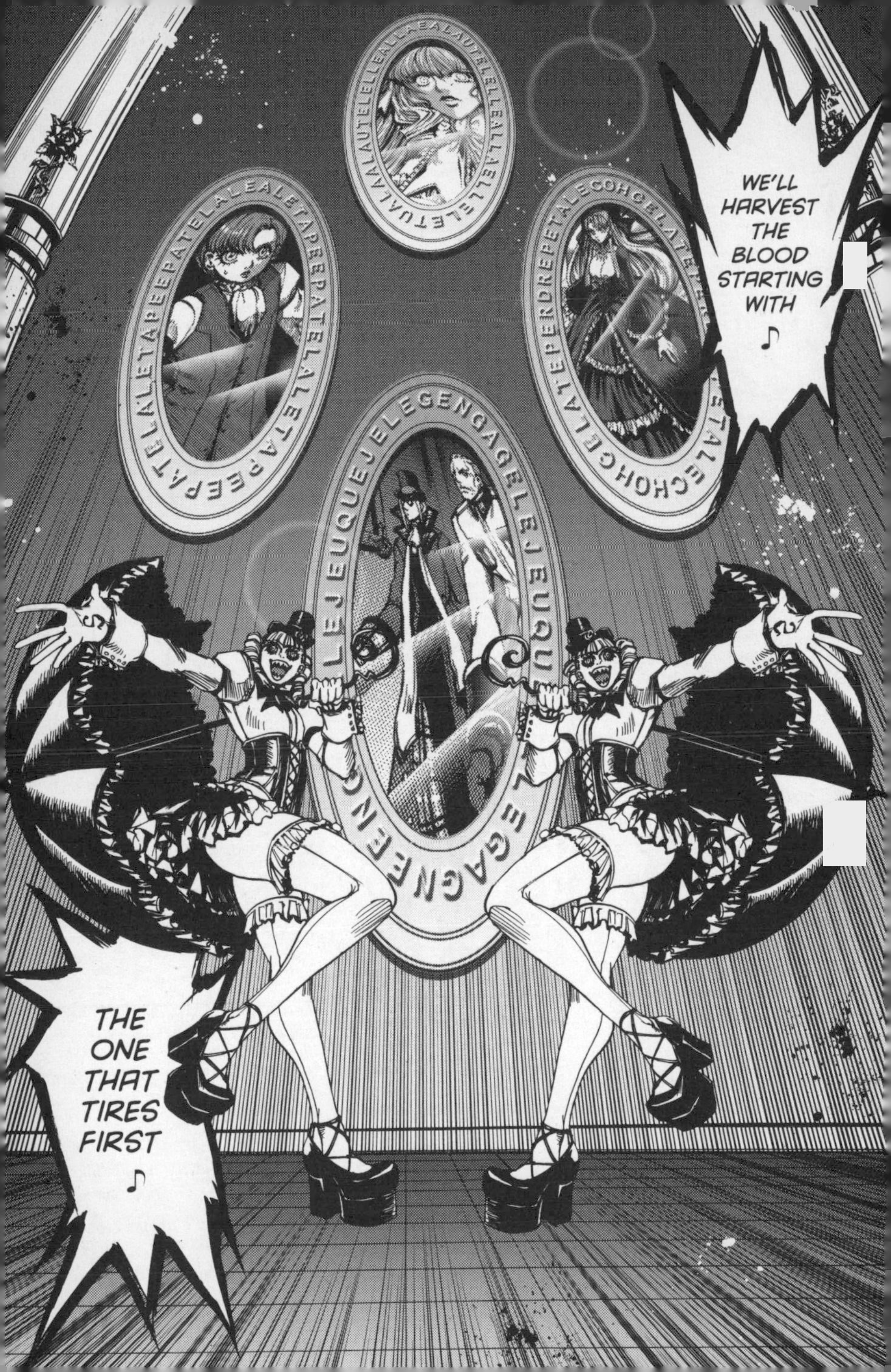
WE'LL HARVEST THE BLOOD STARTING WITH ♪
THE ONE THAT TIRES FIRST ♪

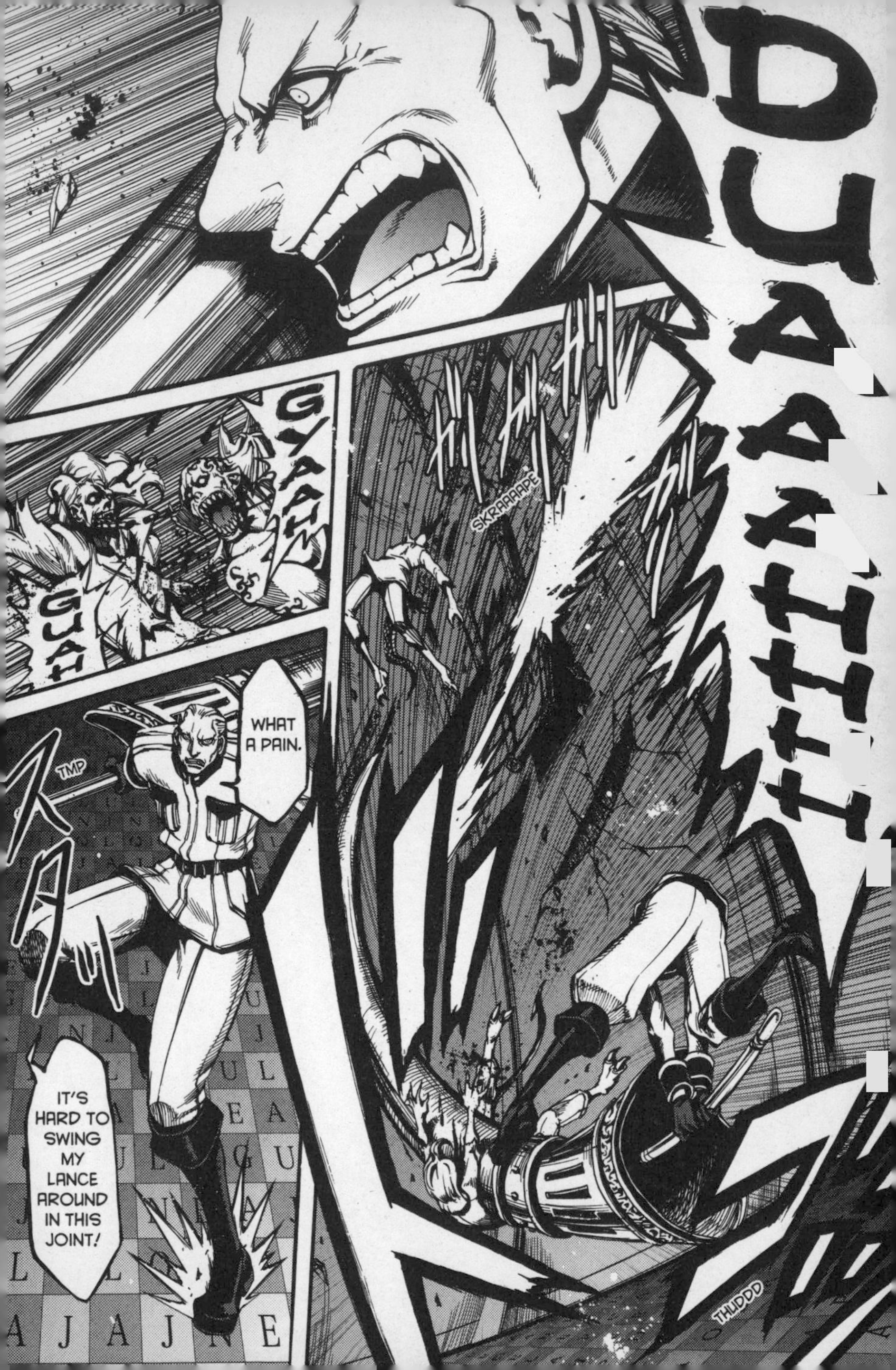
DUAAAHHHH—
SKRAAAAPE
THUDDD
GYAAAH
GUAH
WHAT A PAIN.
TMP
IT'S HARD TO SWING MY LANCE AROUND IN THIS JOINT!

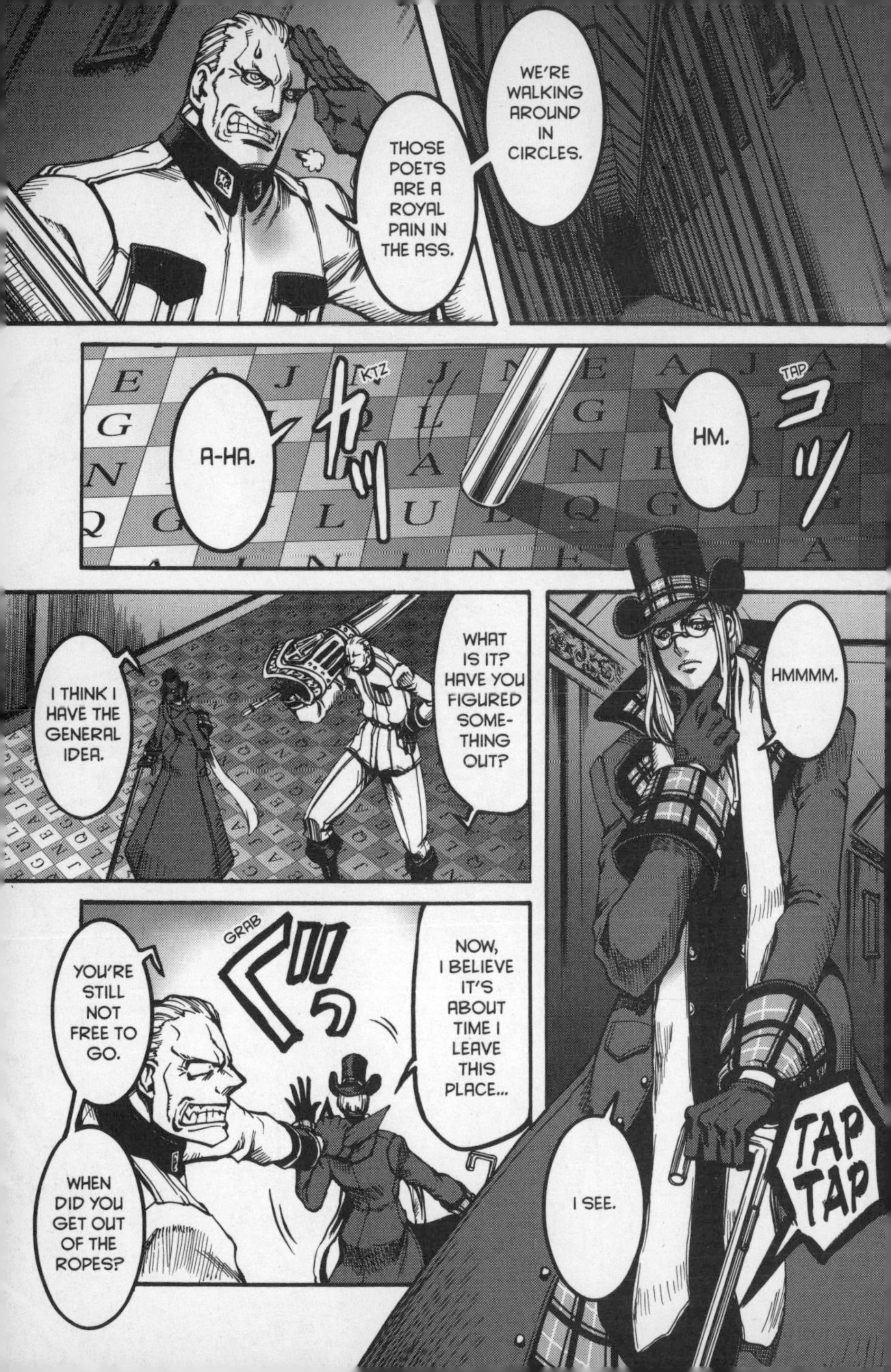
WE'RE WALKING AROUND IN CIRCLES.
THOSE POETS ARE A ROYAL PAIN IN THE ASS.
TAP
HM.
KTZ
A-HA.
HMMMM.
TAP TAP
I SEE.
WHAT IS IT? HAVE YOU FIGURED SOME-THING OUT?
I THINK I HAVE THE GENERAL IDEA.
NOW, I BELIEVE IT'S ABOUT TIME I LEAVE THIS PLACE...
GRAB
YOU'RE STILL NOT FREE TO GO.
WHEN DID YOU GET OUT OF THE ROPES?

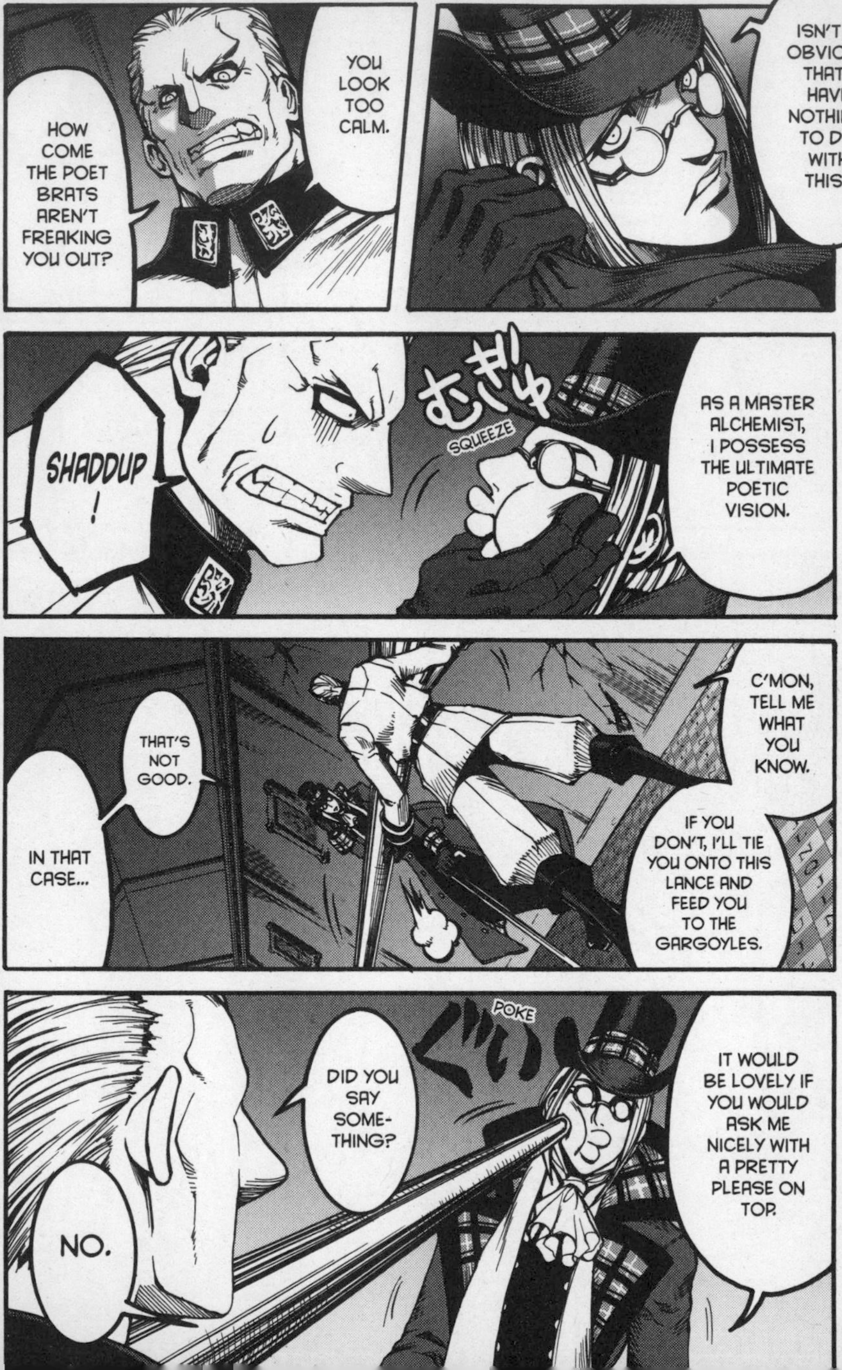
ISN'T IT OBVIOUS THAT I HAVE NOTHING TO DO WITH THIS?
YOU LOOK TOO CALM.
HOW COME THE POET BRATS AREN'T FREAKING YOU OUT?
AS A MASTER ALCHEMIST, I POSSESS THE ULTIMATE POETIC VISION.
むぎゅ
SQUEEZE
SHADDUP!
C'MON, TELL ME WHAT YOU KNOW.
IF YOU DON'T, I'LL TIE YOU ONTO THIS LANCE AND FEED YOU TO THE GARGOYLES.
THAT'S NOT GOOD.
IN THAT CASE...
IT WOULD BE LOVELY IF YOU WOULD ASK ME NICELY WITH A PRETTY PLEASE ON TOP.
ぐいっ
POKE
DID YOU SAY SOMETHING?
NO.

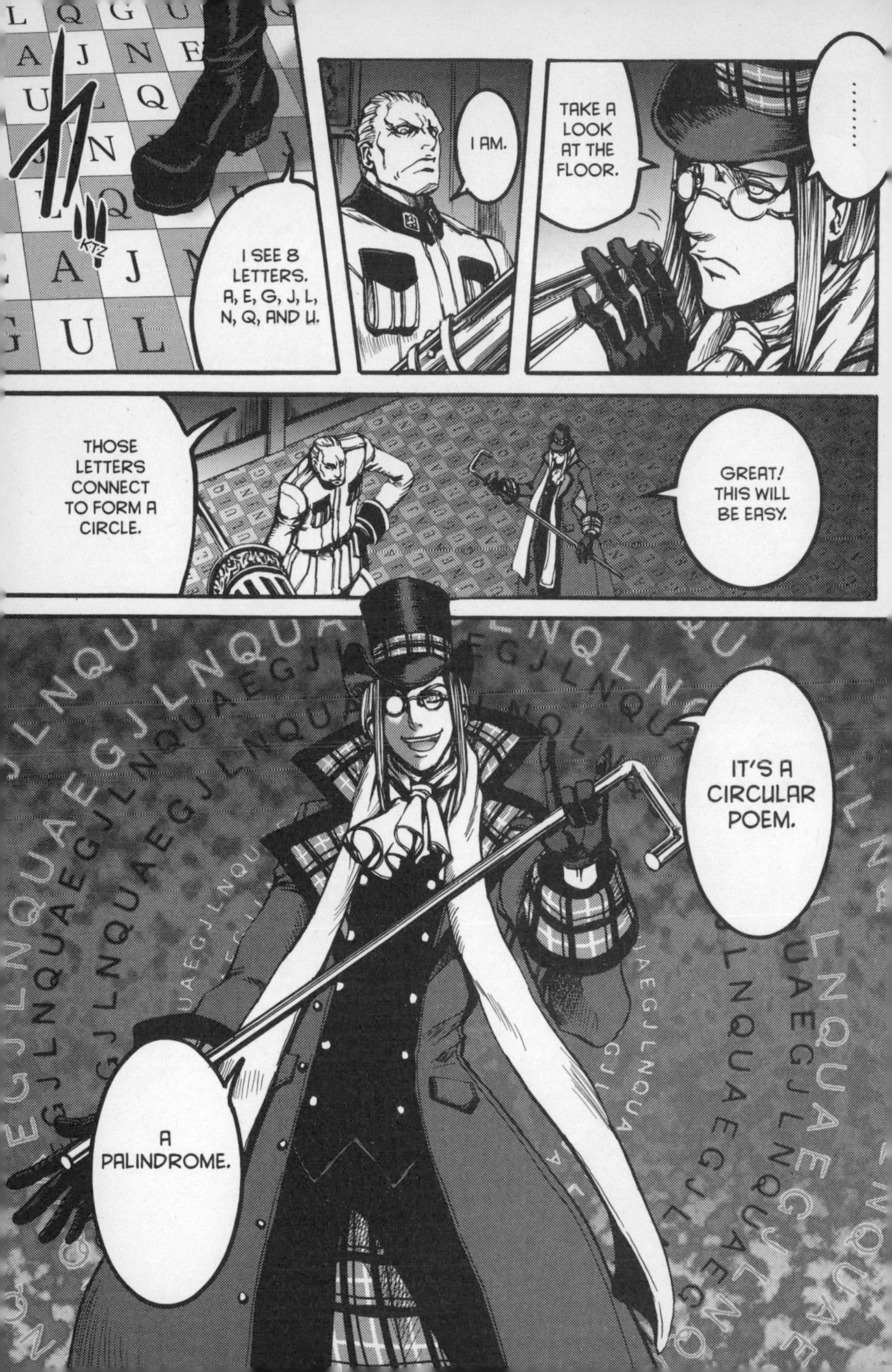
......
TAKE A LOOK AT THE FLOOR.
I AM.
I SEE 8 LETTERS. A, E, G, J, L, N, Q, AND U.
KTZ
GREAT! THIS WILL BE EASY.
THOSE LETTERS CONNECT TO FORM A CIRCLE.
IT'S A CIRCULAR POEM.
A PALINDROME.

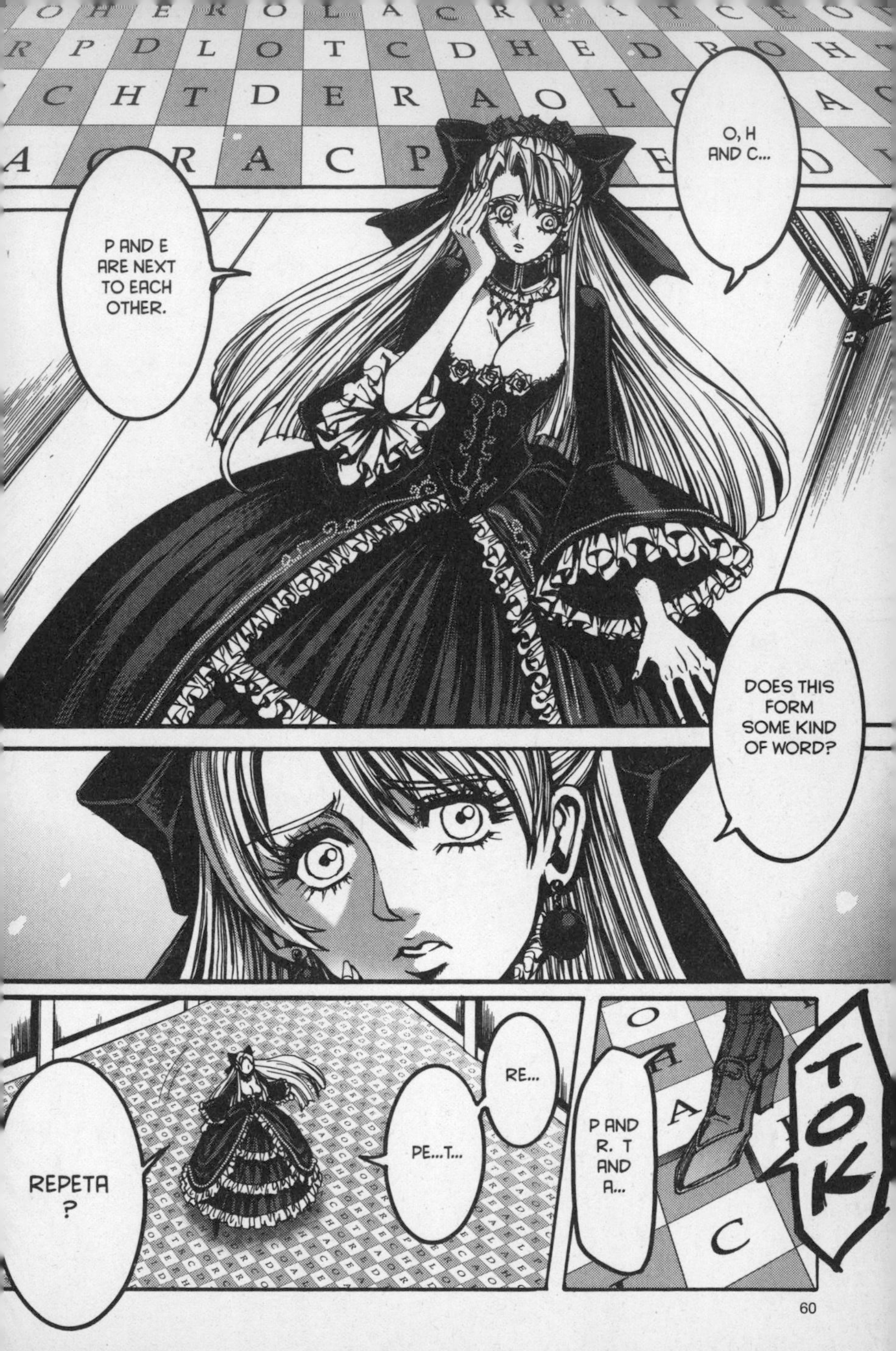
O, H AND C...
P AND E ARE NEXT TO EACH OTHER.
DOES THIS FORM SOME KIND OF WORD?
TOK
P AND R. T AND A...
RE...
PE...T...
REPETA ?

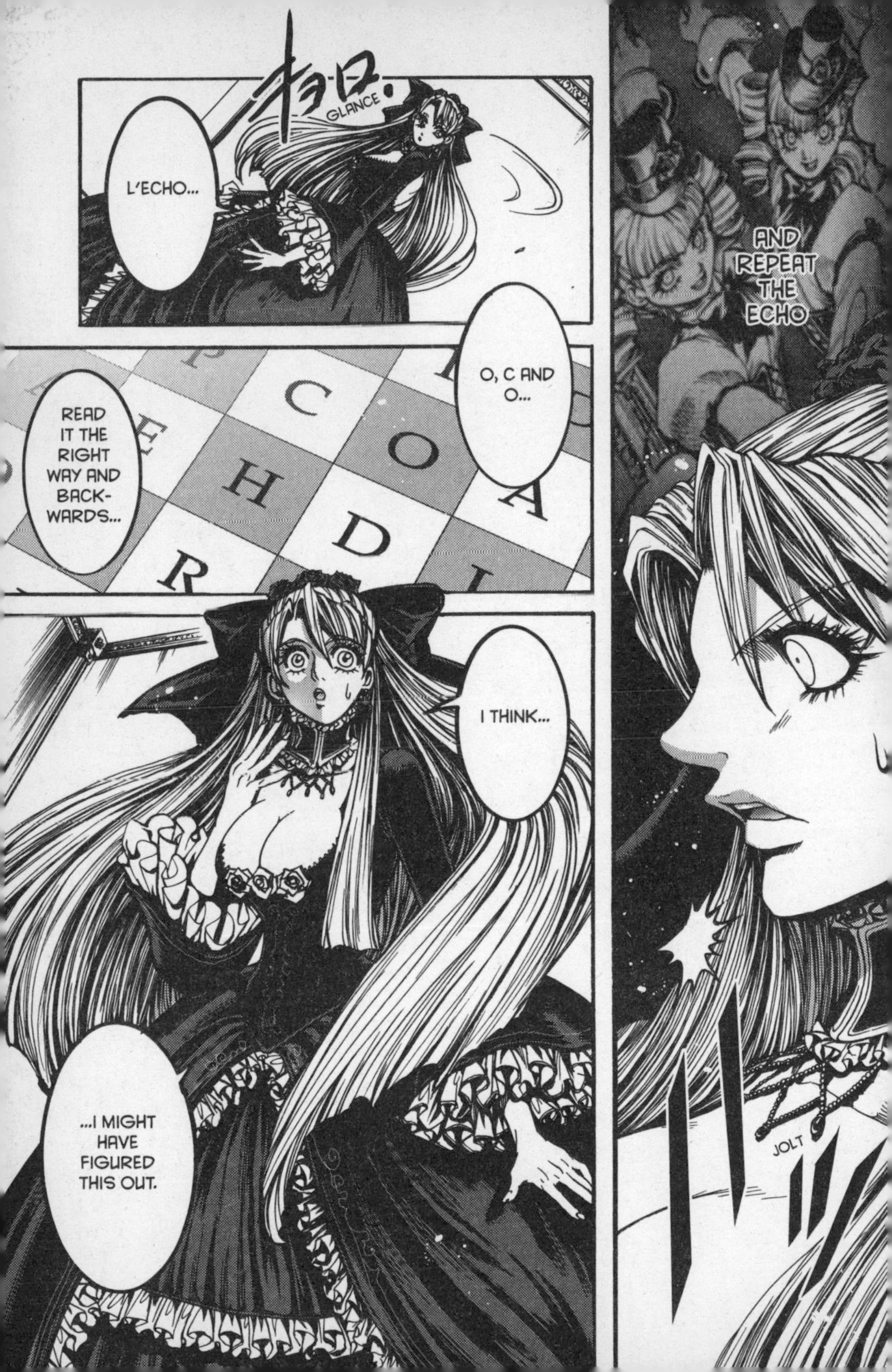
AND REPEAT THE ECHO
JOLT
GLANCE
L'ECHO...
O, C AND O...
READ IT THE RIGHT WAY AND BACK-WARDS...
I THINK...
...I MIGHT HAVE FIGURED THIS OUT.

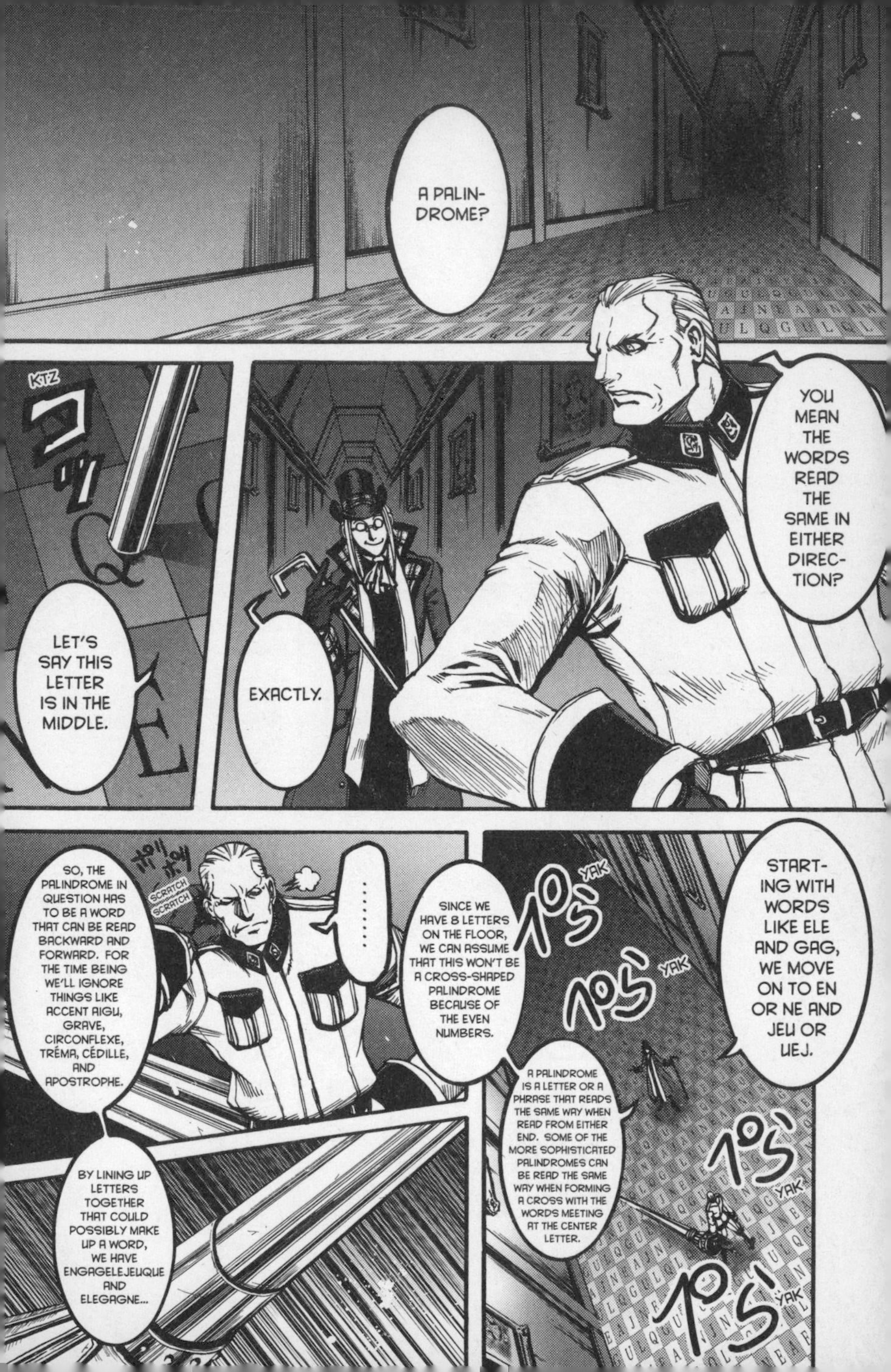

A PALIN-DROME?
YOU MEAN THE WORDS READ THE SAME IN EITHER DIRECTION?
EXACTLY.
KTZ
LET'S SAY THIS LETTER IS IN THE MIDDLE.
STARTING WITH WORDS LIKE ELE AND GAG, WE MOVE ON TO EN OR NE AND JEU OR UEJ.
YAK
YAK
A PALINDROME IS A LETTER OR A PHRASE THAT READS THE SAME WAY WHEN READ FROM EITHER END. SOME OF THE MORE SOPHISTICATED PALINDROMES CAN BE READ THE SAME WAY WHEN FORMING A CROSS WITH THE WORDS MEETING AT THE CENTER LETTER.
YAK
YAK
SINCE WE HAVE 8 LETTERS ON THE FLOOR, WE CAN ASSUME THAT THIS WON'T BE A CROSS-SHAPED PALINDROME BECAUSE OF THE EVEN NUMBERS.
....
SCRATCH SCRATCH
SO, THE PALINDROME IN QUESTION HAS TO BE A WORD THAT CAN BE READ BACKWARD AND FORWARD. FOR THE TIME BEING WE'LL IGNORE THINGS LIKE ACCENT AIGU, GRAVE, CIRCONFLEXE, TRÉMA, CÉDILLE, AND APOSTROPHE.
BY LINING UP LETTERS TOGETHER THAT COULD POSSIBLY MAKE UP A WORD, WE HAVE ENGAGELEJEUQUE AND ELEGAGNE...

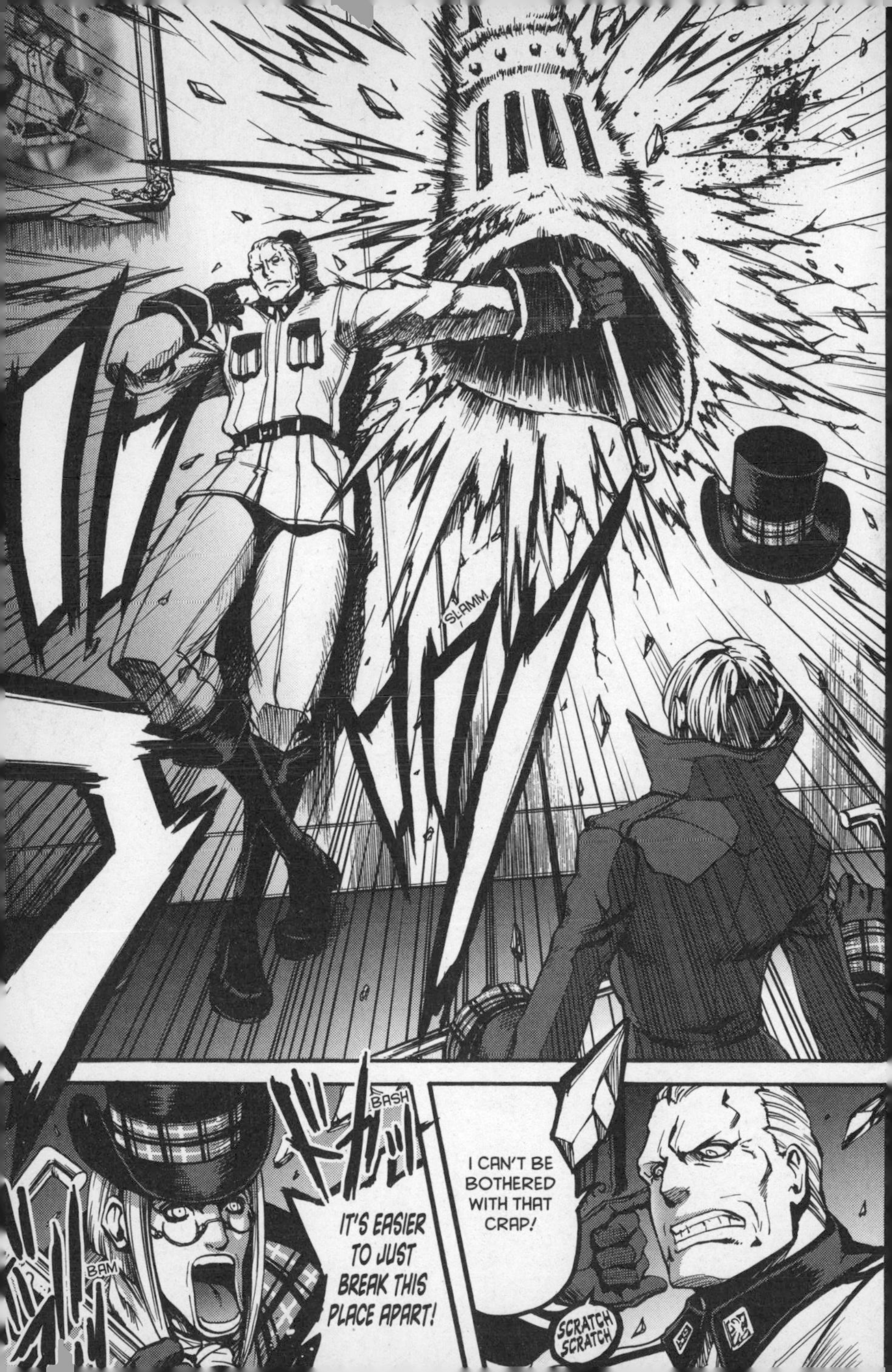
SLAMM
I CAN'T BE BOTHERED WITH THAT CRAP!
SCRATCH SCRATCH
BASH
IT'S EASIER TO JUST BREAK THIS PLACE APART!
BAM

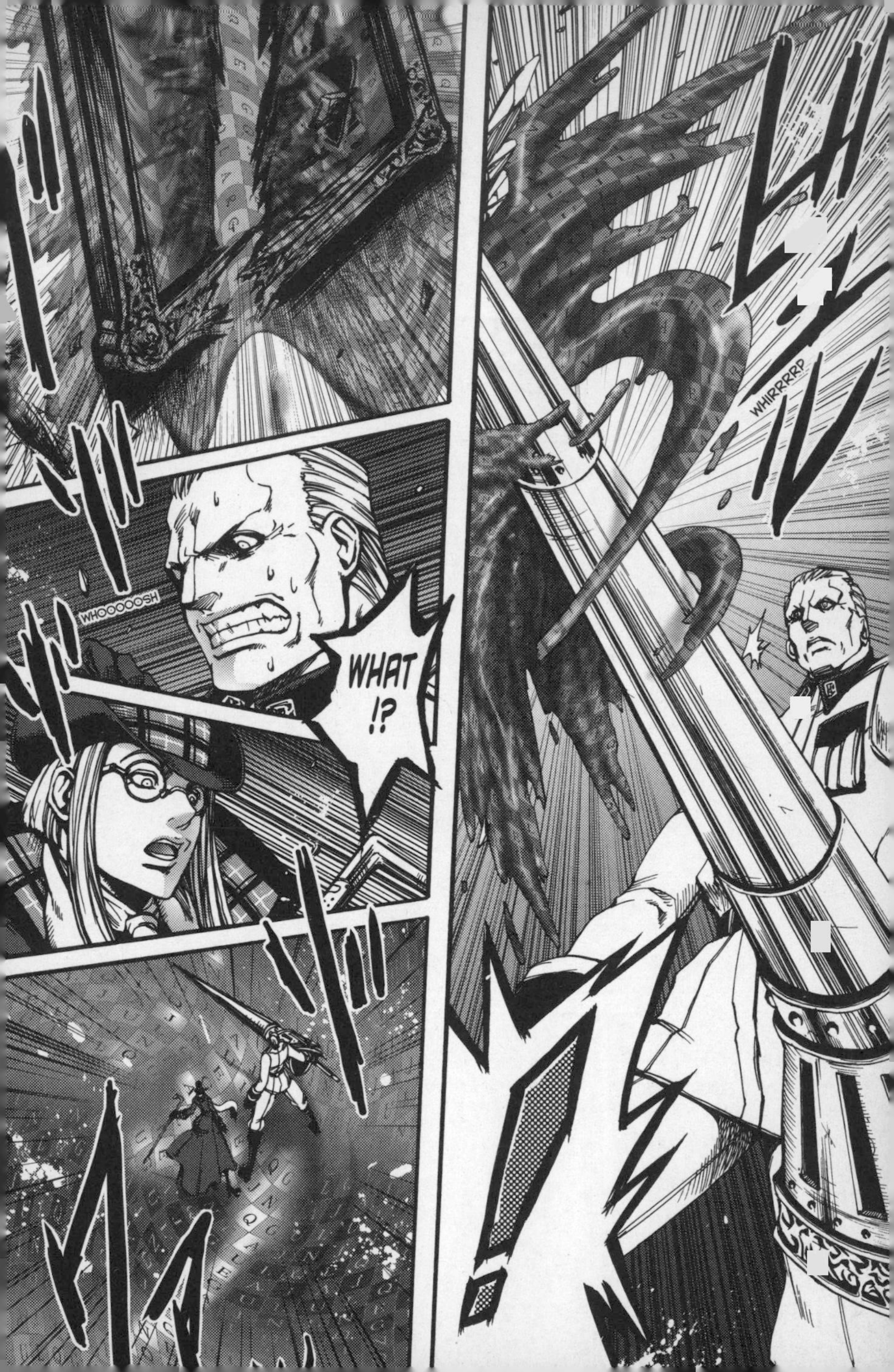
WHIRRRRP
WHOOOOOSH
WHAT !?

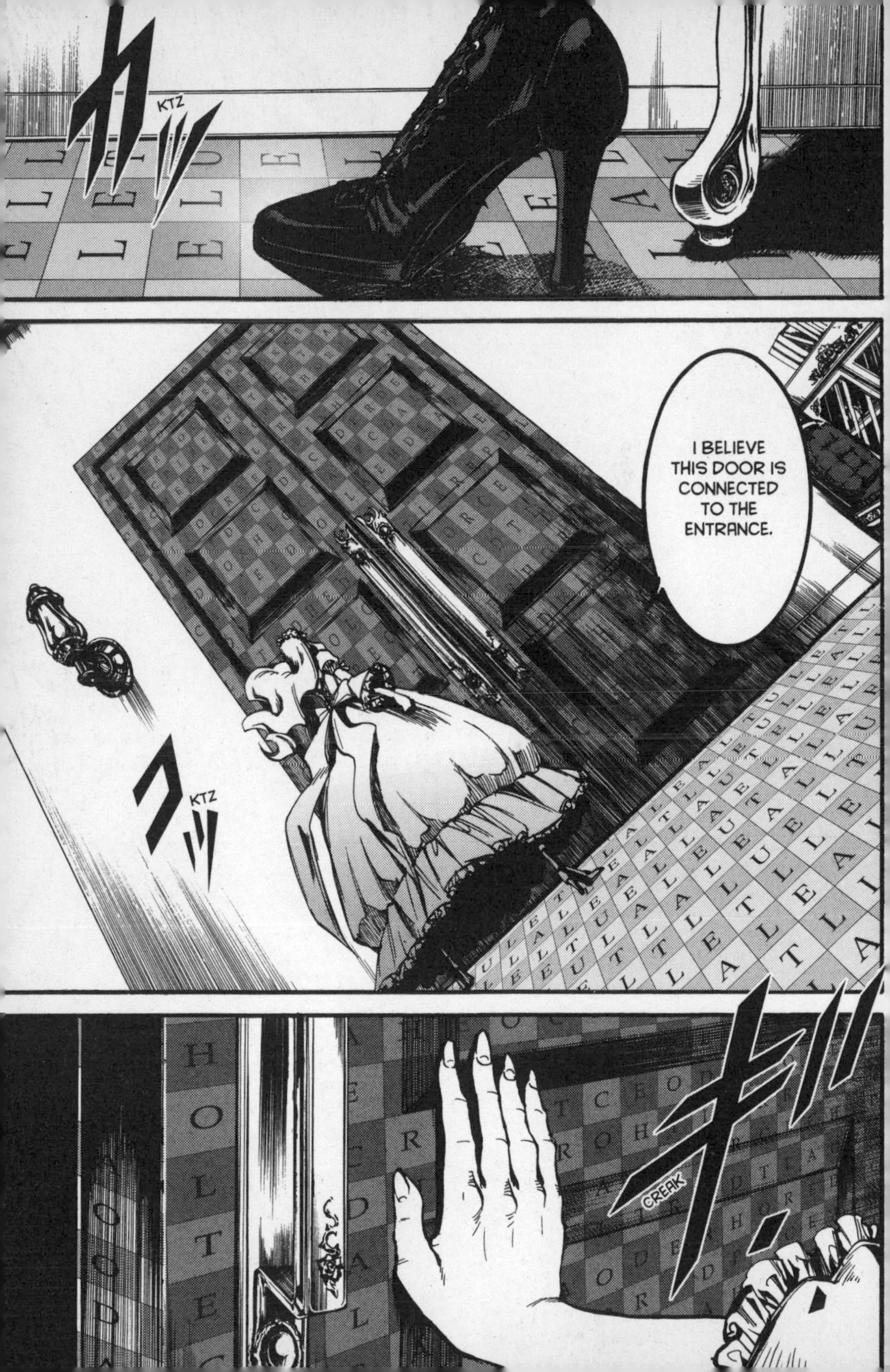
KTZ
I BELIEVE THIS DOOR IS CONNECTED TO THE ENTRANCE.
KTZ
CREAK

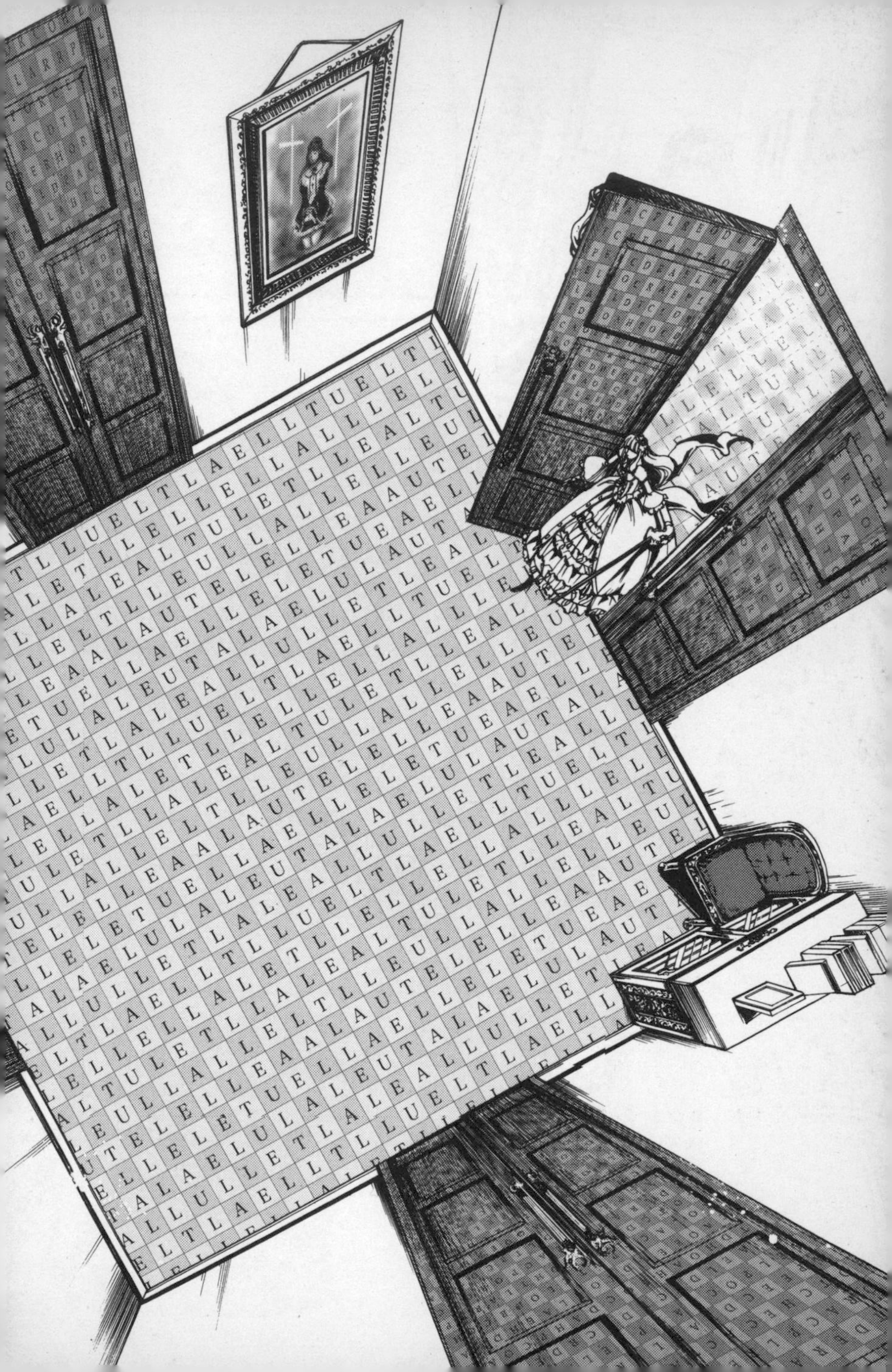

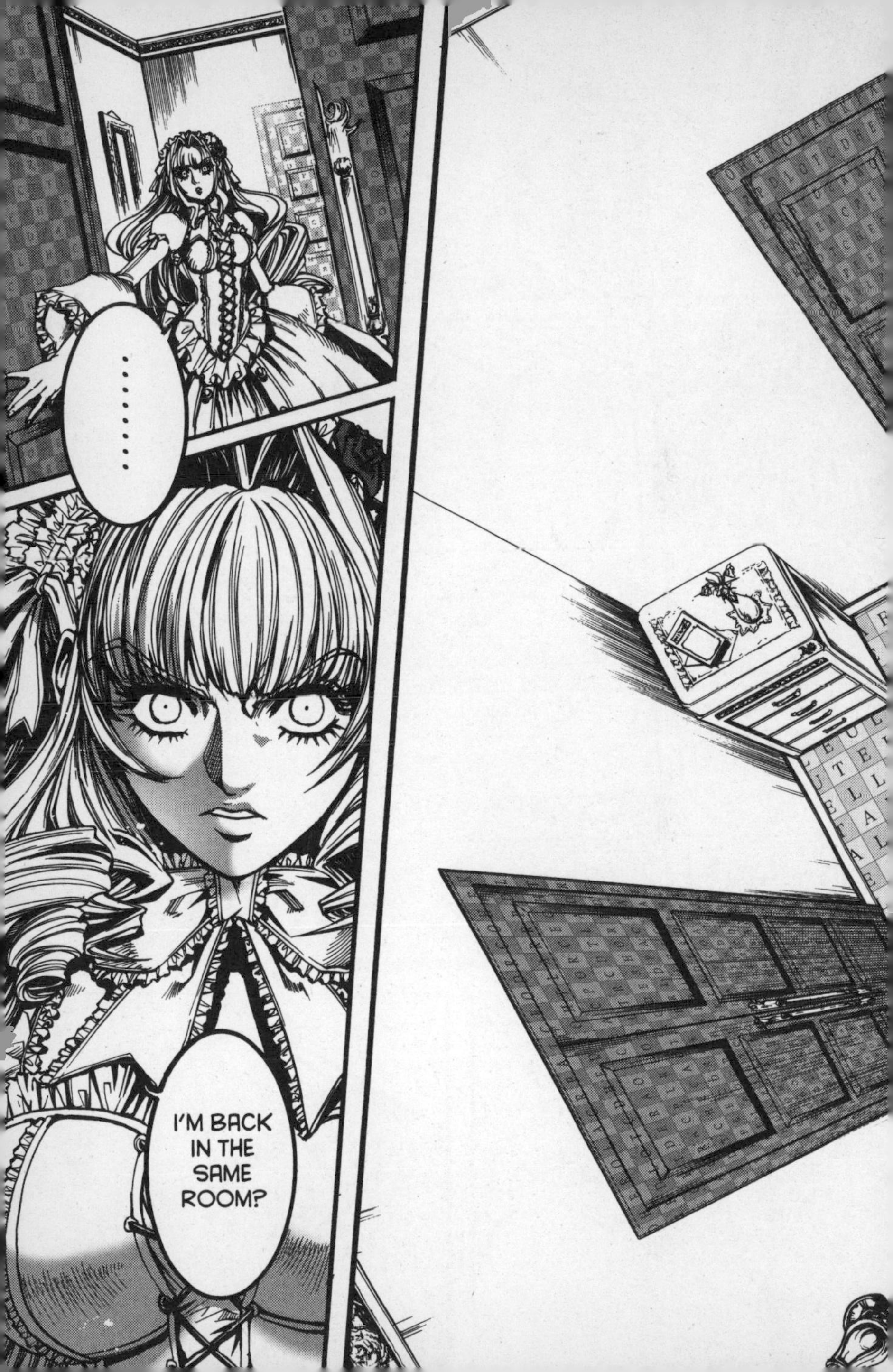
......
I'M BACK IN THE SAME ROOM?

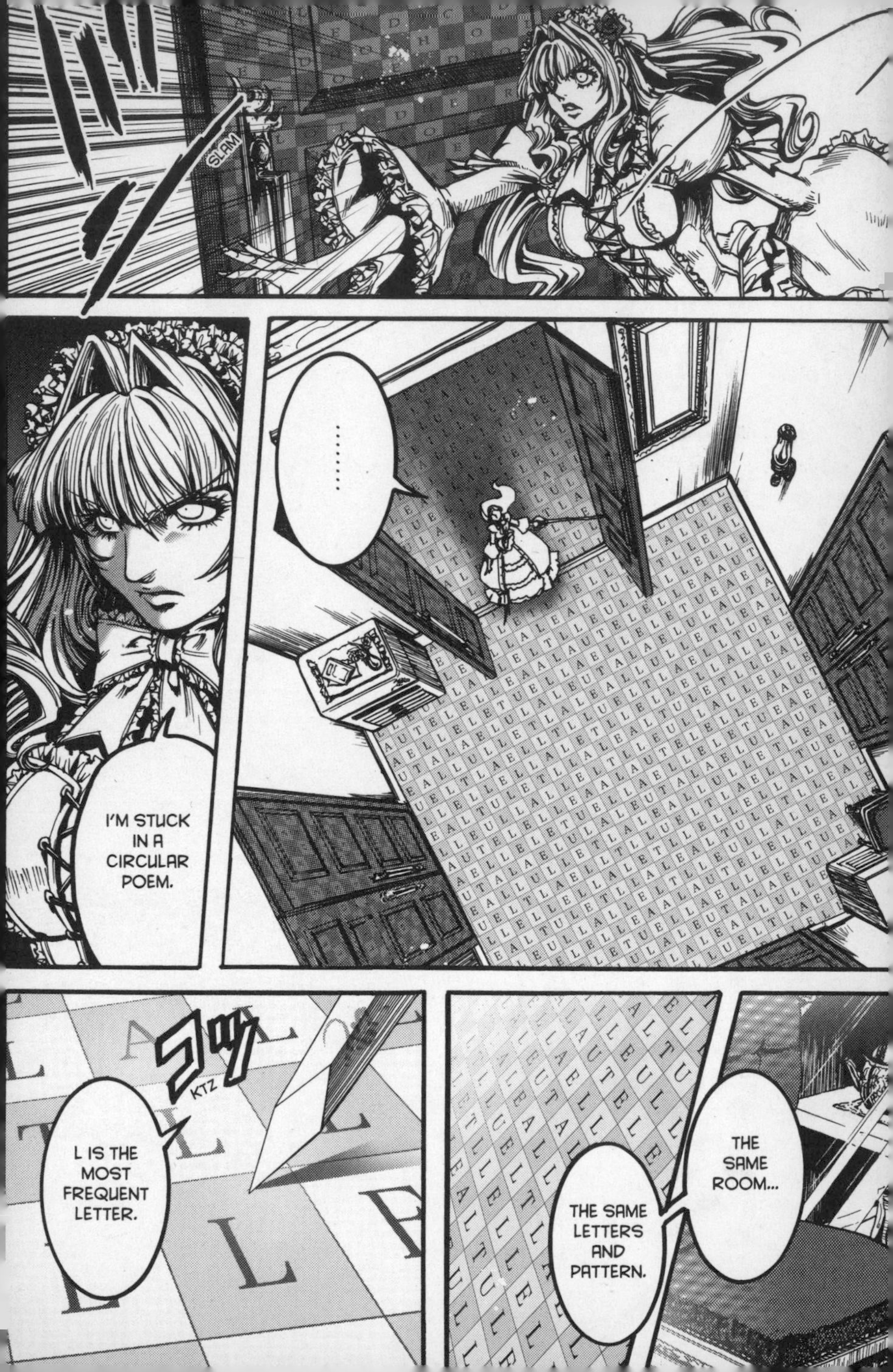
SLAM
......
I'M STUCK IN A CIRCULAR POEM.
THE SAME ROOM...
THE SAME LETTERS AND PATTERN.
KTZ
L IS THE MOST FREQUENT LETTER.

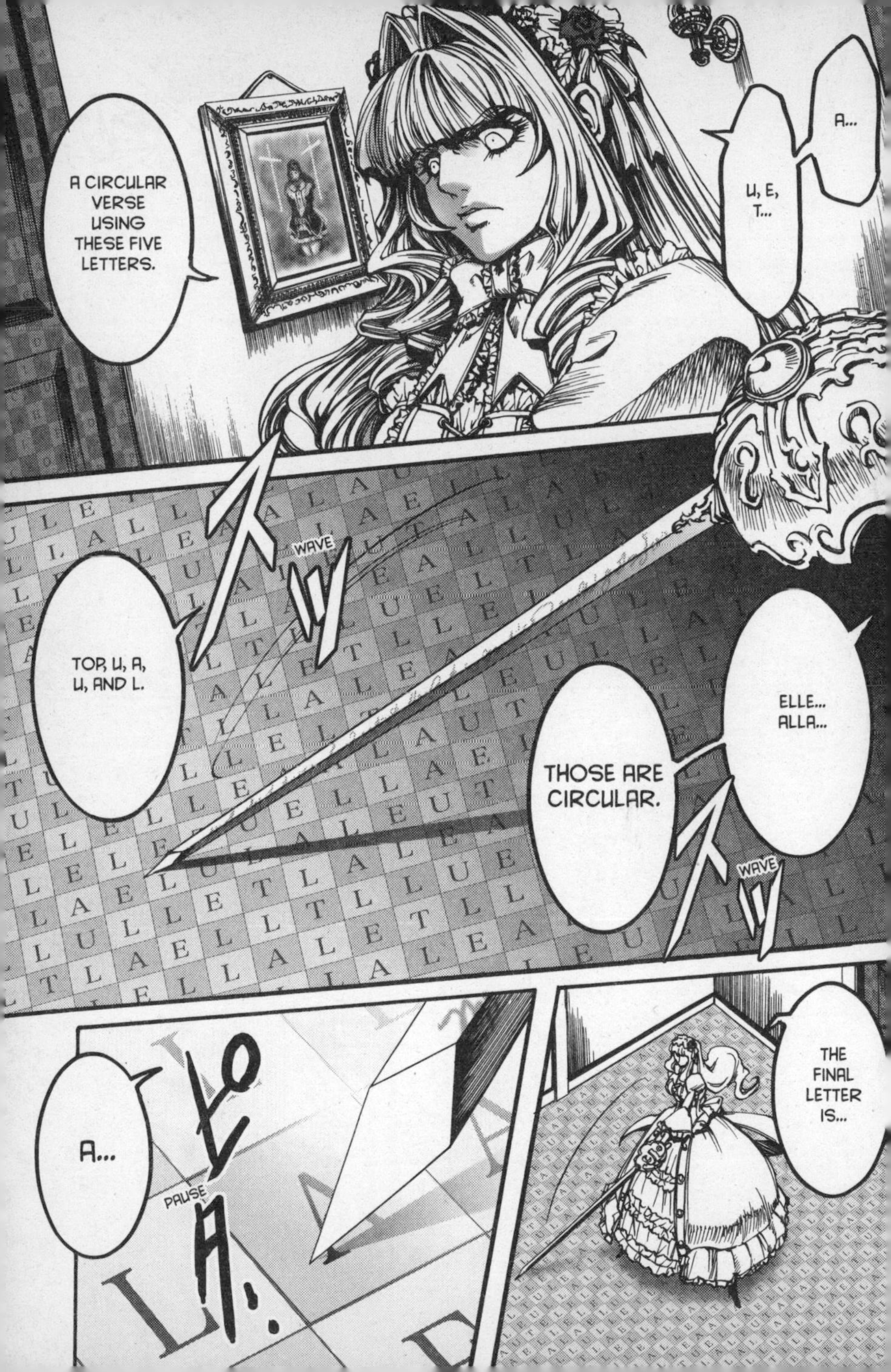
A...
U, E, T...
A CIRCULAR VERSE USING THESE FIVE LETTERS.
ELLE... ALLA...
THOSE ARE CIRCULAR.
WAVE
WAVE
TOP, U, A, U, AND L.
THE FINAL LETTER IS...
A...
PAUSE

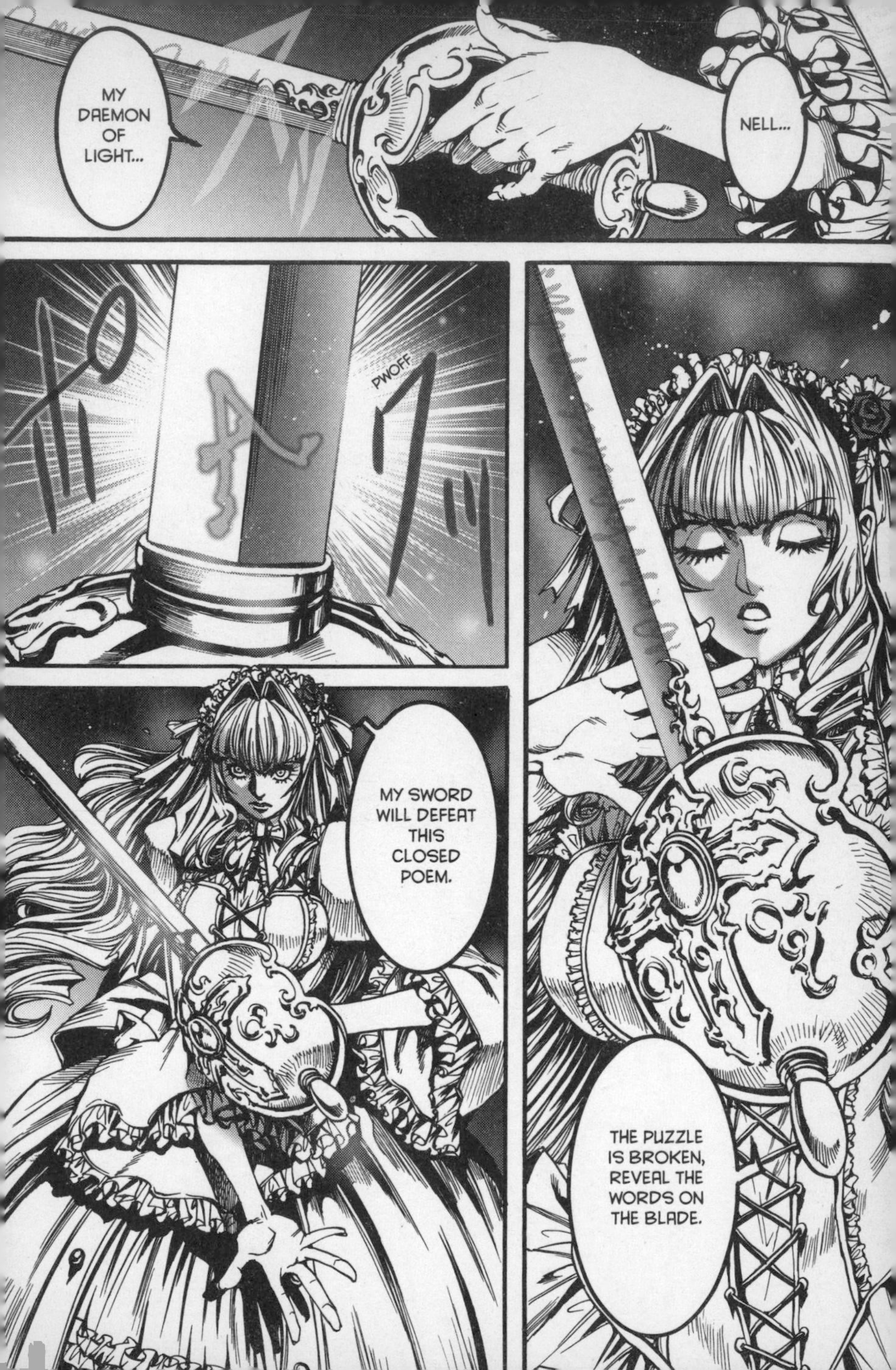
NELL...
MY DAEMON OF LIGHT...
THE PUZZLE IS BROKEN, REVEAL THE WORDS ON THE BLADE.
PWOFF
MY SWORD WILL DEFEAT THIS CLOSED POEM.

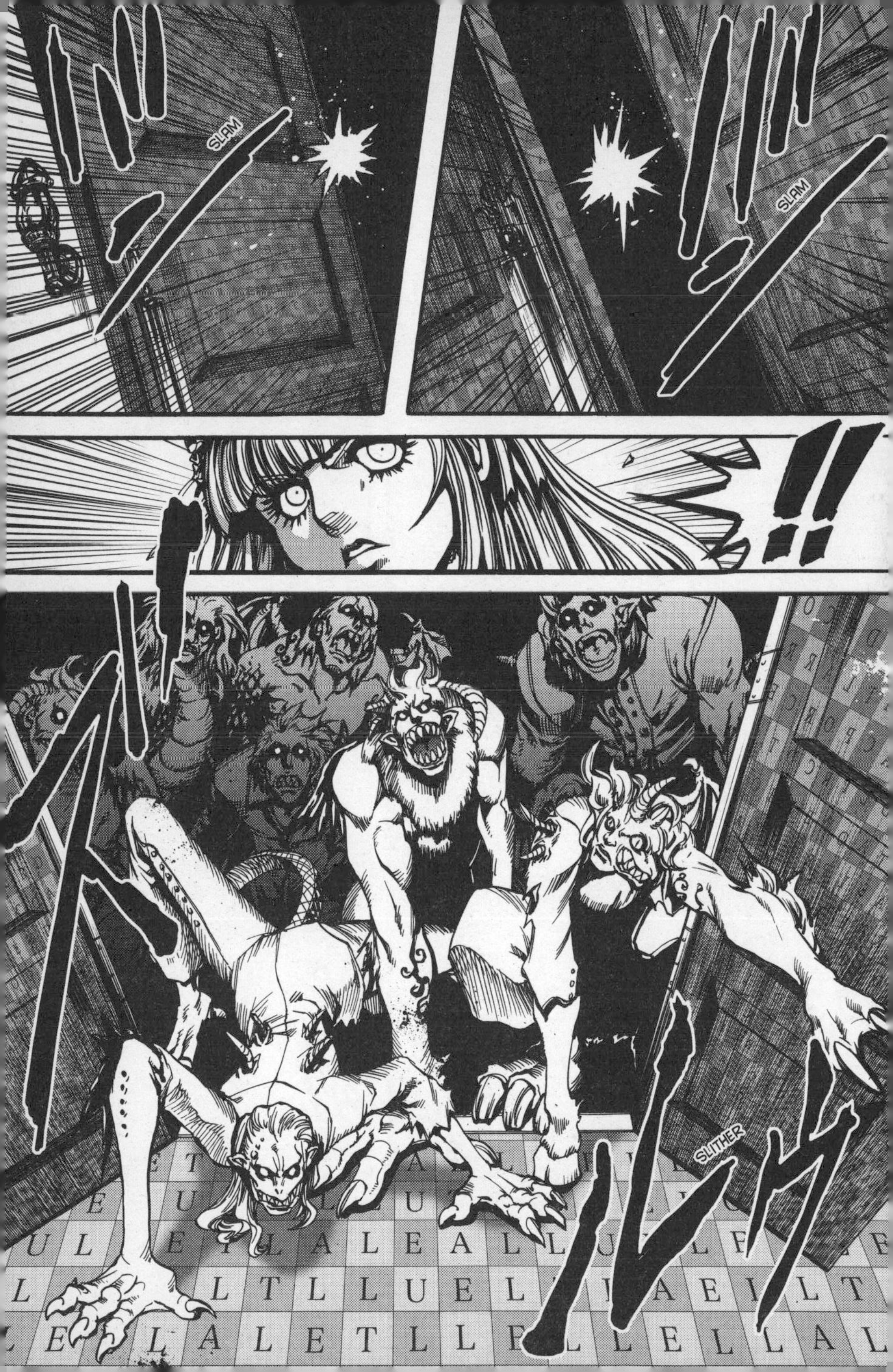
SLAM
SLAM
!!
SLITHER

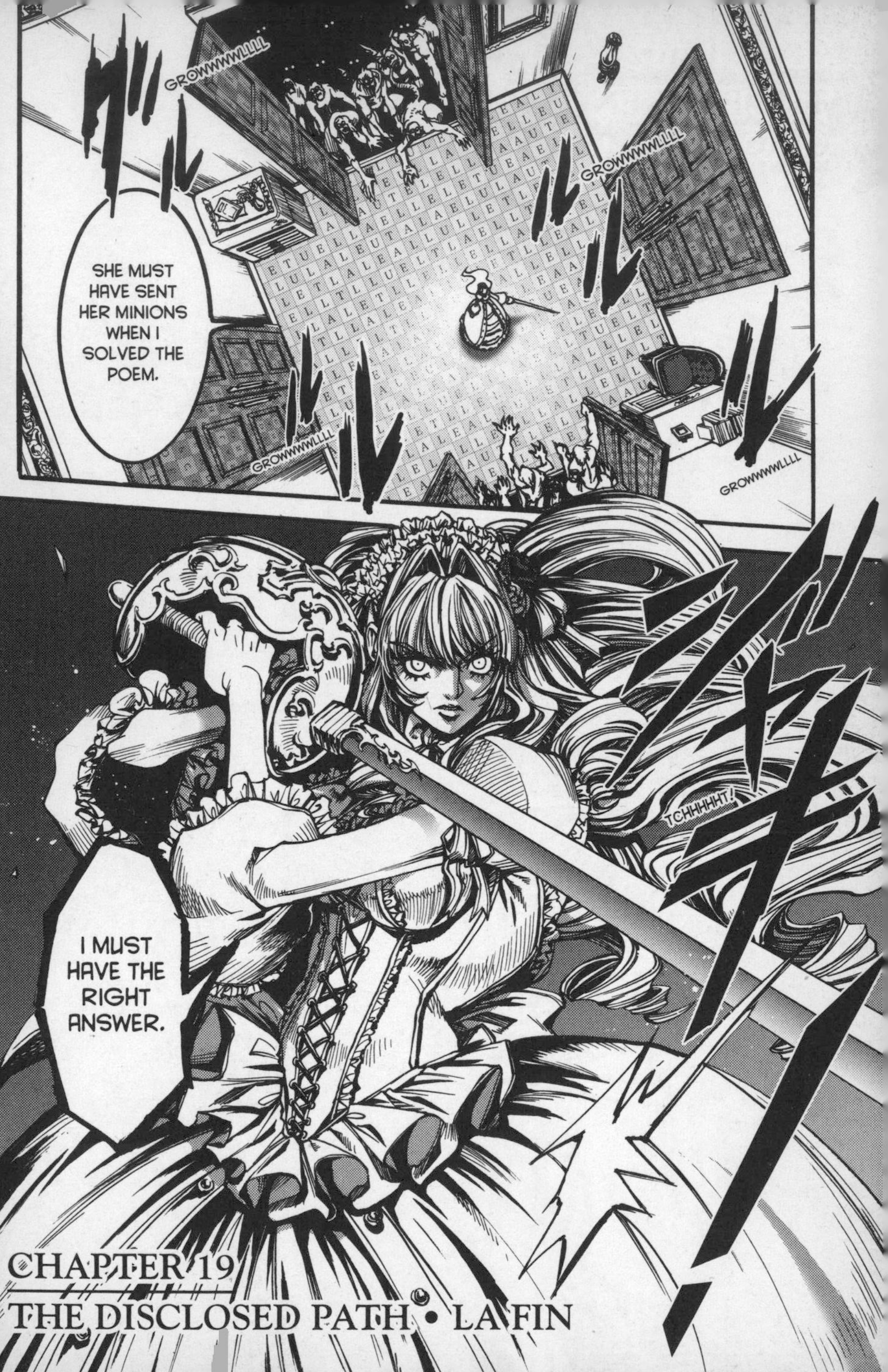
GROWWWWLLLL
GROWWWWLLLL
SHE MUST HAVE SENT HER MINIONS WHEN I SOLVED THE POEM.
GROWWWWLLLL
GROWWWWLLLL
TCHHHHHT!
I MUST HAVE THE RIGHT ANSWER.

CHAPTER 19
THE DISCLOSED PATH • LA FIN

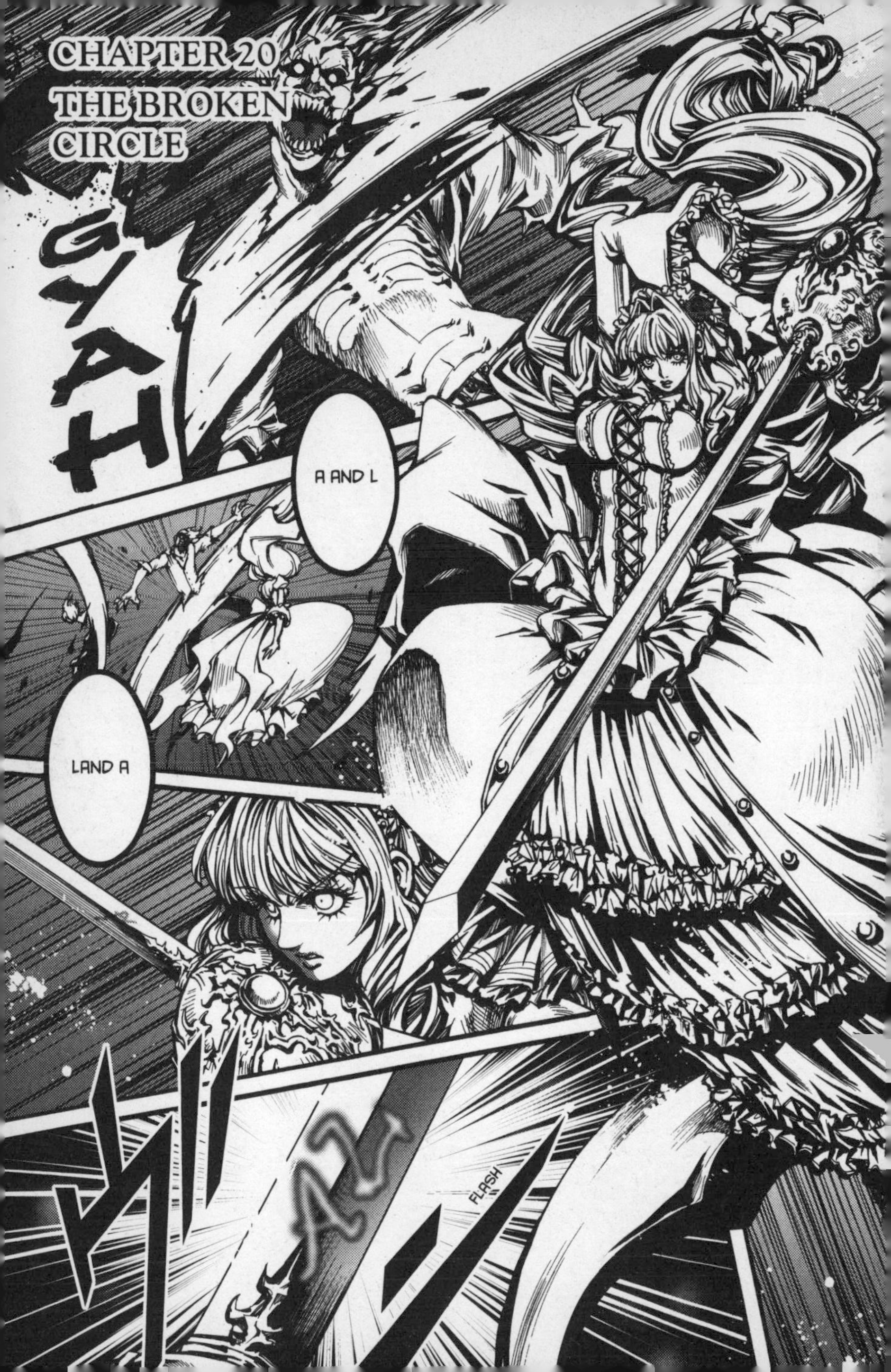
CHAPTER 20
THE BROKEN CIRCLE
GYAH
A AND L
LAND A
FLASH

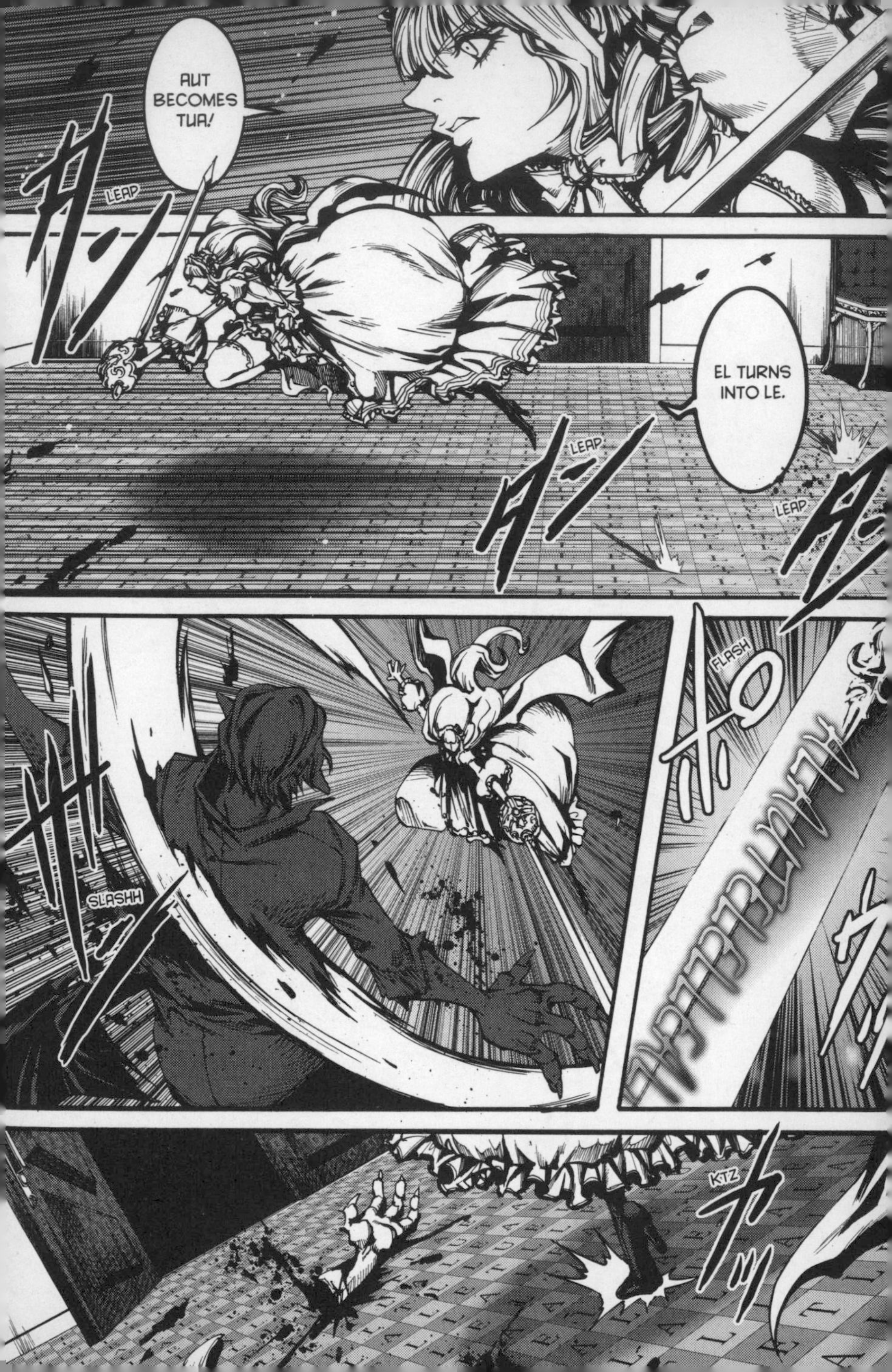
AUT BECOMES TUA!
LEAP
EL TURNS INTO LE.
LEAP
LEAP
FLASH
SLASHH
KTZ

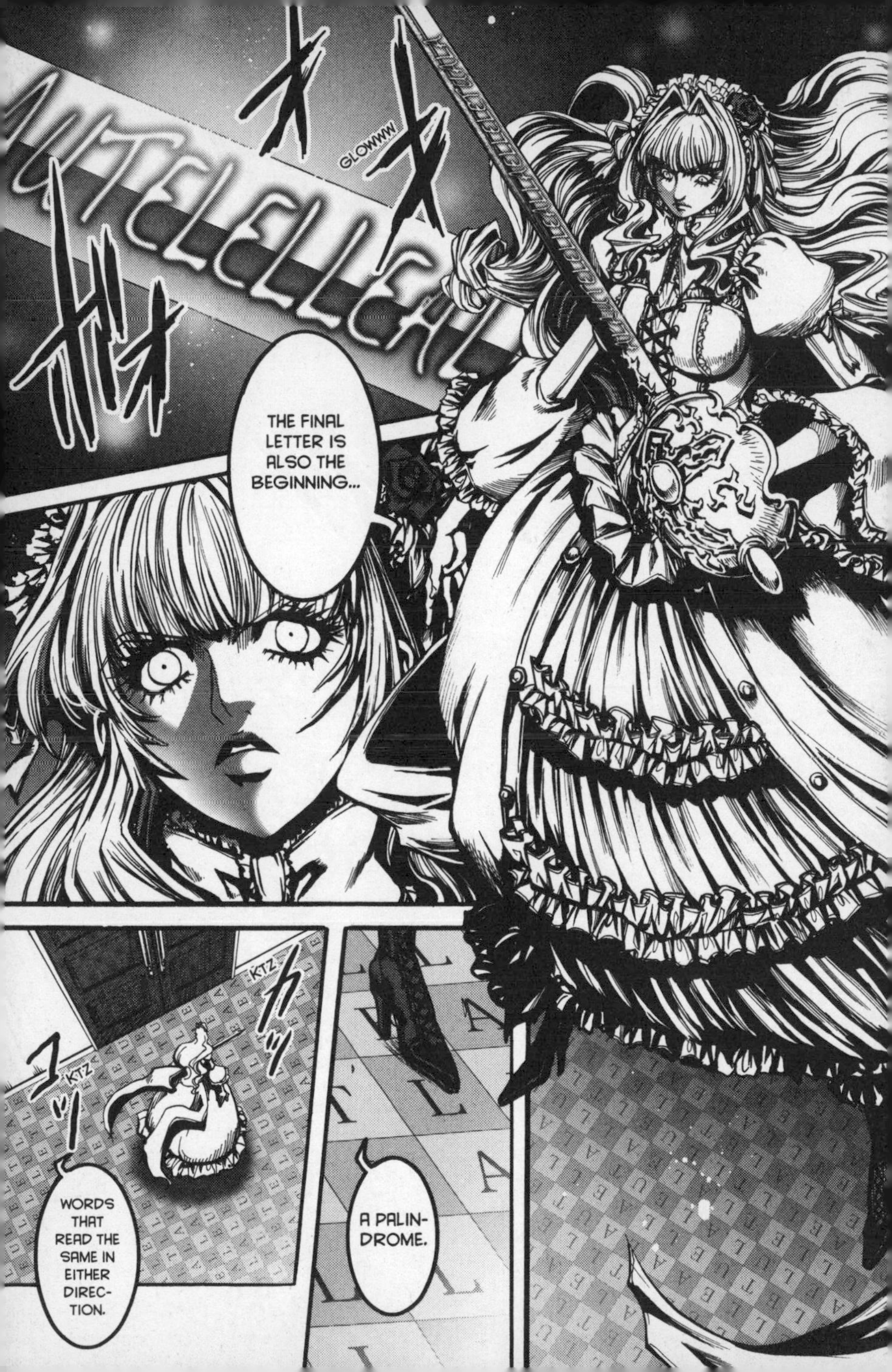
GLOWWW
THE FINAL LETTER IS ALSO THE BEGINNING...
A PALIN-DROME.
KTZ
KTZ
WORDS THAT READ THE SAME IN EITHER DIREC-TION.

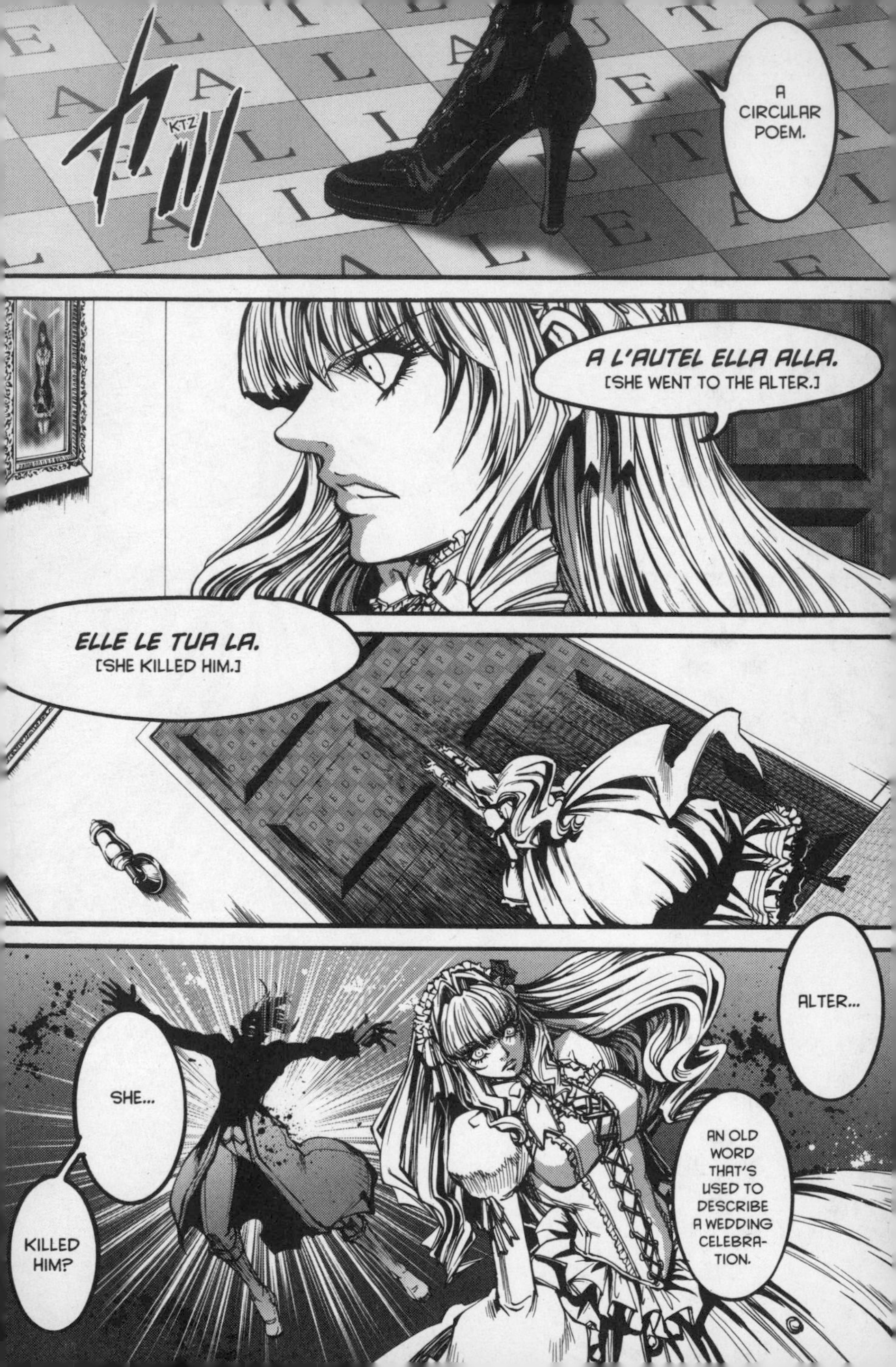
A CIRCULAR POEM.
KTZ
A L'AUTEL ELLA ALLA.
[SHE WENT TO THE ALTER.]
ELLE LE TUA LA.
[SHE KILLED HIM.]
ALTER...
AN OLD WORD THAT'S USED TO DESCRIBE A WEDDING CELEBRA-TION.
SHE...
KILLED HIM?

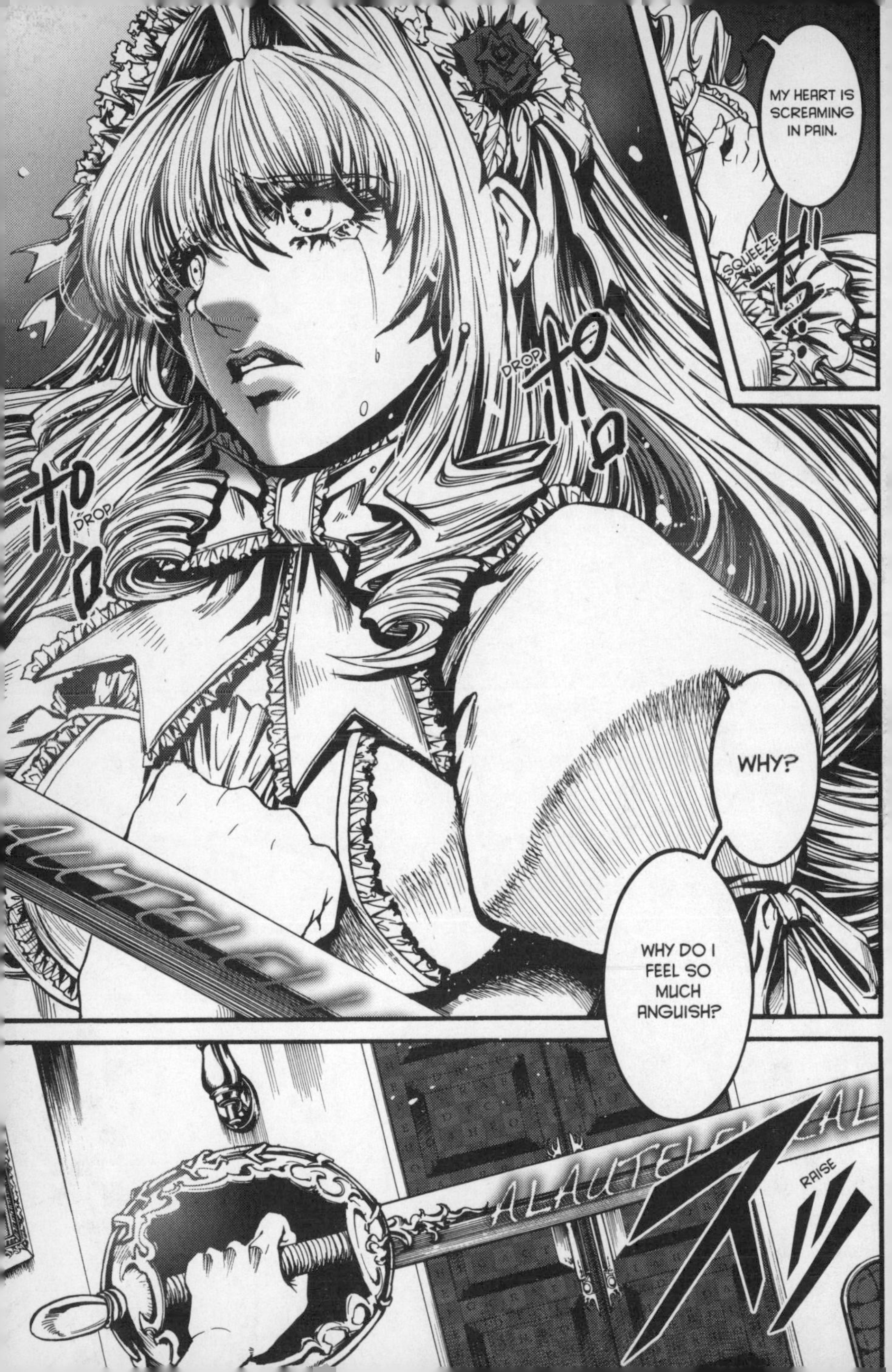
MY HEART IS SCREAMING IN PAIN.
SQUEEZE
DROP
DROP
WHY?
WHY DO I FEEL SO MUCH ANGUISH?
RAISE

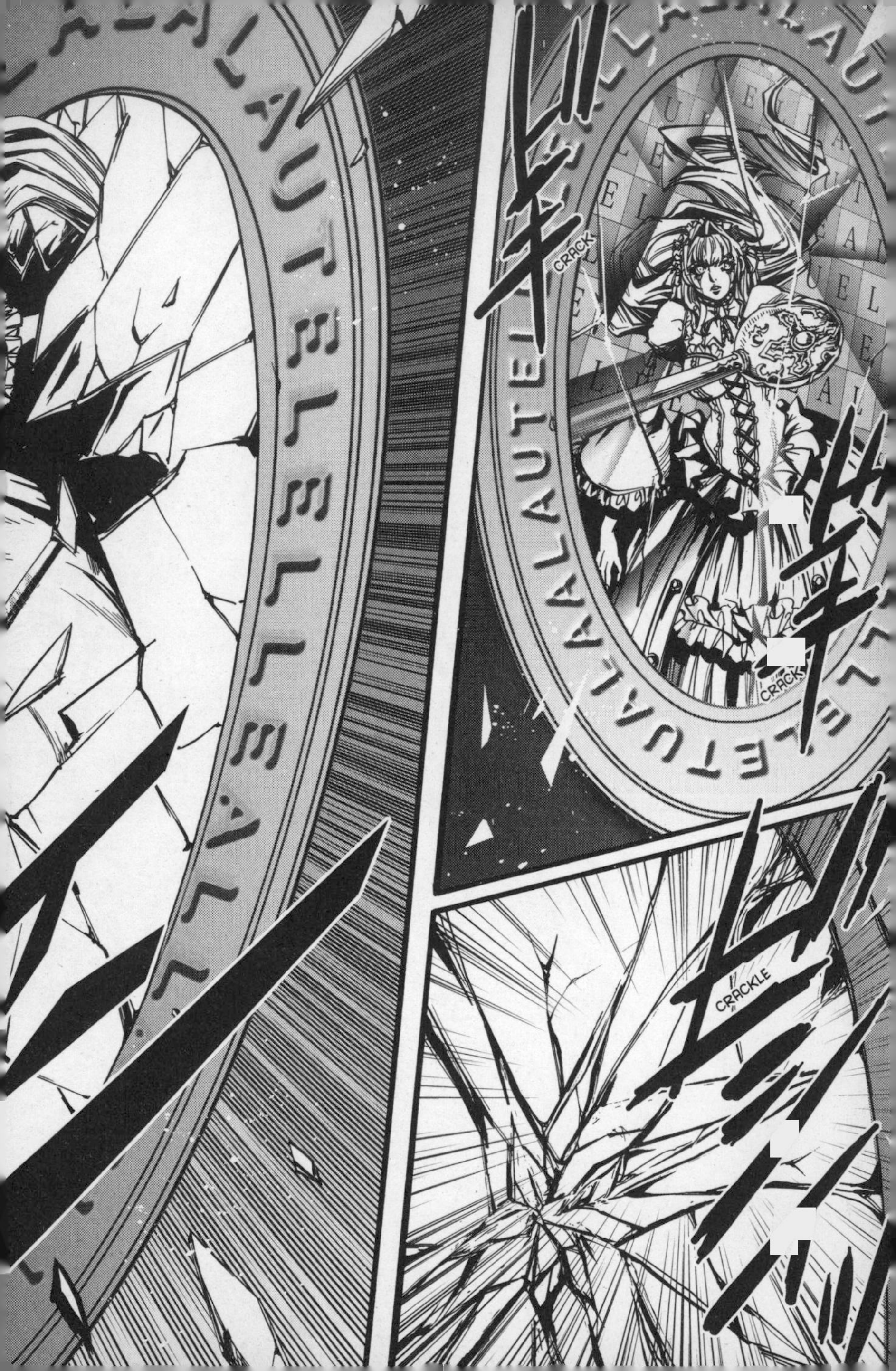
CRACK
CRACK
CRACKLE

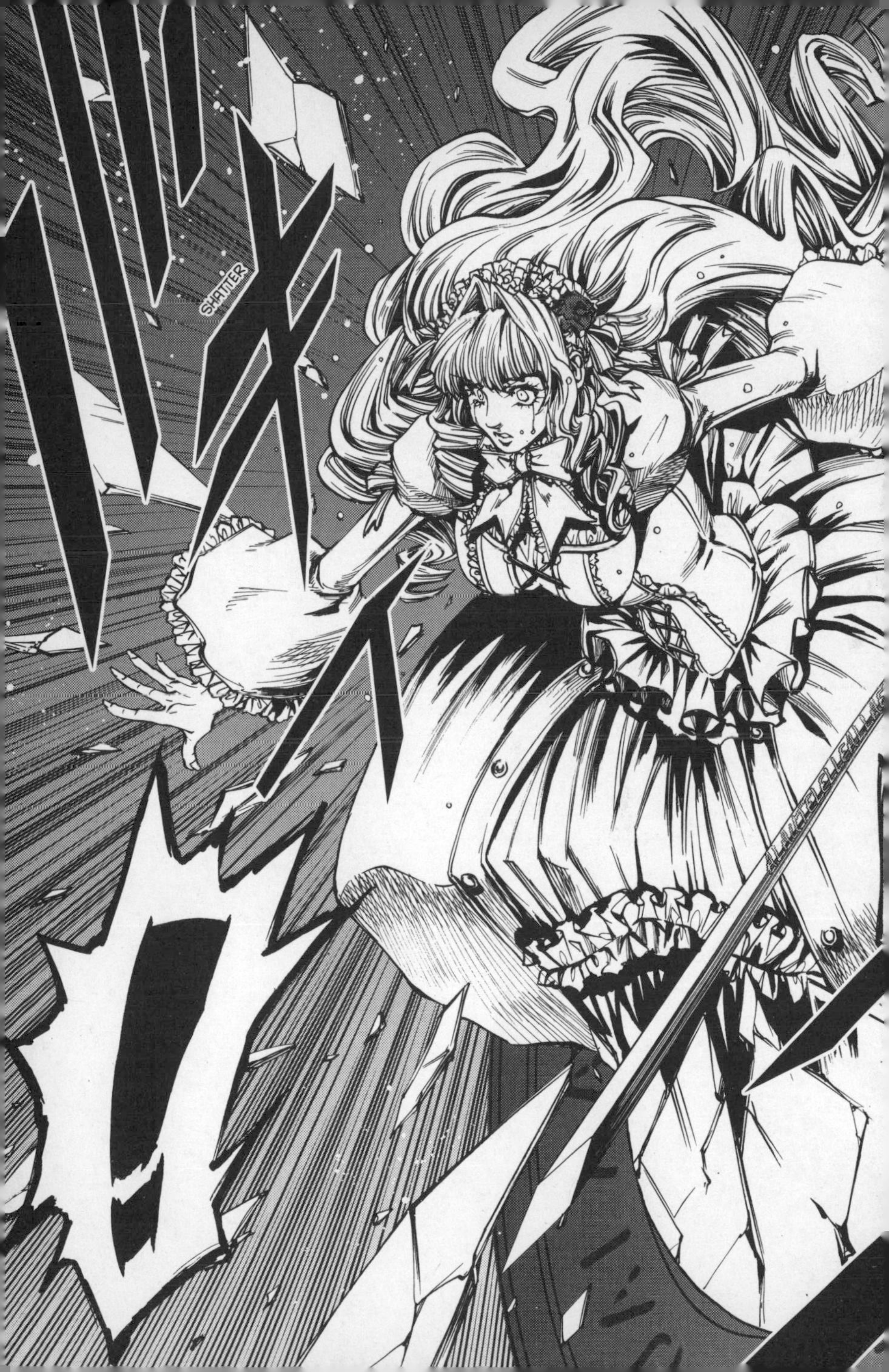
SHATTER

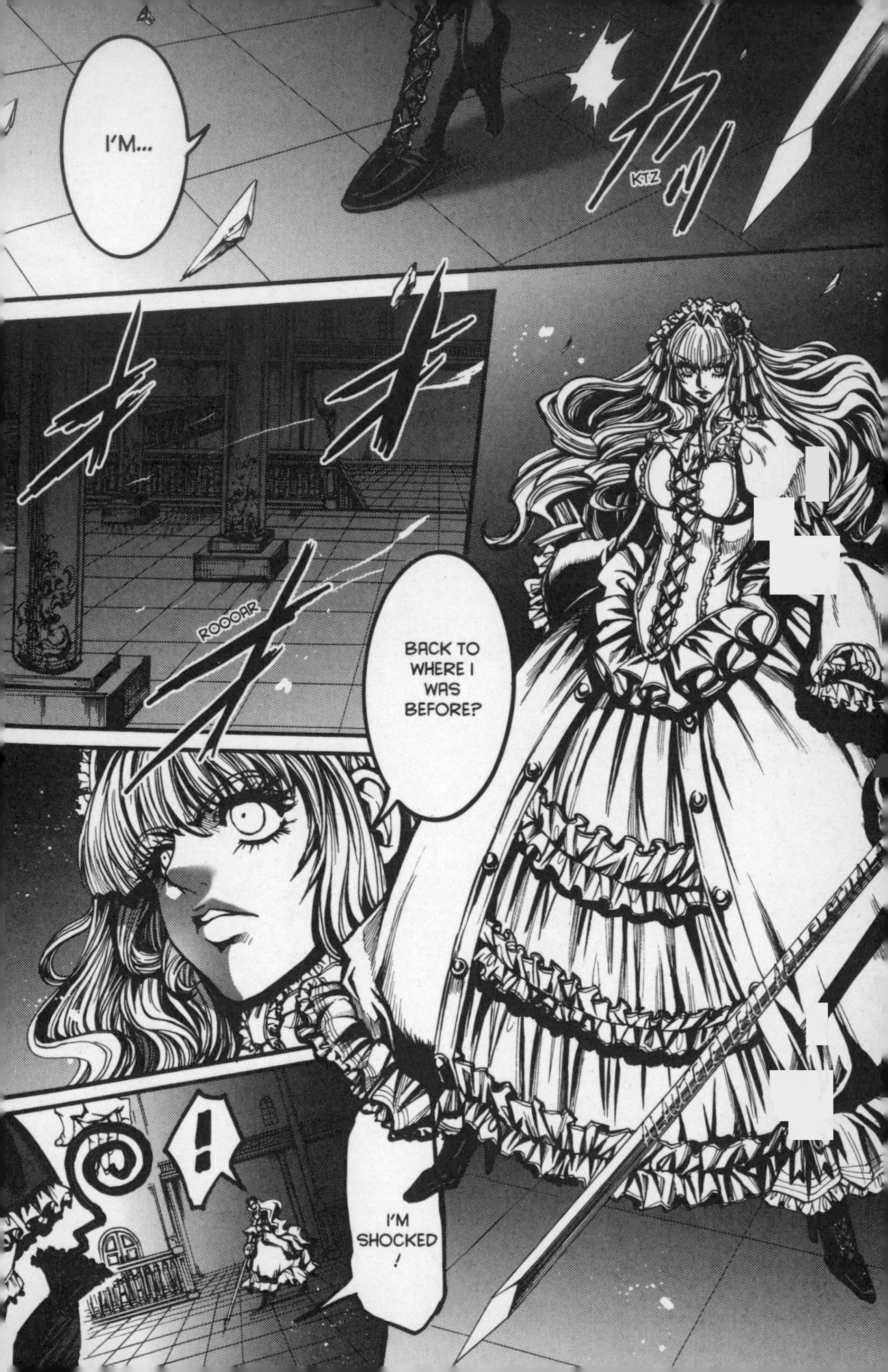
KTZ
I'M...
BACK TO WHERE I WAS BEFORE?
I'M SHOCKED!
ROOOAR
!

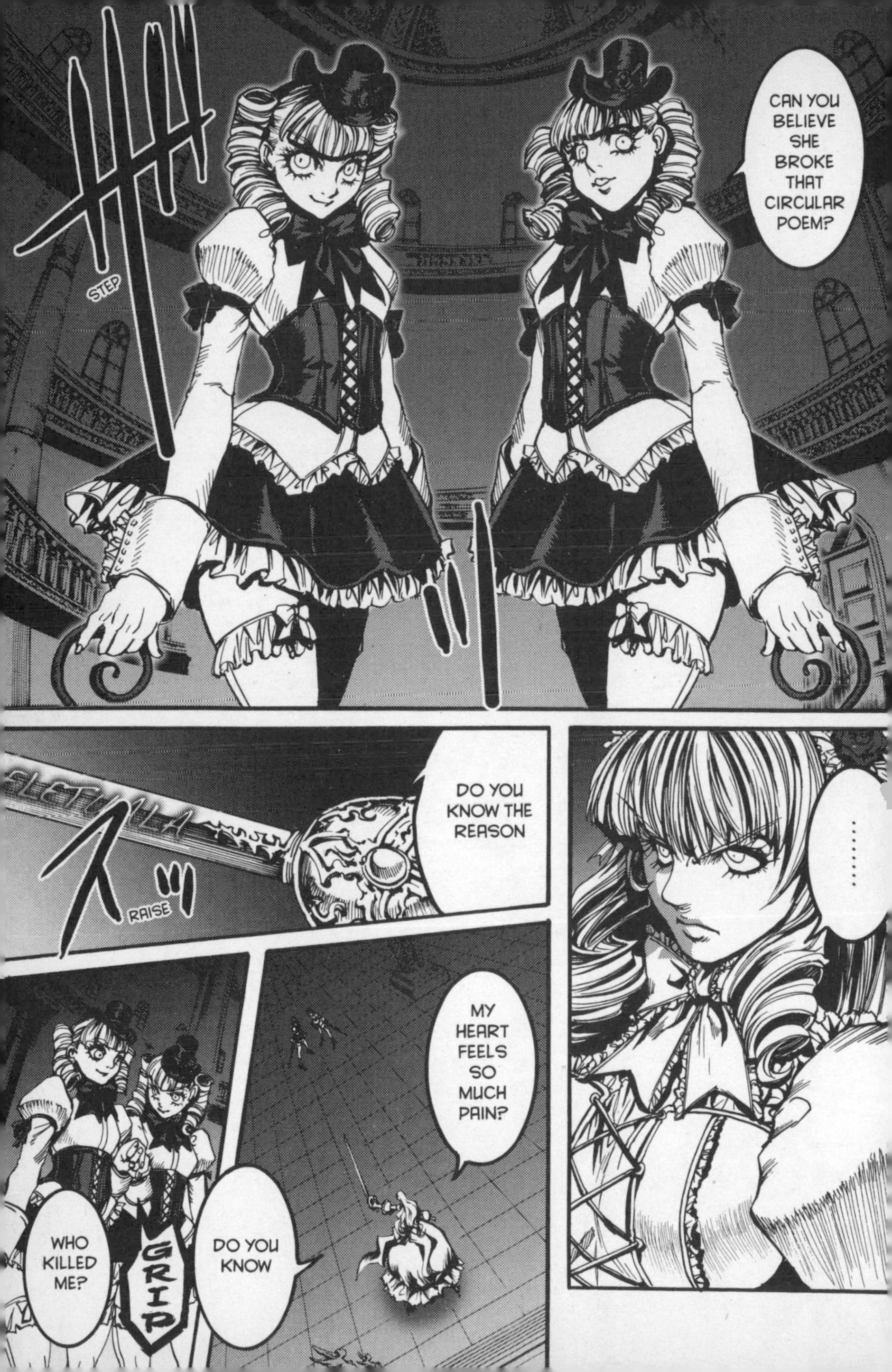
CAN YOU BELIEVE SHE BROKE THAT CIRCULAR POEM?
STEP
......
DO YOU KNOW THE REASON
RAISE
MY HEART FEELS SO MUCH PAIN?
DO YOU KNOW
GRIP
WHO KILLED ME?

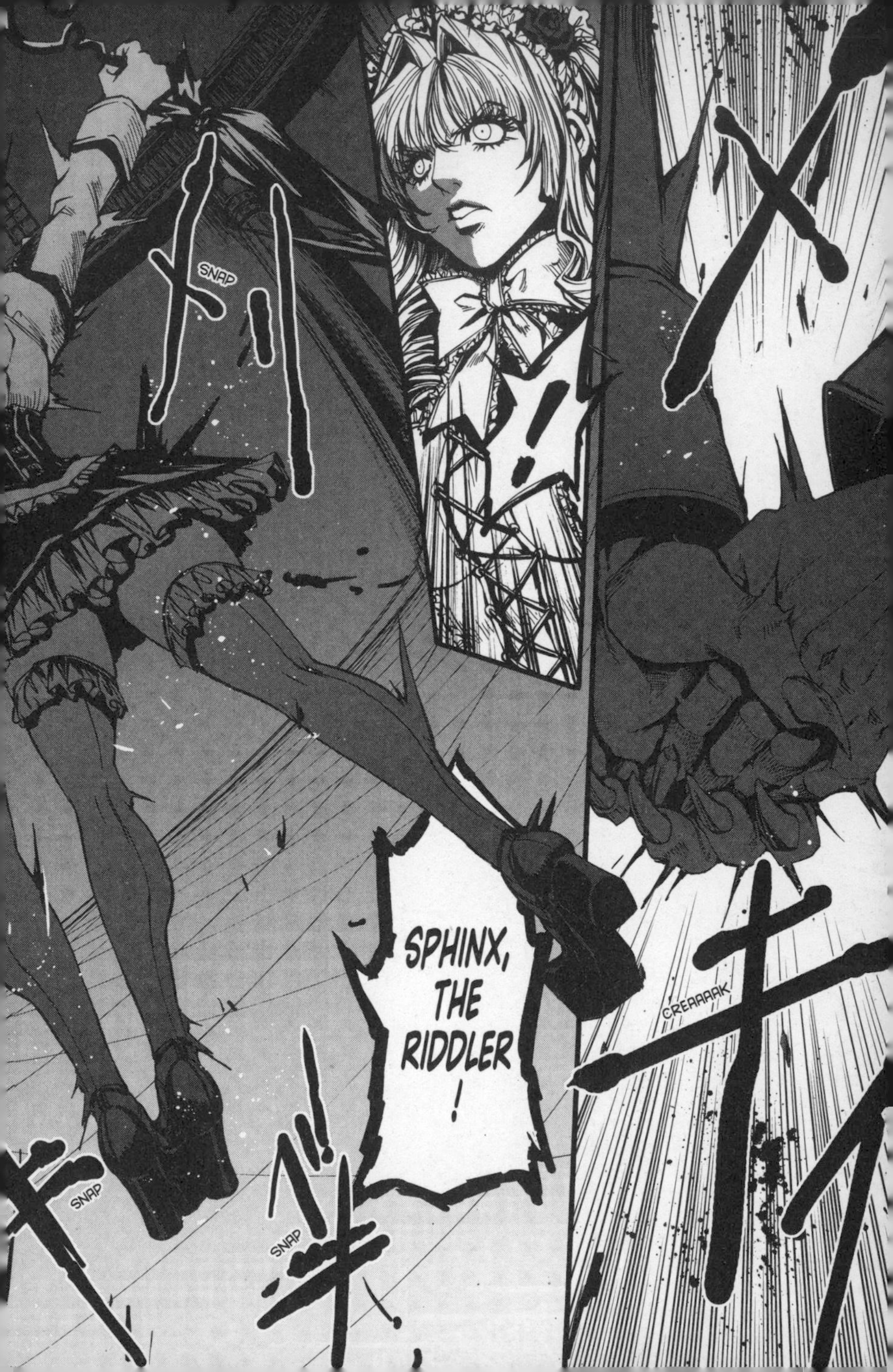
CREAAAAK
SNAP
SPHINX, THE RIDDLER !
SNAP
SNAP

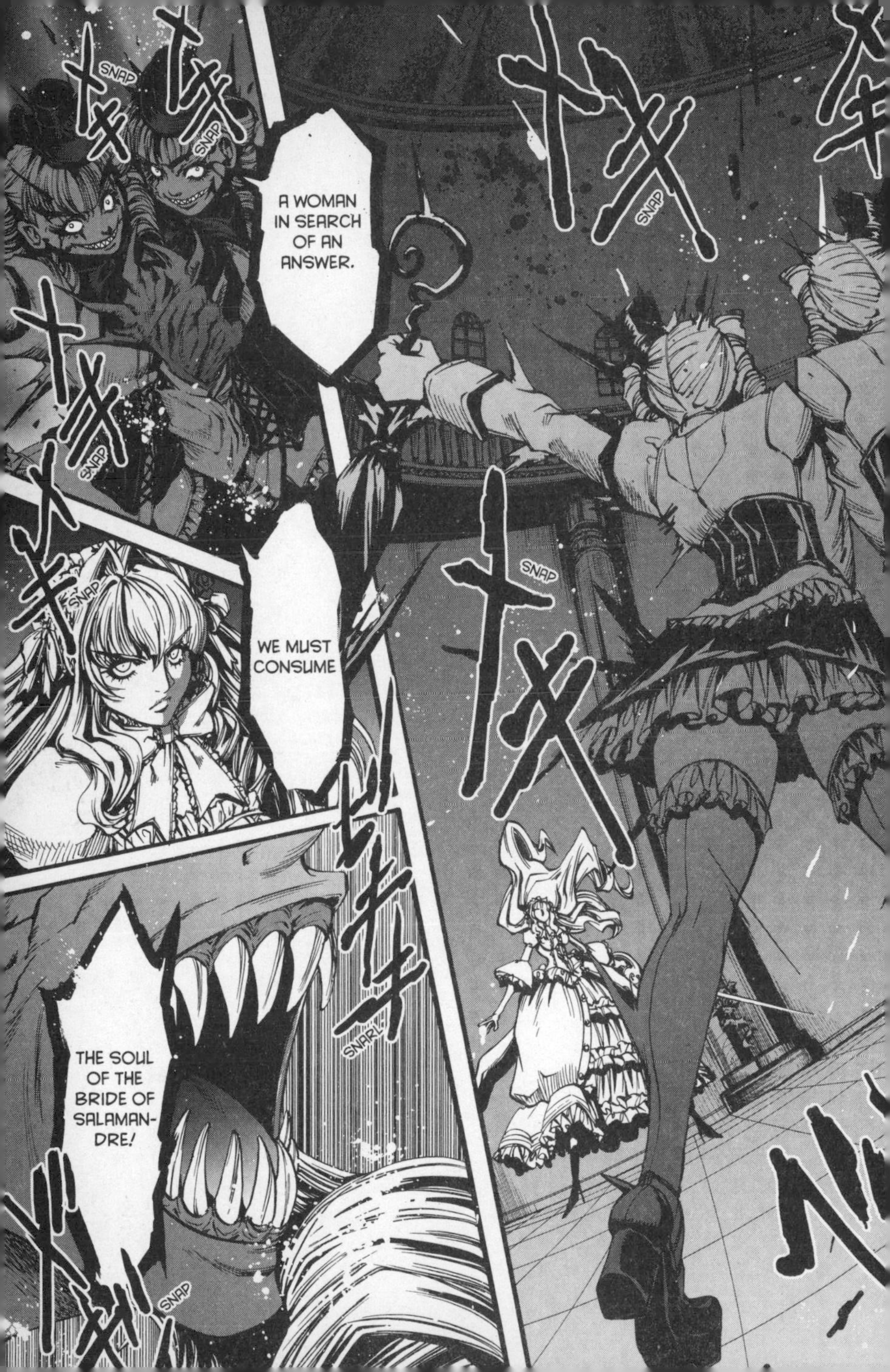
SNAP
SNAP
SNAP
SNAP
A WOMAN IN SEARCH OF AN ANSWER.
SNAP
SNAP
WE MUST CONSUME
SNARL
THE SOUL OF THE BRIDE OF SALAMANDRE!
SNAP

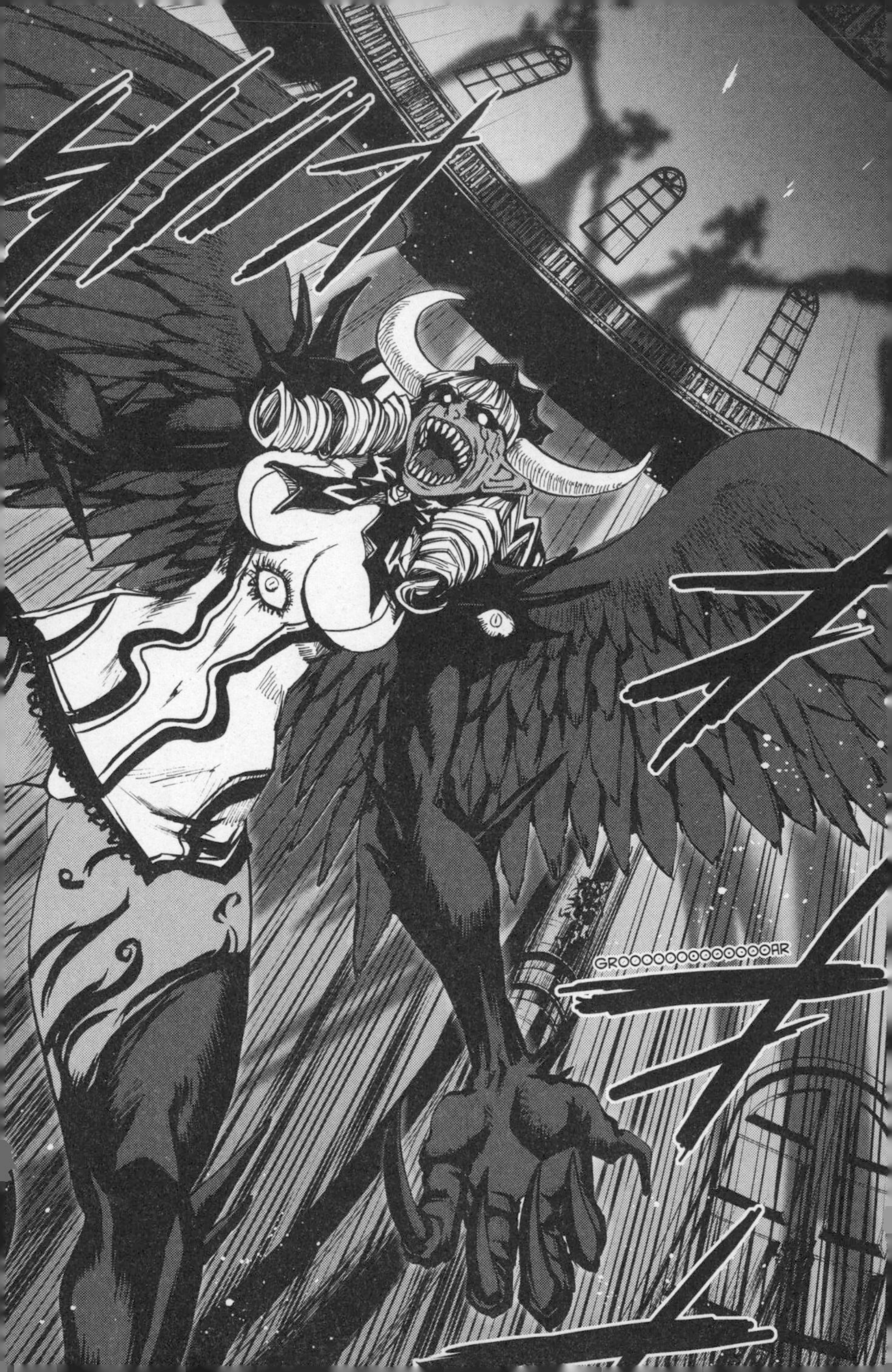
GROOOOOOOOOOOOOOAR

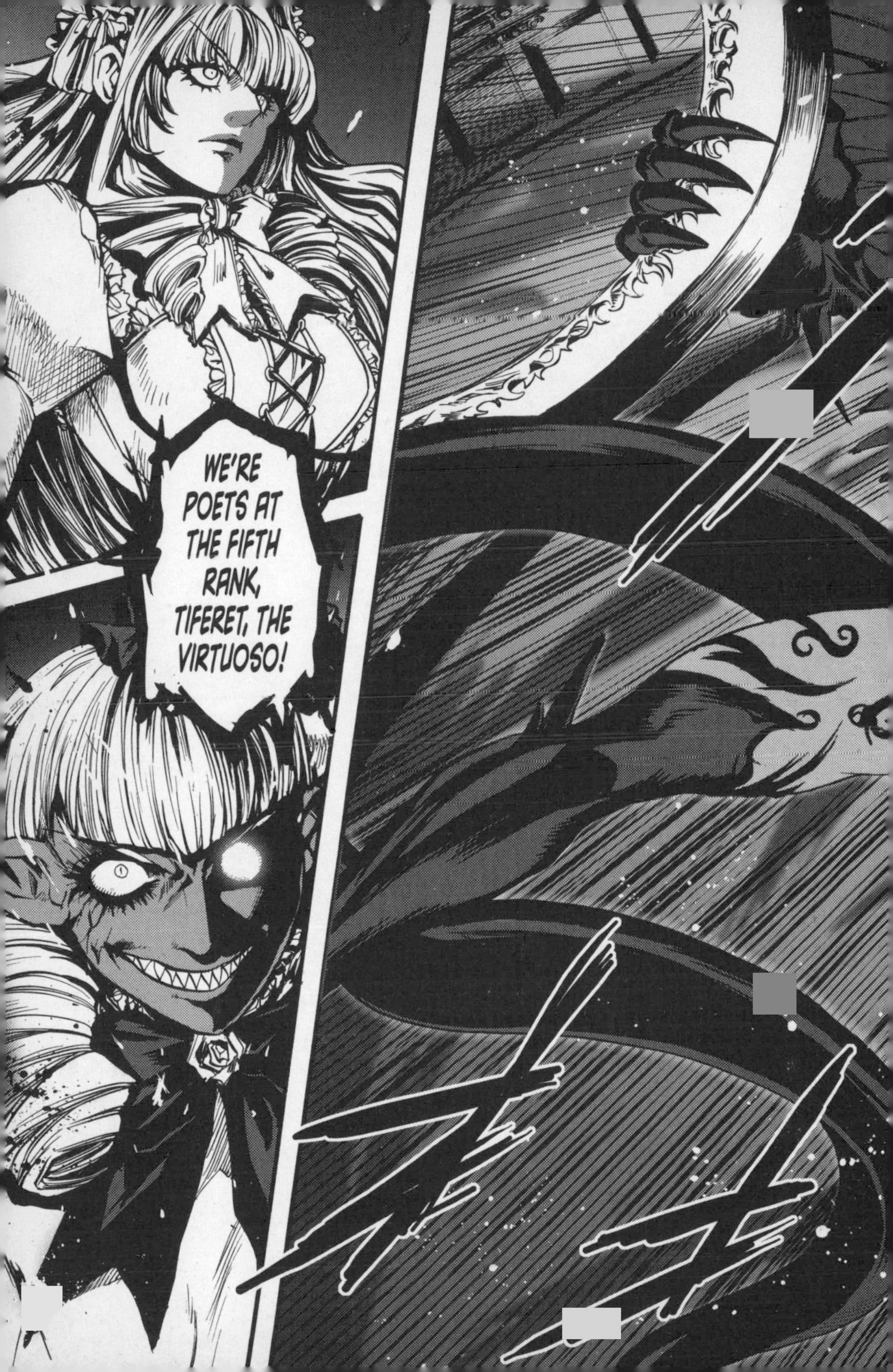
WE'RE POETS AT THE FIFTH RANK, TIFERET, THE VIRTUOSO!

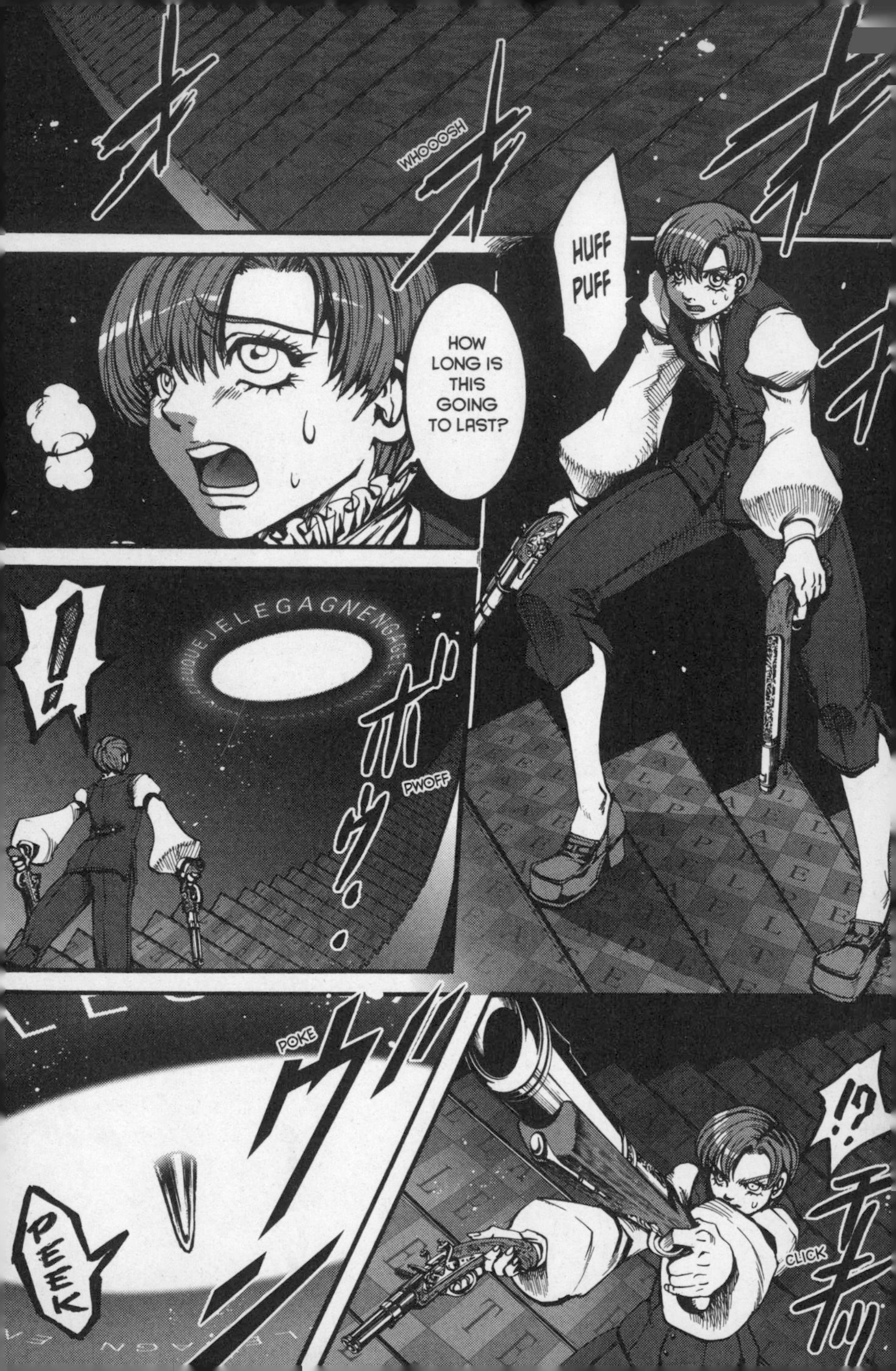
WHOOOSH
HUFF PUFF
HOW LONG IS THIS GOING TO LAST?
!
PWOFF
!?
CLICK
POKE
PEEK

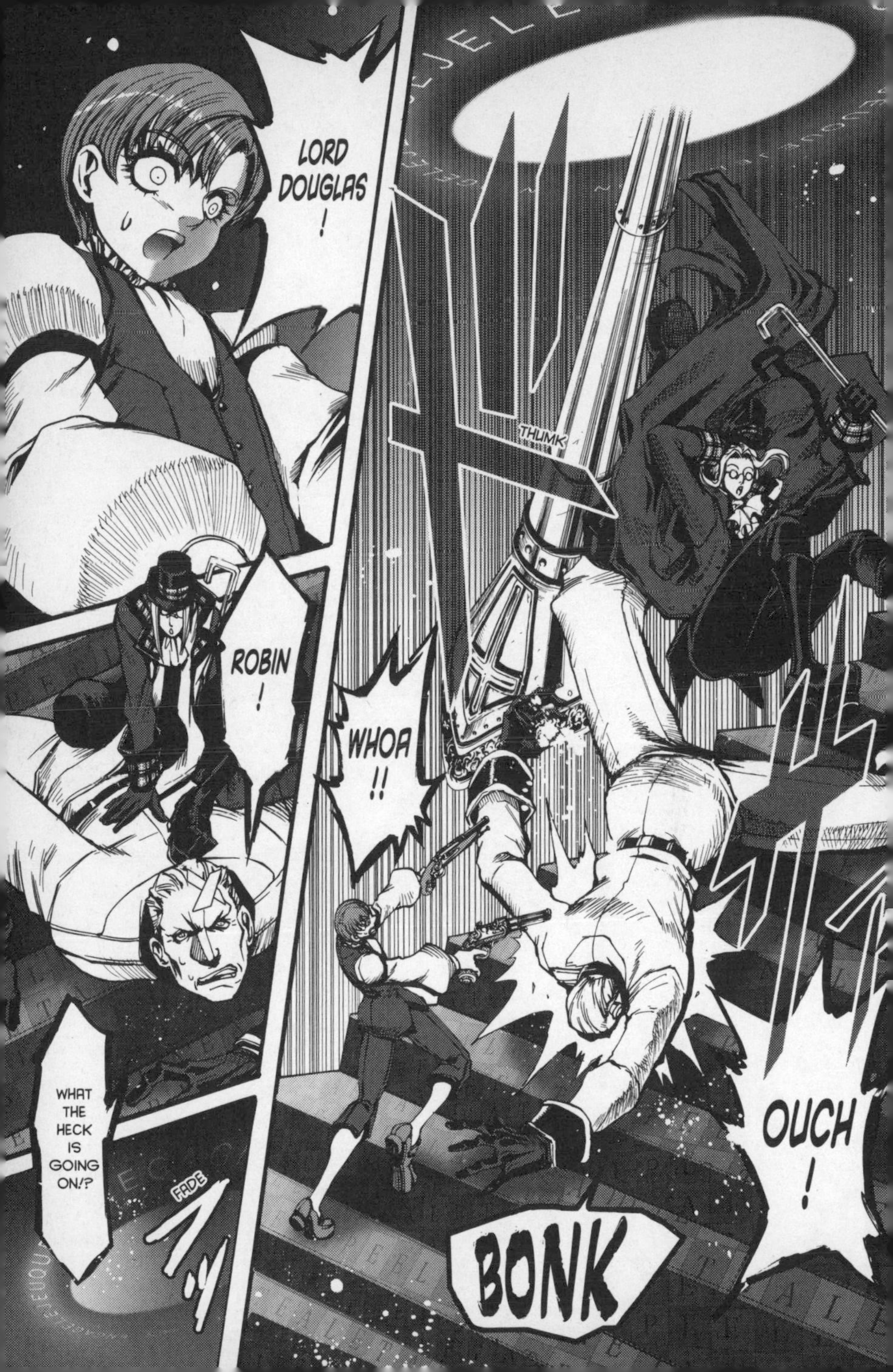
THUMK
WHOA !!
OUCH !
BONK
LORD DOUGLAS !
ROBIN !
WHAT THE HECK IS GOING ON!?
FADE

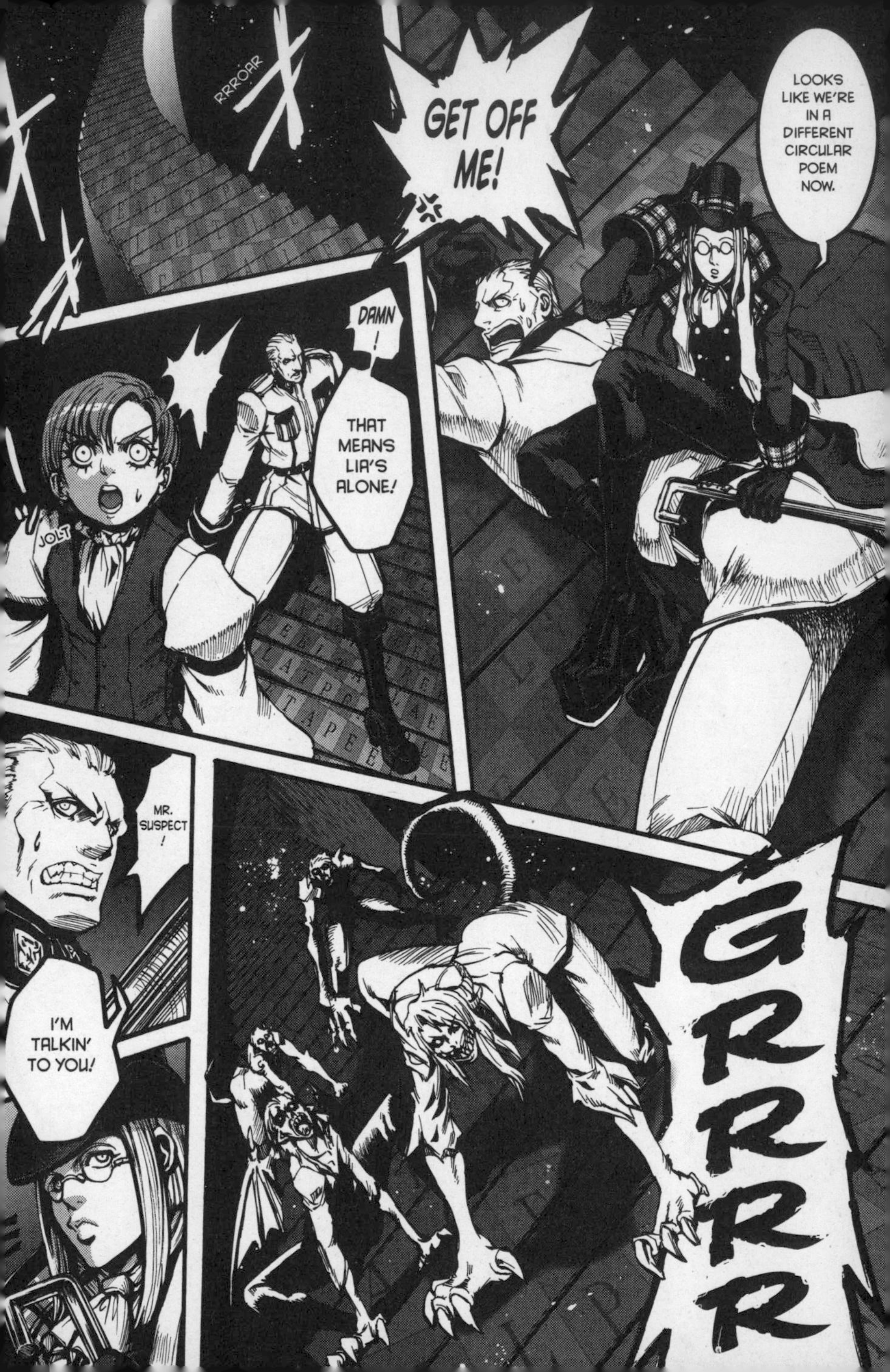
LOOKS LIKE WE'RE IN A DIFFERENT CIRCULAR POEM NOW.
GET OFF ME!
RRROAR
DAMN!
THAT MEANS LIA'S ALONE!
JOLT
GRRRR
MR. SUSPECT!
I'M TALKIN' TO YOU!

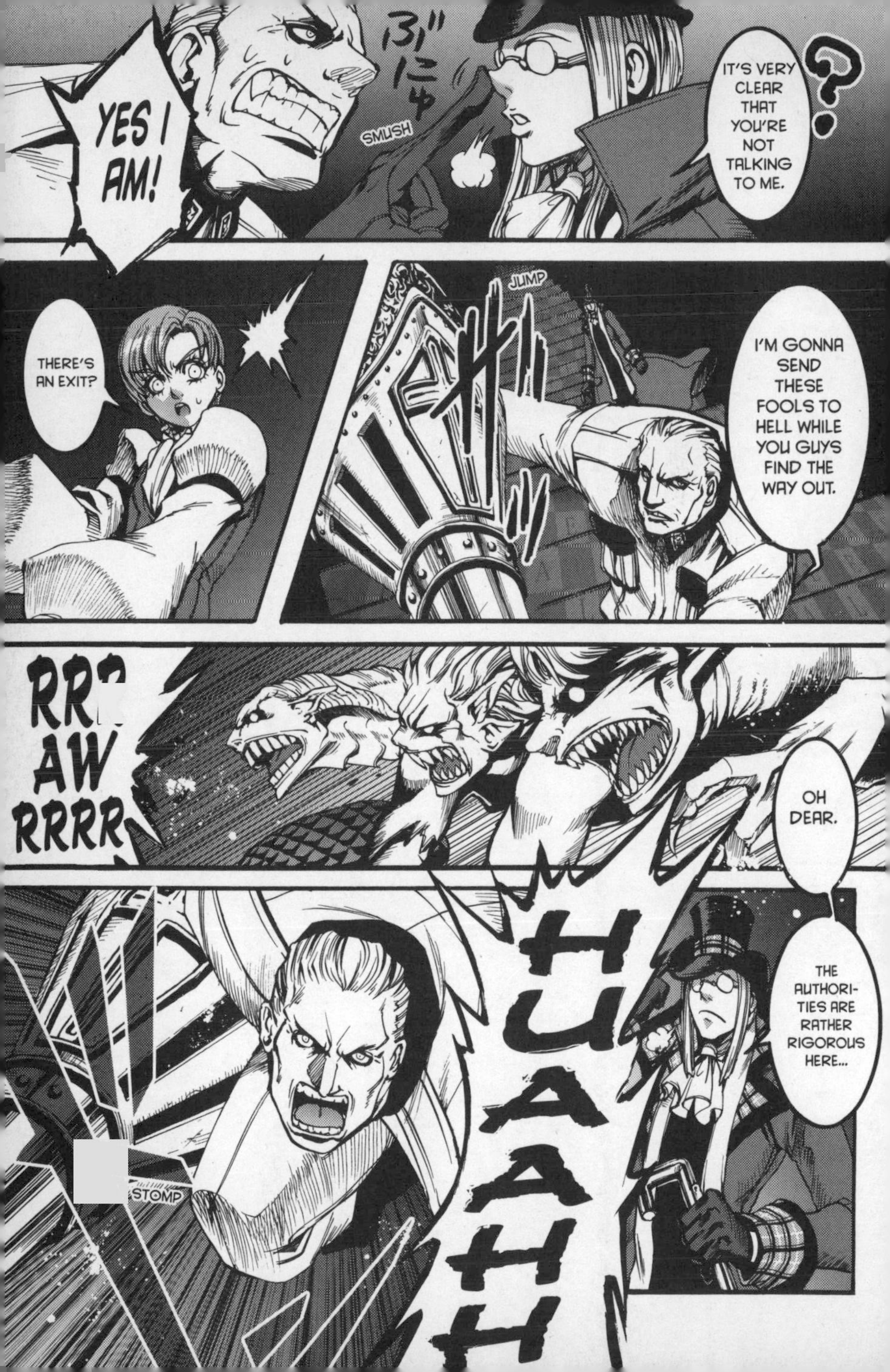
IT'S VERY CLEAR THAT YOU'RE NOT TALKING TO ME.
ぶにゅ
SMUSH
YES I AM!
JUMP
I'M GONNA SEND THESE FOOLS TO HELL WHILE YOU GUYS FIND THE WAY OUT.
THERE'S AN EXIT?
RR AW RRRR
OH DEAR.
THE AUTHORI-TIES ARE RATHER RIGOROUS HERE...
HUAAHH
STOMP

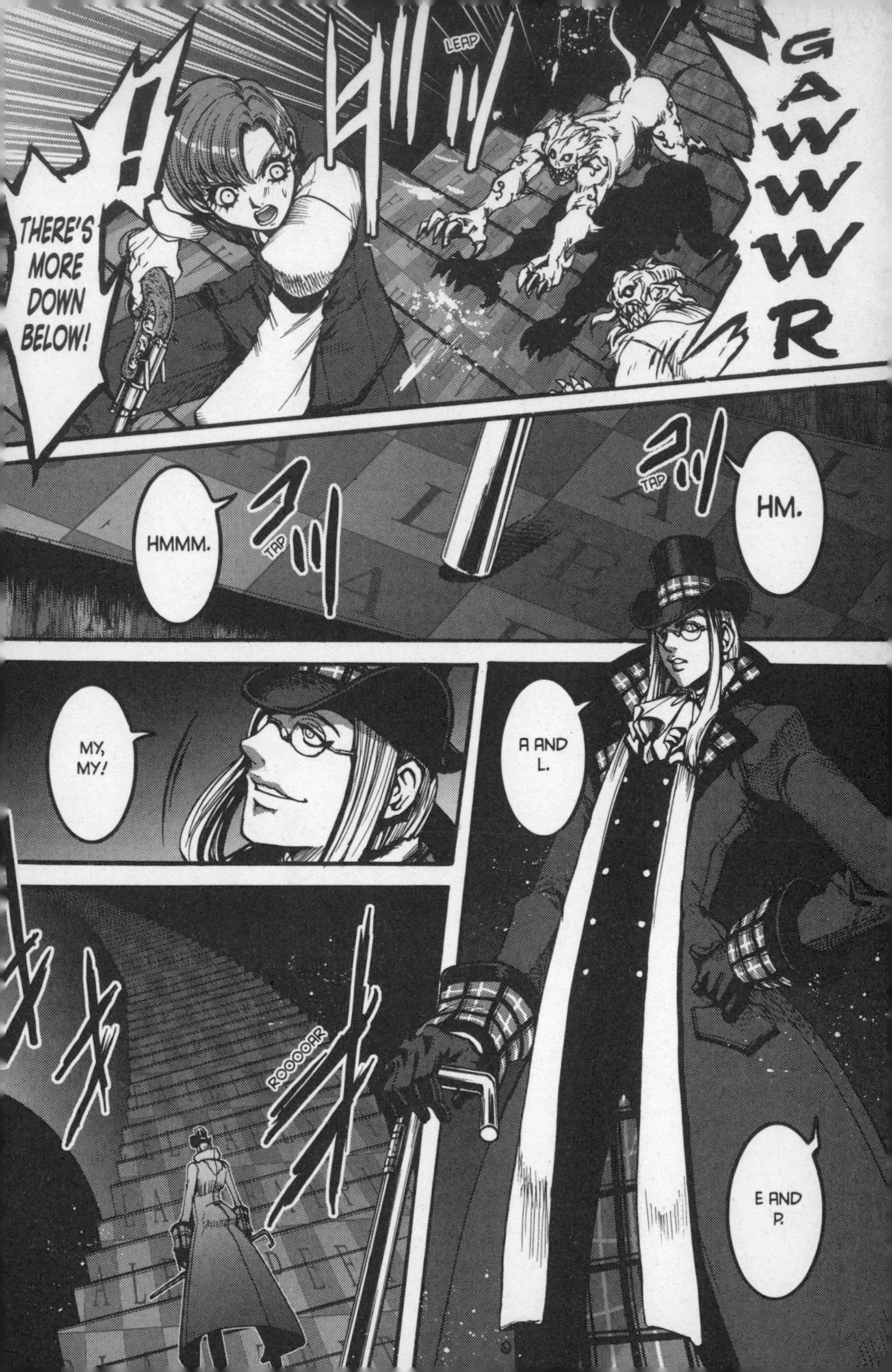
GAWWR
LEAP
THERE'S MORE DOWN BELOW!
HM.
TAP
HMMM.
TAP
A AND L.
E AND P.
MY, MY!
ROOOOAR

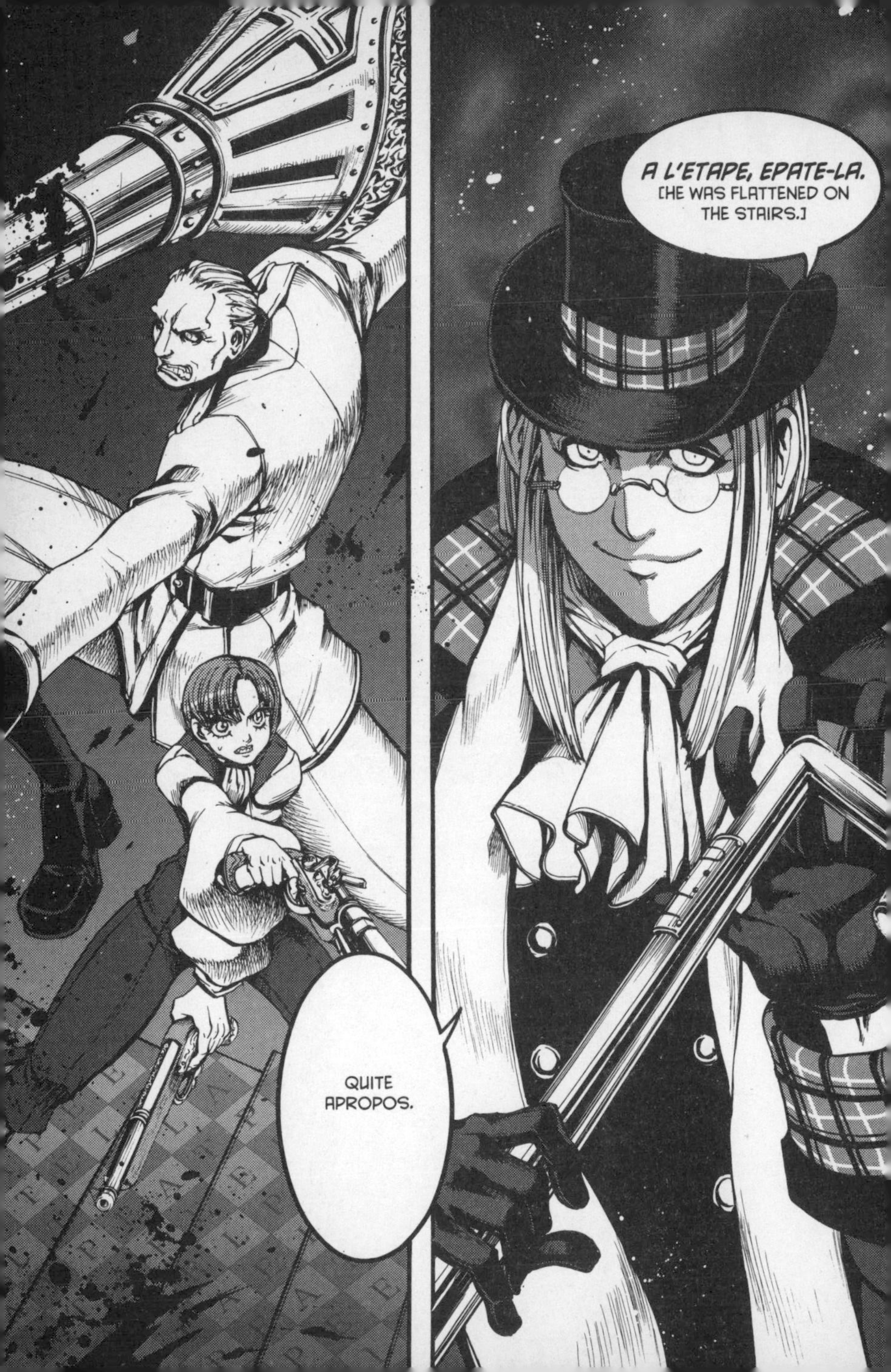
A L'ETAPE, EPATE-LA.
[HE WAS FLATTENED ON THE STAIRS.]
QUITE APROPOS.

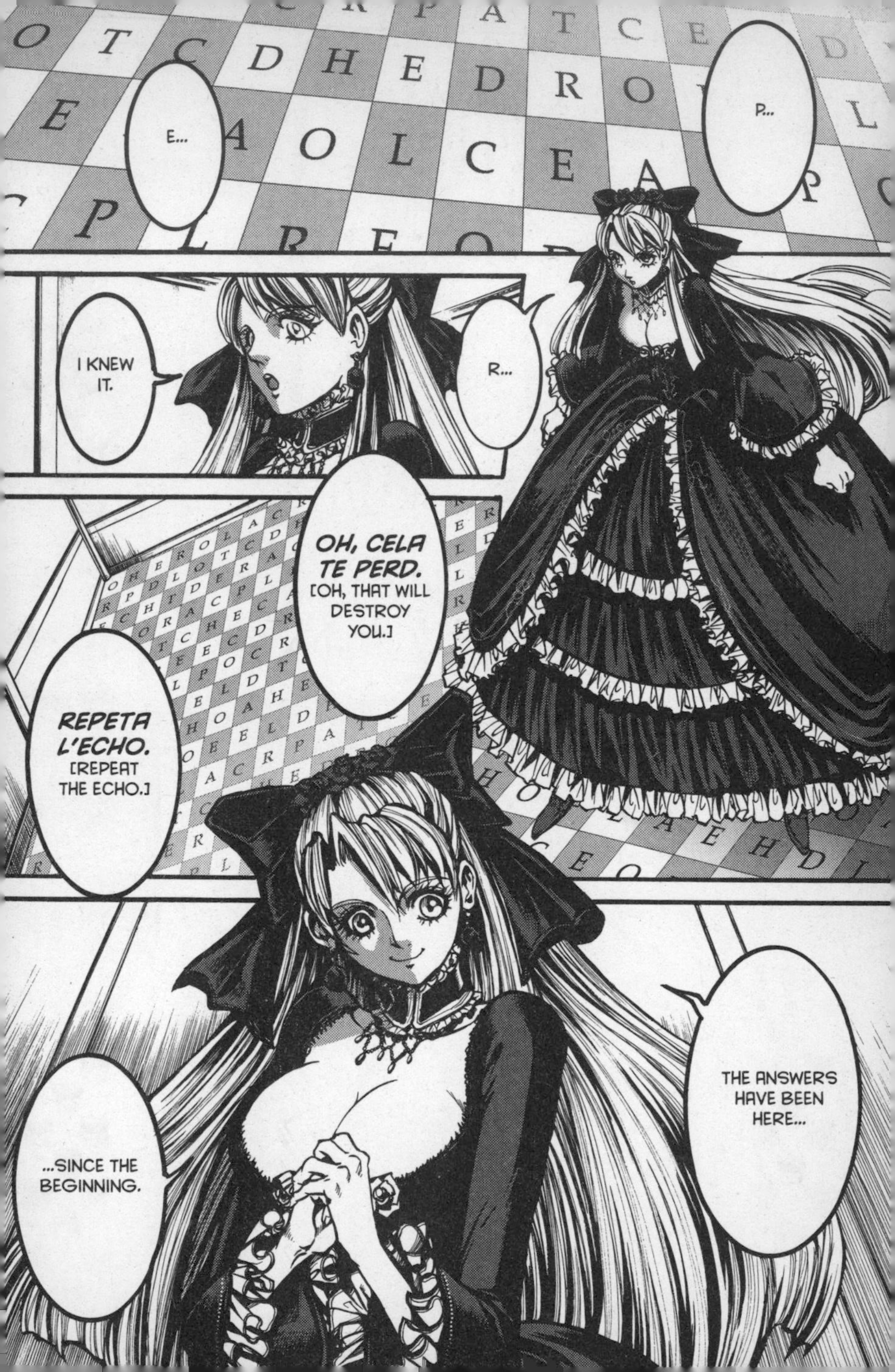
P...
E...
R...
I KNEW IT.
OH, CELA TE PERD. [OH, THAT WILL DESTROY YOU.]
REPETA L'ECHO. [REPEAT THE ECHO.]
THE ANSWERS HAVE BEEN HERE...
...SINCE THE BEGINNING.

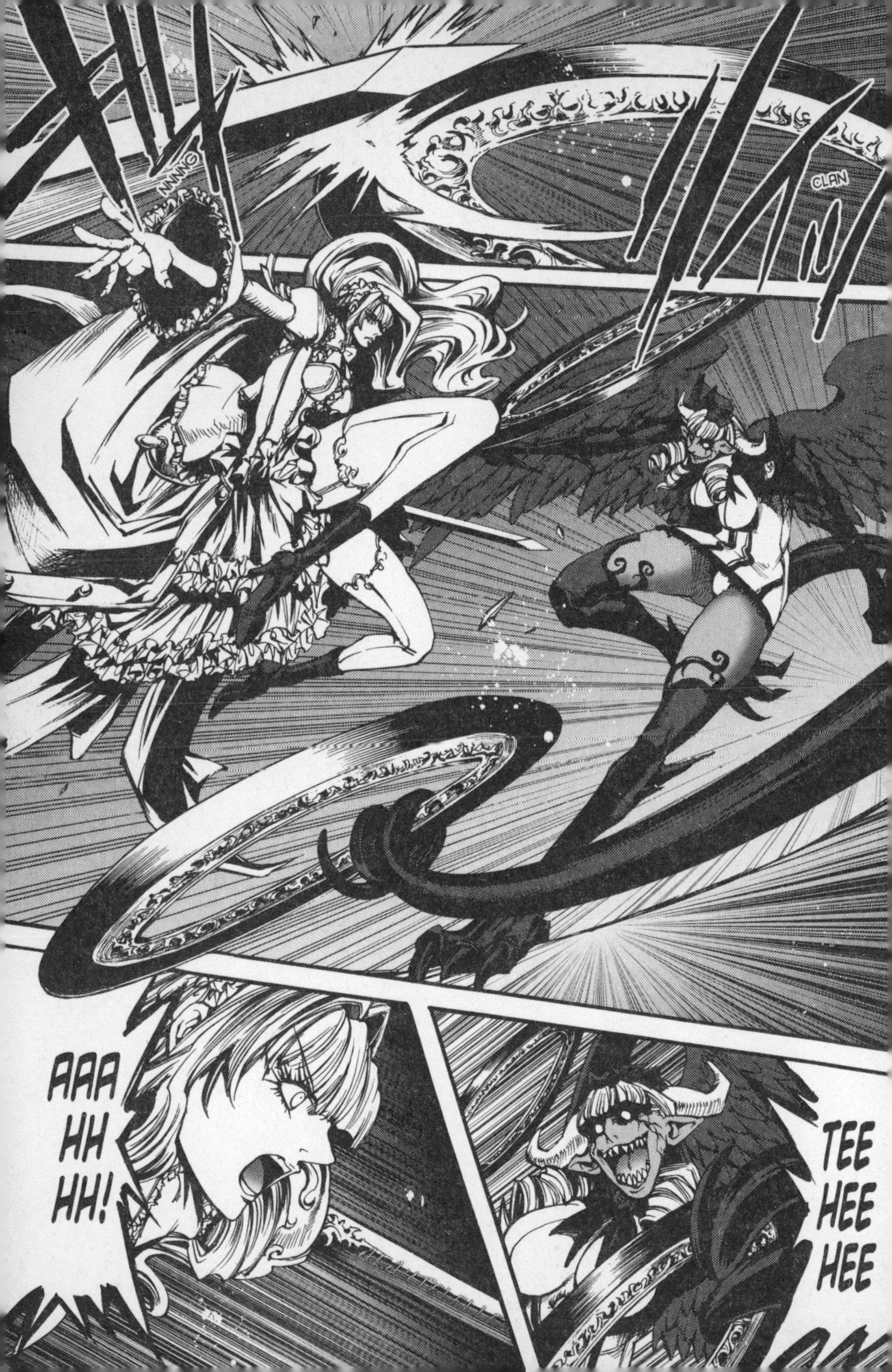
CLAN
NNNNG
TEE HEE HEE
AAAHHHHH!

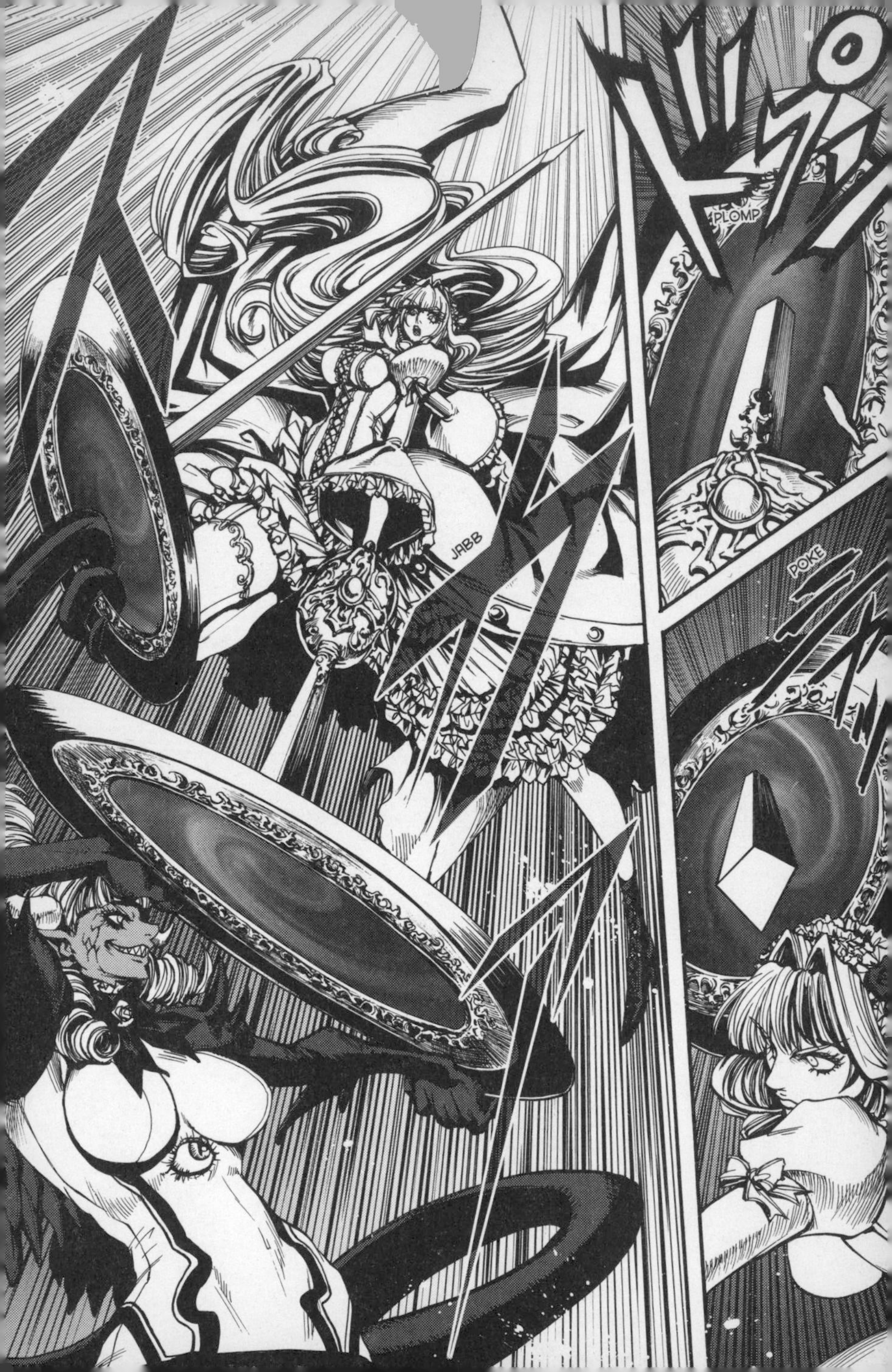
PLOMP
POKE
JABB

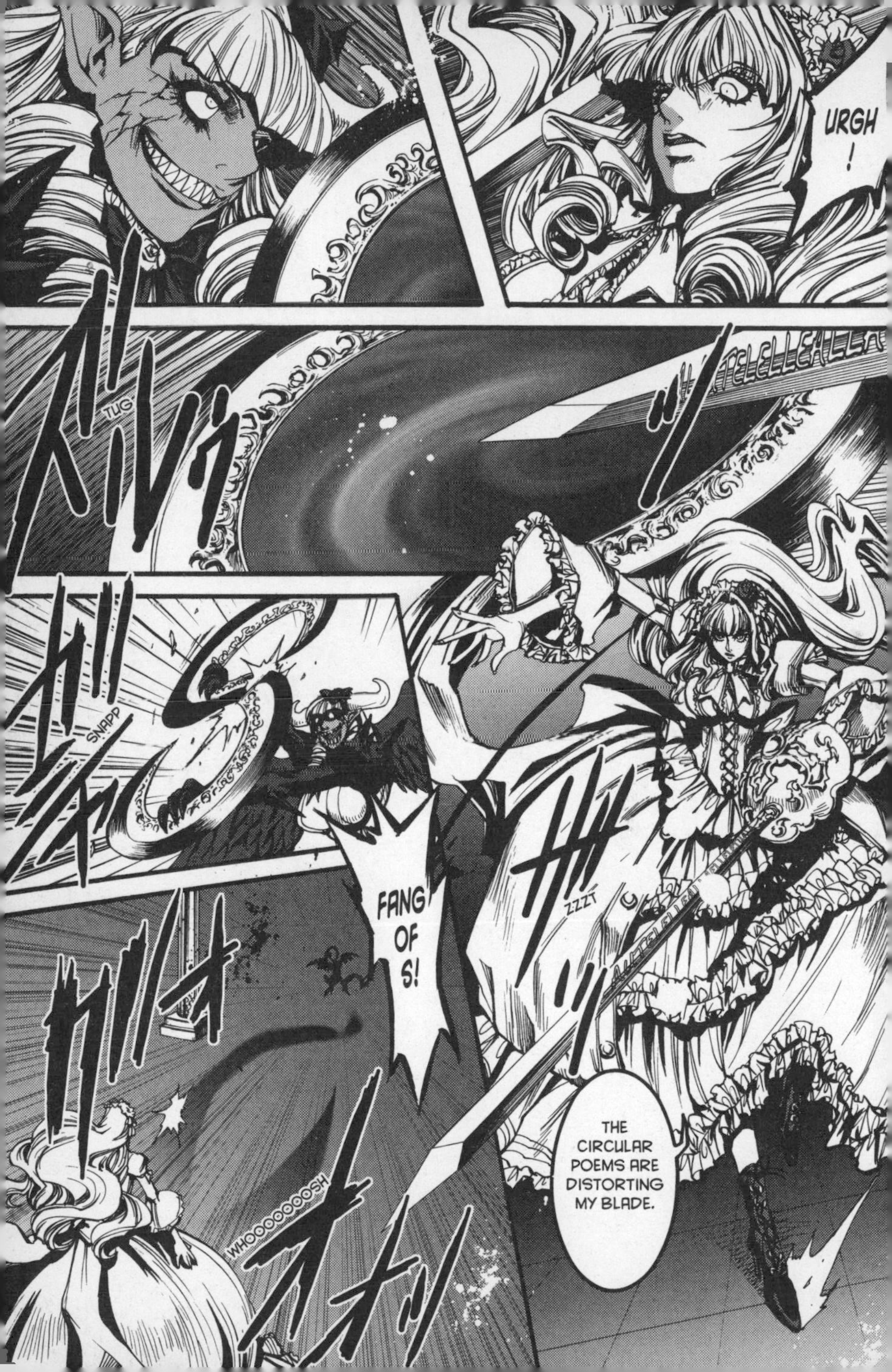
URGH !
TUG
FANG OF S!
ZZZT
THE CIRCULAR POEMS ARE DISTORTING MY BLADE.
SNAPP
WHOOOOOOOSH

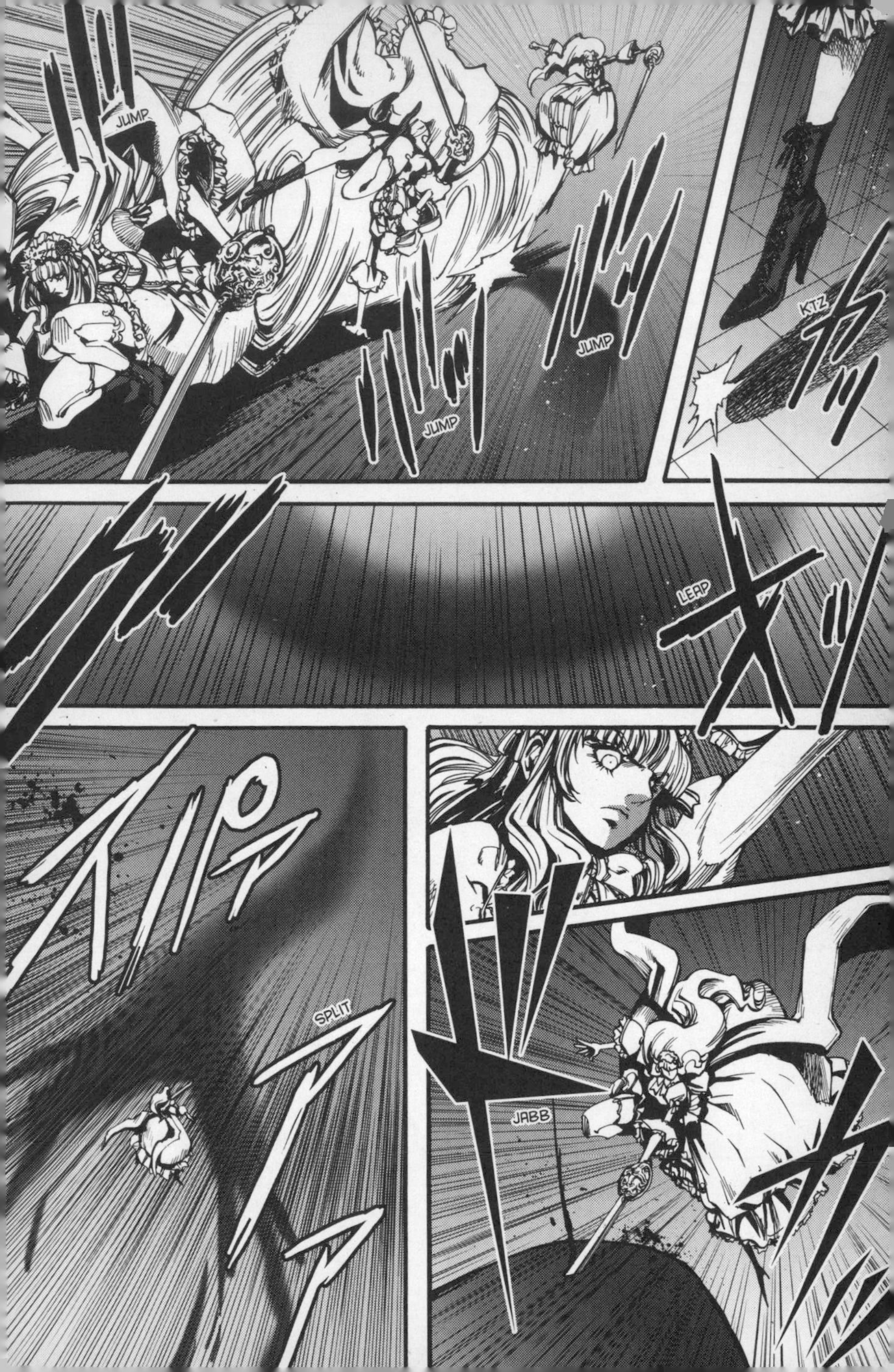
KTZ
JUMP
JUMP
JUMP
LEAP
JABB
SPLIT

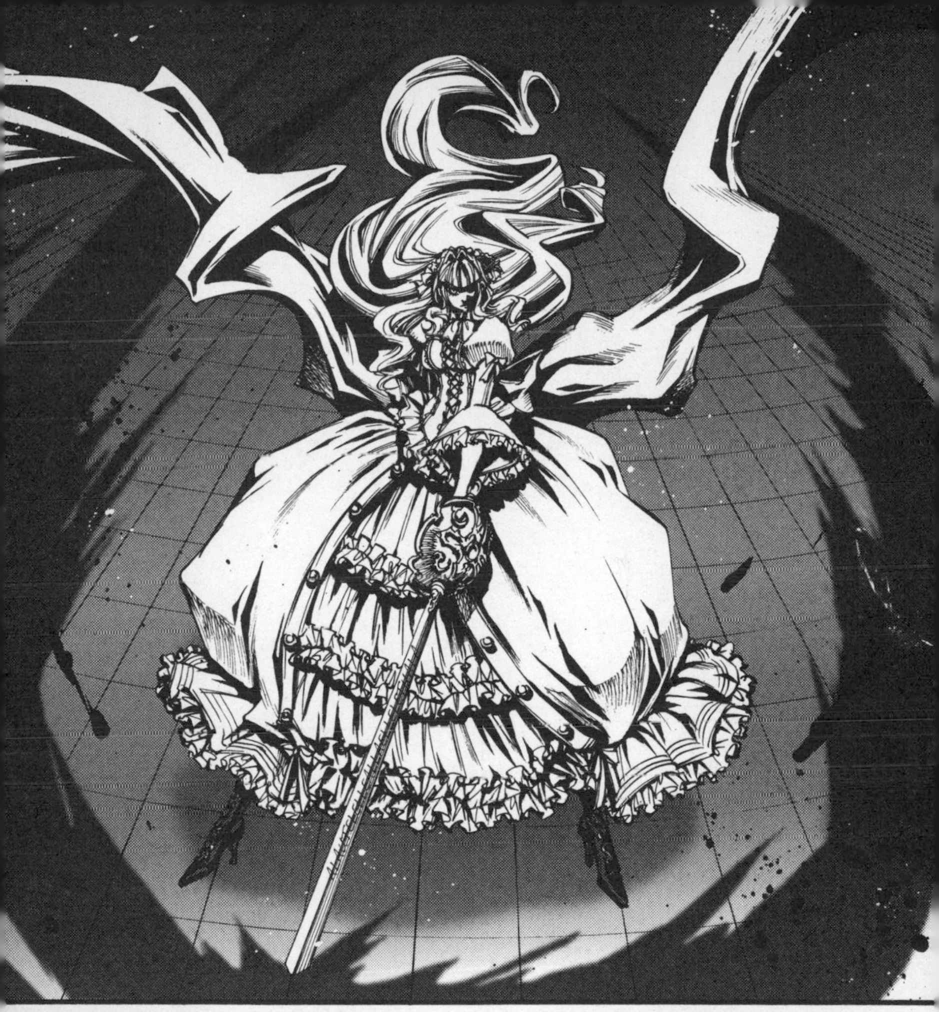
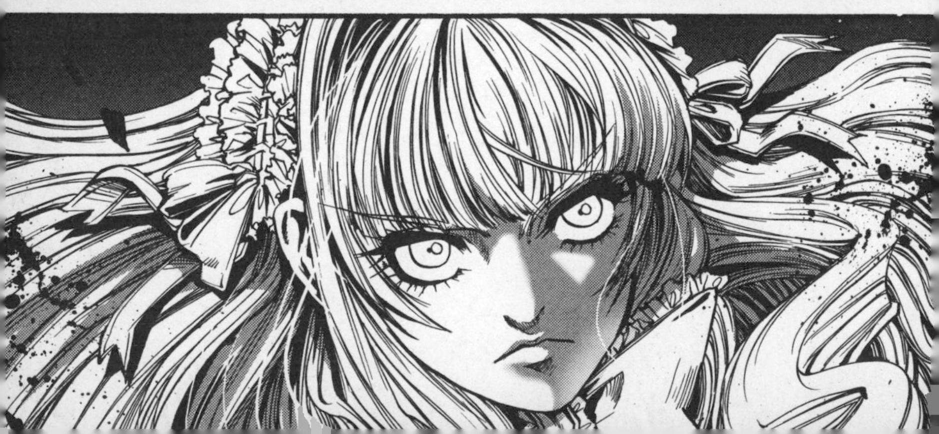

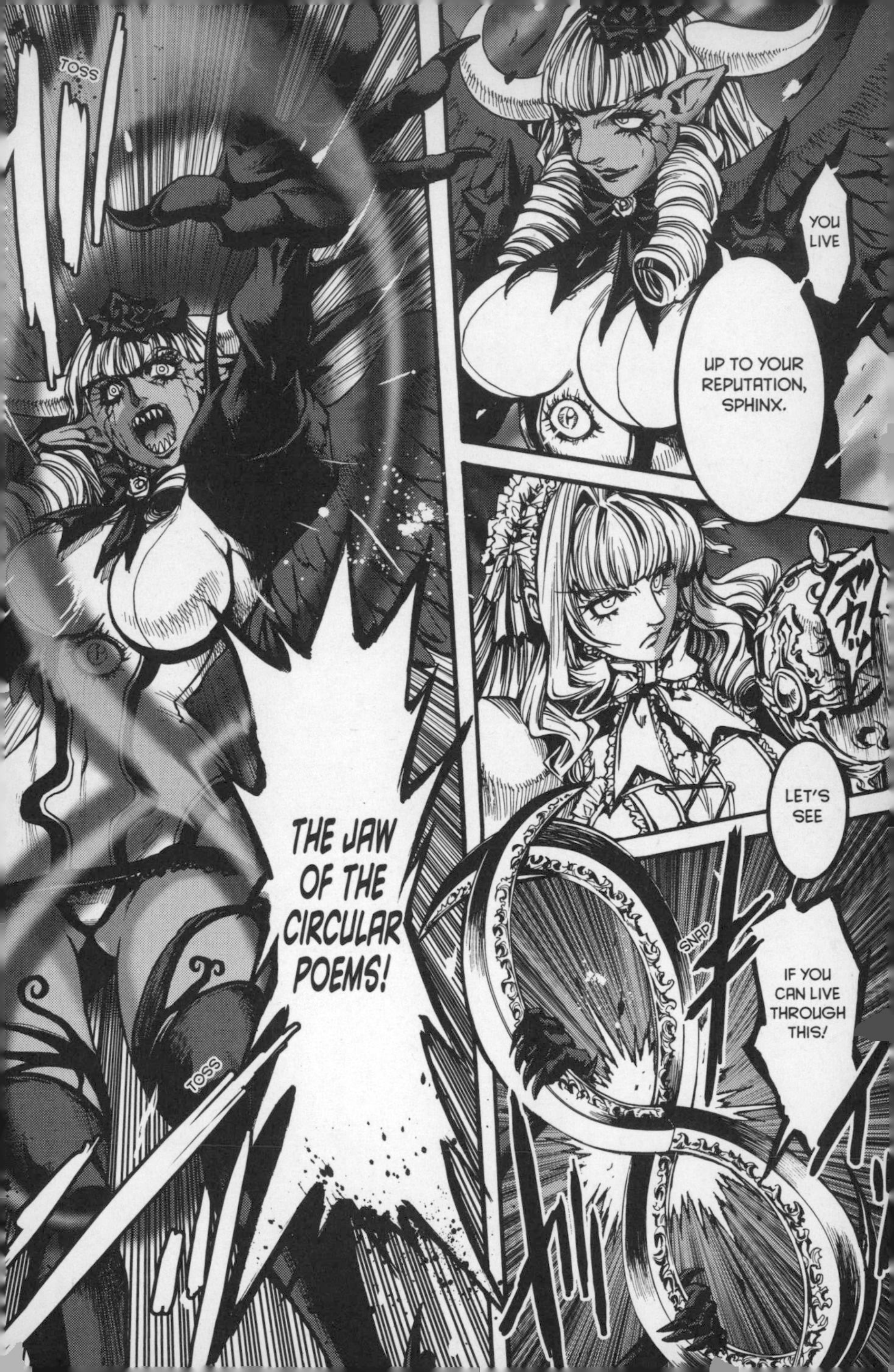
YOU LIVE
UP TO YOUR REPUTATION, SPHINX.
LET'S SEE
SNAP
IF YOU CAN LIVE THROUGH THIS!
TOSS
THE JAW OF THE CIRCULAR POEMS!
TOSS

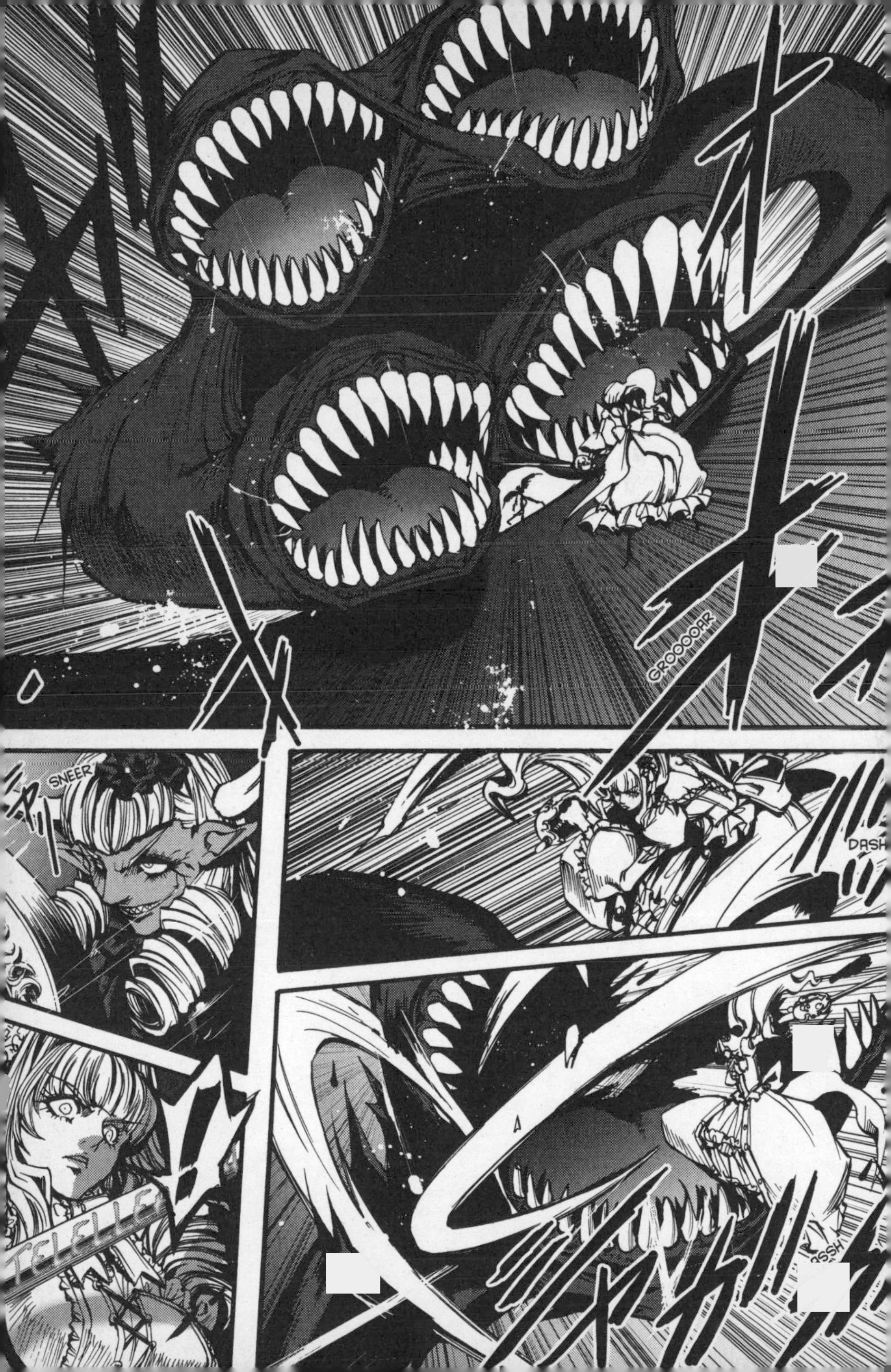
GROOOOAR
DASH
SNEER
TELELLE!
SSH

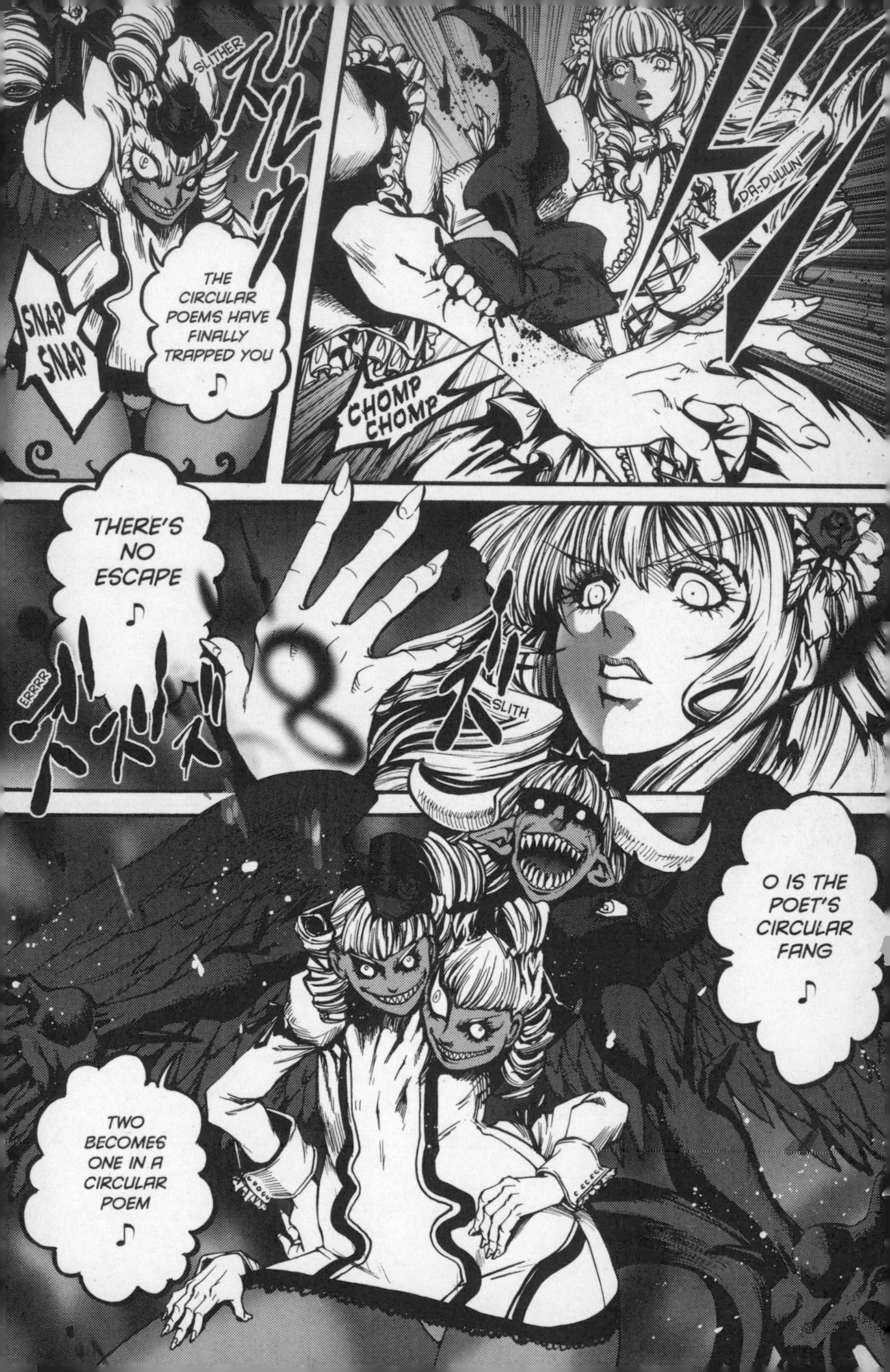

DA-DUUUN
CHOMP CHOMP
SLITHER
THE CIRCULAR POEMS HAVE FINALLY TRAPPED YOU ♪
SNAP SNAP
SLITH
THERE'S NO ESCAPE ♪
ERRRR
O IS THE POET'S CIRCULAR FANG ♪
TWO BECOMES ONE IN A CIRCULAR POEM ♪

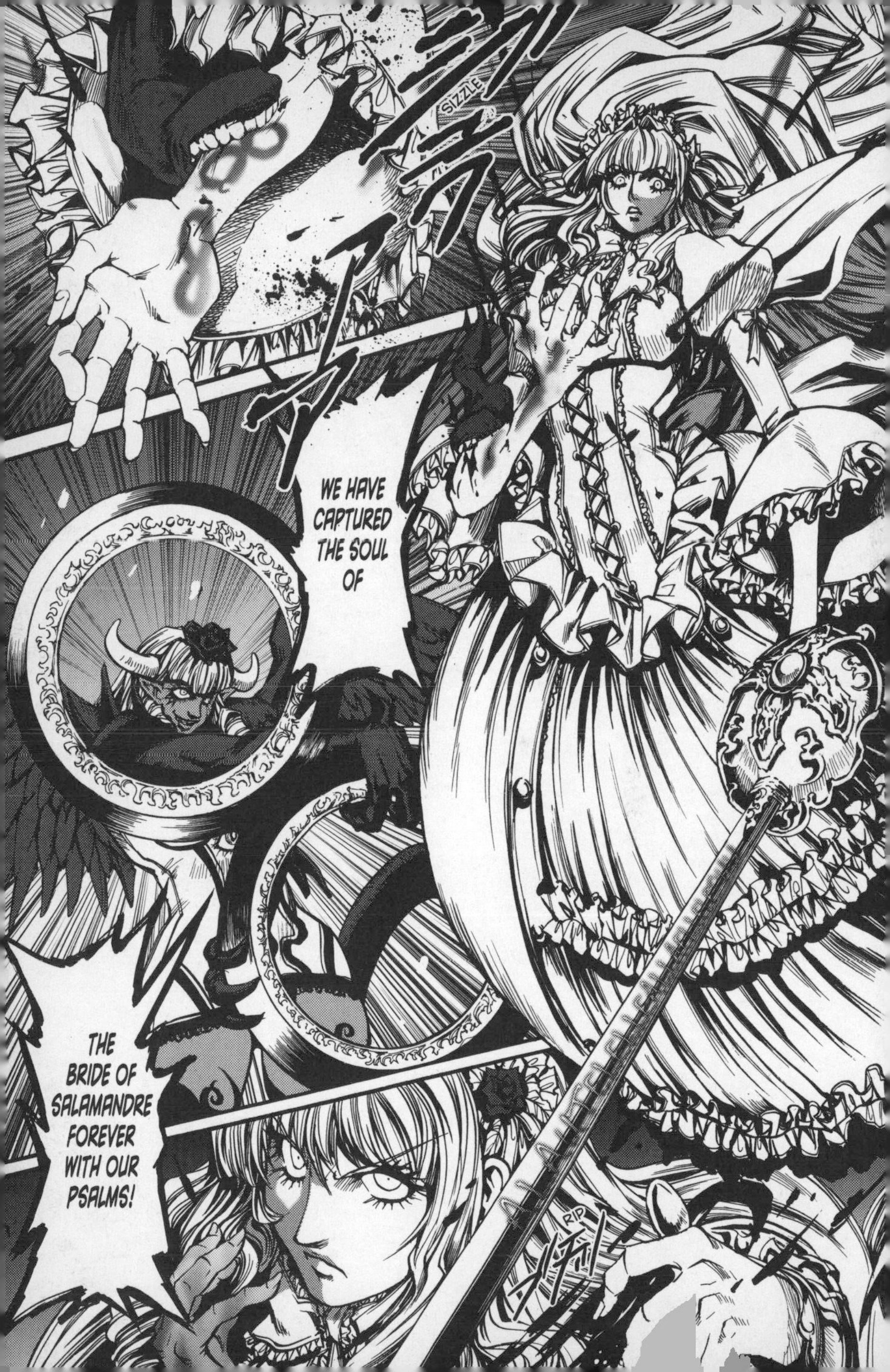
SIZZLE
WE HAVE CAPTURED THE SOUL OF
THE BRIDE OF SALAMANDRE FOREVER WITH OUR PSALMS!
RIP

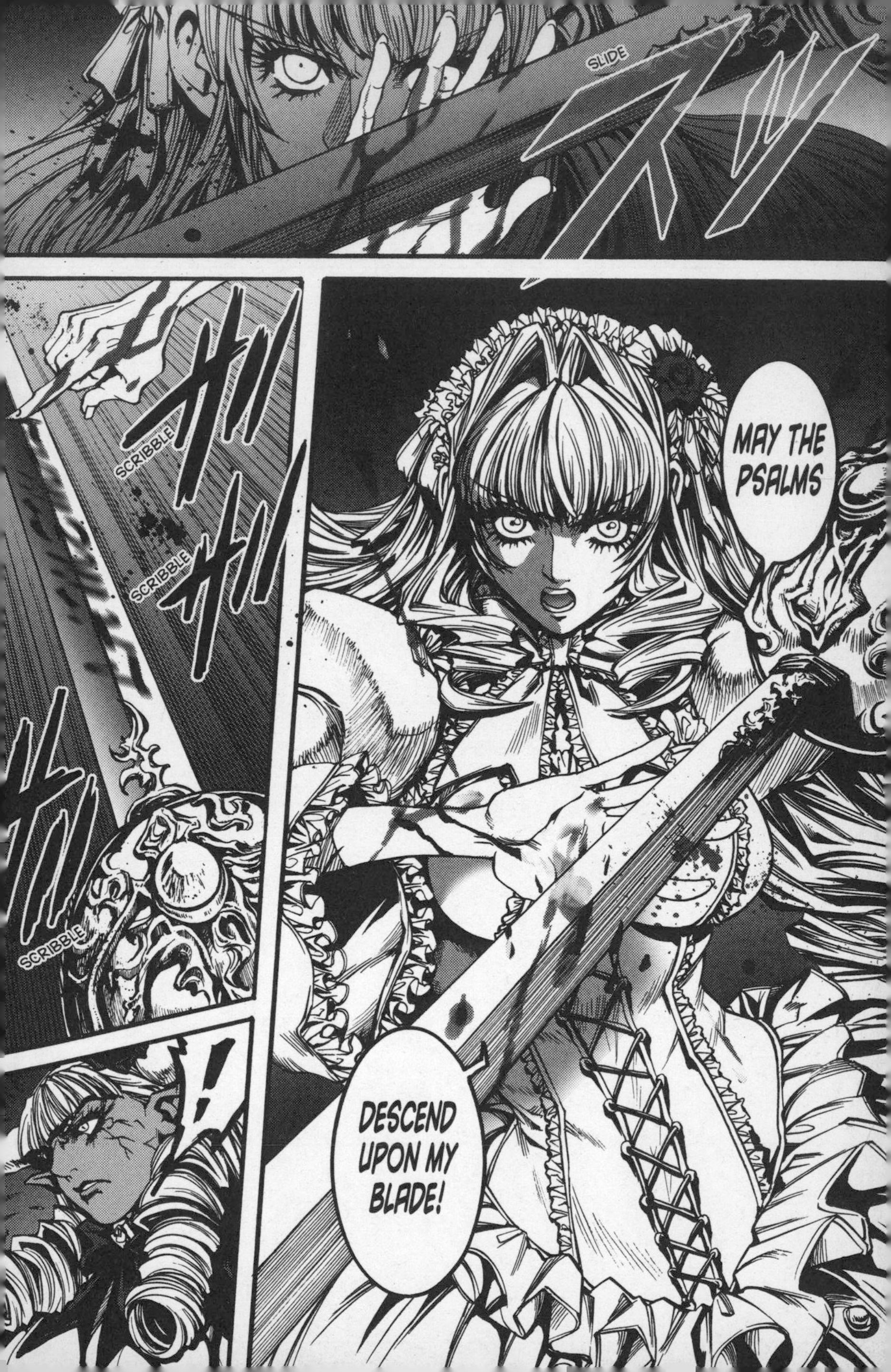
SLIDE
MAY THE PSALMS
DESCEND UPON MY BLADE!
SCRIBBLE
SCRIBBLE
SCRIBBLE
!

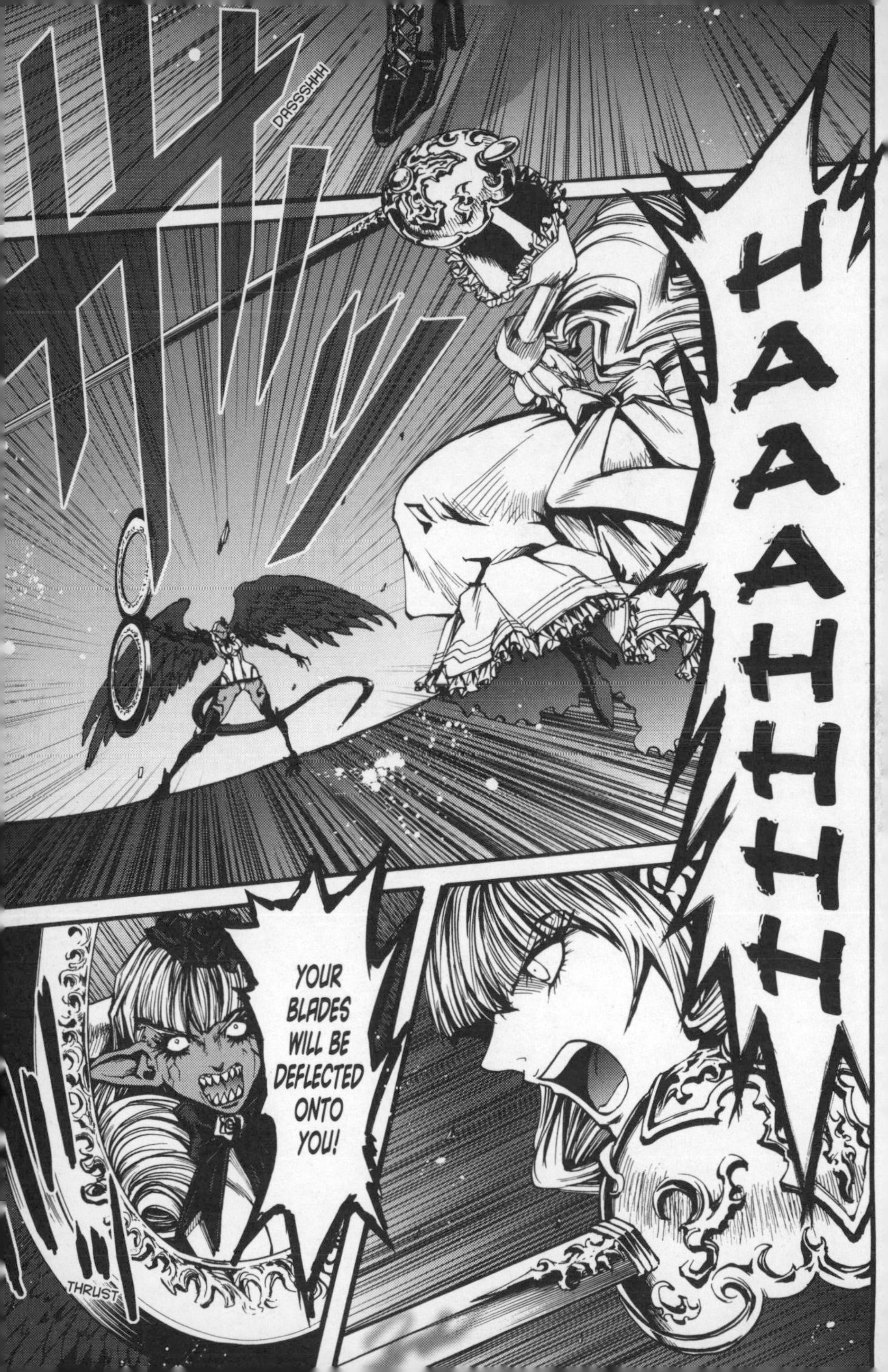
HAAAHHHH
DASSSHHH
YOUR BLADES WILL BE DEFLECTED ONTO YOU!
THRUST

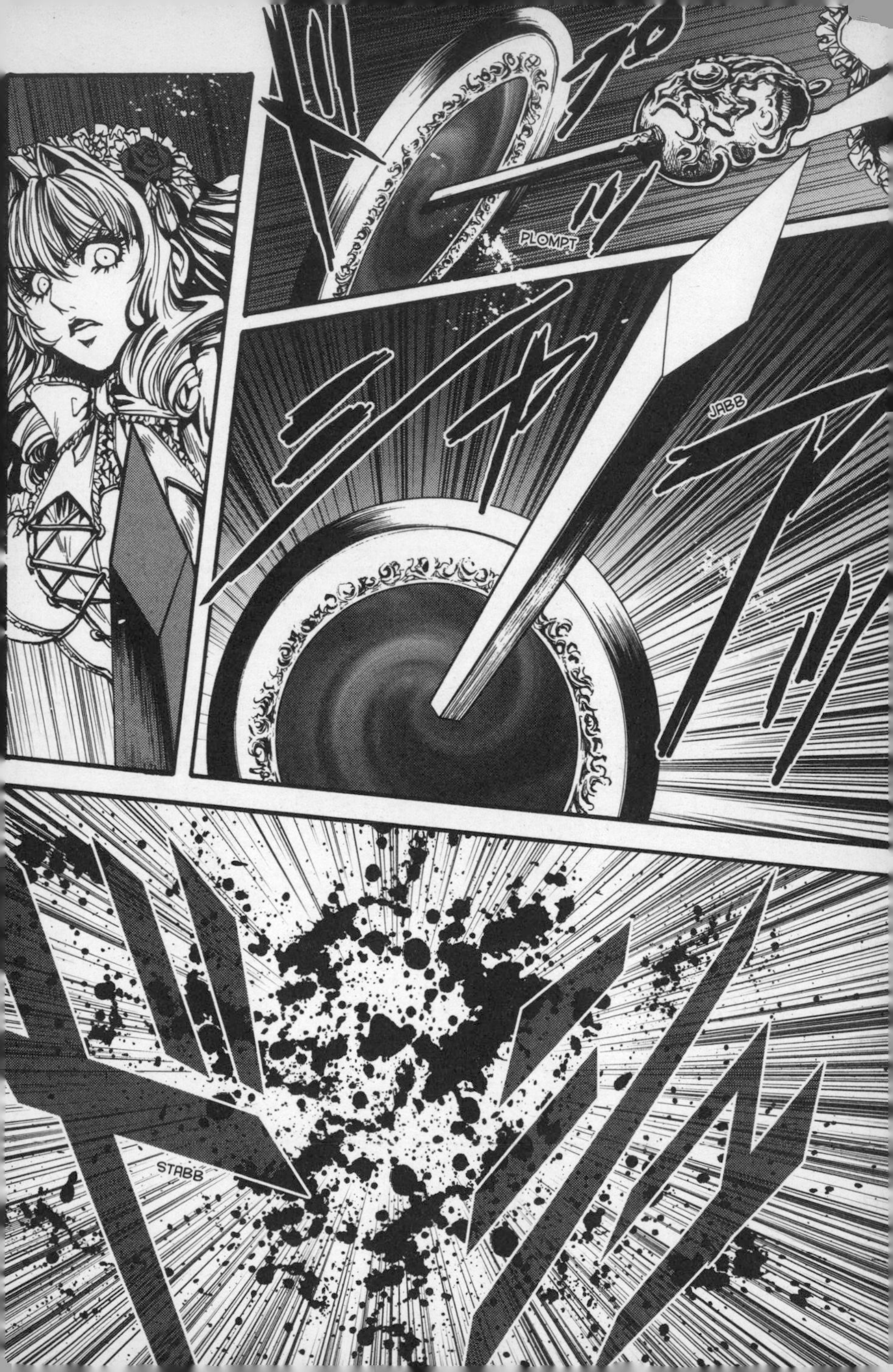
PLOMPT
JABB
STABB

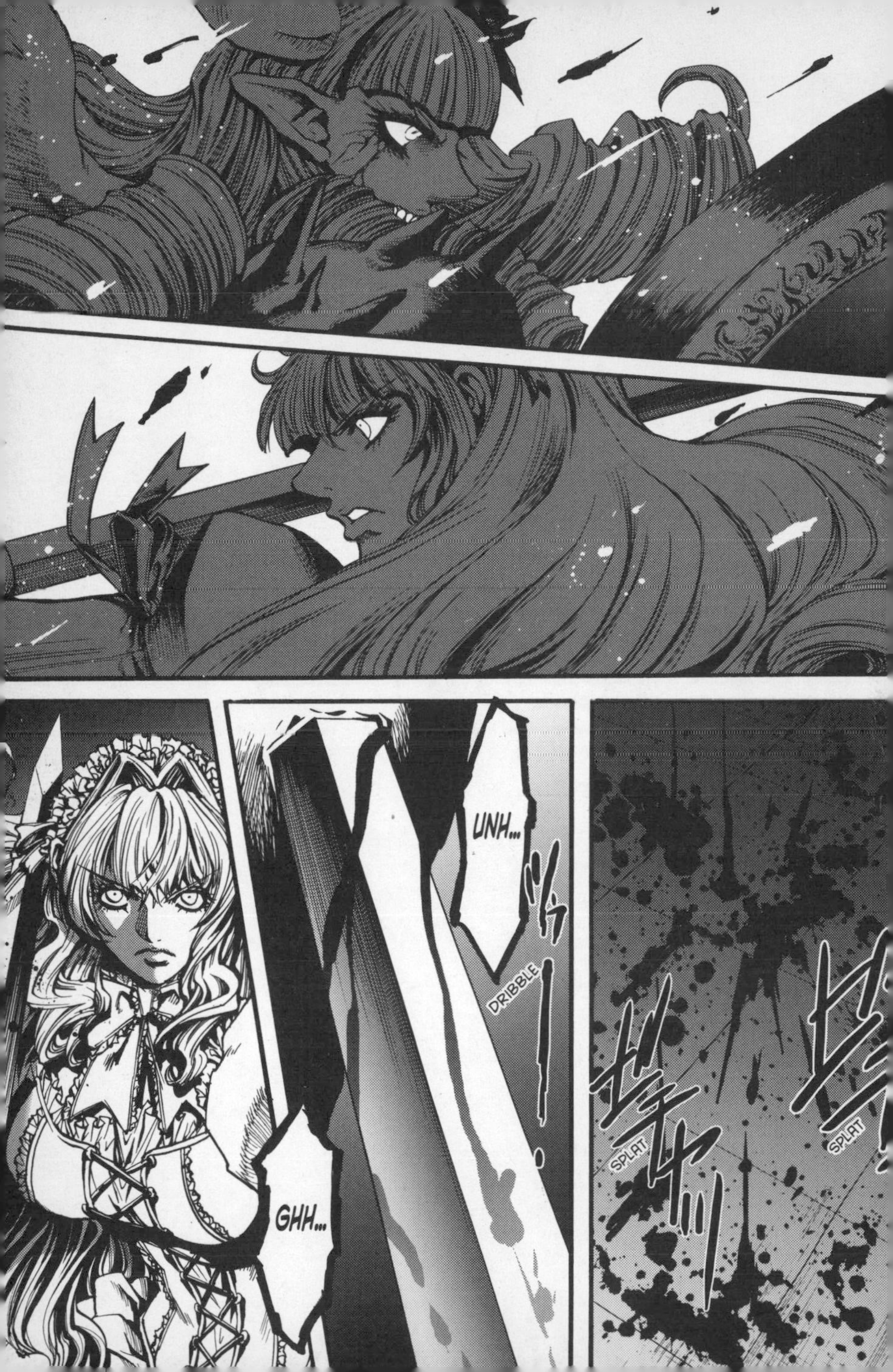
SPLAT
SPLAT
UNH...
DRIBBLE
GHH...

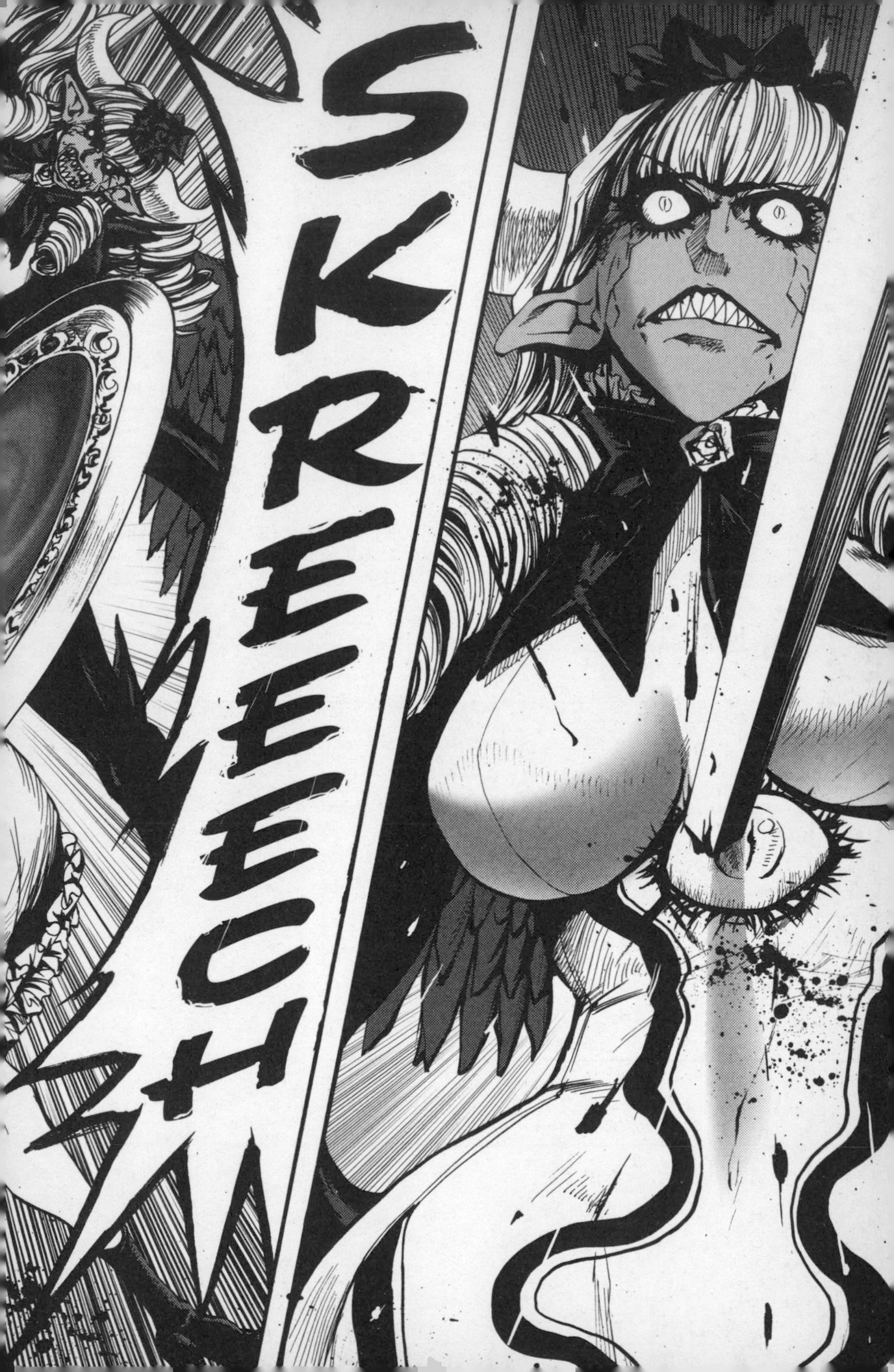
SKREEEECH

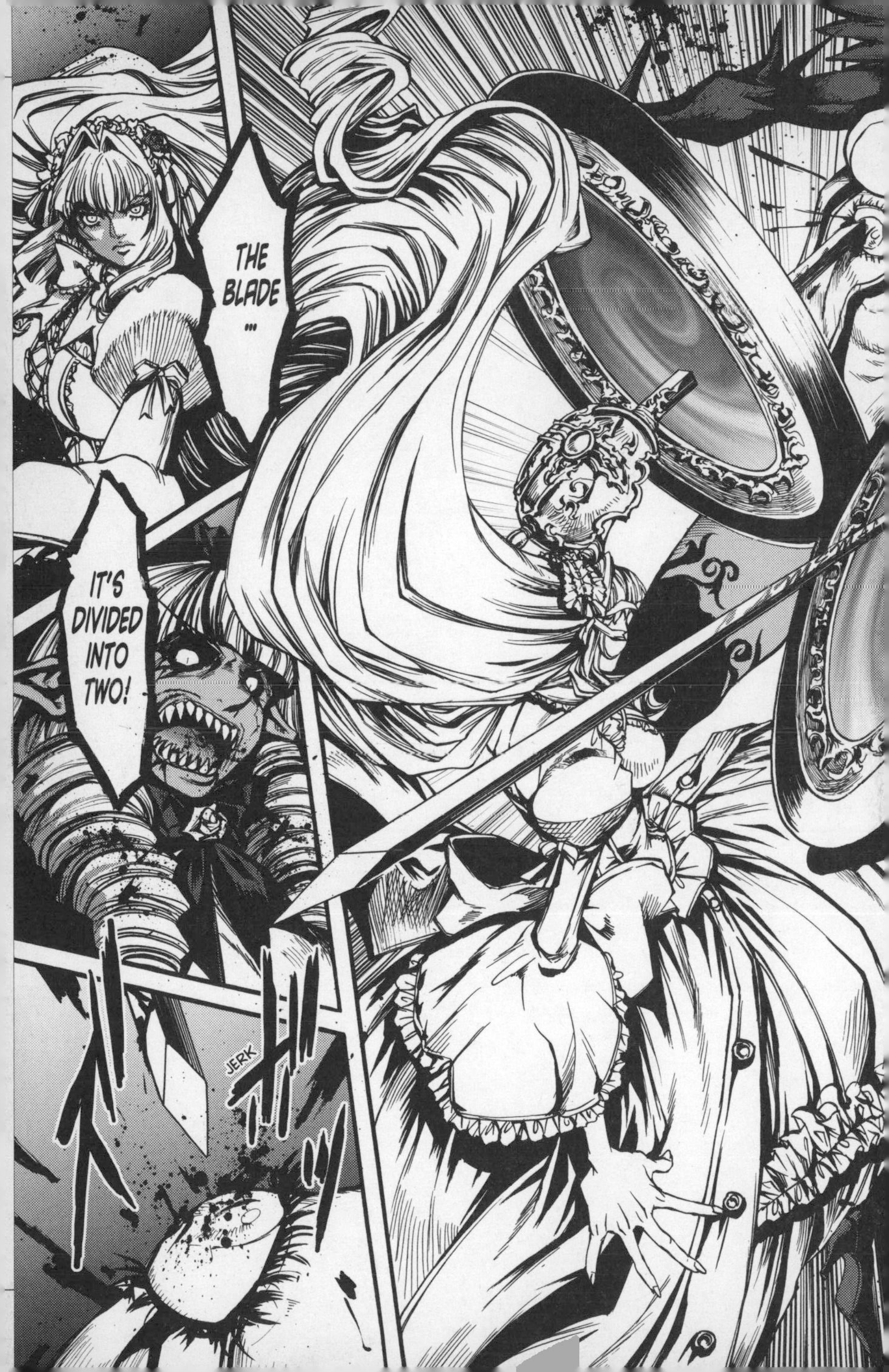
THE BLADE ...
IT'S DIVIDED INTO TWO!
JERK

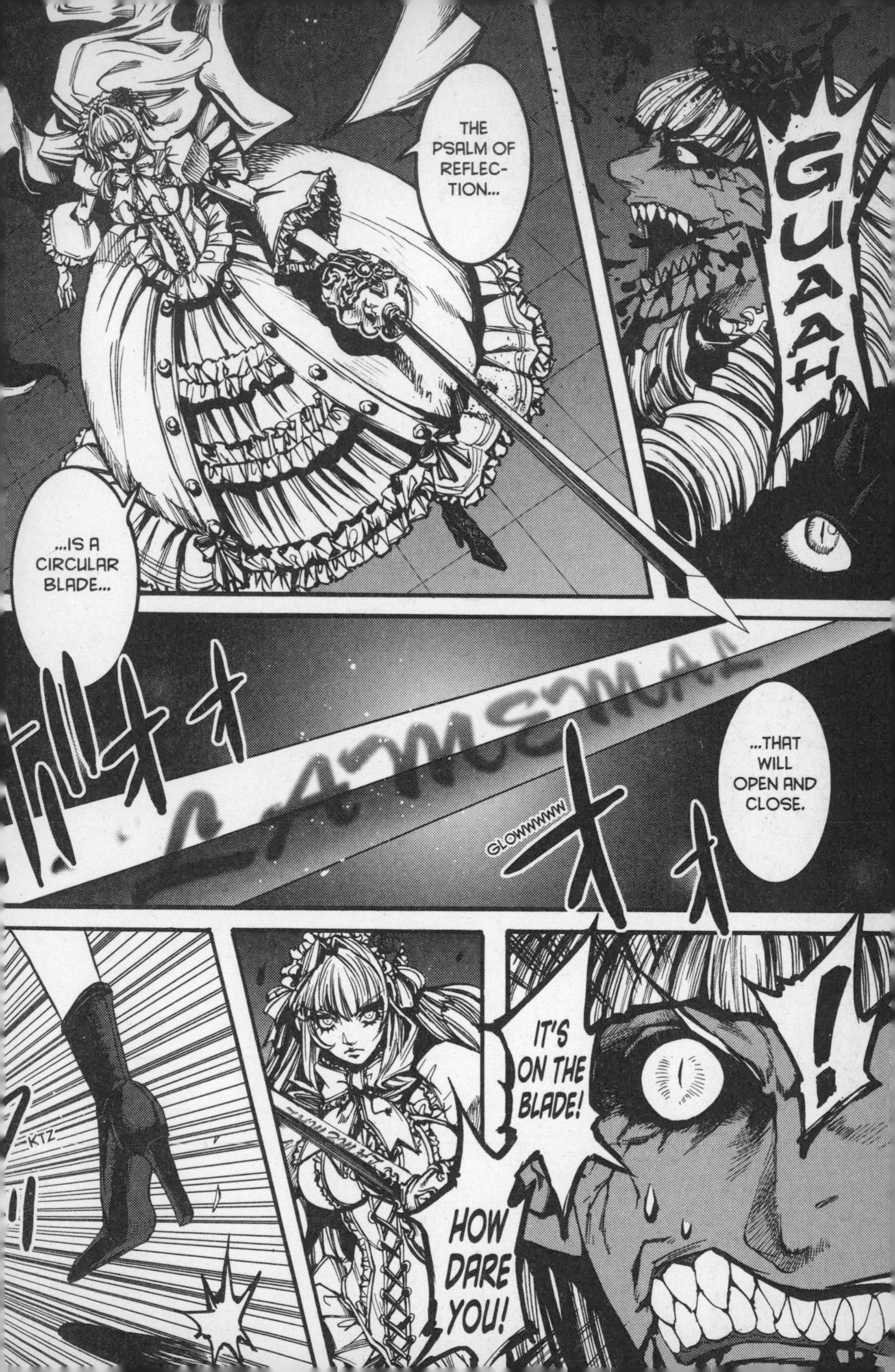
GUAAAH!
THE PSALM OF REFLECTION...
...IS A CIRCULAR BLADE...
...THAT WILL OPEN AND CLOSE.
GLOWWWWW
!
IT'S ON THE BLADE!
HOW DARE YOU!
KTZ
!

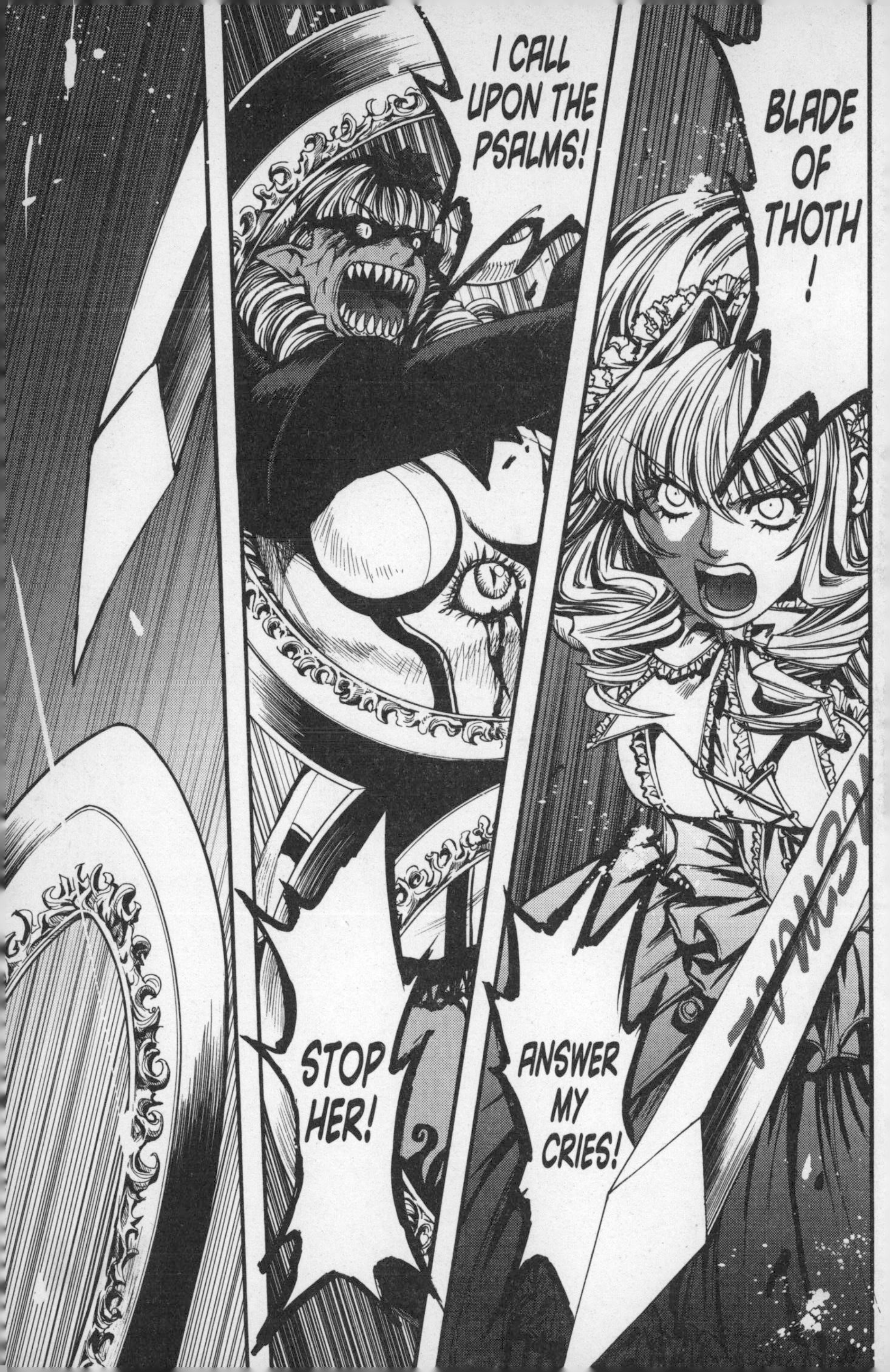
BLADE OF THOTH!
ANSWER MY CRIES!
I CALL UPON THE PSALMS!
STOP HER!

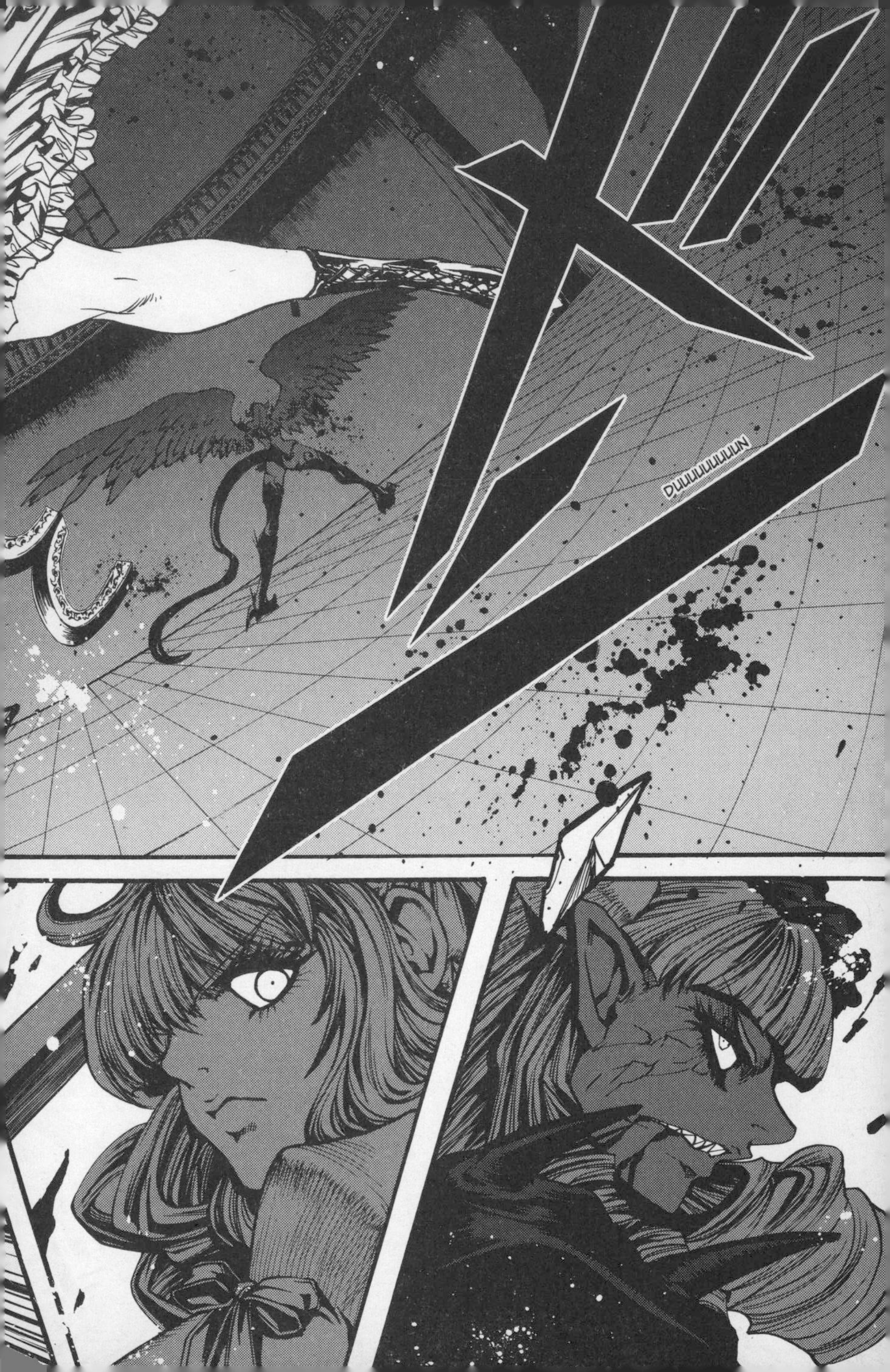
Duuuuuuuun

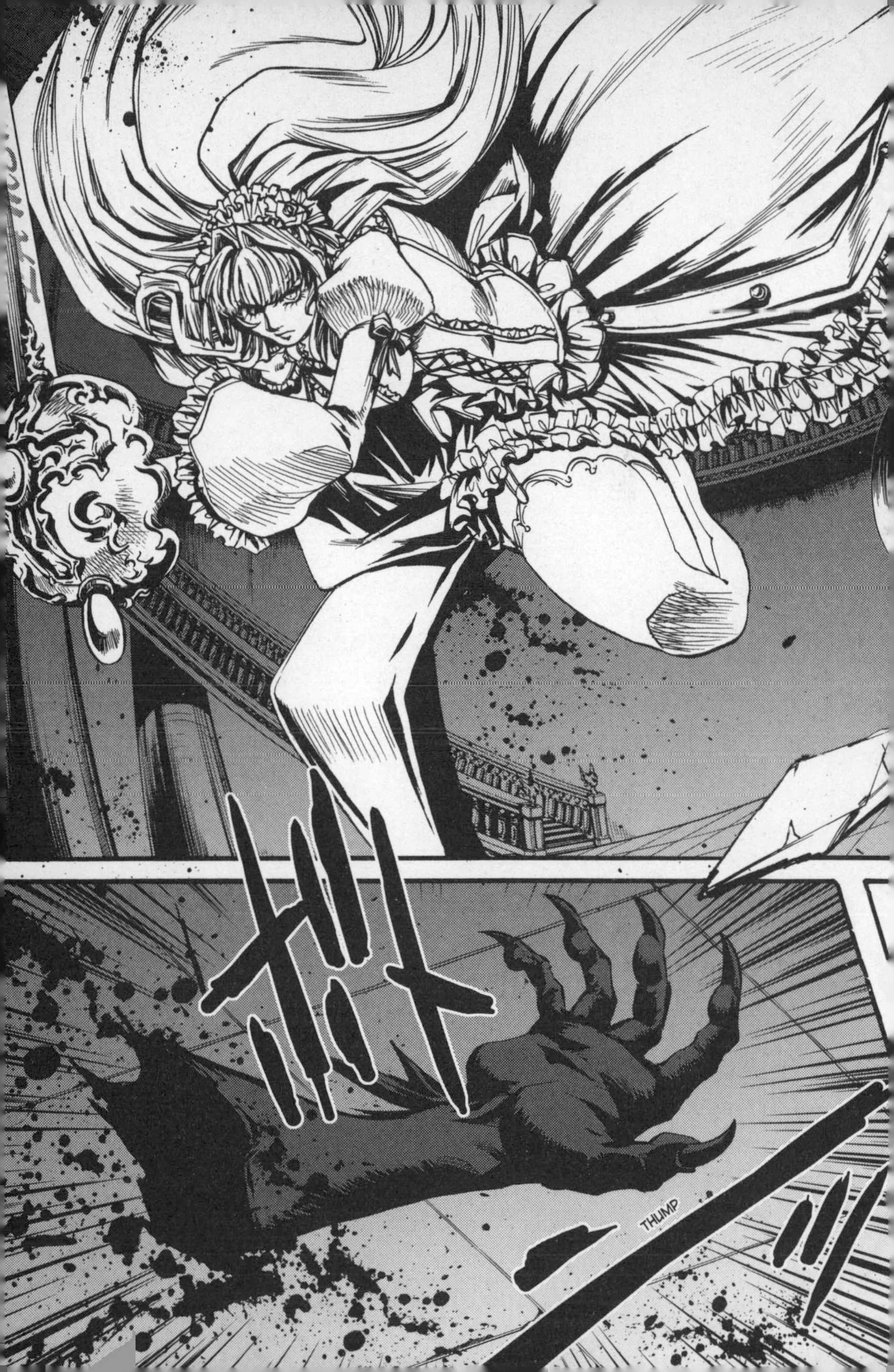
THUMP

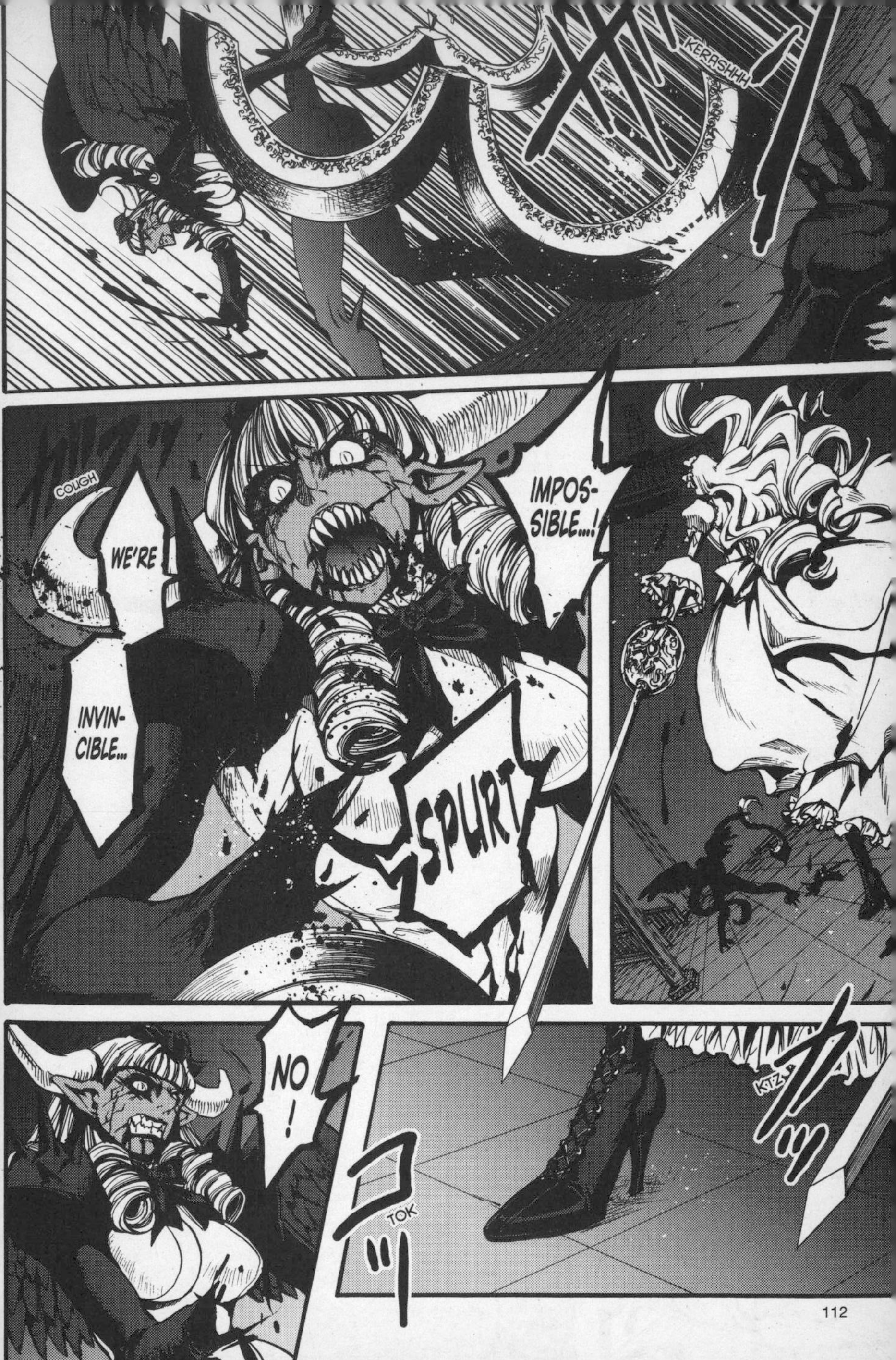
KERASHHH
IMPOS-
SIBLE...!
COUGH
WE'RE
INVIN-
CIBLE...
SPURT
KTZ
TOK
NO
!

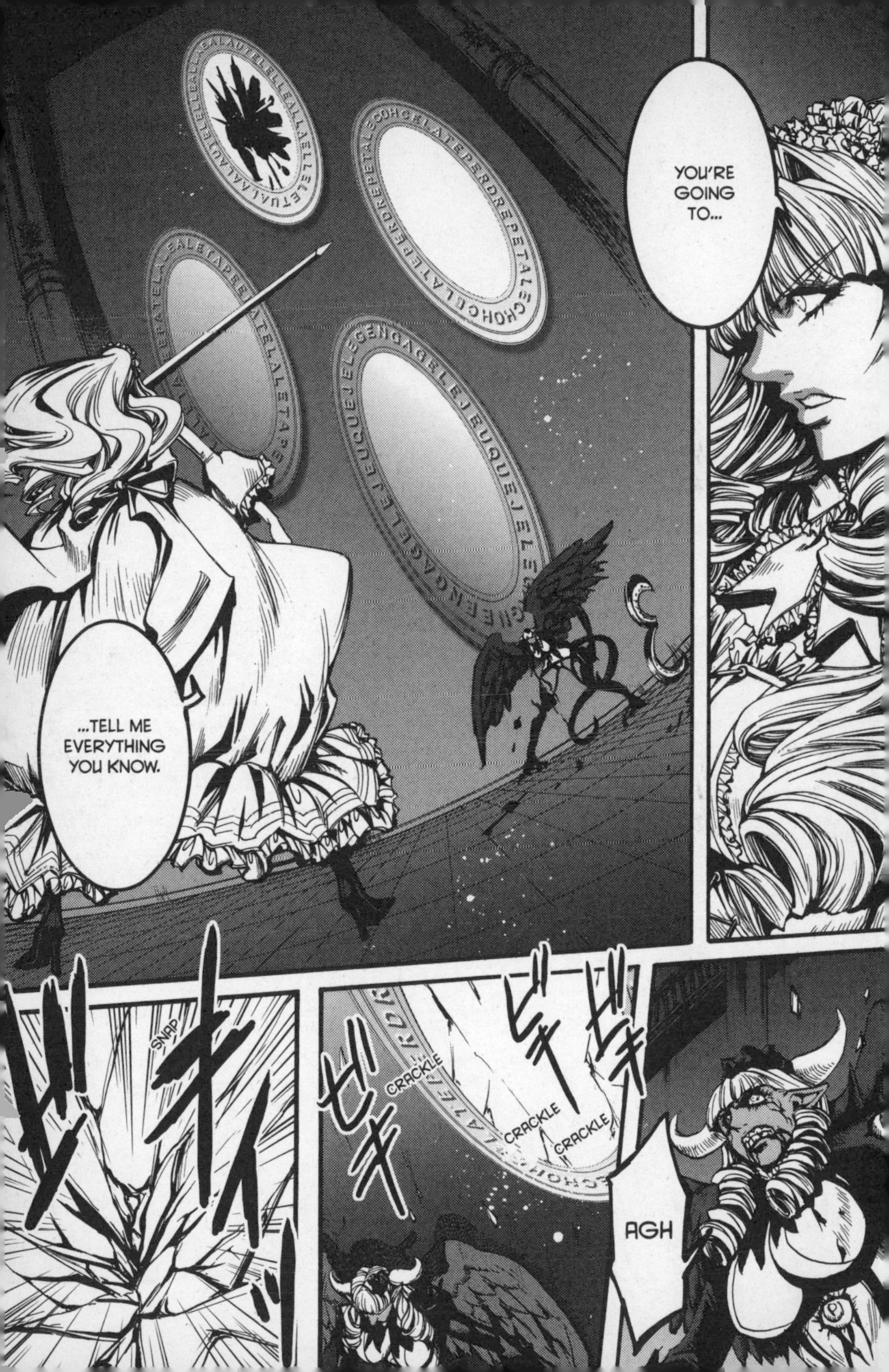
YOU'RE GOING TO...
...TELL ME EVERYTHING YOU KNOW.
AGH
CRACKLE
CRACKLE
CRACKLE
SNAP

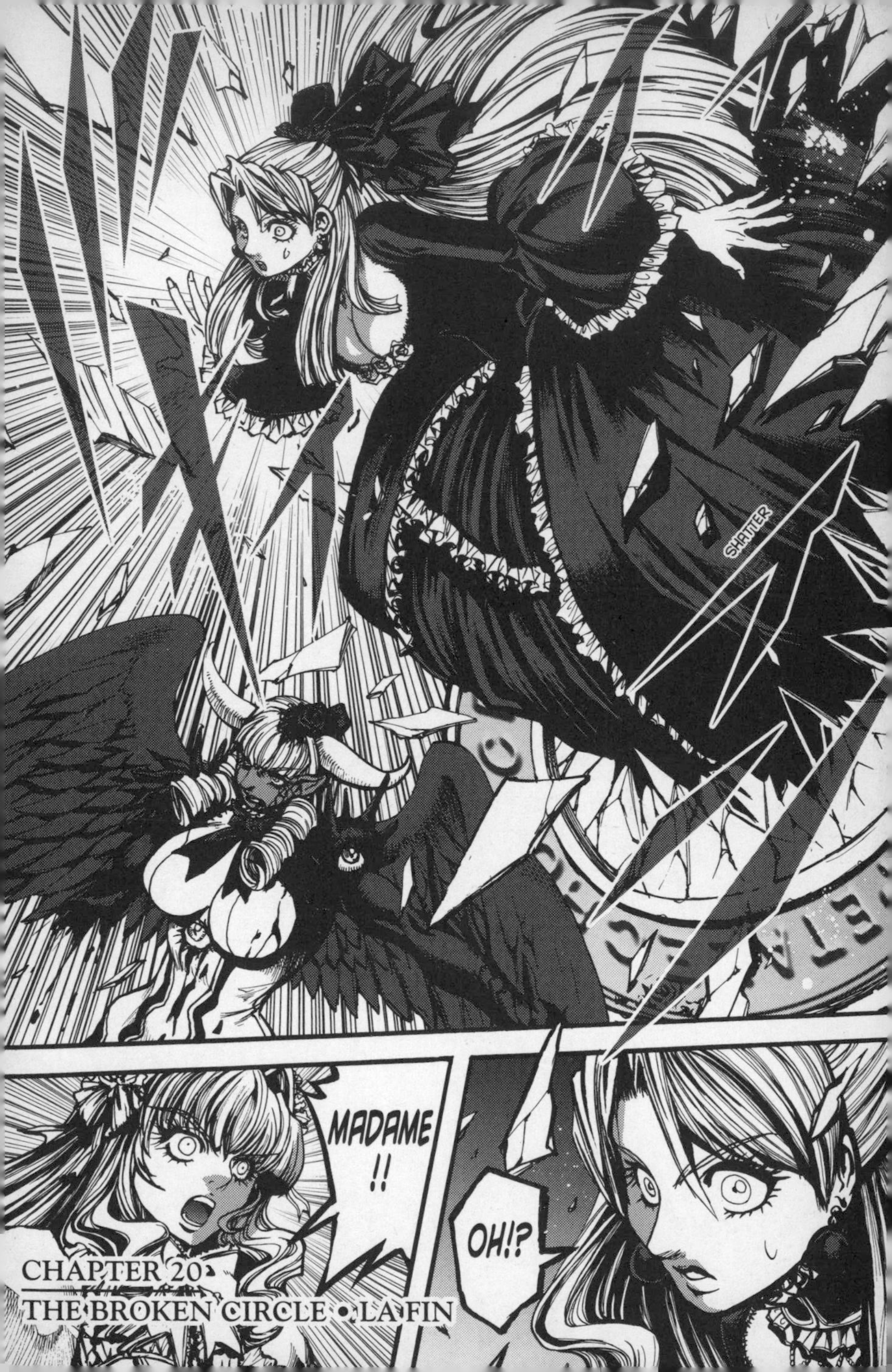
SHATTER
OH!?
MADAME !!

CHAPTER 20 THE BROKEN CIRCLE • LA FIN

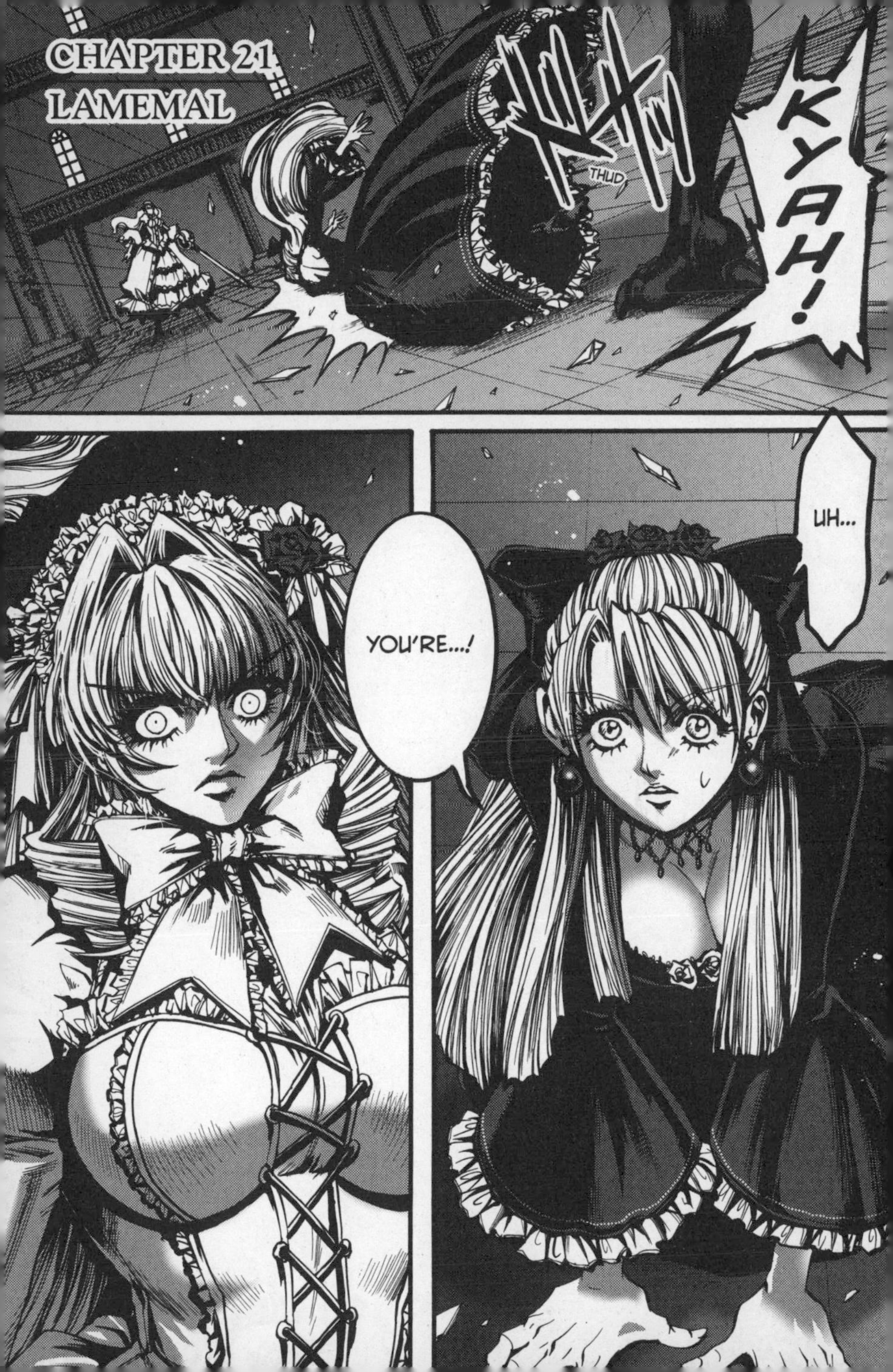
CHAPTER 21
LAMEMAL
KYAH!
THUD
UH...
YOU'RE...!

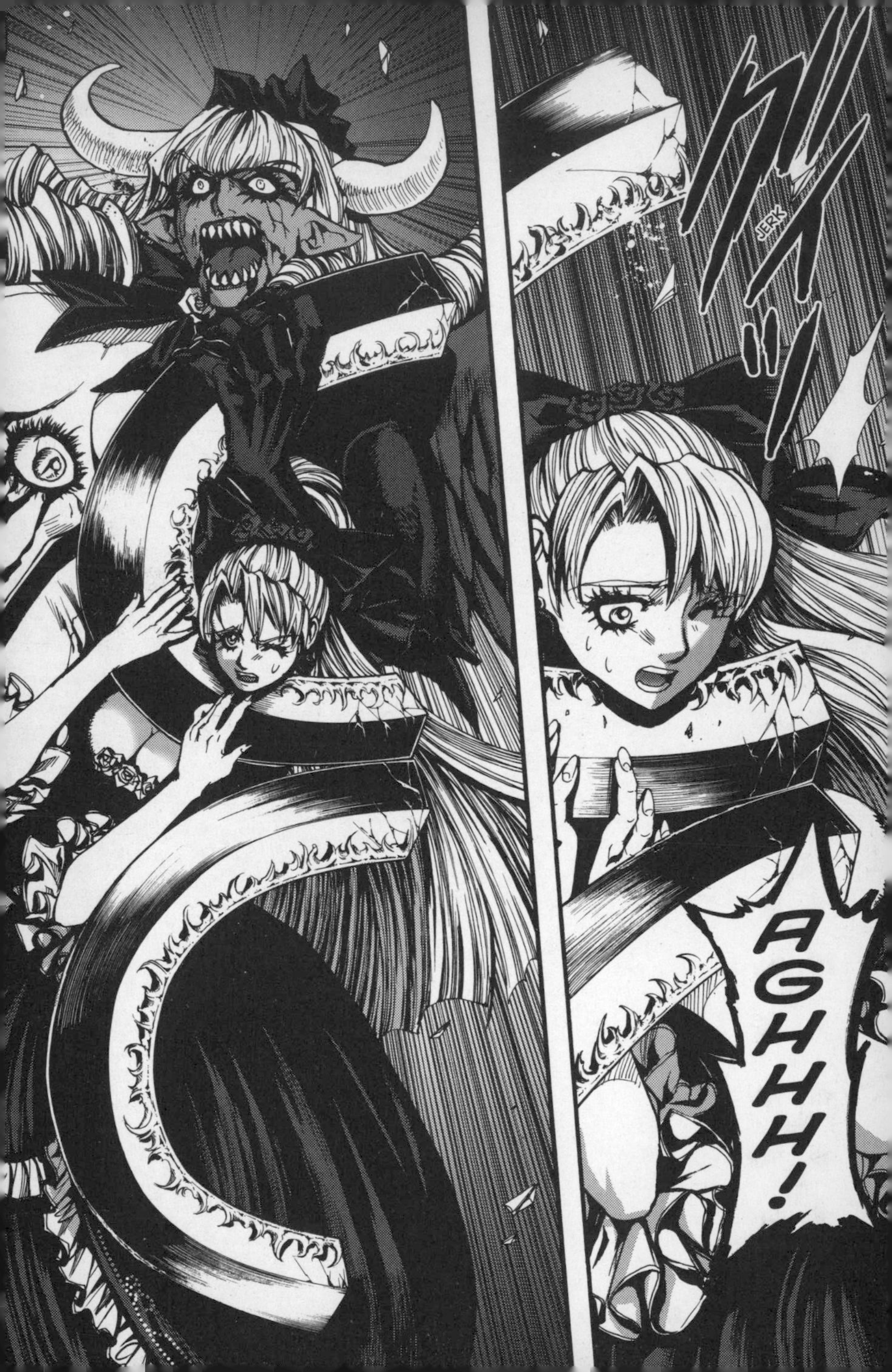
JERK
AGHHH!

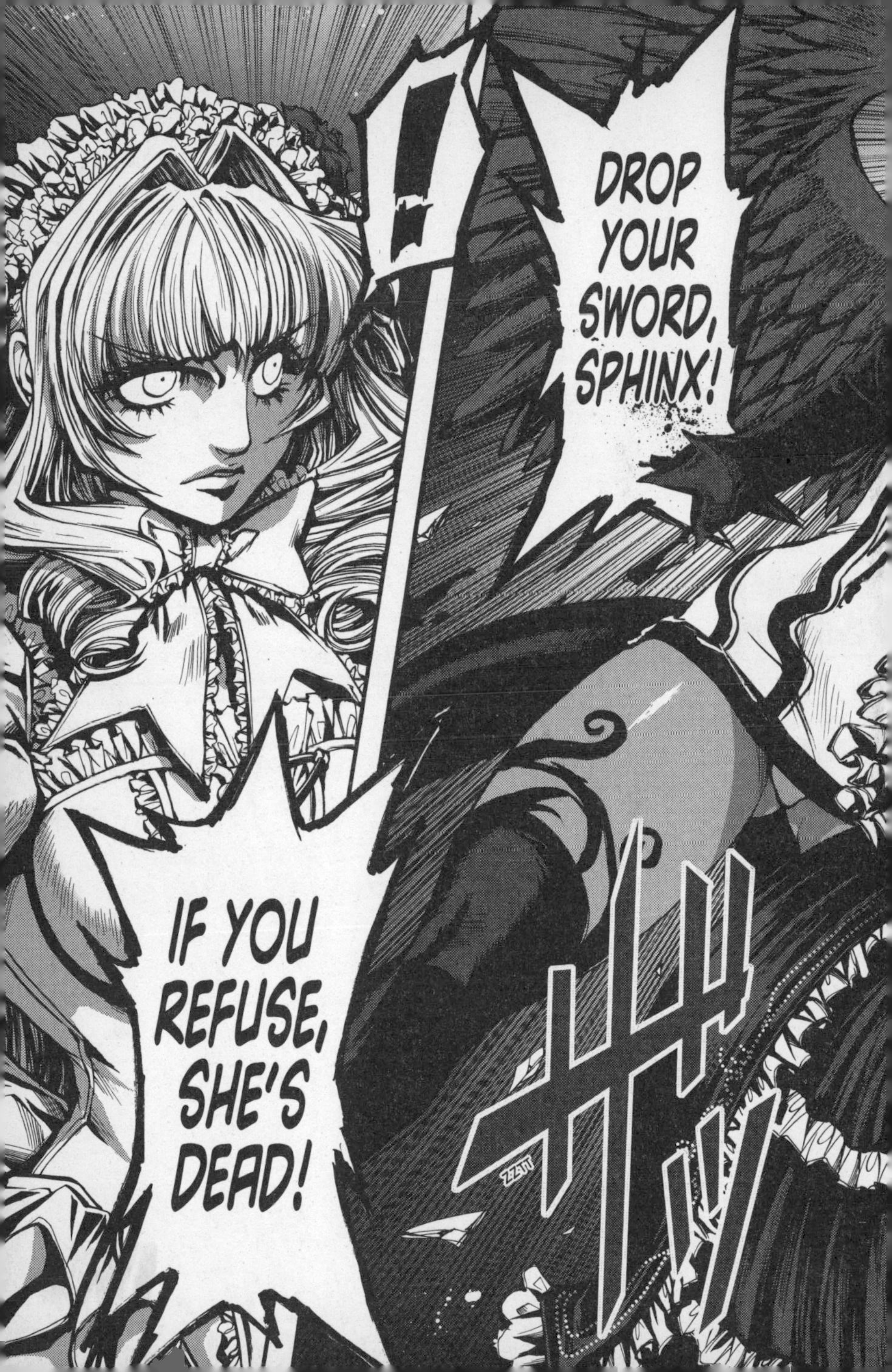
!
DROP YOUR SWORD, SPHINX!
IF YOU REFUSE, SHE'S DEAD!
ZZAN

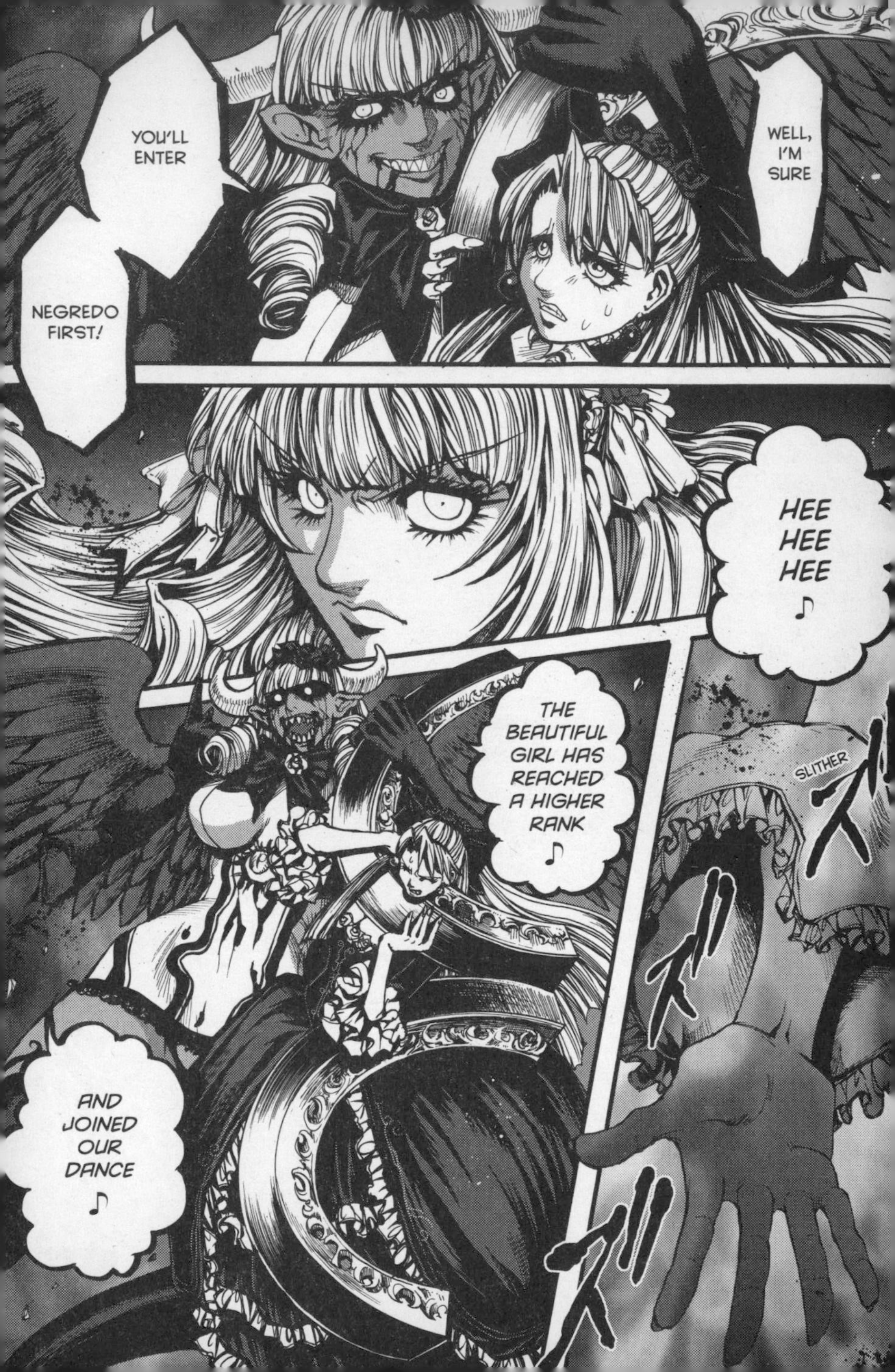
WELL, I'M SURE
YOU'LL ENTER
NEGREDO FIRST!
HEE HEE HEE ♪
THE BEAUTIFUL GIRL HAS REACHED A HIGHER RANK ♪
SLITHER
AND JOINED OUR DANCE ♪

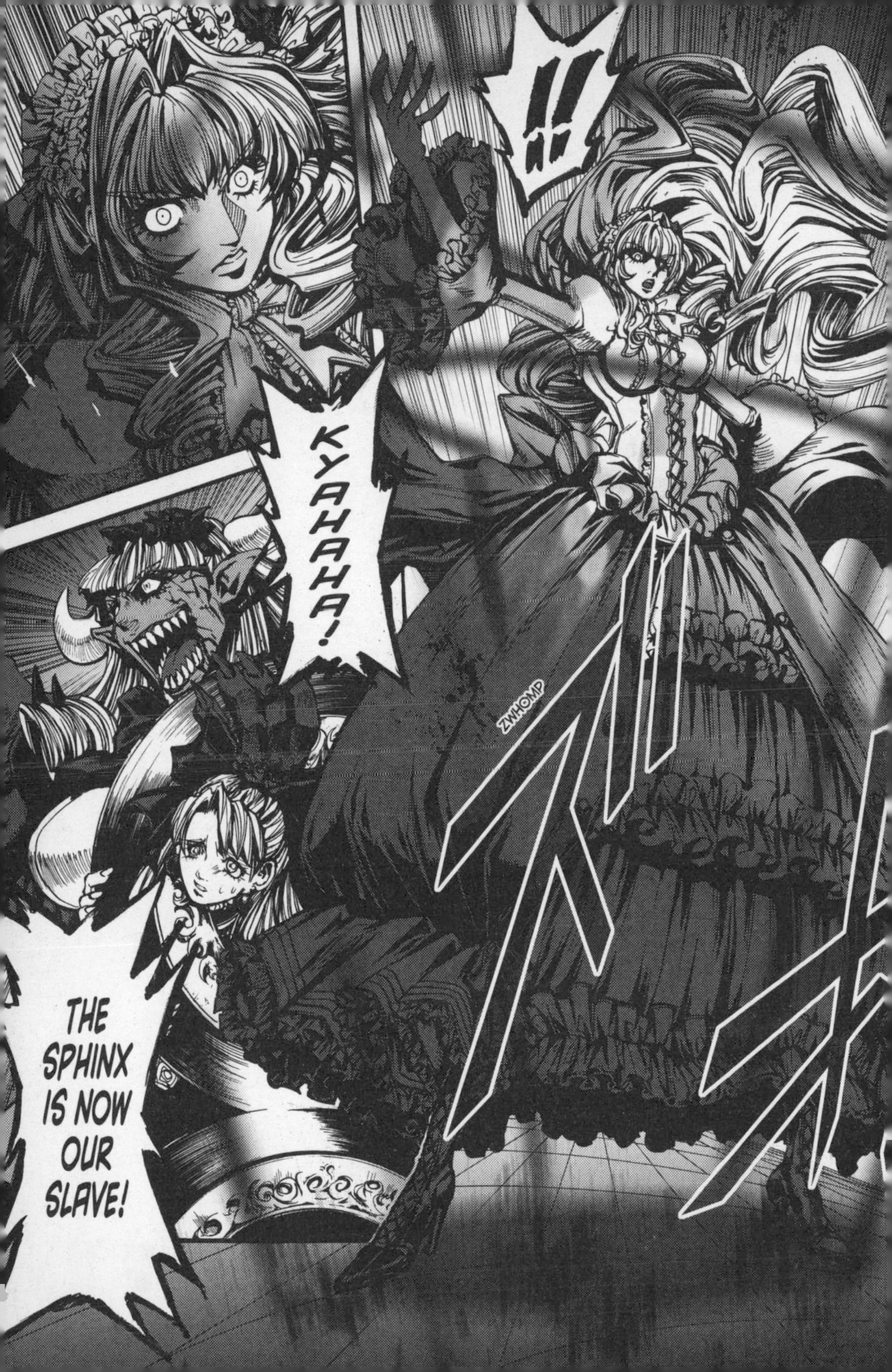
!!
ZWHOMP
KYAHAHA!
THE SPHINX IS NOW OUR SLAVE!

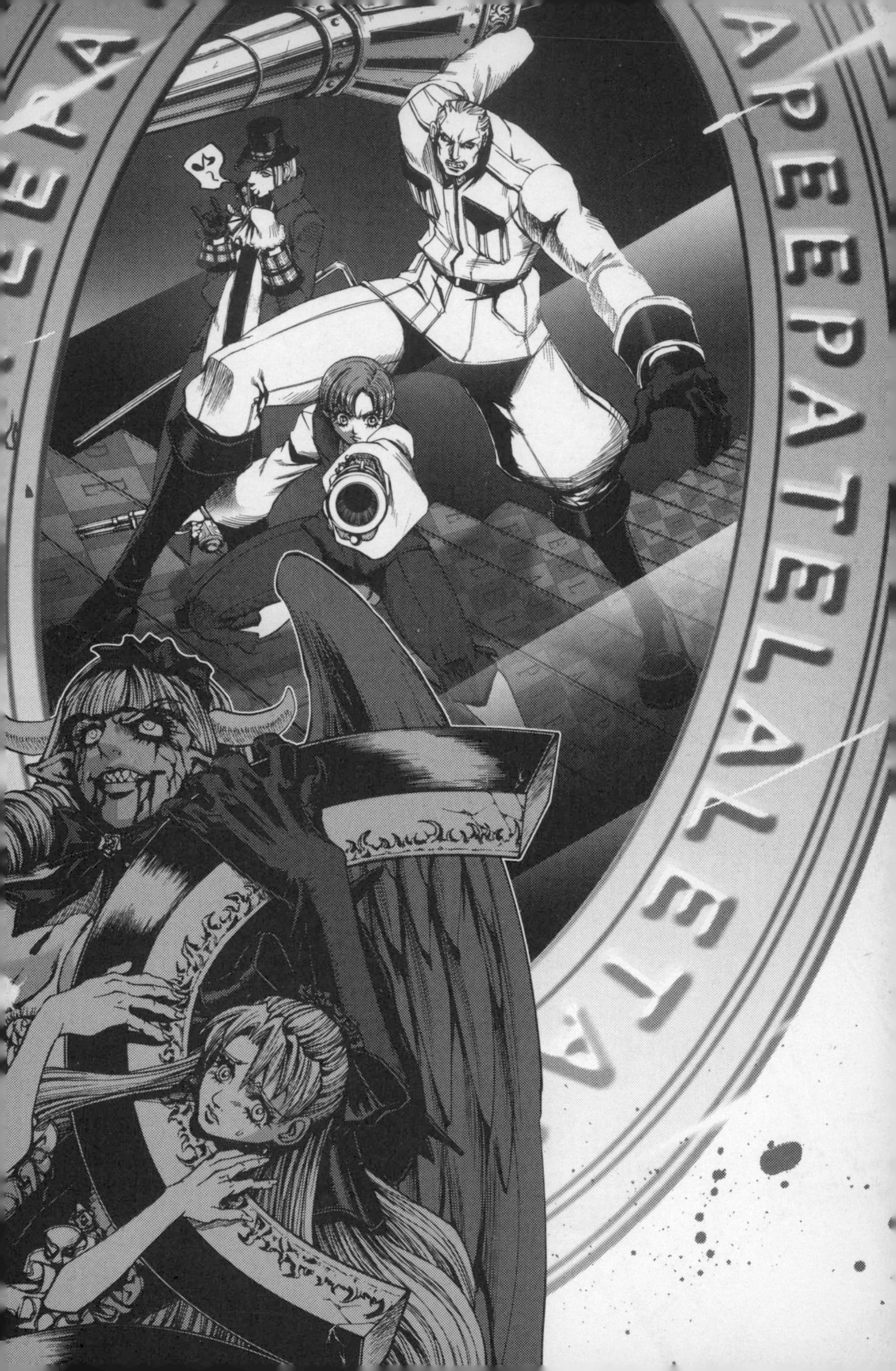

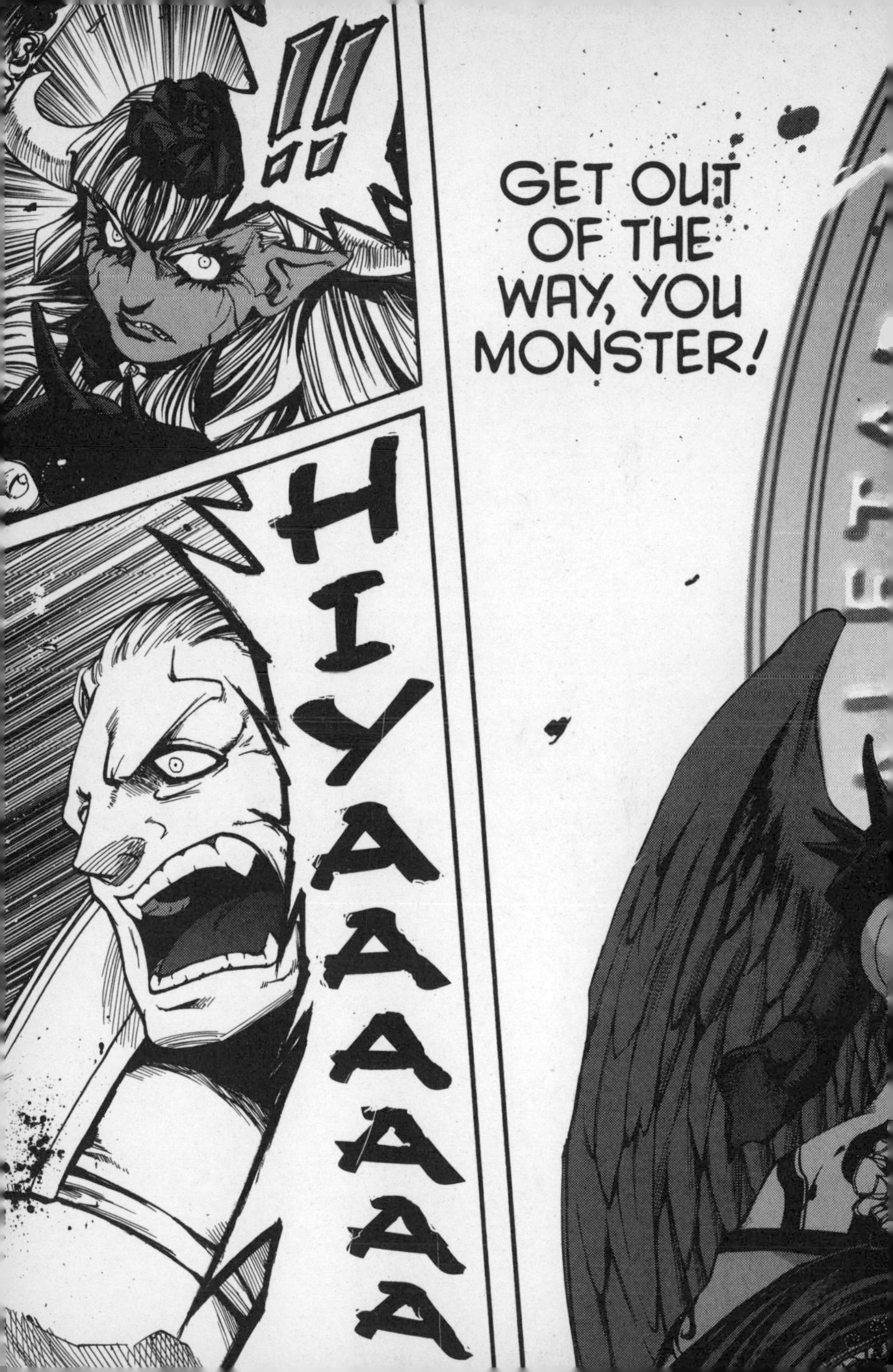
GET OUT OF THE WAY, YOU MONSTER!
!!
HIYAAAAAA

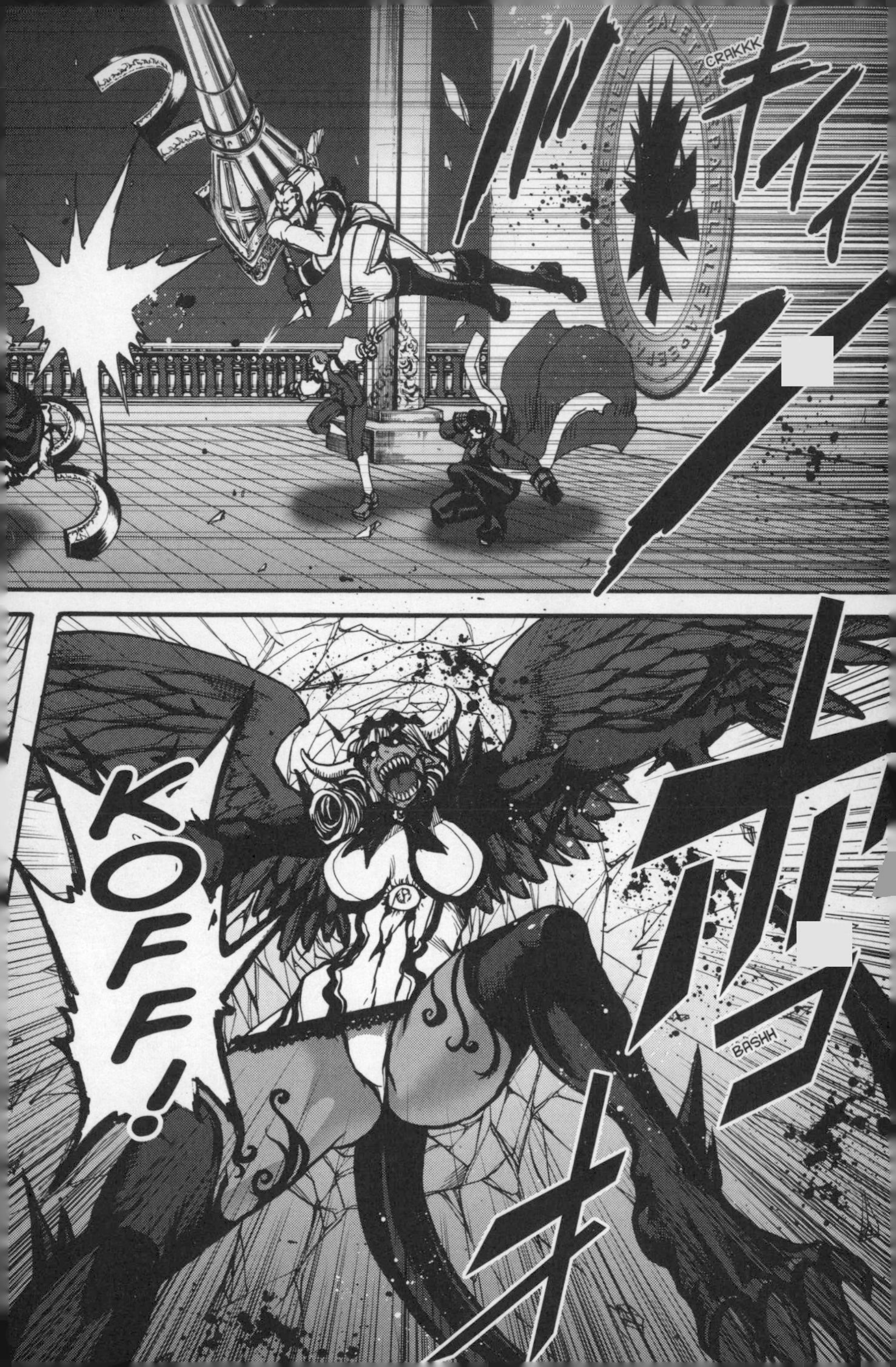
CRAKKK
BASHH
KOFF!

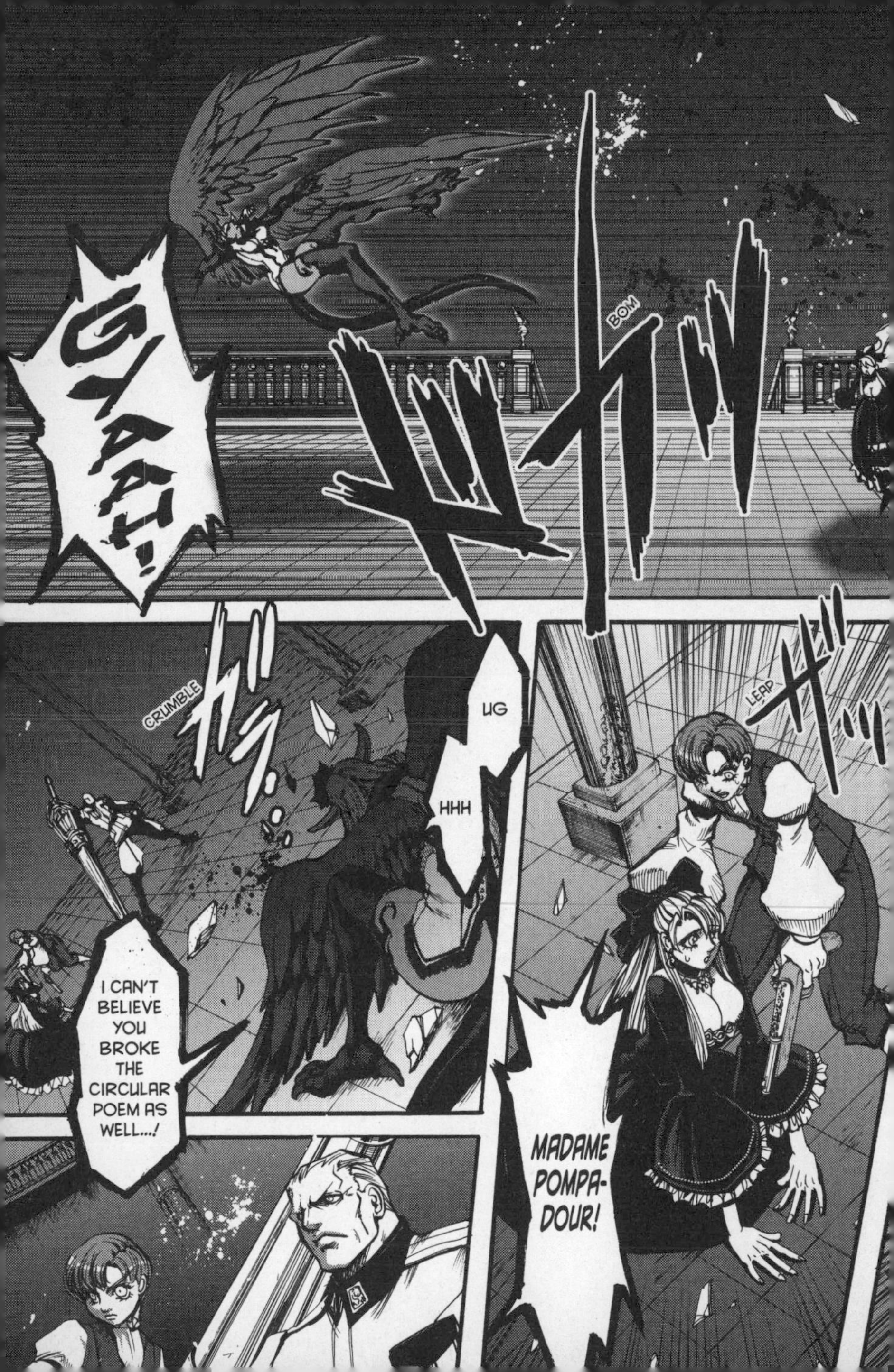
BOM
GYAAH!
LEAP
MADAME POMPADOUR!
CRUMBLE
UG
HHH
I CAN'T BELIEVE YOU BROKE THE CIRCULAR POEM AS WELL...!

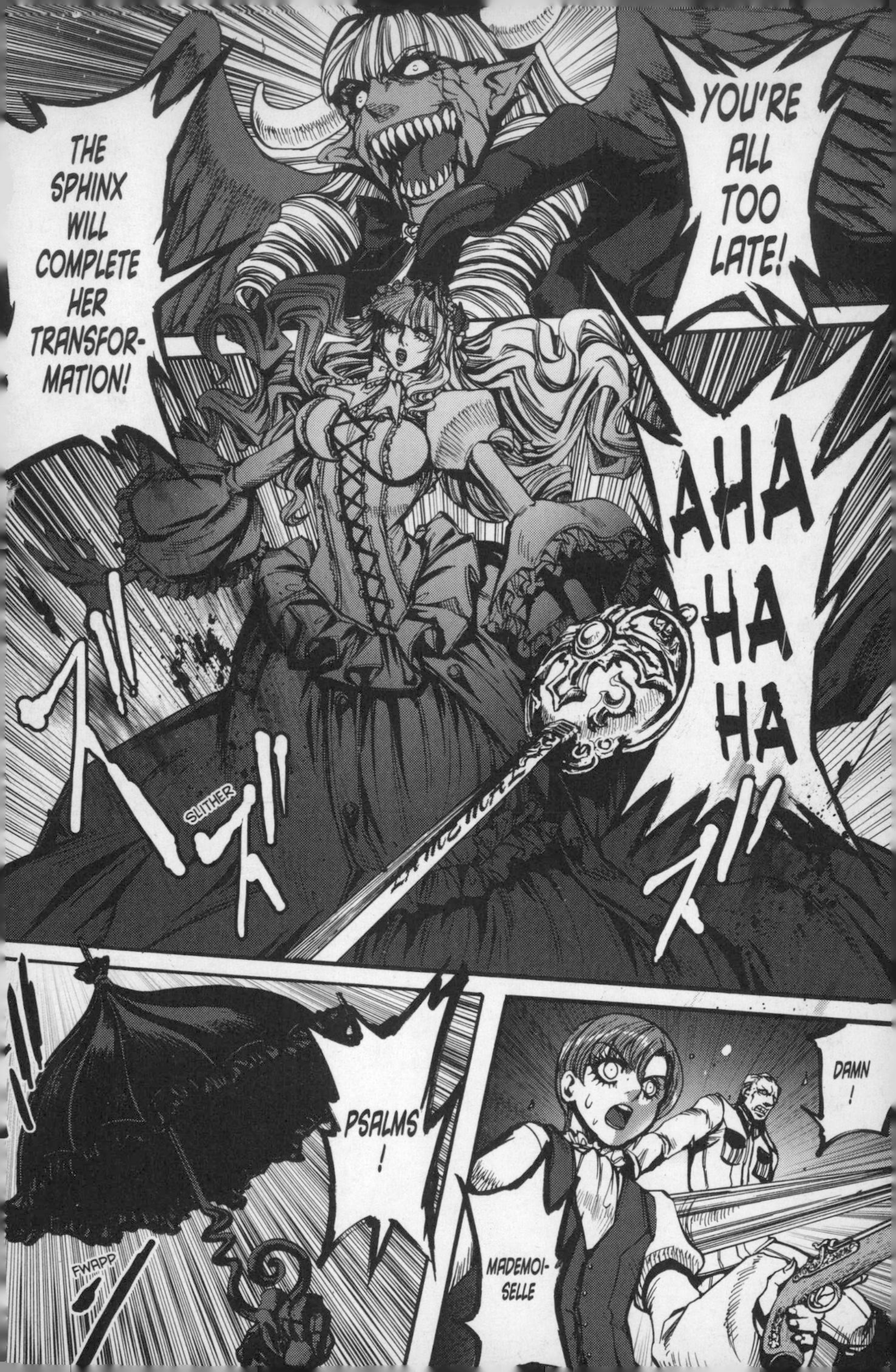

YOU'RE ALL TOO LATE!
THE SPHINX WILL COMPLETE HER TRANSFOR-MATION!
AHA HA HA HA
SLITHER
DAMN!
MADEMOI-SELLE
PSALMS!
FWAPP

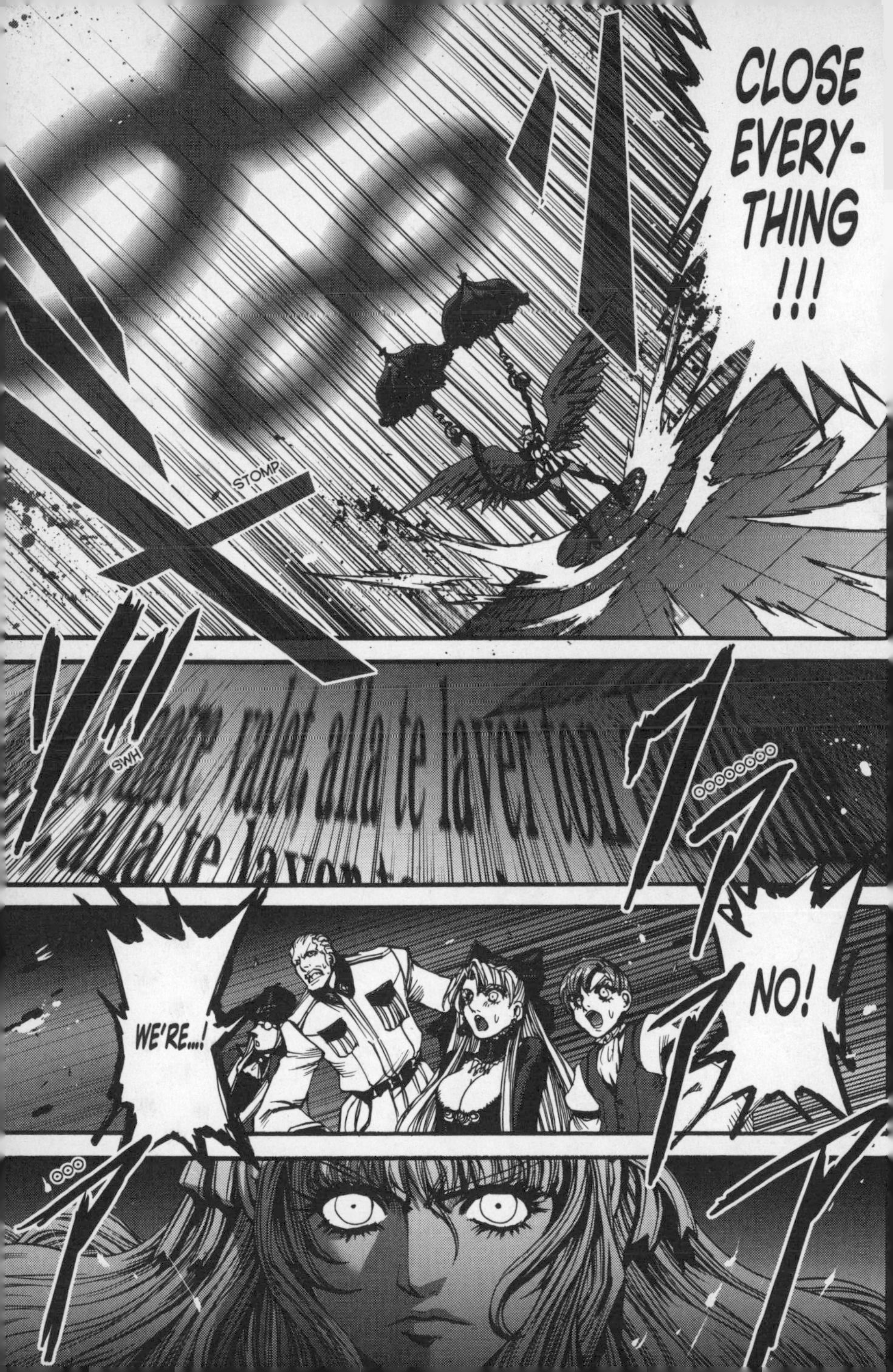
CLOSE EVERY-THING!!!
STOMP
SWH
NO!
WE'RE...!

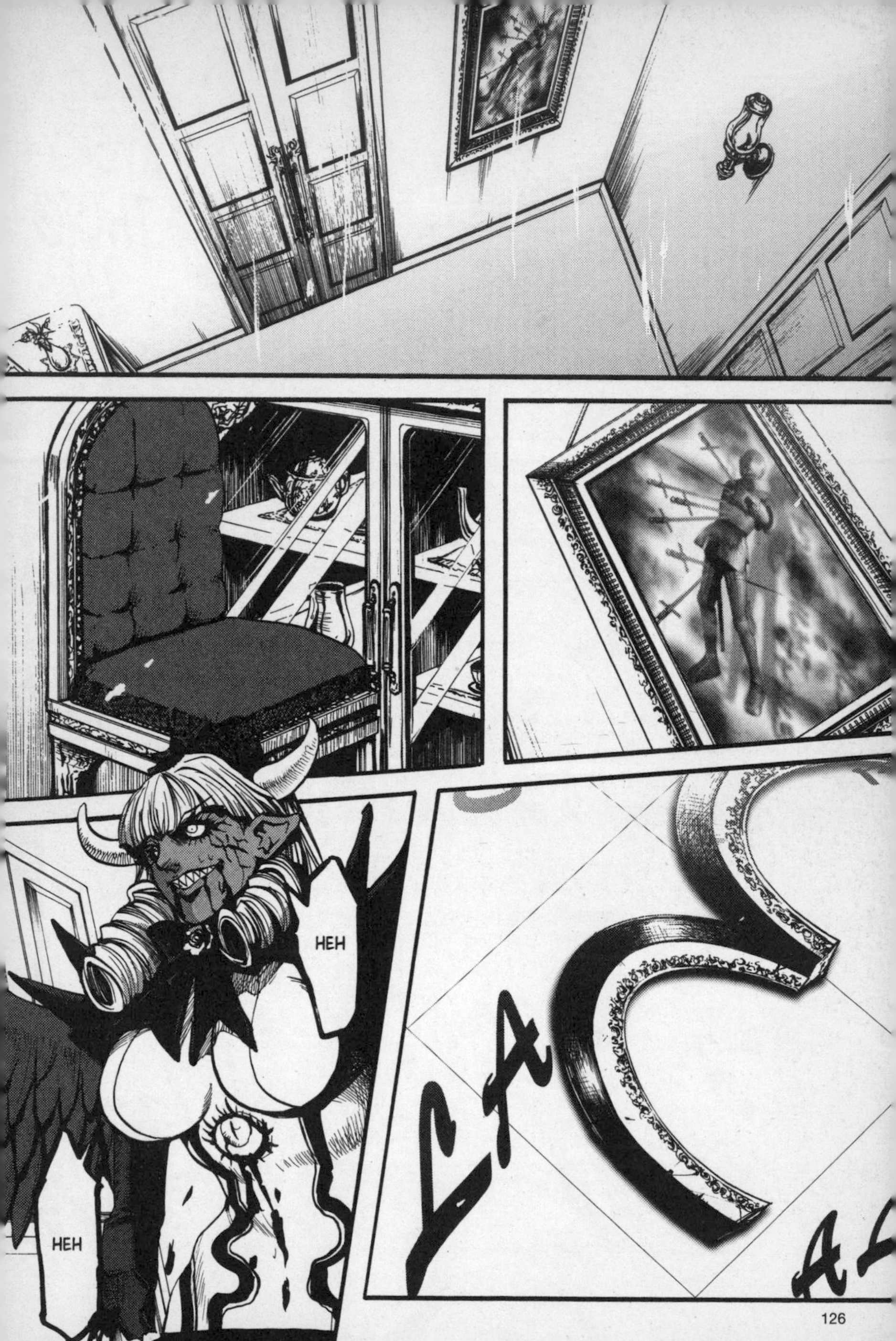
LAC
AL
HEH
HEH

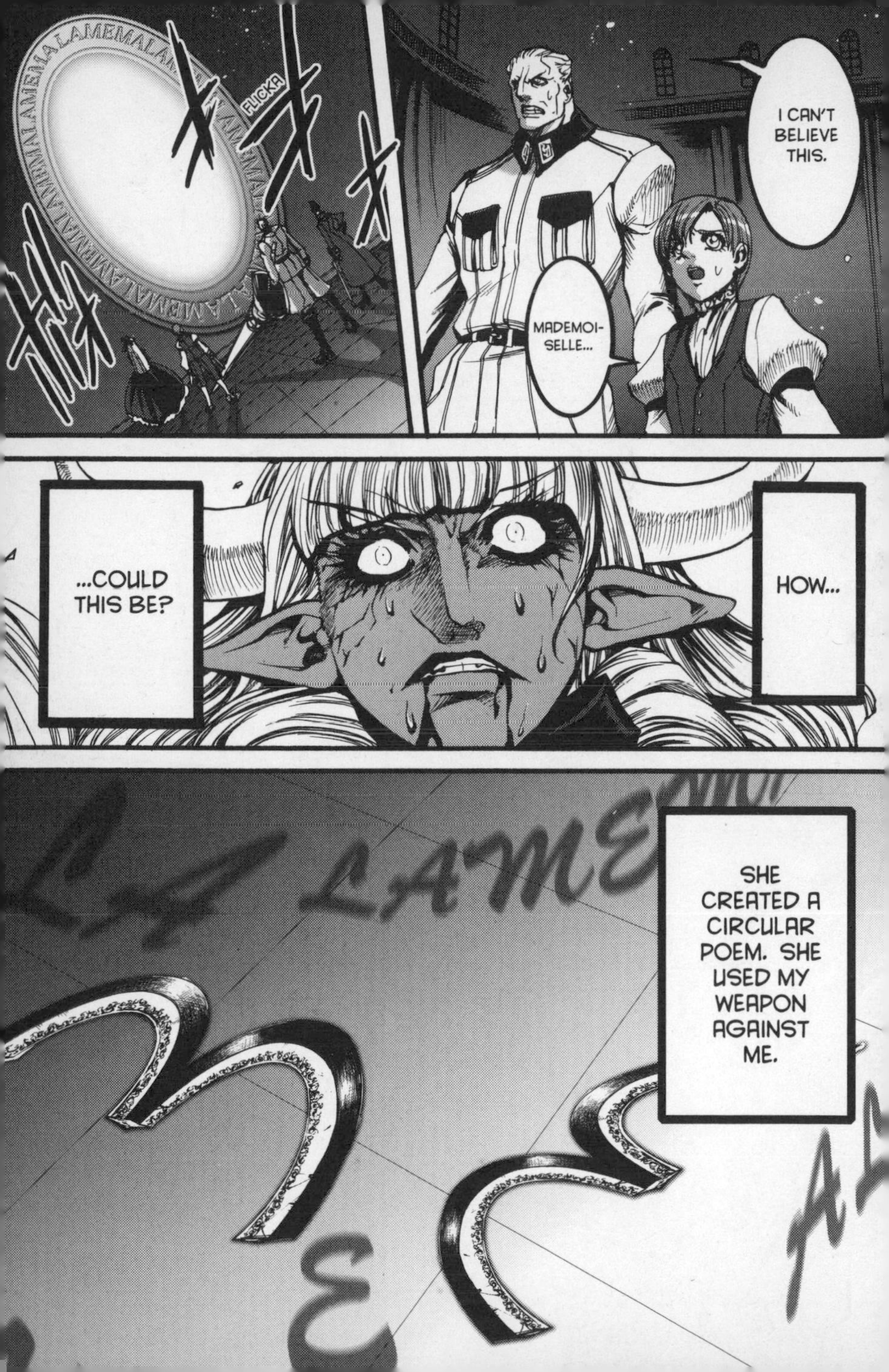
I CAN'T BELIEVE THIS.
MADEMOI-SELLE...
FLICKA
HOW...
...COULD THIS BE?
SHE CREATED A CIRCULAR POEM. SHE USED MY WEAPON AGAINST ME.

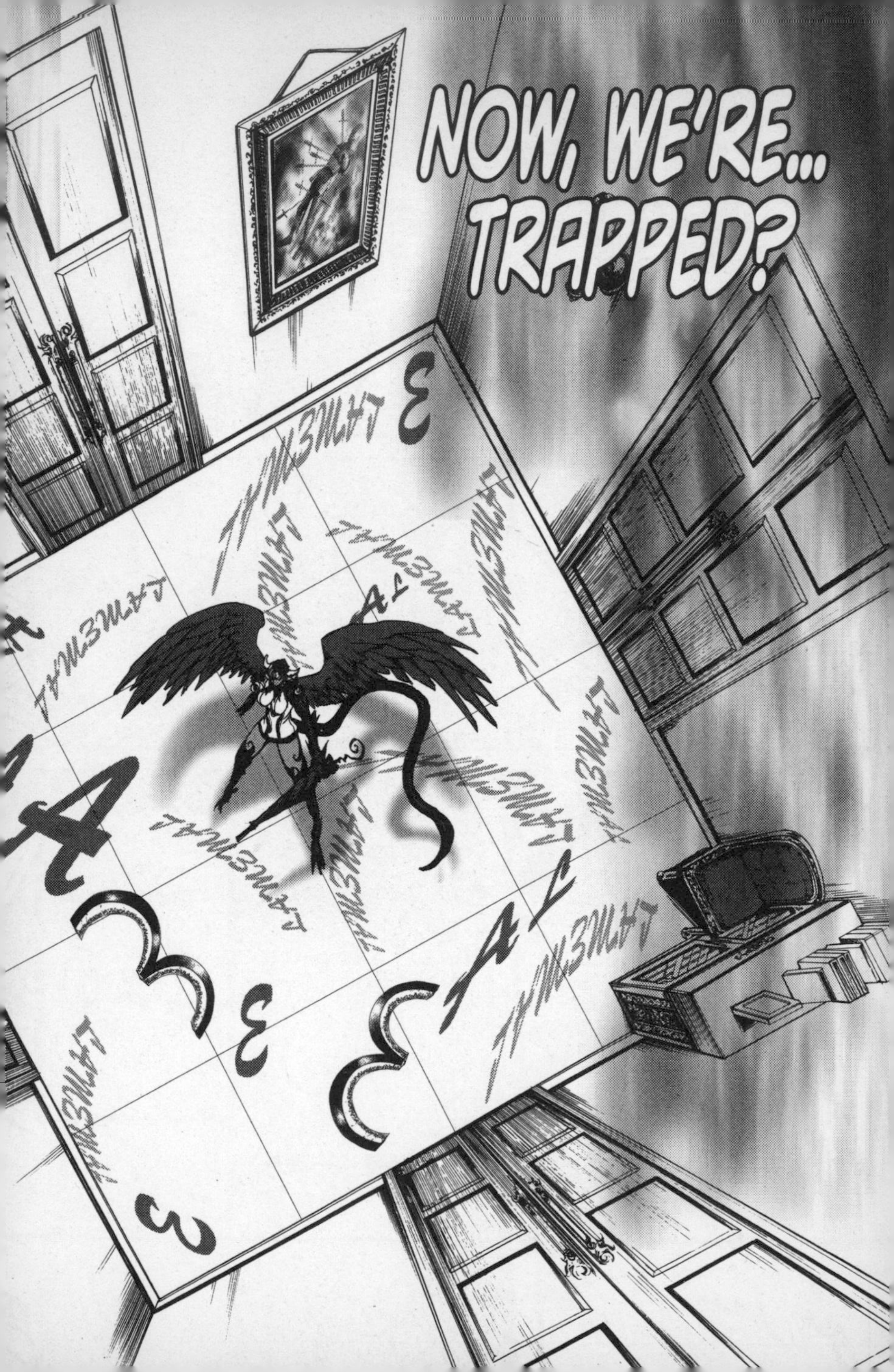
NOW, WE'RE... TRAPPED?

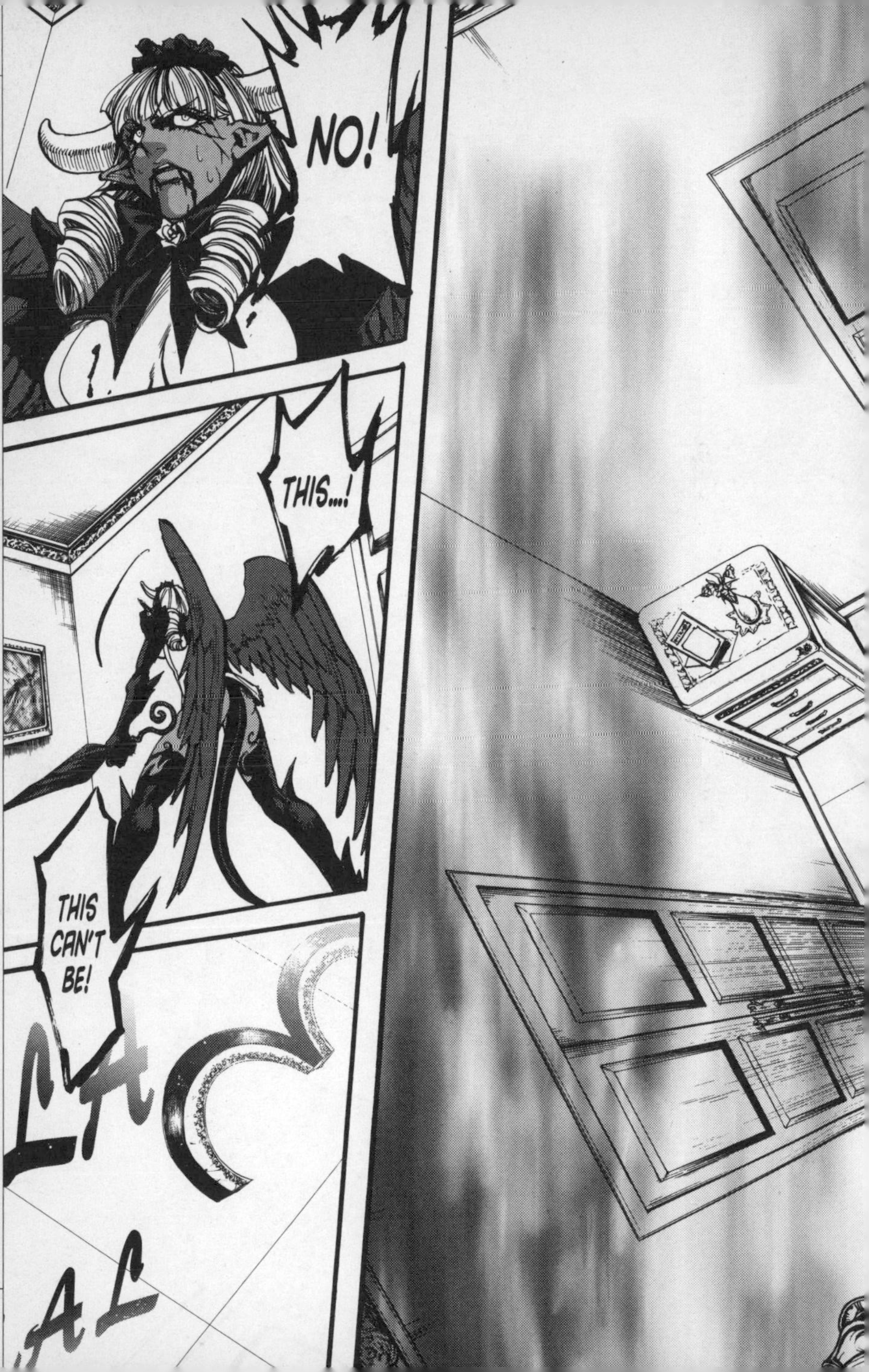
NO!
THIS...!
THIS CAN'T BE!

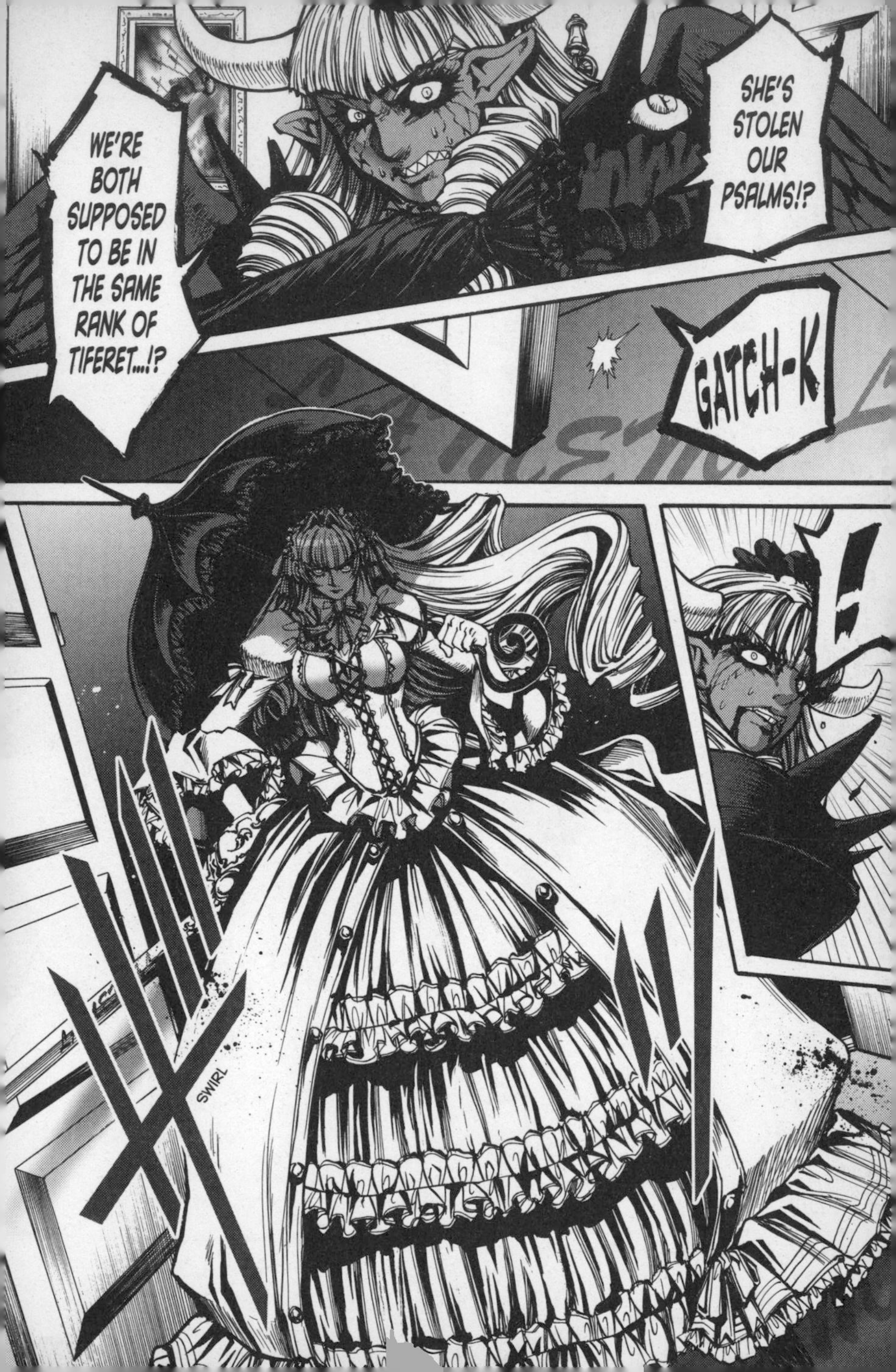
SHE'S STOLEN OUR PSALMS!?
WE'RE BOTH SUPPOSED TO BE IN THE SAME RANK OF TIFERET...!?
GATCH-K
!!
SWIRL

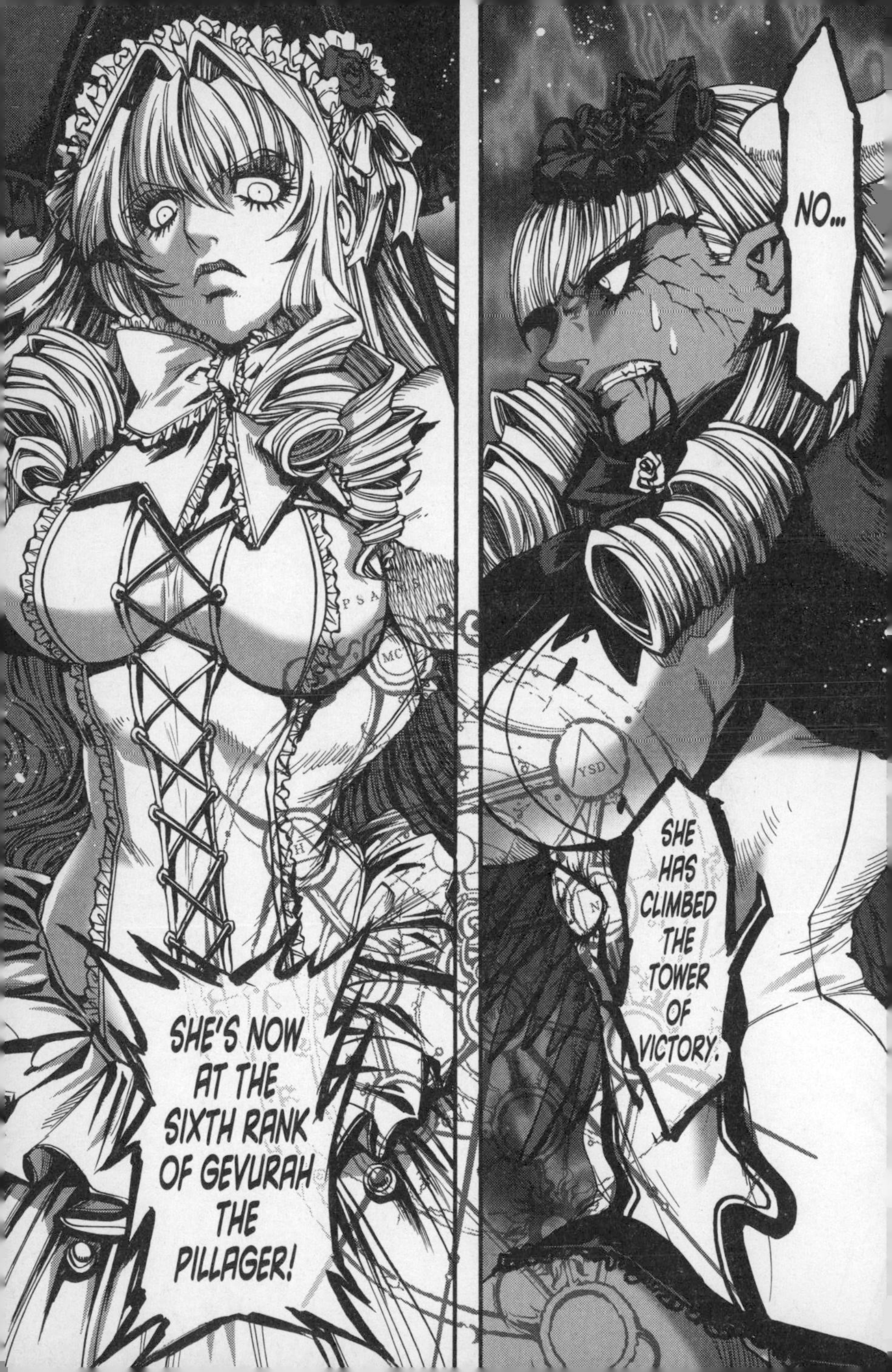
NO...
SHE HAS CLIMBED THE TOWER OF VICTORY.
SHE'S NOW AT THE SIXTH RANK OF GEVURAH THE PILLAGER!

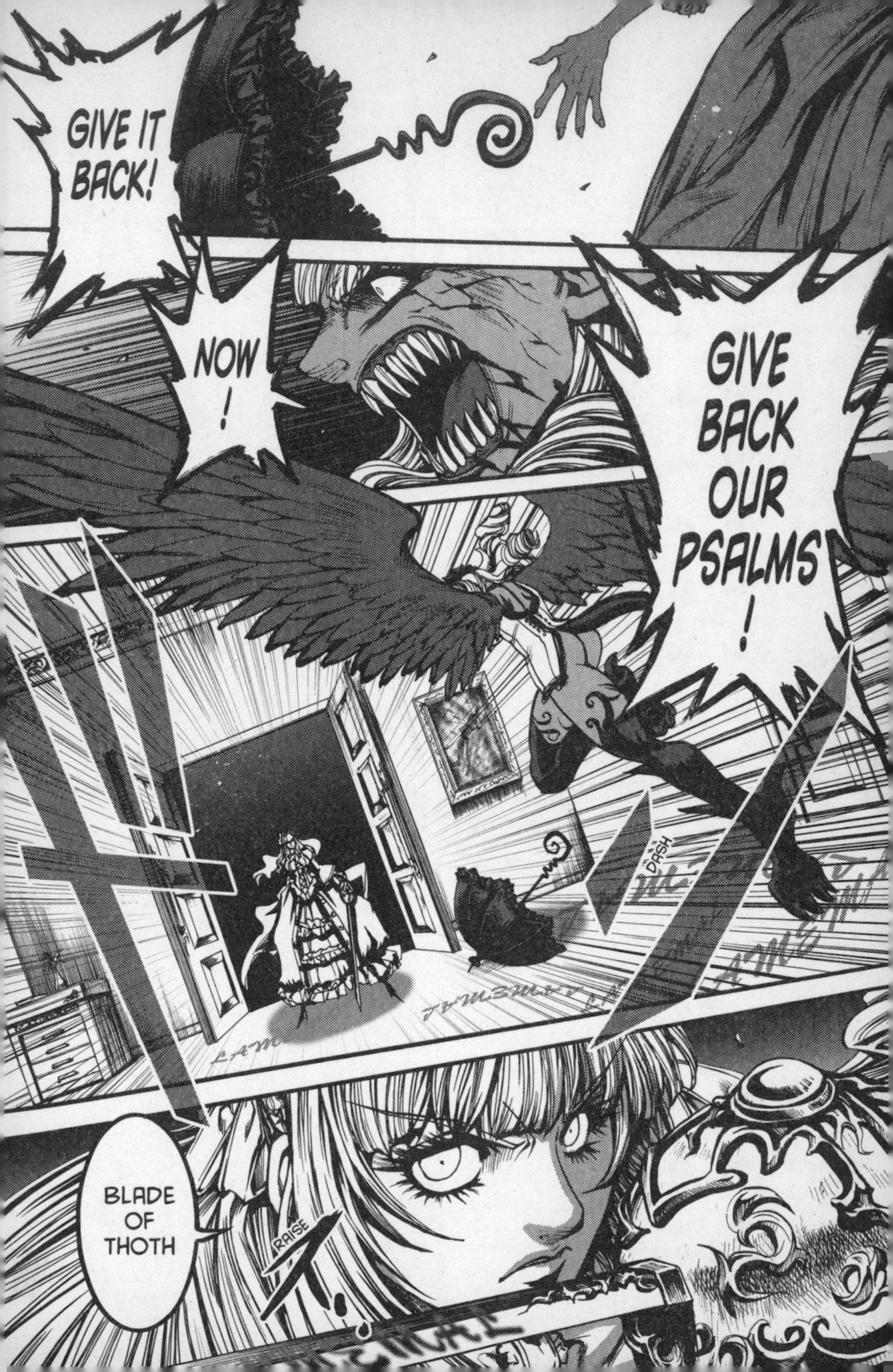
GIVE IT BACK!
NOW!
GIVE BACK OUR PSALMS!
DASH
BLADE OF THOTH
RAISE

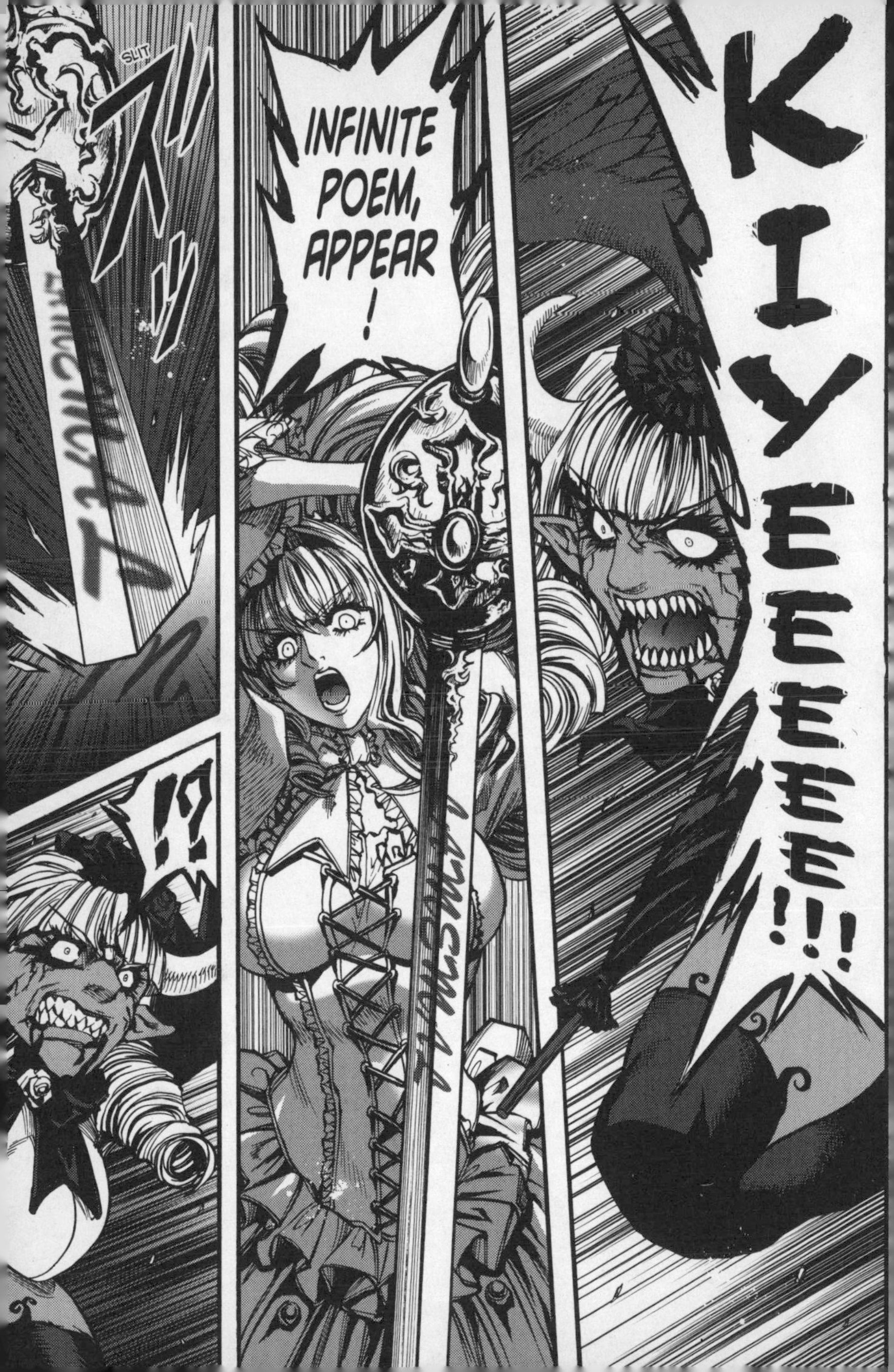
KIYEEEEEE!!!
INFINITE POEM, APPEAR!
SLIT
!?

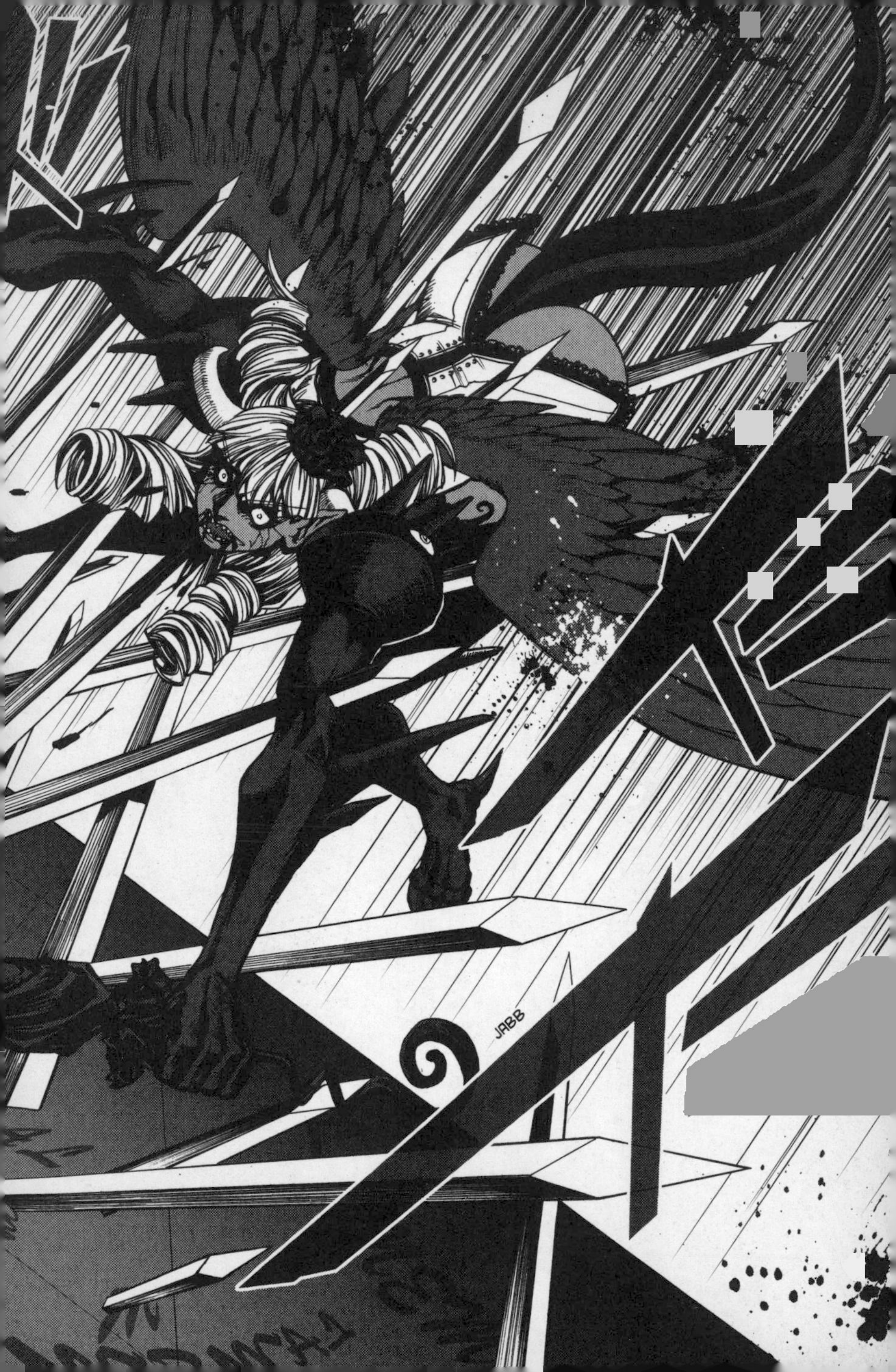
JABB

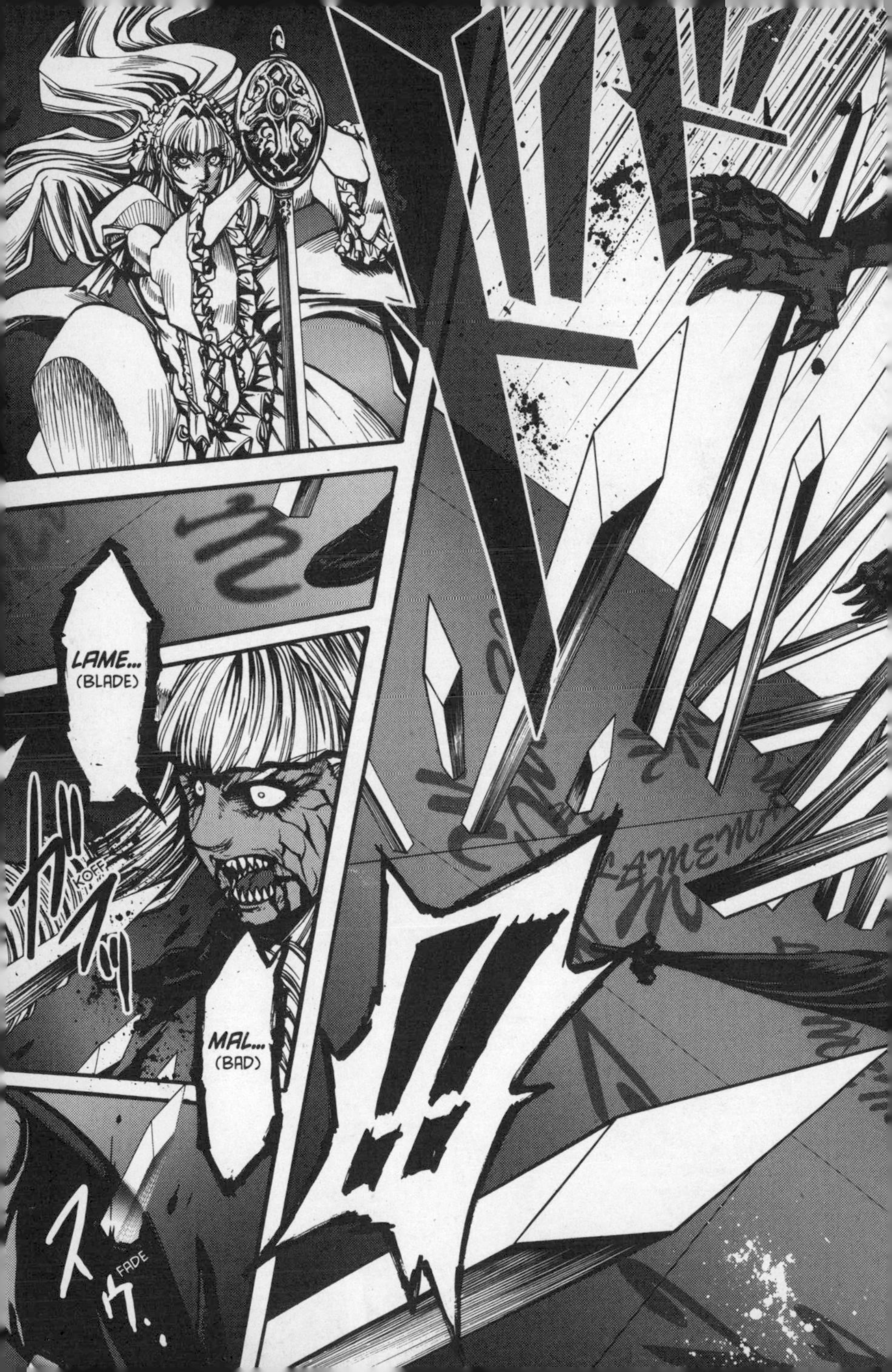
LAME...
(BLADE)
KOFF
MAL...
(BAD)
FADE

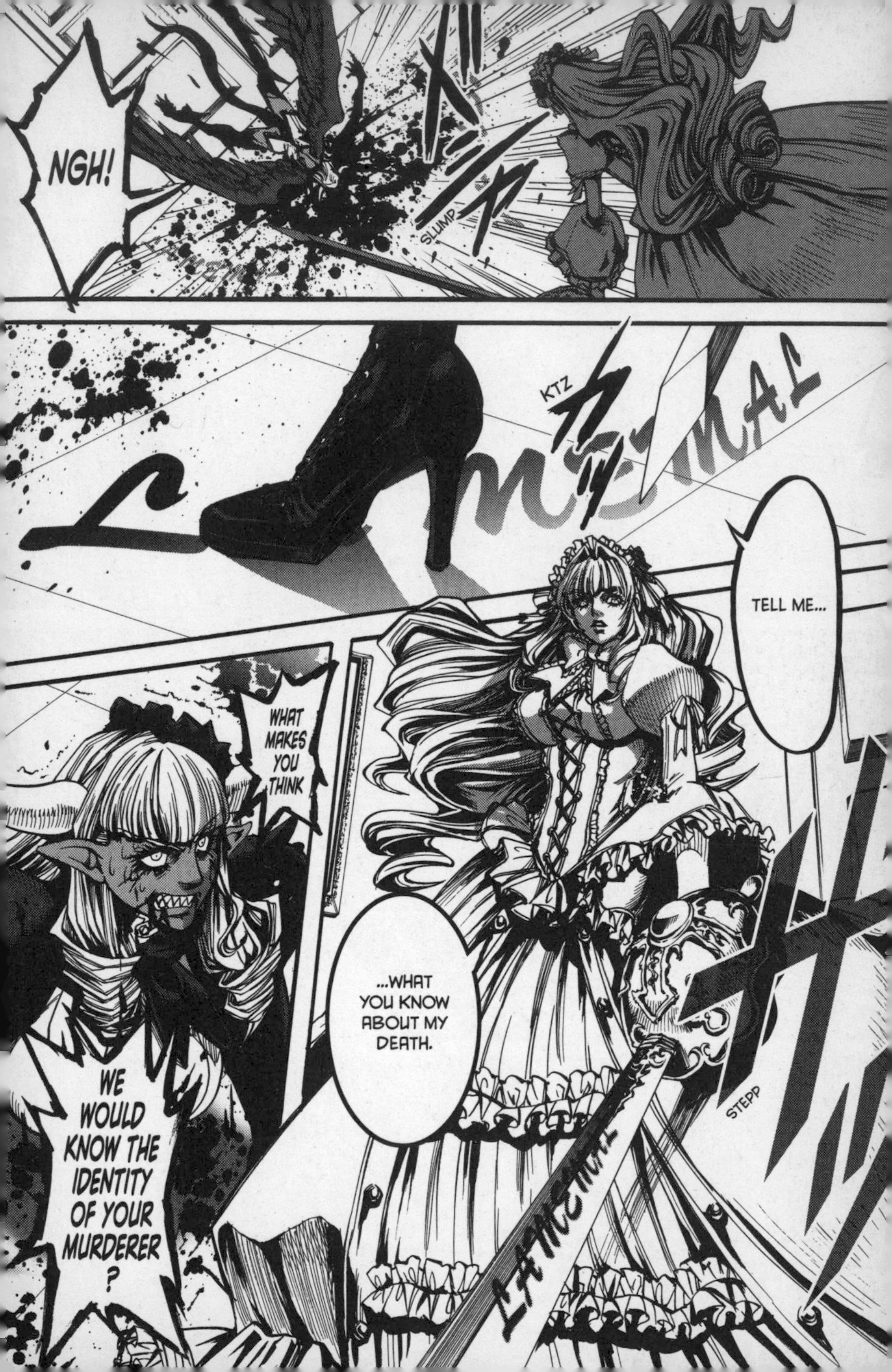
SLUMP
NGH!
KTZ
TELL ME...
STEPP
...WHAT YOU KNOW ABOUT MY DEATH.
WHAT MAKES YOU THINK
WE WOULD KNOW THE IDENTITY OF YOUR MURDERER?

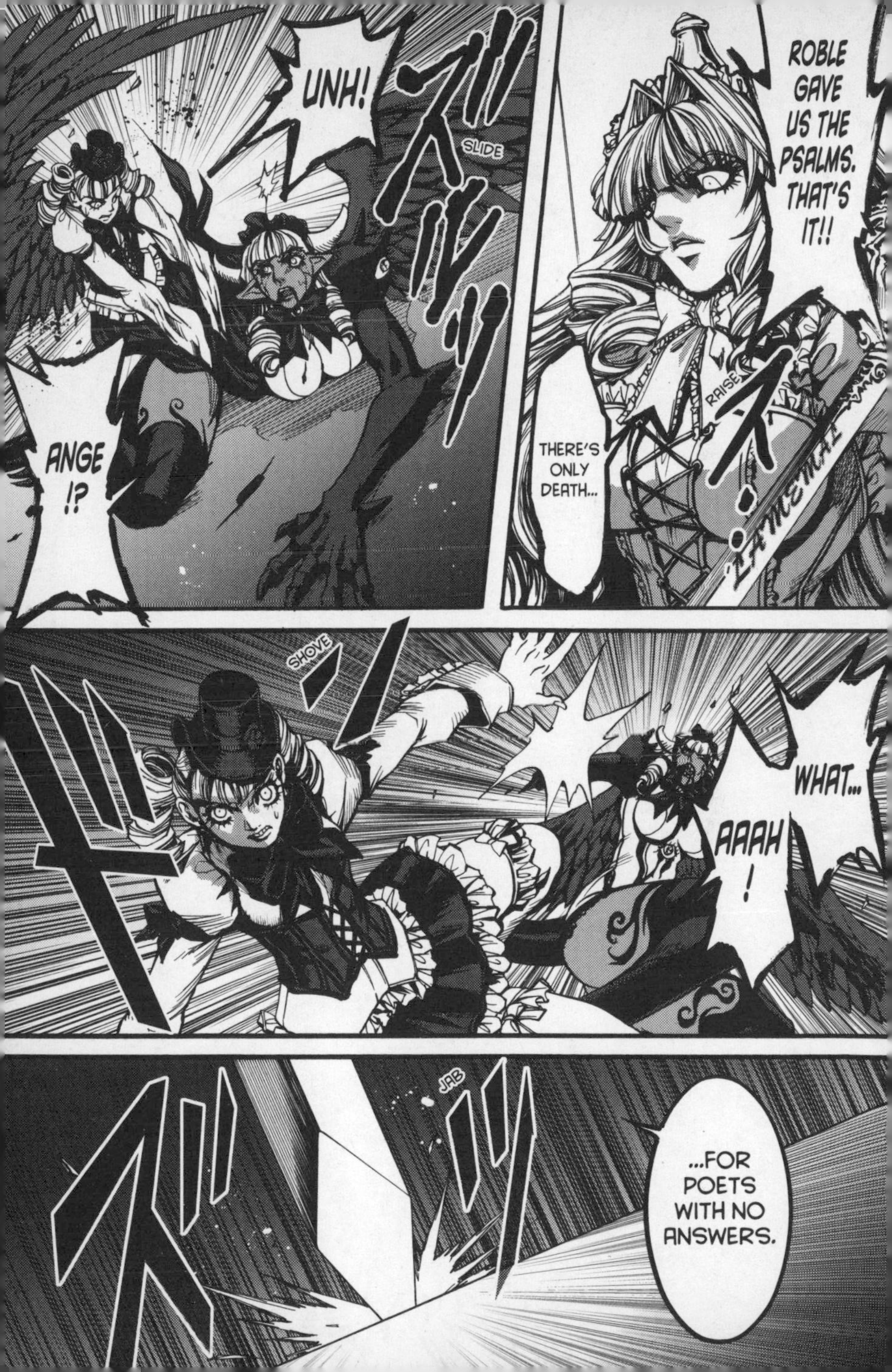
ROBLE GAVE US THE PSALMS. THAT'S IT!!
RAISE
THERE'S ONLY DEATH...
UNH!
SLIDE
ANGE !?
WHAT...
AAAH!
SHOVE
...FOR POETS WITH NO ANSWERS.
JAB

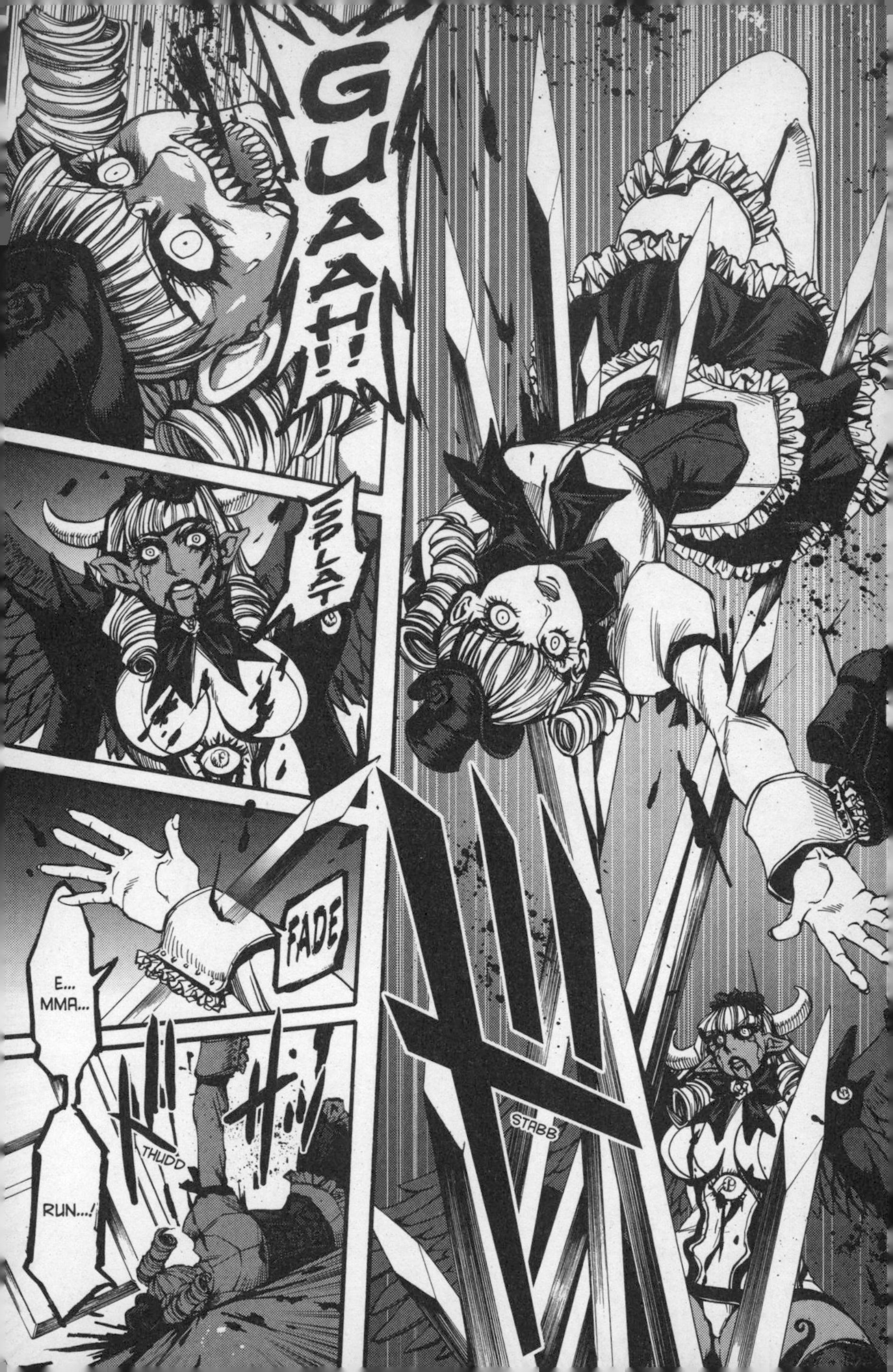
STABB
GUAH!!
SPLAT
FADE
E... MMA...
THUDD
RUN...!

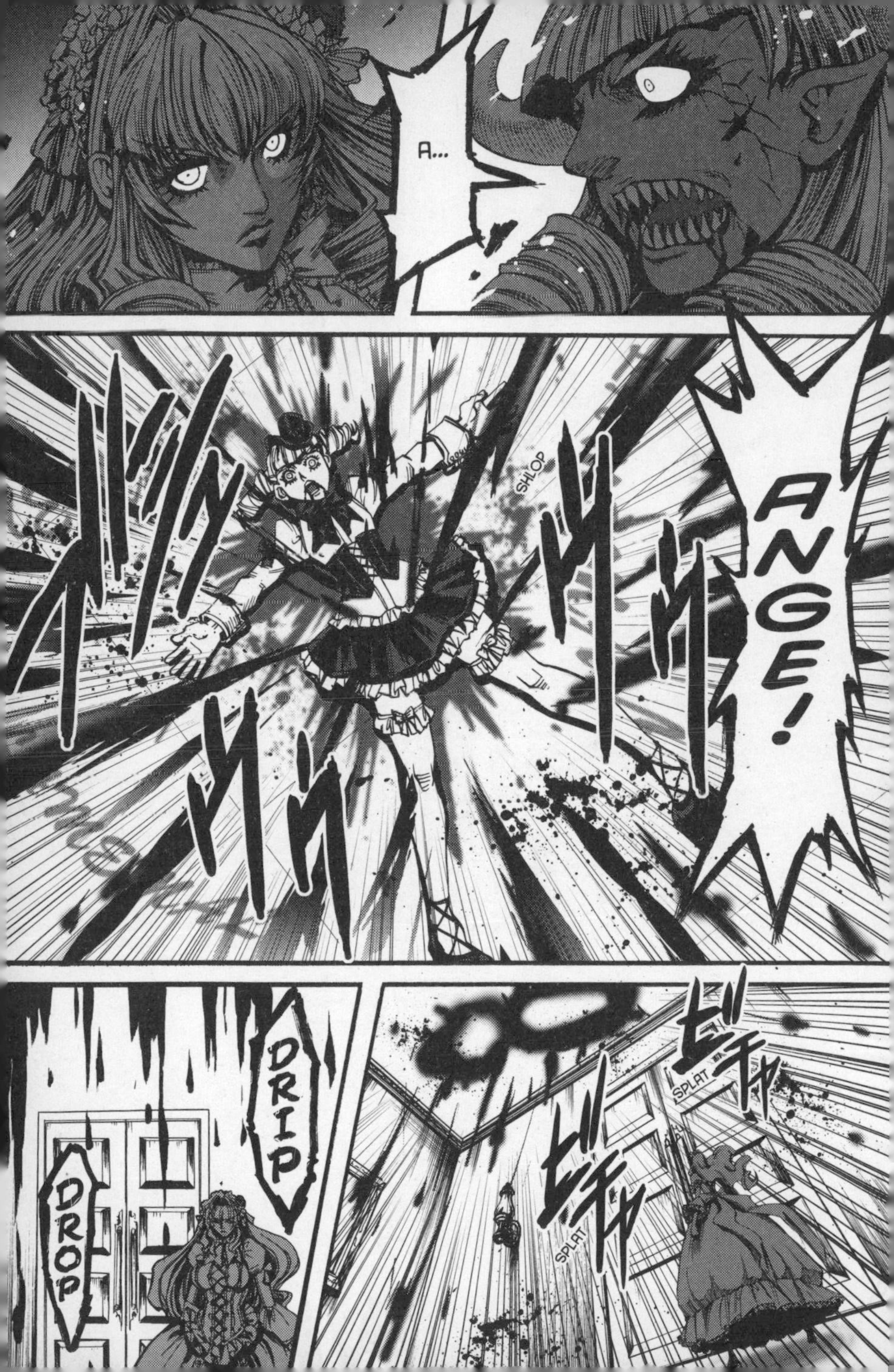
A...
ANGE!
SHLOP
SPLAT
SPLAT
DRIP
DROP

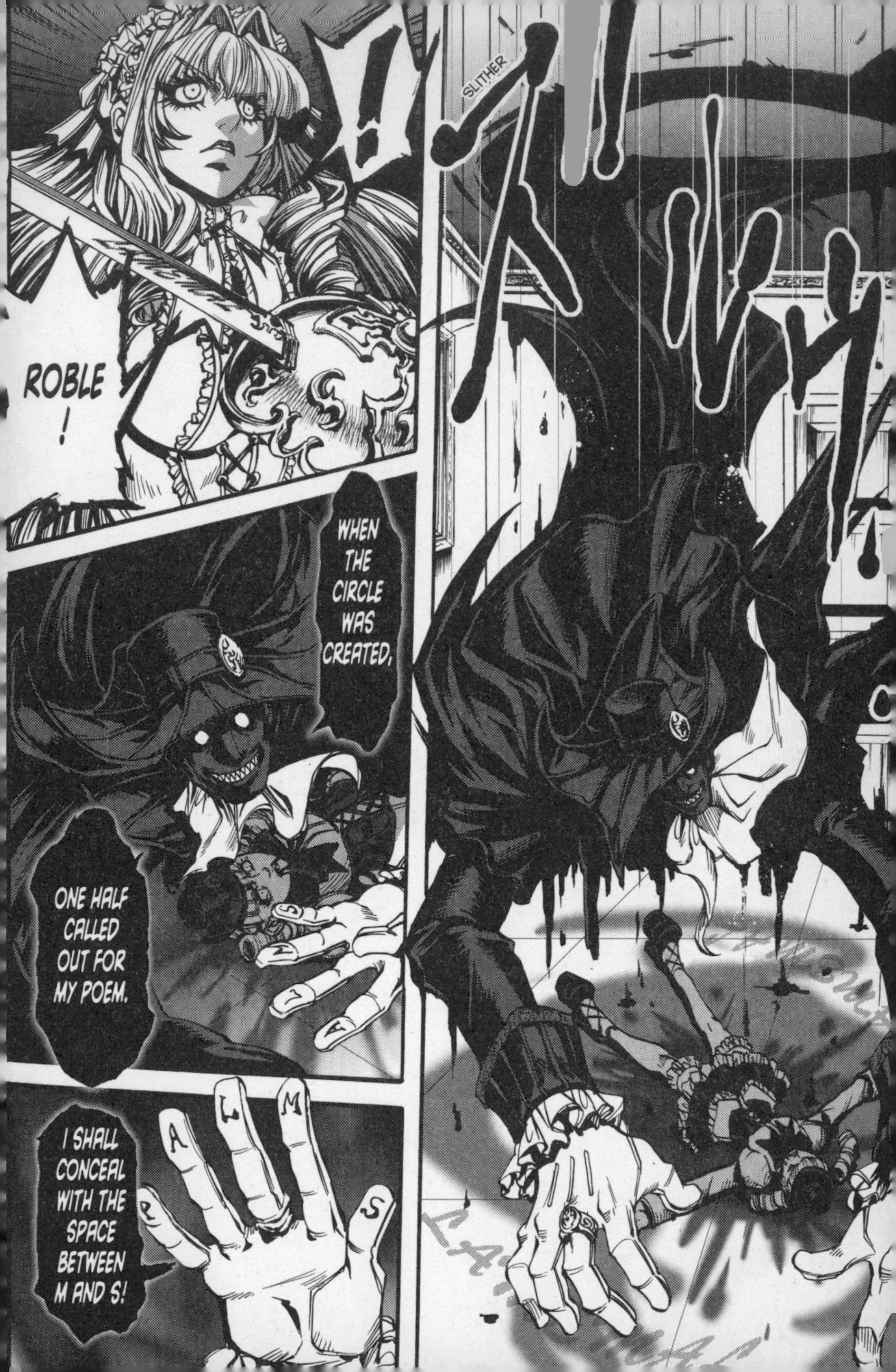
SLITHER
ROBLE !
WHEN THE CIRCLE WAS CREATED,
ONE HALF CALLED OUT FOR MY POEM.
I SHALL CONCEAL WITH THE SPACE BETWEEN M AND S!

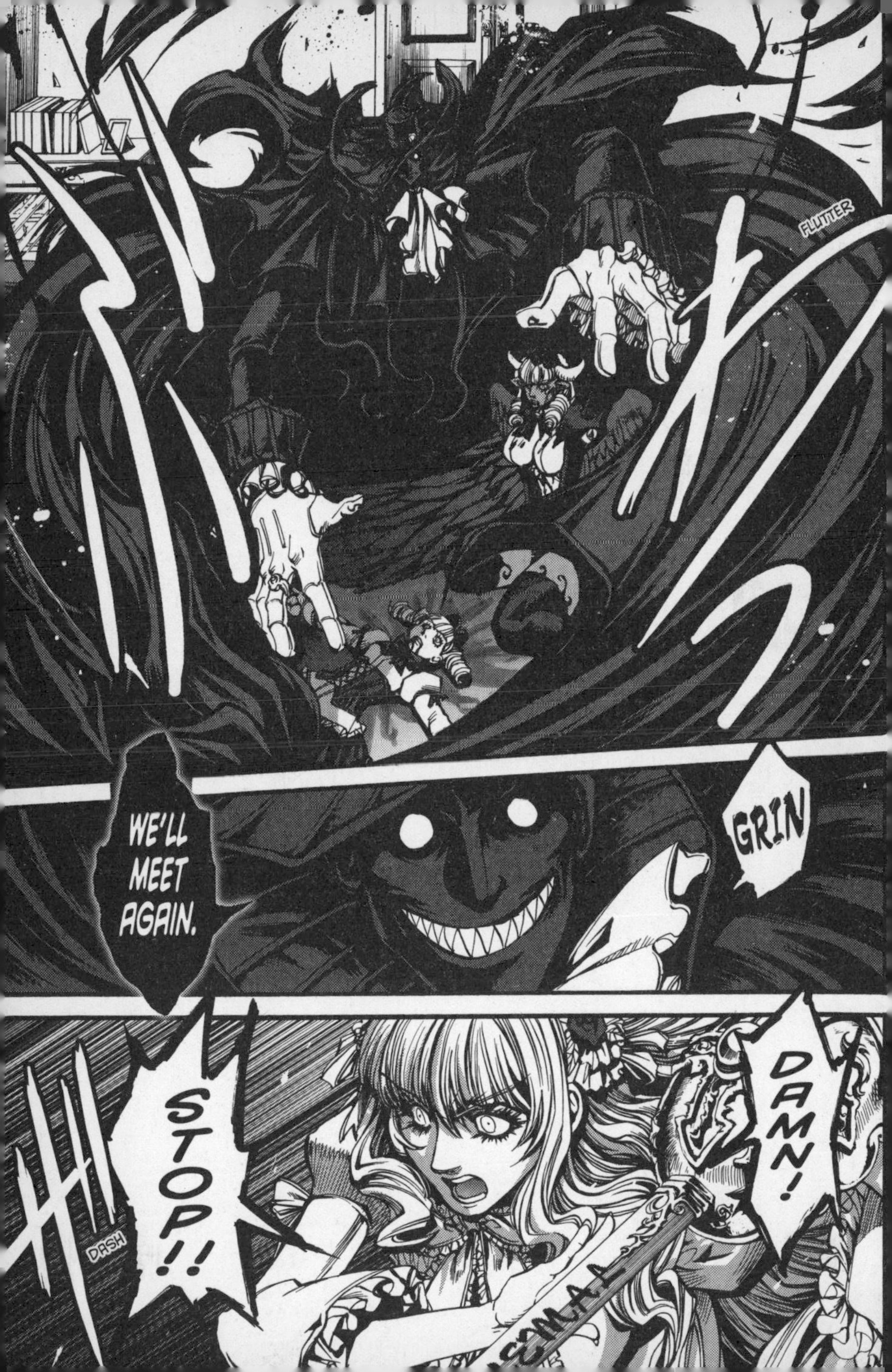
FLUTTER
GRIN
WE'LL MEET AGAIN.
DAMN!
STOP!!
DASH

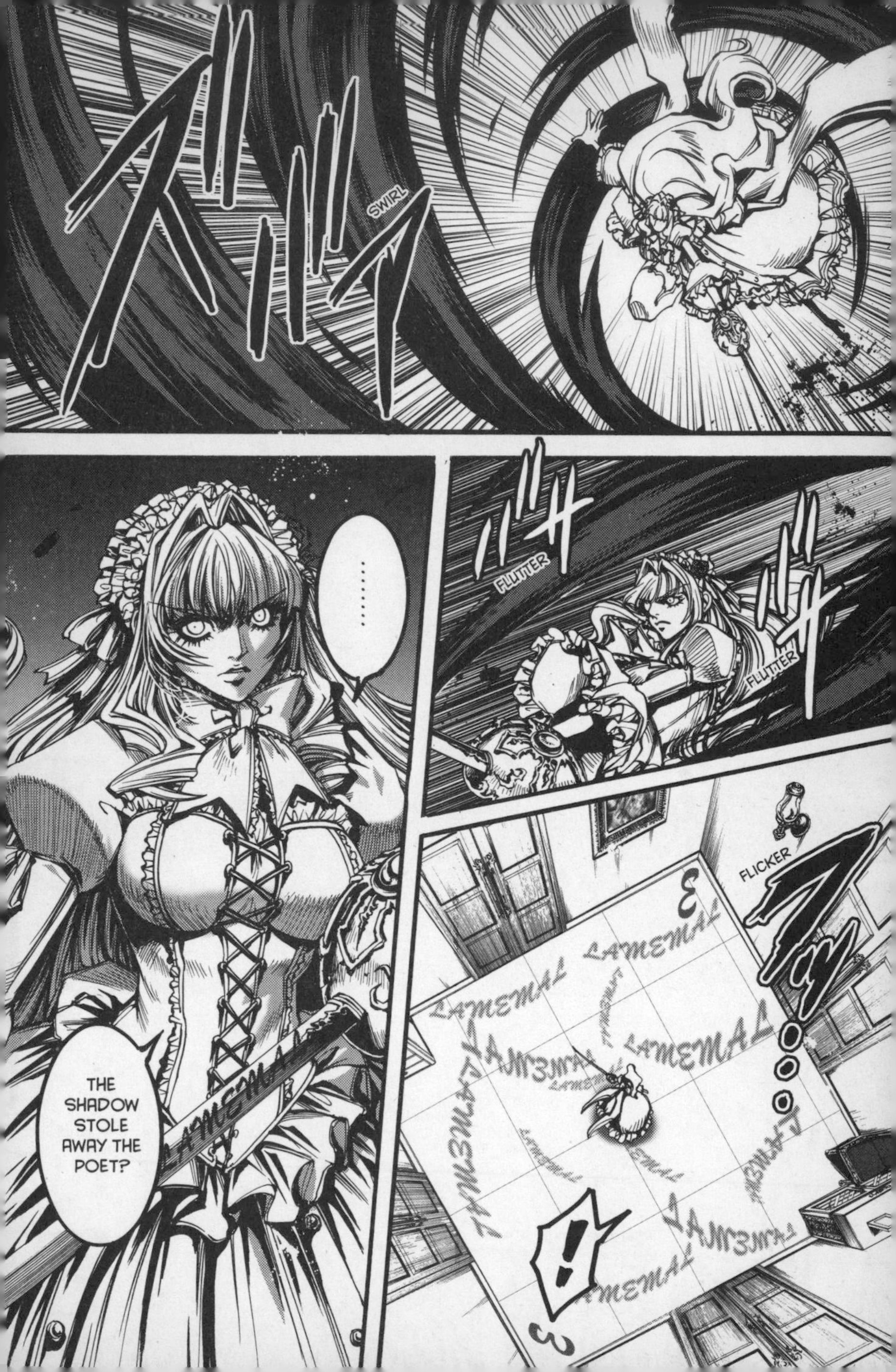
SWIRL
FLUTTER
FLUTTER
FLICKER
LAMEMAL
!
......
THE SHADOW STOLE AWAY THE POET?

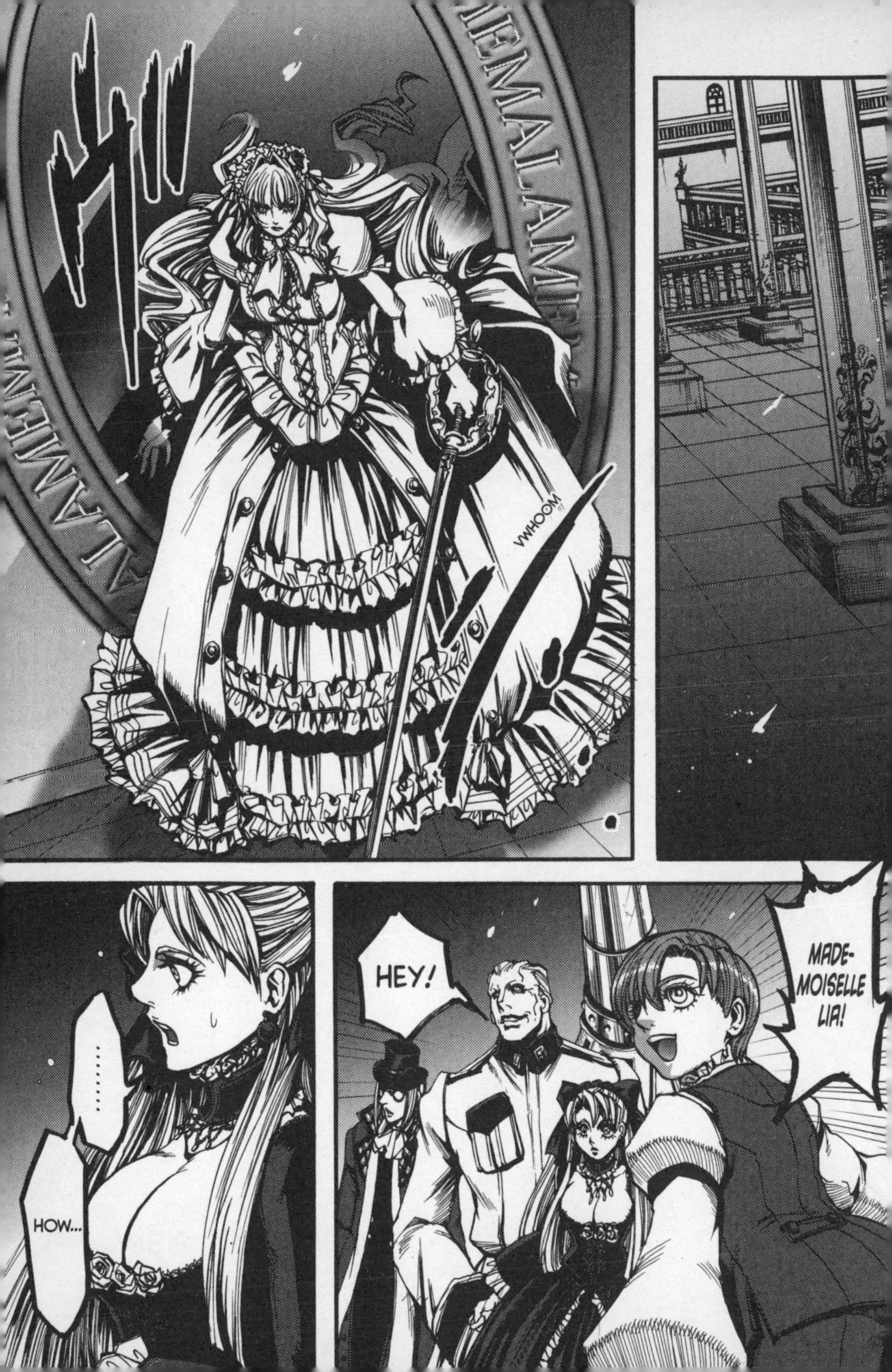
VWHOOM
MADE-MOISELLE LIA!
HEY!
....
HOW...

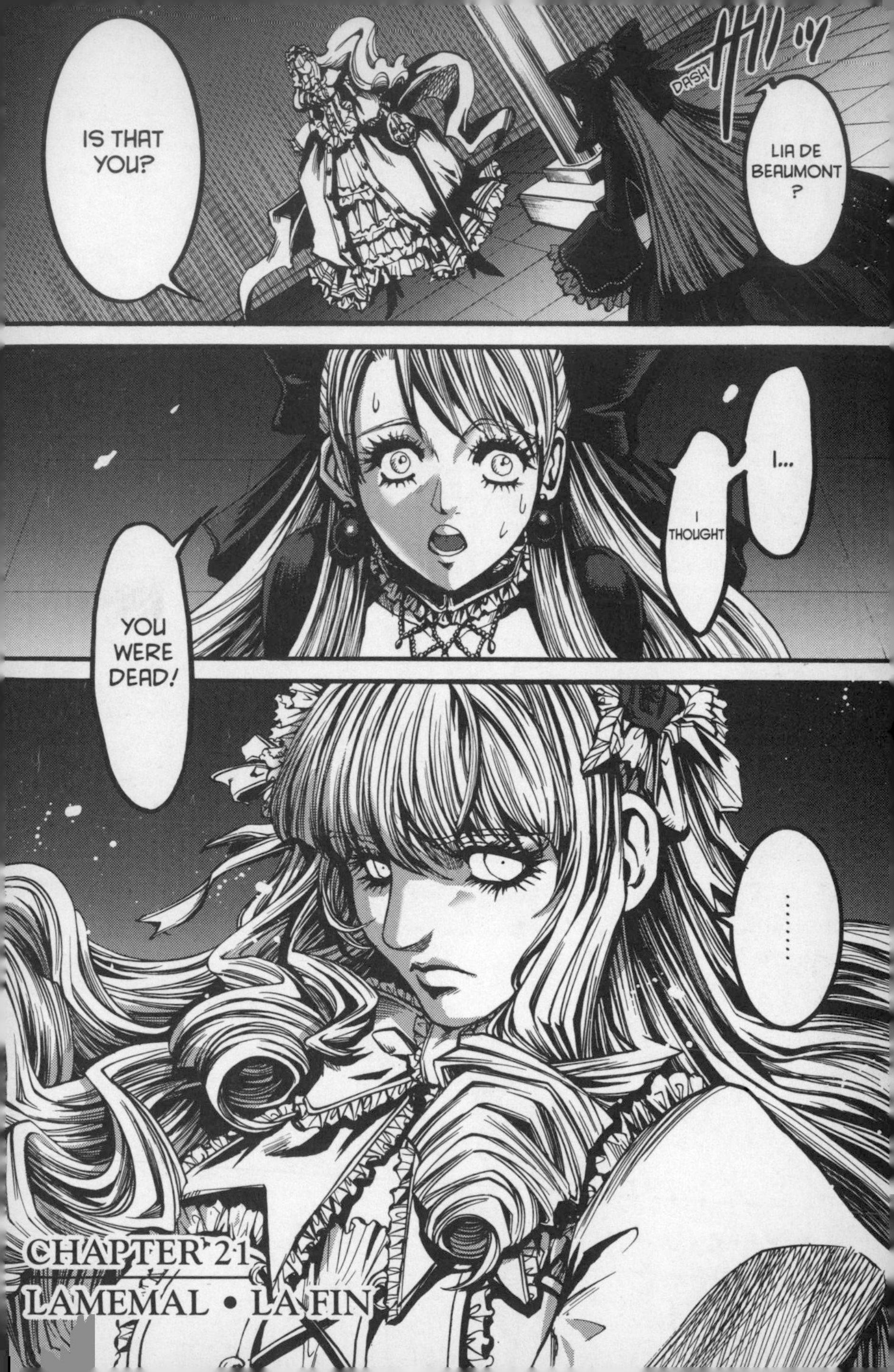
DASH
LIA DE BEAUMONT ?
IS THAT YOU?
I... I THOUGHT
YOU WERE DEAD!
......
CHAPTER 21
LAMEMAL • LA FIN

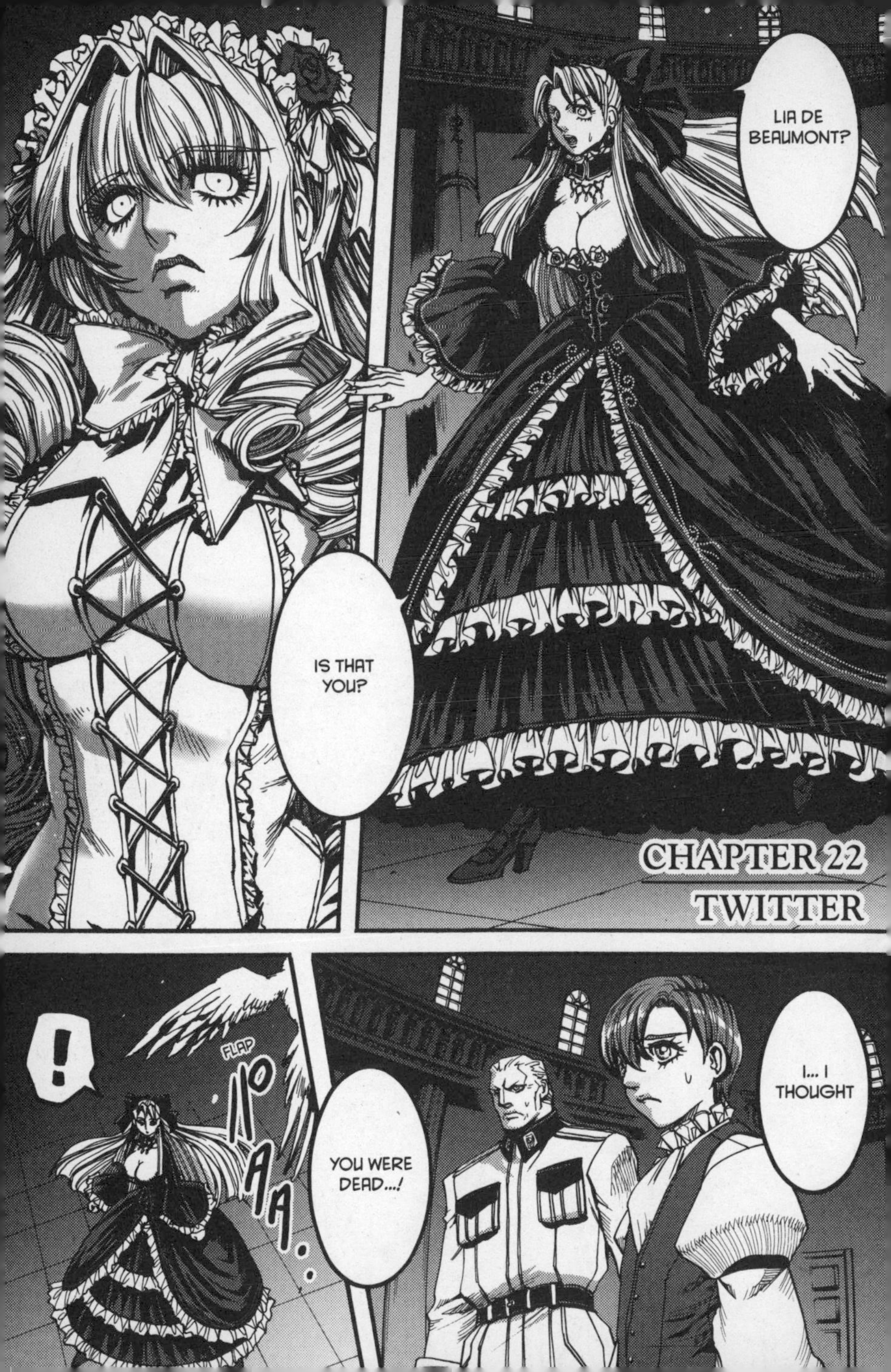
LIA DE BEAUMONT?
IS THAT YOU?
CHAPTER 22
TWITTER
I... I THOUGHT
YOU WERE DEAD...!
!
FLAP

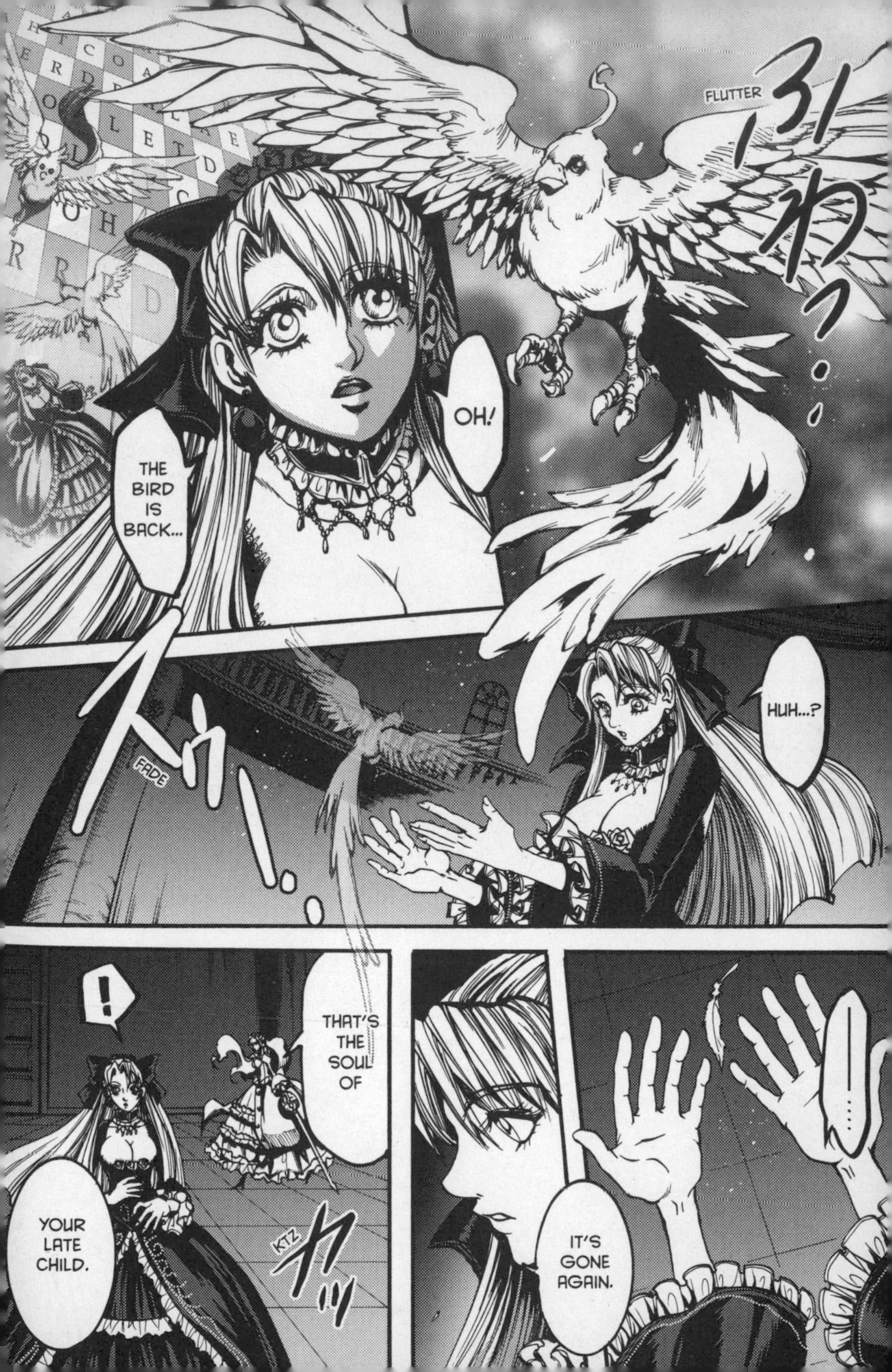
FLUTTER
OH!
THE BIRD IS BACK...
HUH...?
FADE
IT'S GONE AGAIN.
!
THAT'S THE SOUL OF
YOUR LATE CHILD.
KTZ

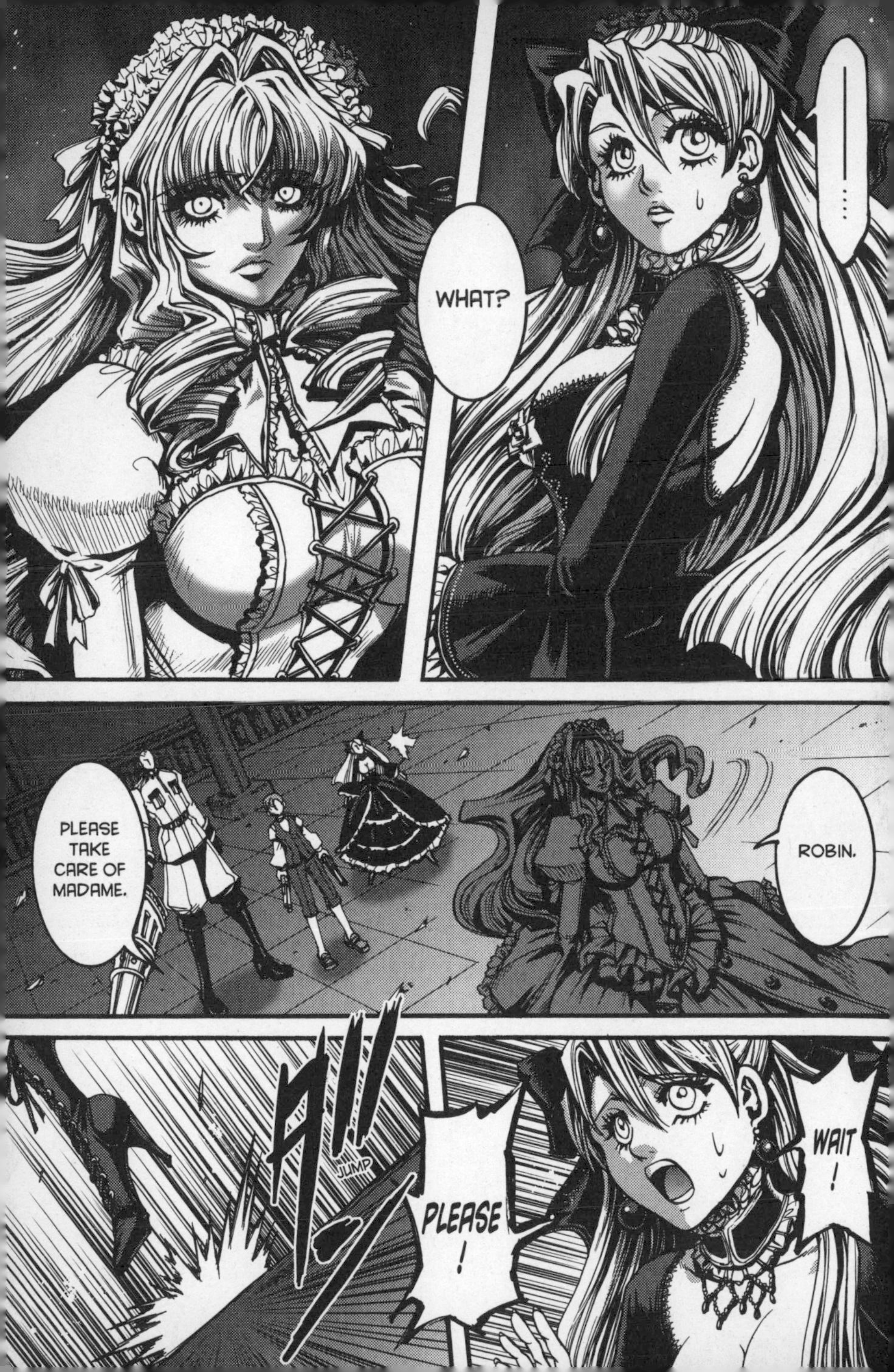

!....
WHAT?
ROBIN.
PLEASE TAKE CARE OF MADAME.
WAIT!
PLEASE!
JUMP

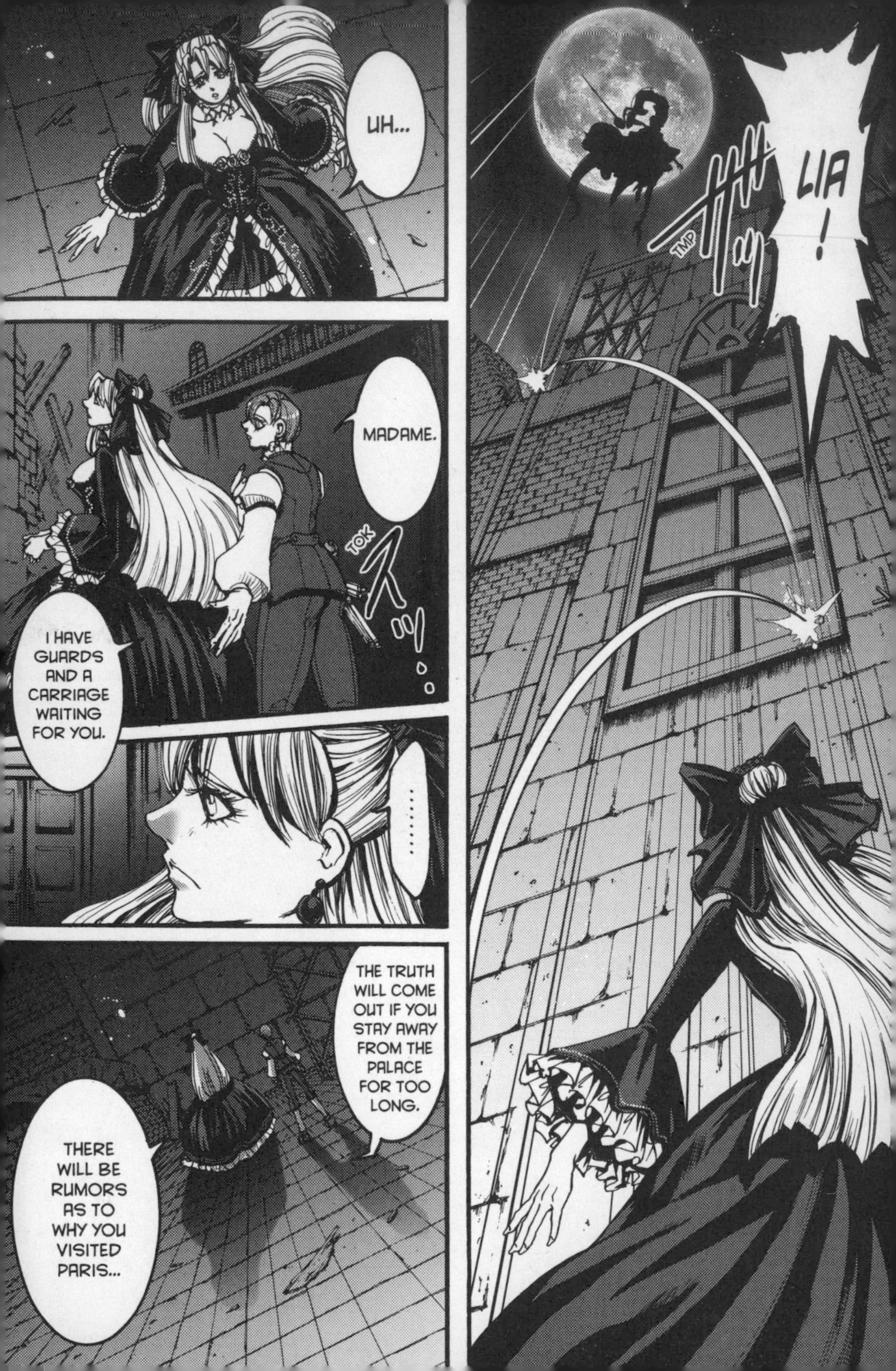
TMP
LIA!
UH...
MADAME.
TOK
I HAVE GUARDS AND A CARRIAGE WAITING FOR YOU.
......
THE TRUTH WILL COME OUT IF YOU STAY AWAY FROM THE PALACE FOR TOO LONG.
THERE WILL BE RUMORS AS TO WHY YOU VISITED PARIS...

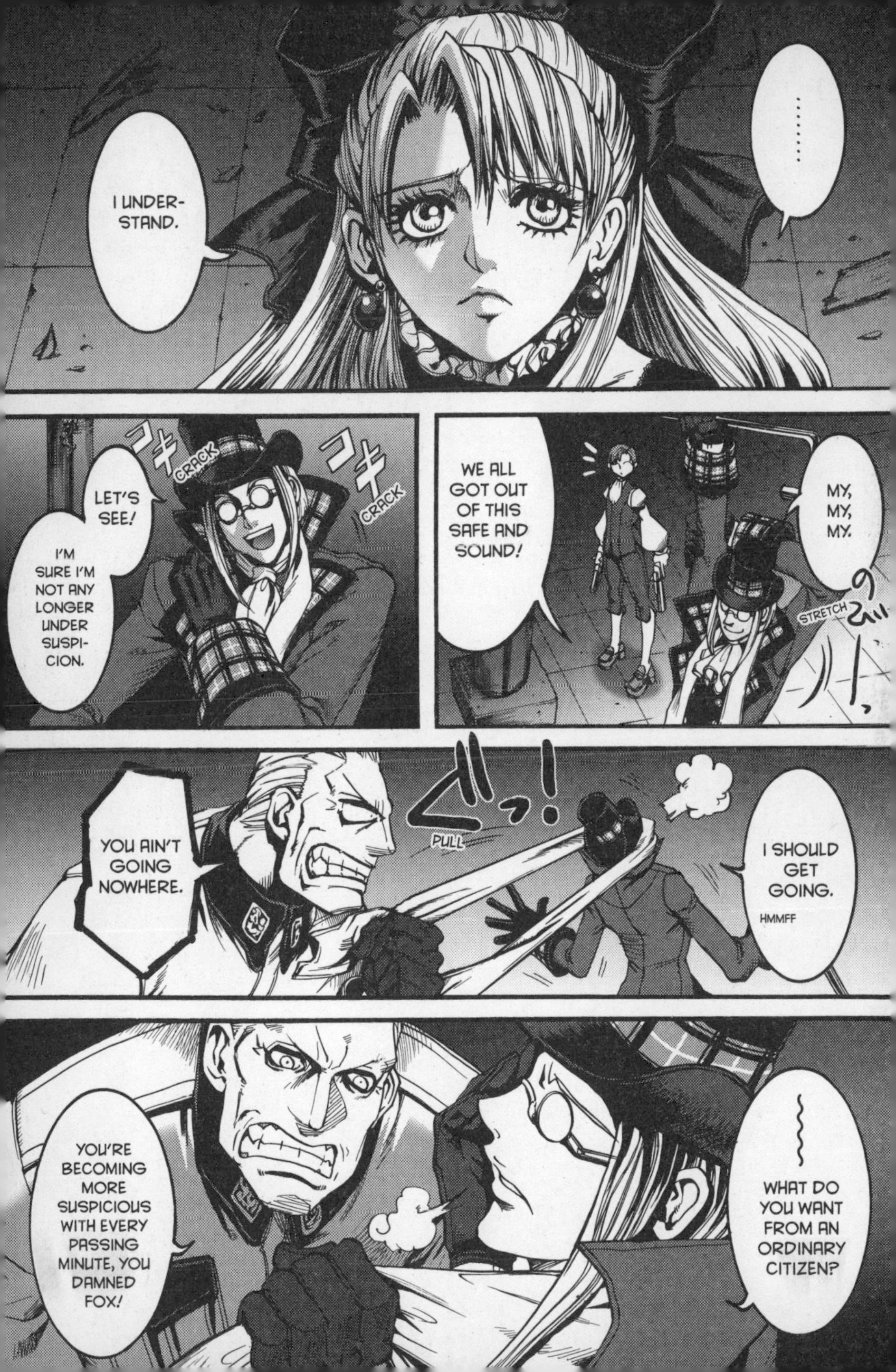
……
I UNDER-STAND.
MY, MY, MY.
STRETCH
WE ALL GOT OUT OF THIS SAFE AND SOUND!
CRACK
CRACK
LET'S SEE!
I'M SURE I'M NOT ANY LONGER UNDER SUSPI-CION.
I SHOULD GET GOING.
HMMFF
PULL
YOU AIN'T GOING NOWHERE.
WHAT DO YOU WANT FROM AN ORDINARY CITIZEN?
YOU'RE BECOMING MORE SUSPICIOUS WITH EVERY PASSING MINUTE, YOU DAMNED FOX!

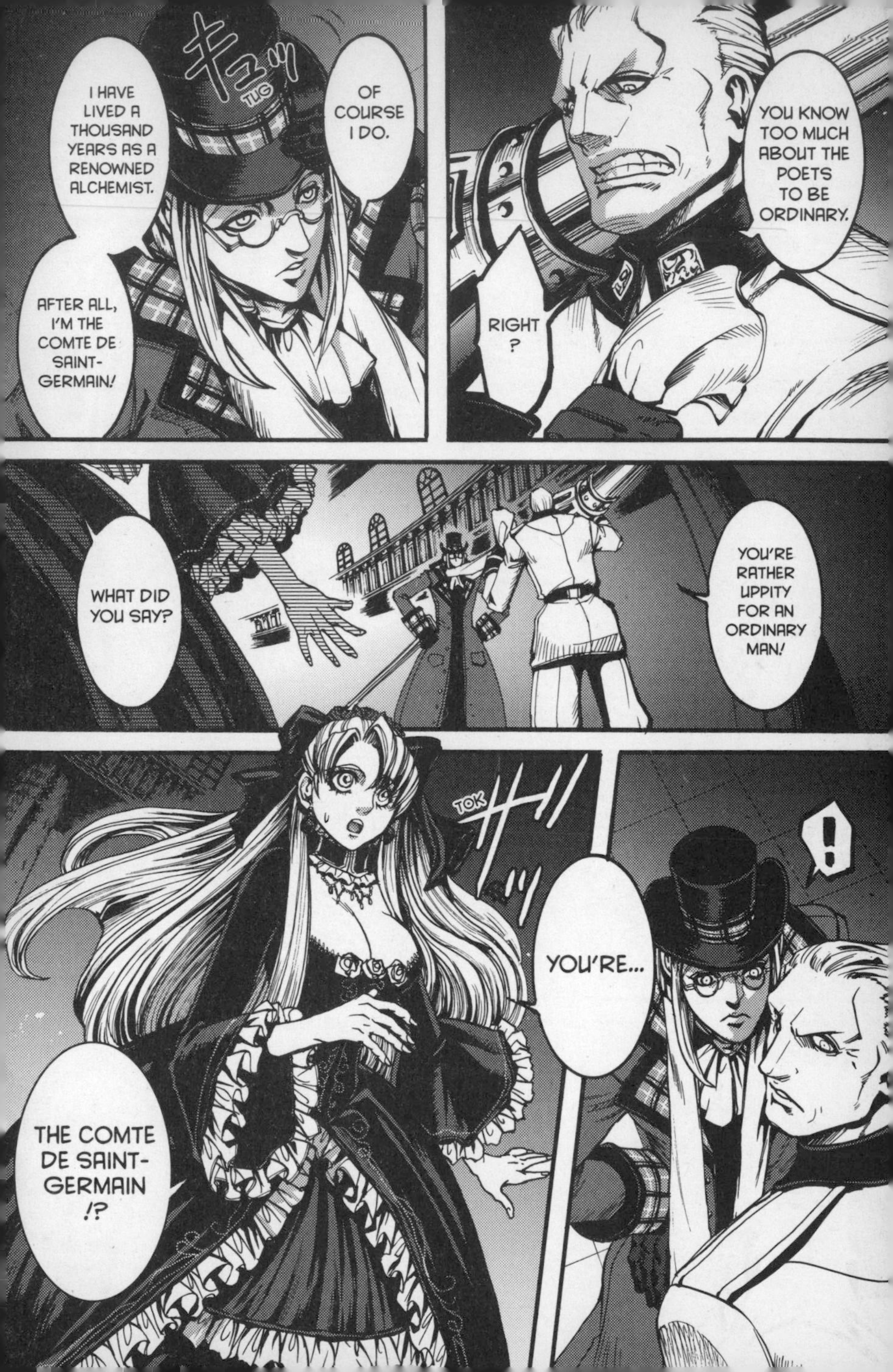
YOU KNOW TOO MUCH ABOUT THE POETS TO BE ORDINARY.
RIGHT?
キュッ
TUG
OF COURSE I DO.
I HAVE LIVED A THOUSAND YEARS AS A RENOWNED ALCHEMIST.
AFTER ALL, I'M THE COMTE DE SAINT-GERMAIN!
YOU'RE RATHER UPPITY FOR AN ORDINARY MAN!
WHAT DID YOU SAY?
!
YOU'RE...
TOK
THE COMTE DE SAINT-GERMAIN!?

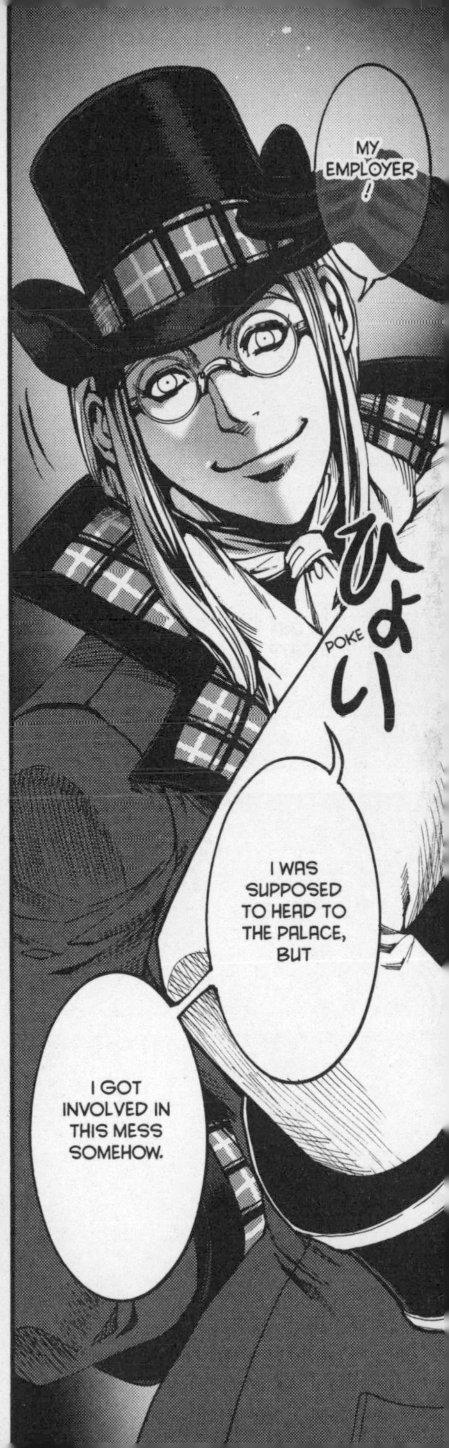
MY EMPLOYER!
ひょい
POKE
I WAS SUPPOSED TO HEAD TO THE PALACE, BUT
I GOT INVOLVED IN THIS MESS SOMEHOW.

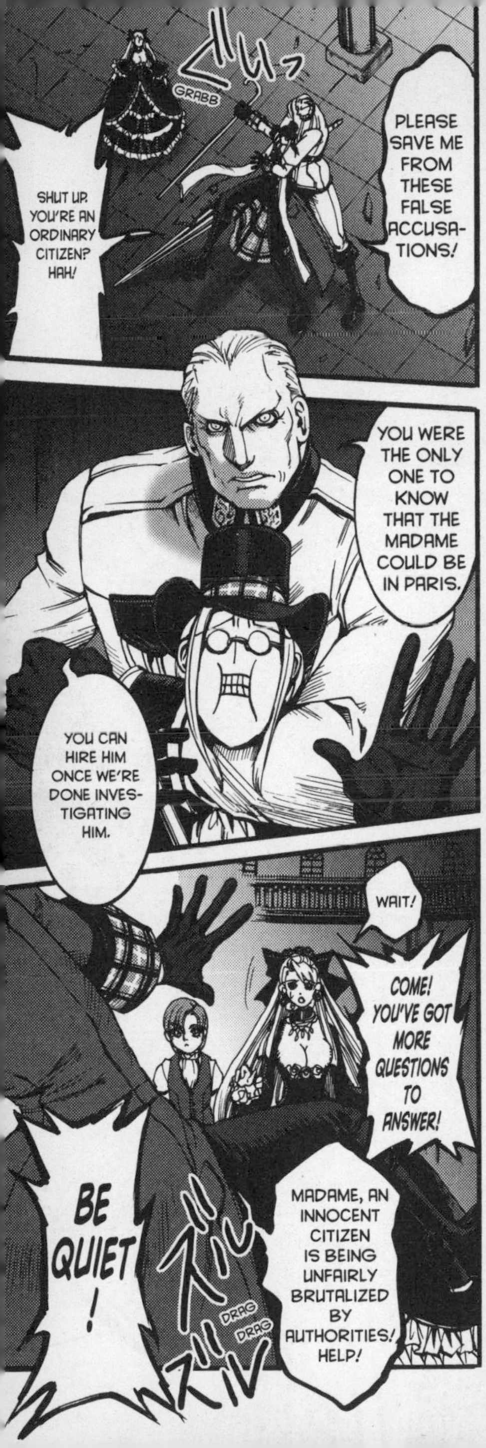
PLEASE SAVE ME FROM THESE FALSE ACCUSATIONS!
ぐいっ
GRABB
SHUT UP. YOU'RE AN ORDINARY CITIZEN? HAH!
YOU WERE THE ONLY ONE TO KNOW THAT THE MADAME COULD BE IN PARIS.
YOU CAN HIRE HIM ONCE WE'RE DONE INVESTIGATING HIM.
WAIT!
COME! YOU'VE GOT MORE QUESTIONS TO ANSWER!
MADAME, AN INNOCENT CITIZEN IS BEING UNFAIRLY BRUTALIZED BY AUTHORITIES! HELP!
ズル ズル
DRAG DRAG
BE QUIET!

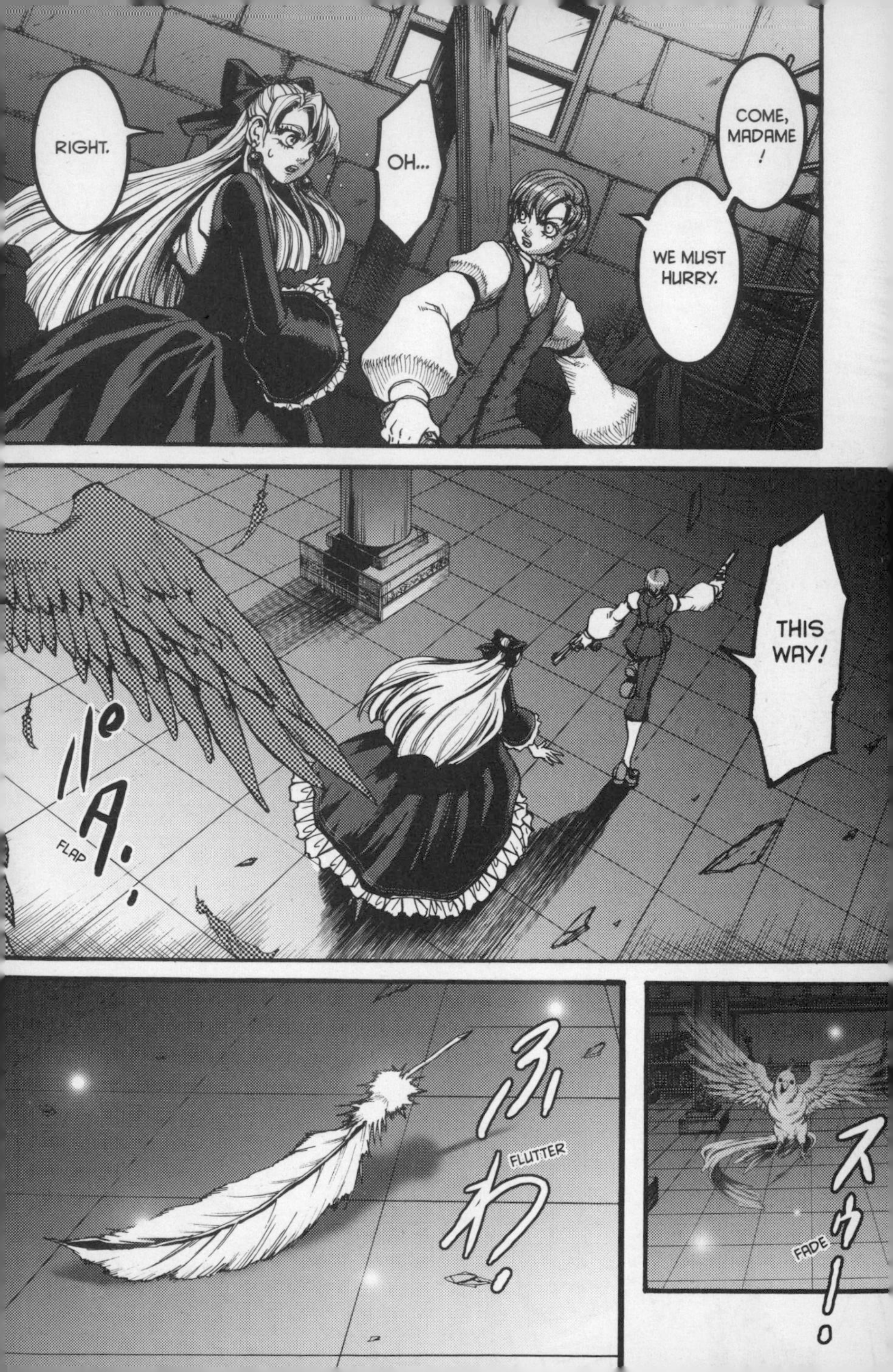
COME, MADAME!
WE MUST HURRY.
OH...
RIGHT.
THIS WAY!
FLAP
スゥー
FADE
ふわ
FLUTTER

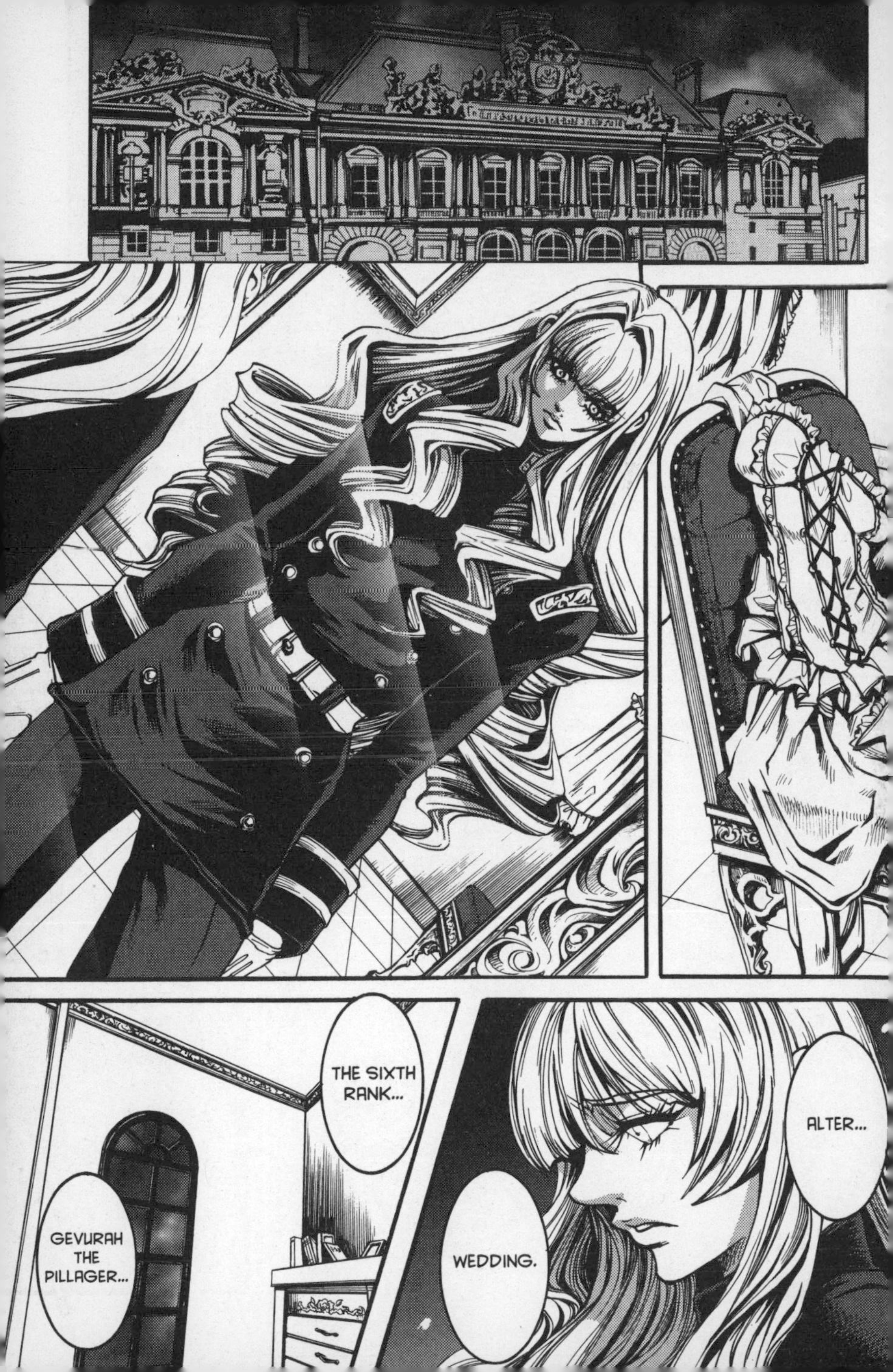
ALTER...
WEDDING.
THE SIXTH RANK...
GEVURAH THE PILLAGER...

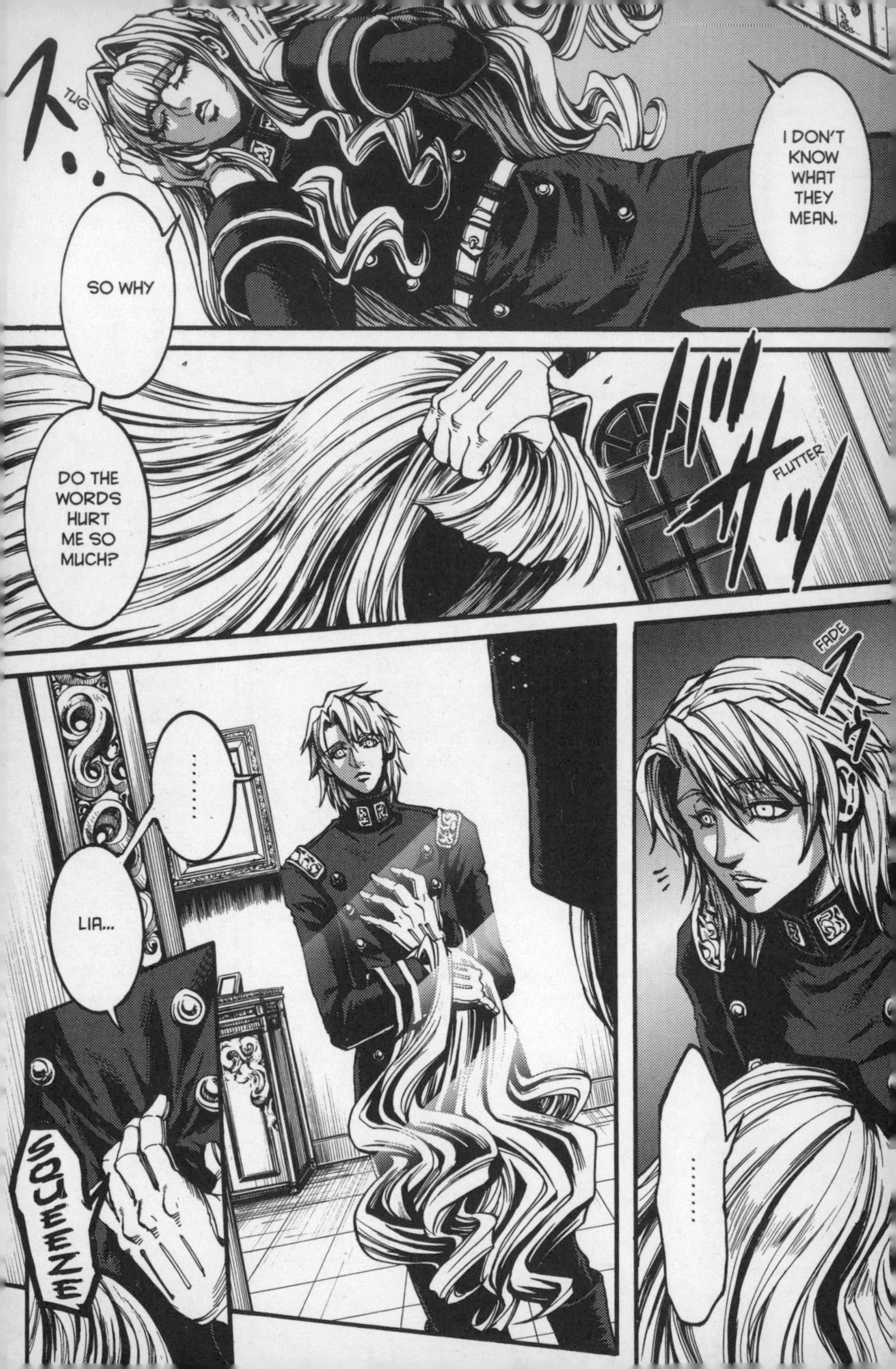
I DON'T KNOW WHAT THEY MEAN.
TUG
SO WHY
FLUTTER
DO THE WORDS HURT ME SO MUCH?
FADE
......
......
LIA...
SQUEEZE

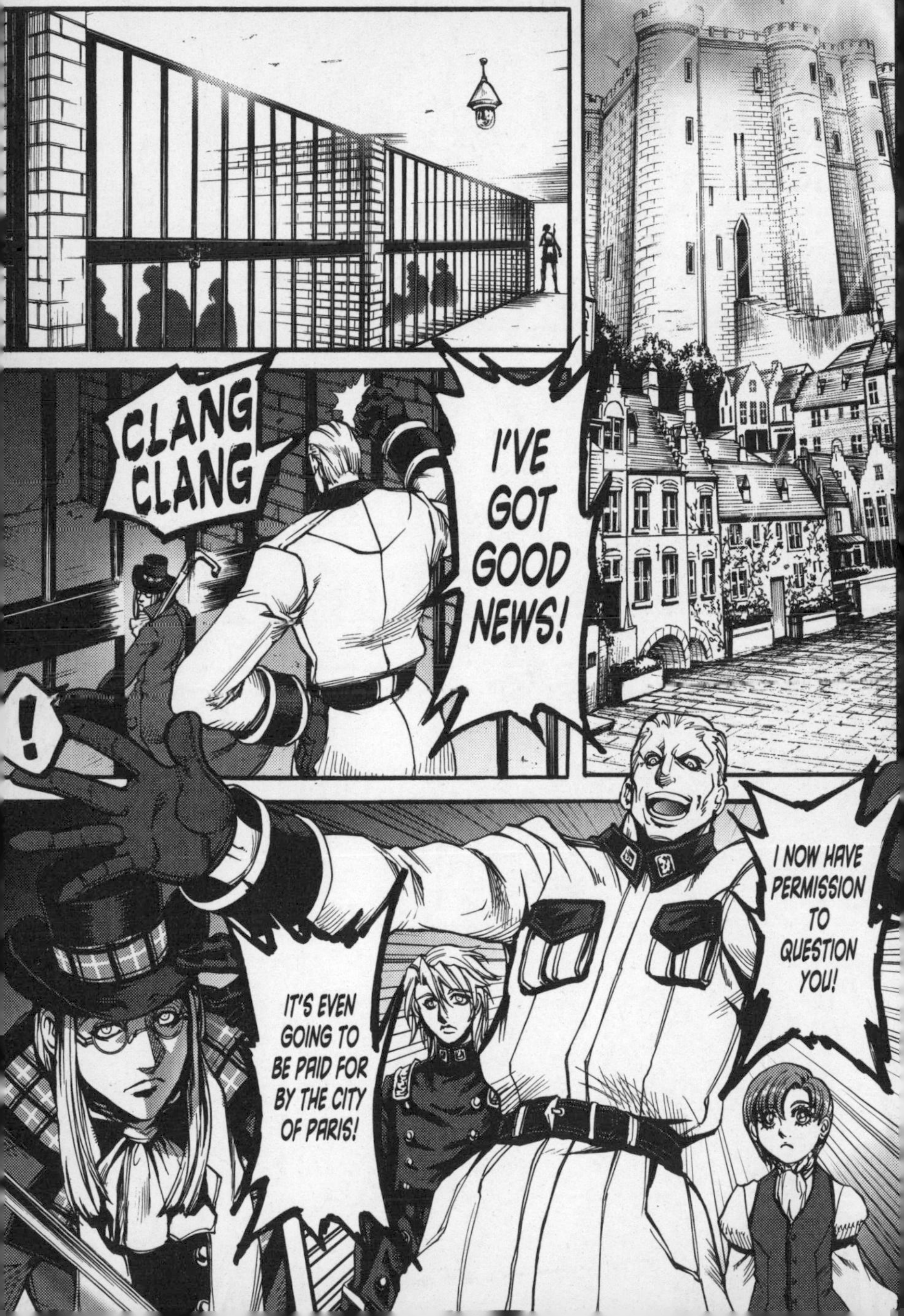
I'VE GOT GOOD NEWS!
CLANG CLANG
I NOW HAVE PERMISSION TO QUESTION YOU!
IT'S EVEN GOING TO BE PAID FOR BY THE CITY OF PARIS!
!

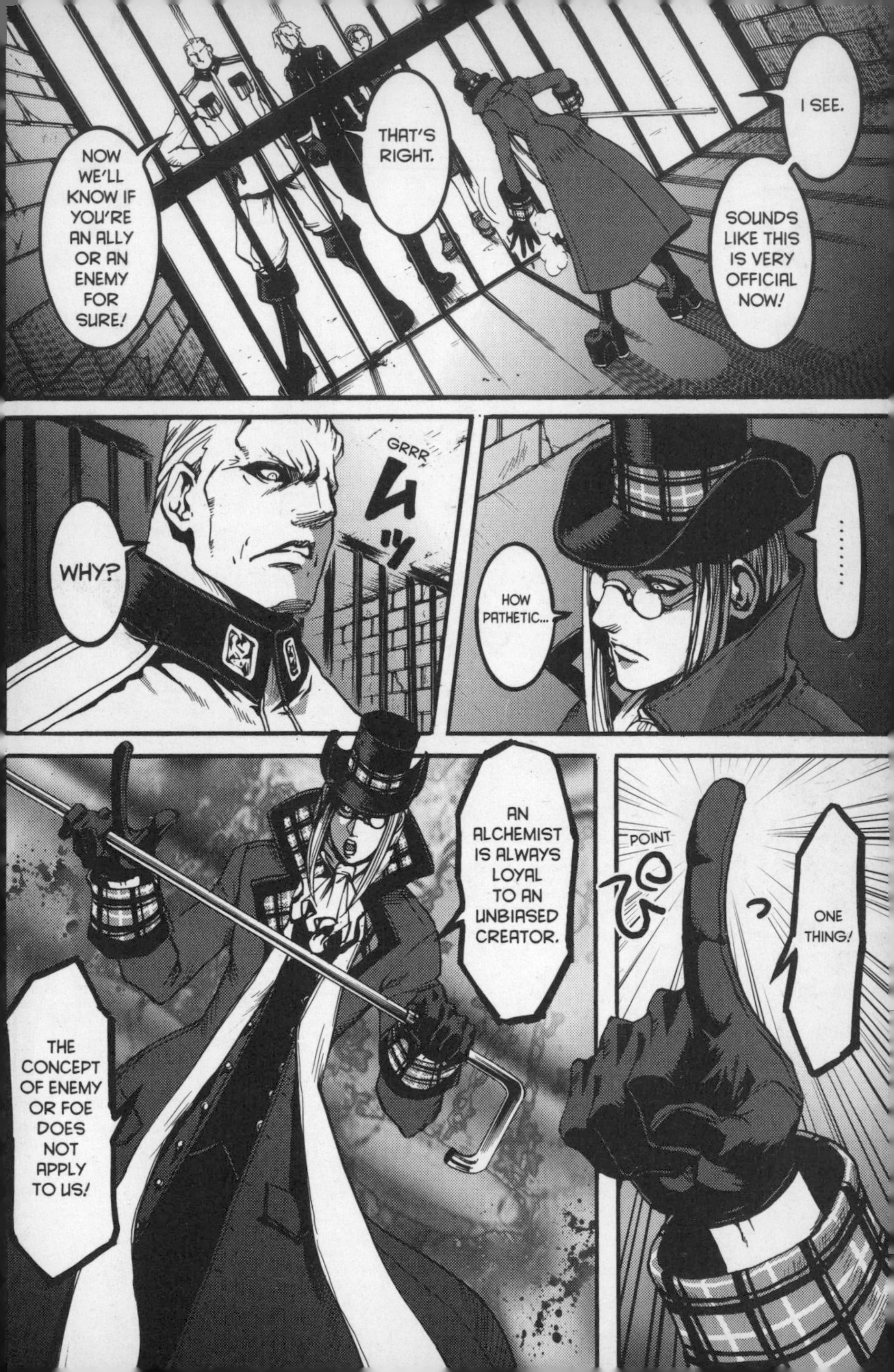
I SEE.
SOUNDS LIKE THIS IS VERY OFFICIAL NOW!
THAT'S RIGHT.
NOW WE'LL KNOW IF YOU'RE AN ALLY OR AN ENEMY FOR SURE!
......
HOW PATHETIC...
GRRR
ムッ
WHY?
ONE THING!
POINT
AN ALCHEMIST IS ALWAYS LOYAL TO AN UNBIASED CREATOR.
THE CONCEPT OF ENEMY OR FOE DOES NOT APPLY TO US!

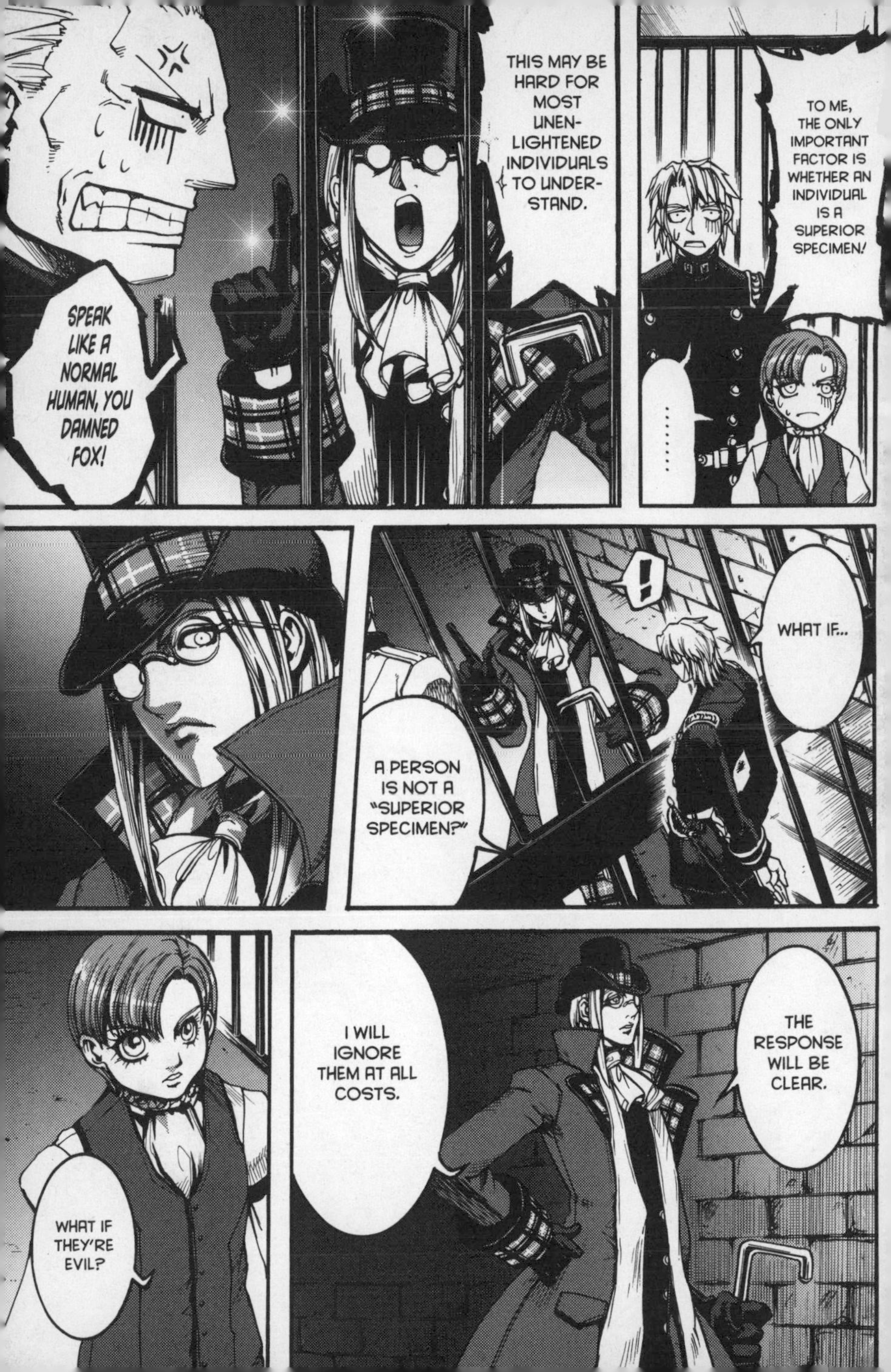
TO ME, THE ONLY IMPORTANT FACTOR IS WHETHER AN INDIVIDUAL IS A SUPERIOR SPECIMEN!
......
THIS MAY BE HARD FOR MOST UNEN-LIGHTENED INDIVIDUALS TO UNDER-STAND.
SPEAK LIKE A NORMAL HUMAN, YOU DAMNED FOX!
!
WHAT IF...
A PERSON IS NOT A "SUPERIOR SPECIMEN?"
THE RESPONSE WILL BE CLEAR.
I WILL IGNORE THEM AT ALL COSTS.
WHAT IF THEY'RE EVIL?

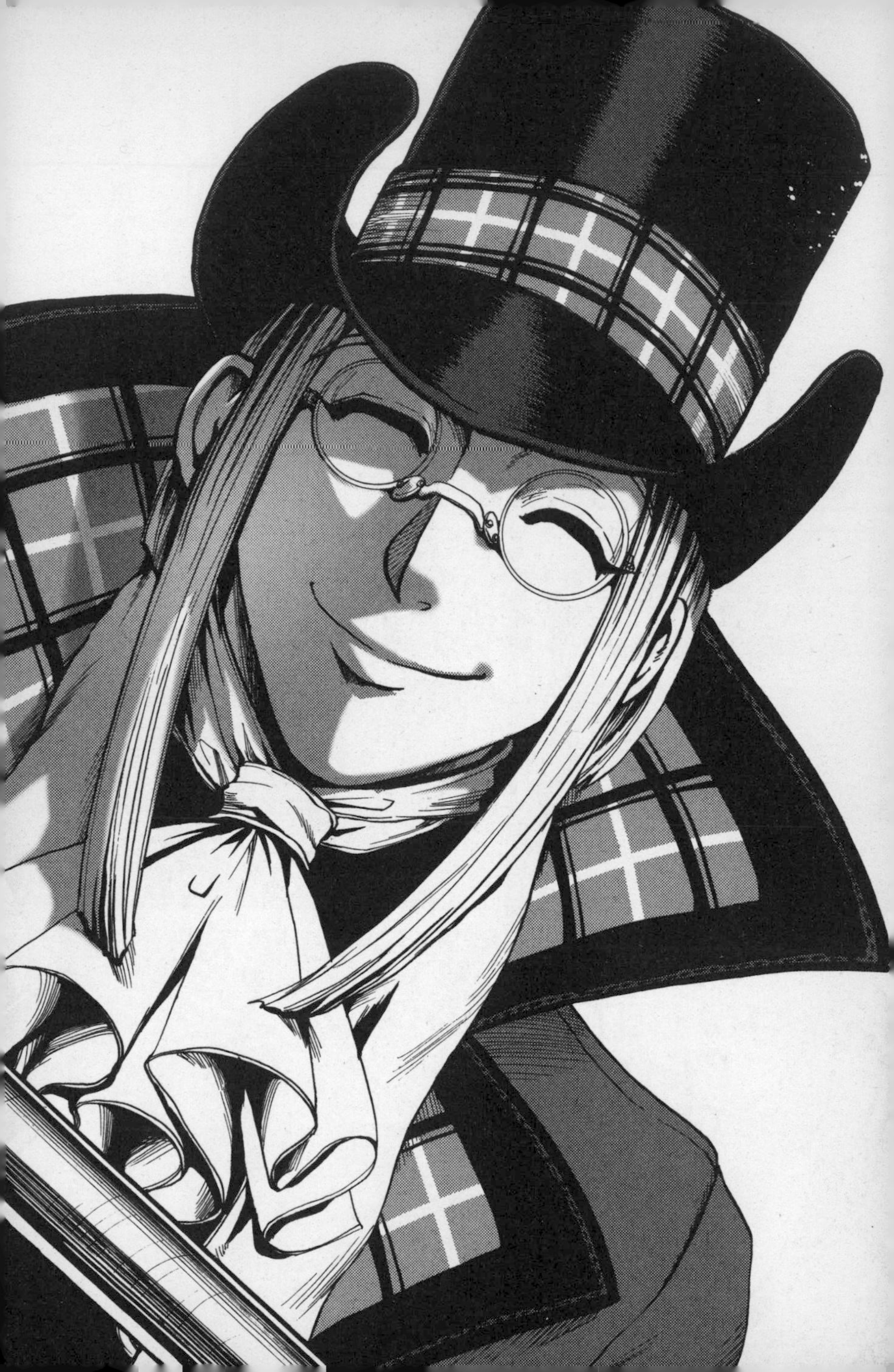

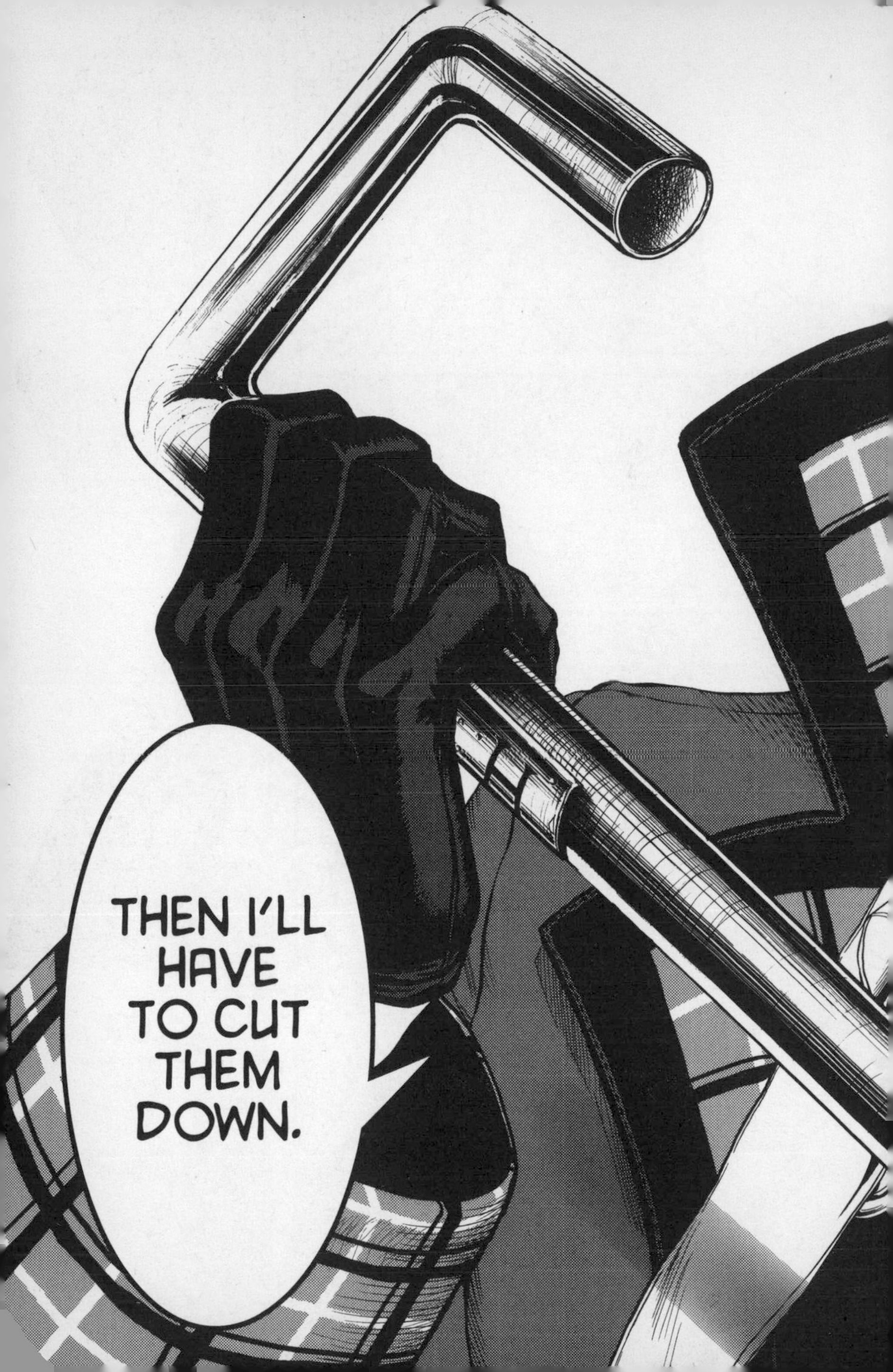
THEN I'LL HAVE TO CUT THEM DOWN.

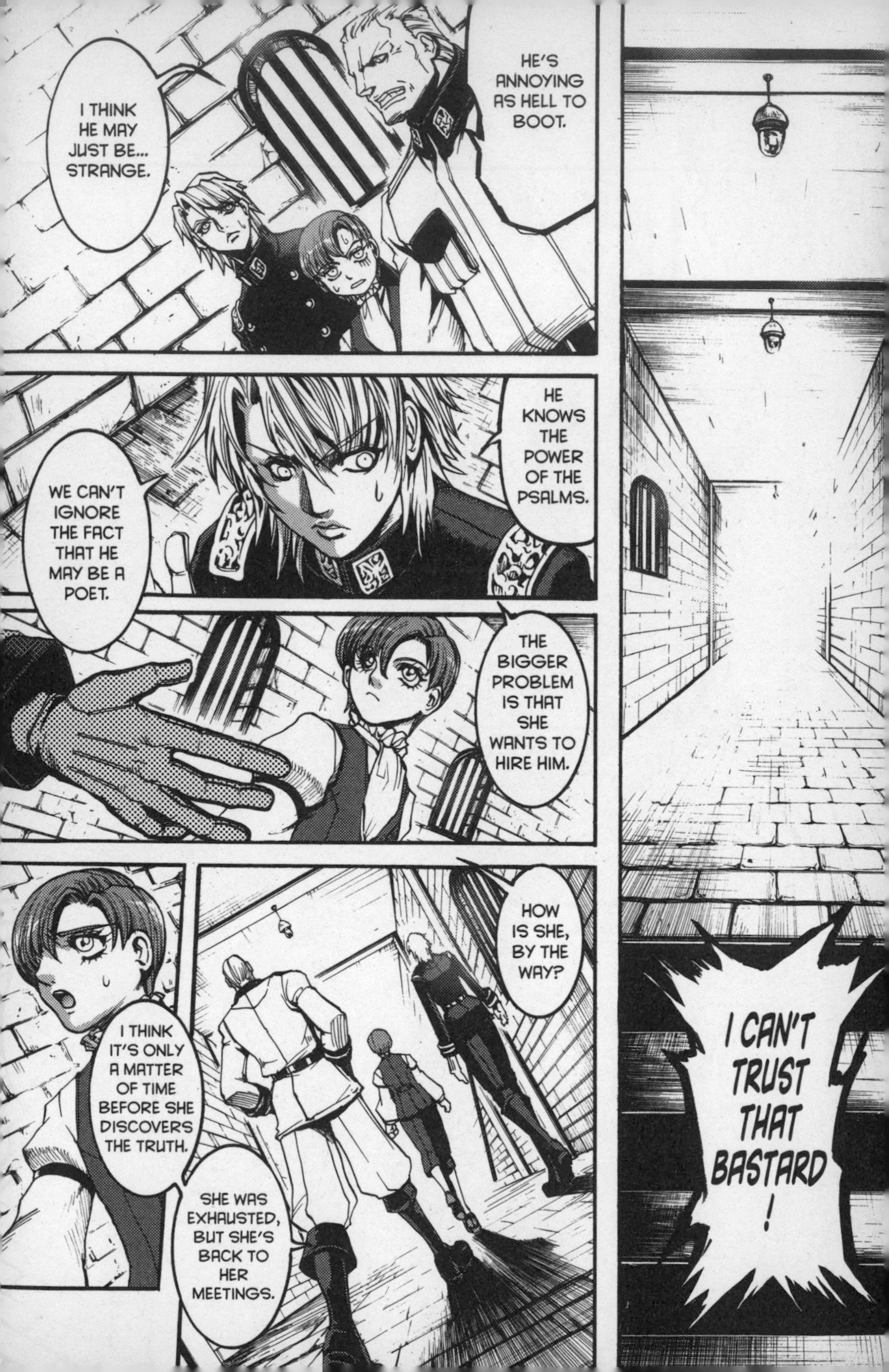
HE'S ANNOYING AS HELL TO BOOT.
I THINK HE MAY JUST BE... STRANGE.
HE KNOWS THE POWER OF THE PSALMS.
WE CAN'T IGNORE THE FACT THAT HE MAY BE A POET.
THE BIGGER PROBLEM IS THAT SHE WANTS TO HIRE HIM.
HOW IS SHE, BY THE WAY?
SHE WAS EXHAUSTED, BUT SHE'S BACK TO HER MEETINGS.
I THINK IT'S ONLY A MATTER OF TIME BEFORE SHE DISCOVERS THE TRUTH.
I CAN'T TRUST THAT BASTARD!

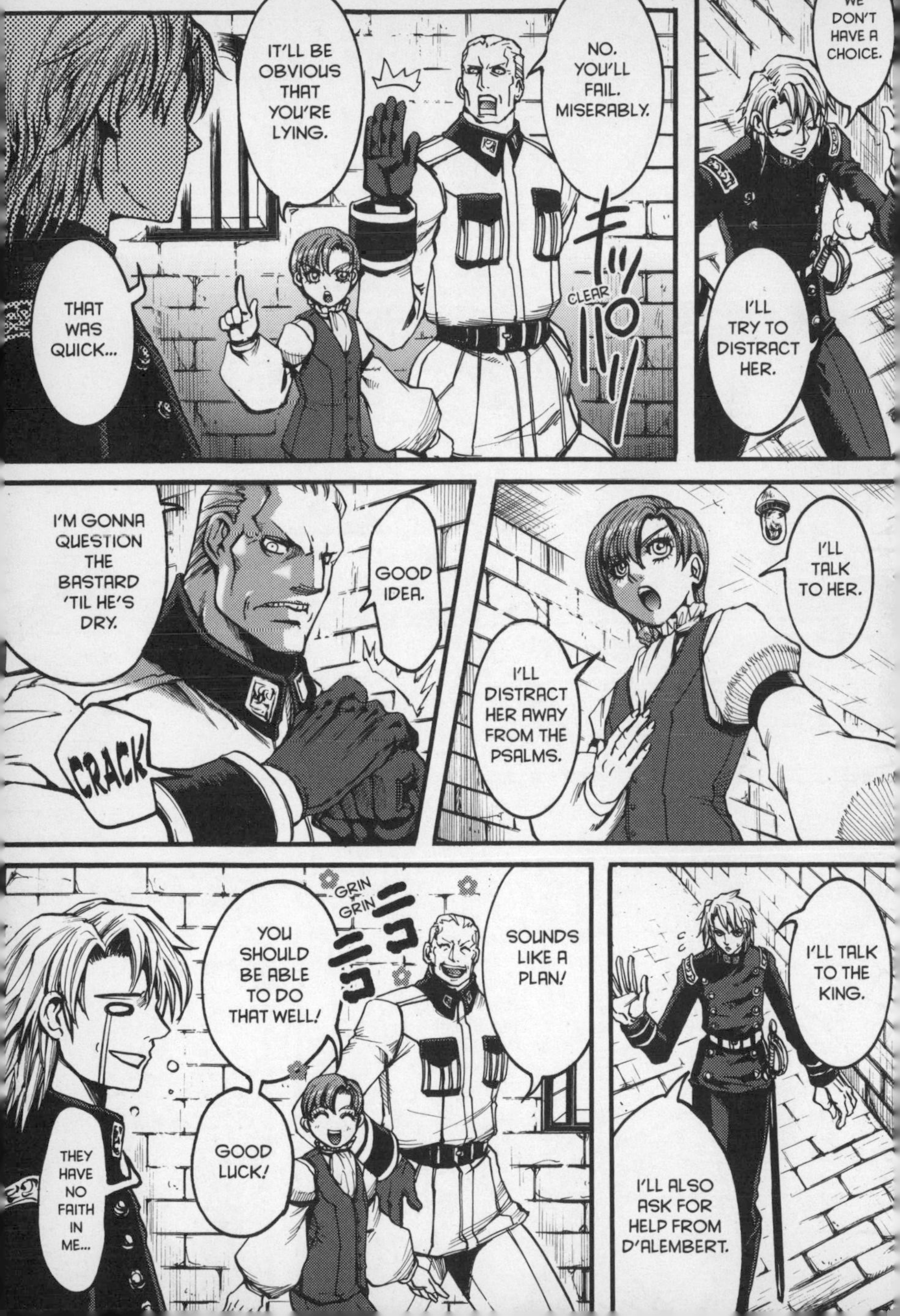
WE DON'T HAVE A CHOICE.
I'LL TRY TO DISTRACT HER.
NO. YOU'LL FAIL. MISERABLY.
CLEAR
IT'LL BE OBVIOUS THAT YOU'RE LYING.
THAT WAS QUICK...
I'LL TALK TO HER.
I'LL DISTRACT HER AWAY FROM THE PSALMS.
GOOD IDEA.
I'M GONNA QUESTION THE BASTARD 'TIL HE'S DRY.
CRACK
I'LL TALK TO THE KING.
I'LL ALSO ASK FOR HELP FROM D'ALEMBERT.
SOUNDS LIKE A PLAN!
GRIN GRIN
YOU SHOULD BE ABLE TO DO THAT WELL!
GOOD LUCK!
THEY HAVE NO FAITH IN ME...

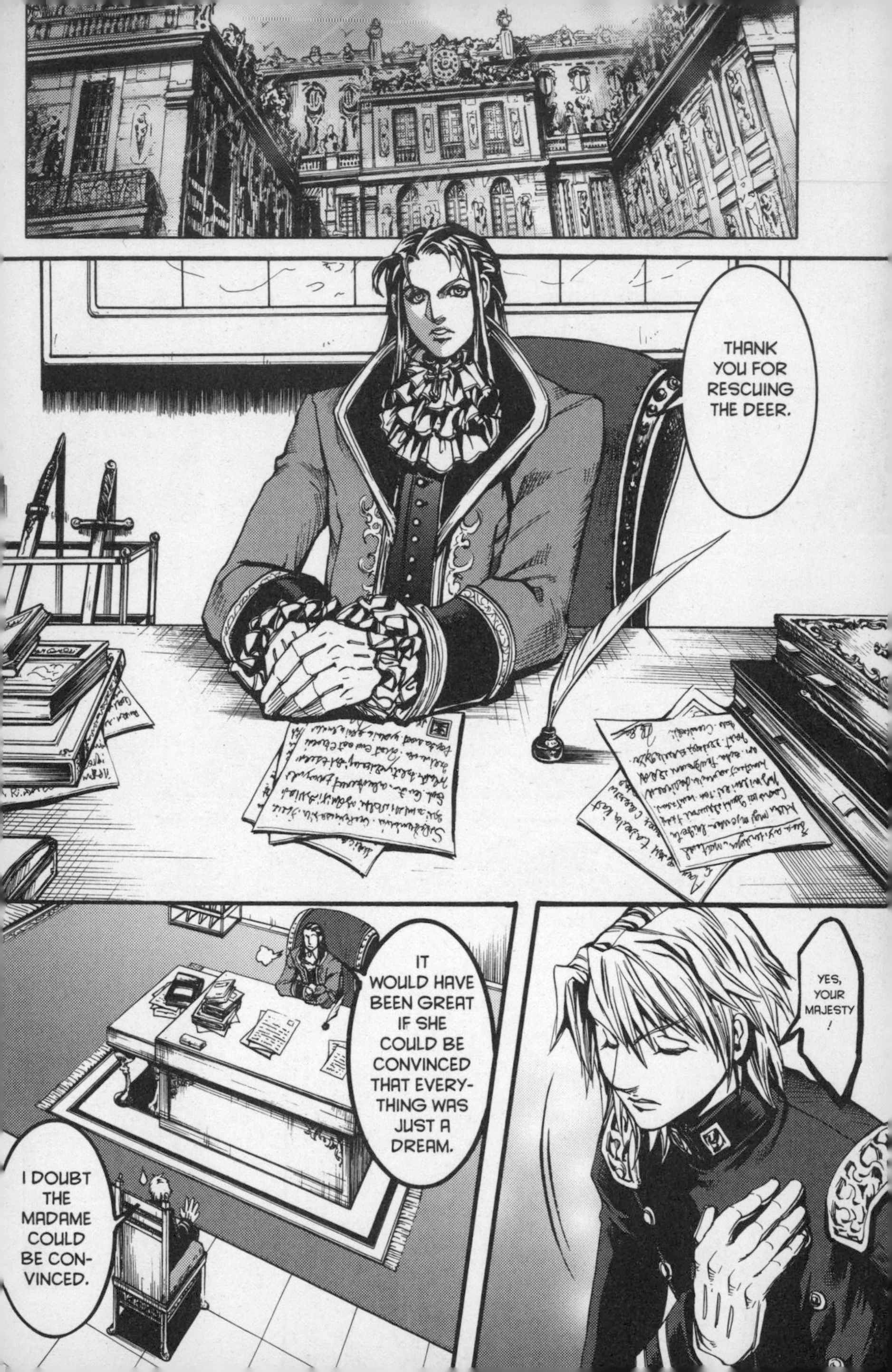
THANK YOU FOR RESCUING THE DEER.
YES, YOUR MAJESTY!
IT WOULD HAVE BEEN GREAT IF SHE COULD BE CONVINCED THAT EVERY-THING WAS JUST A DREAM.
I DOUBT THE MADAME COULD BE CON-VINCED.

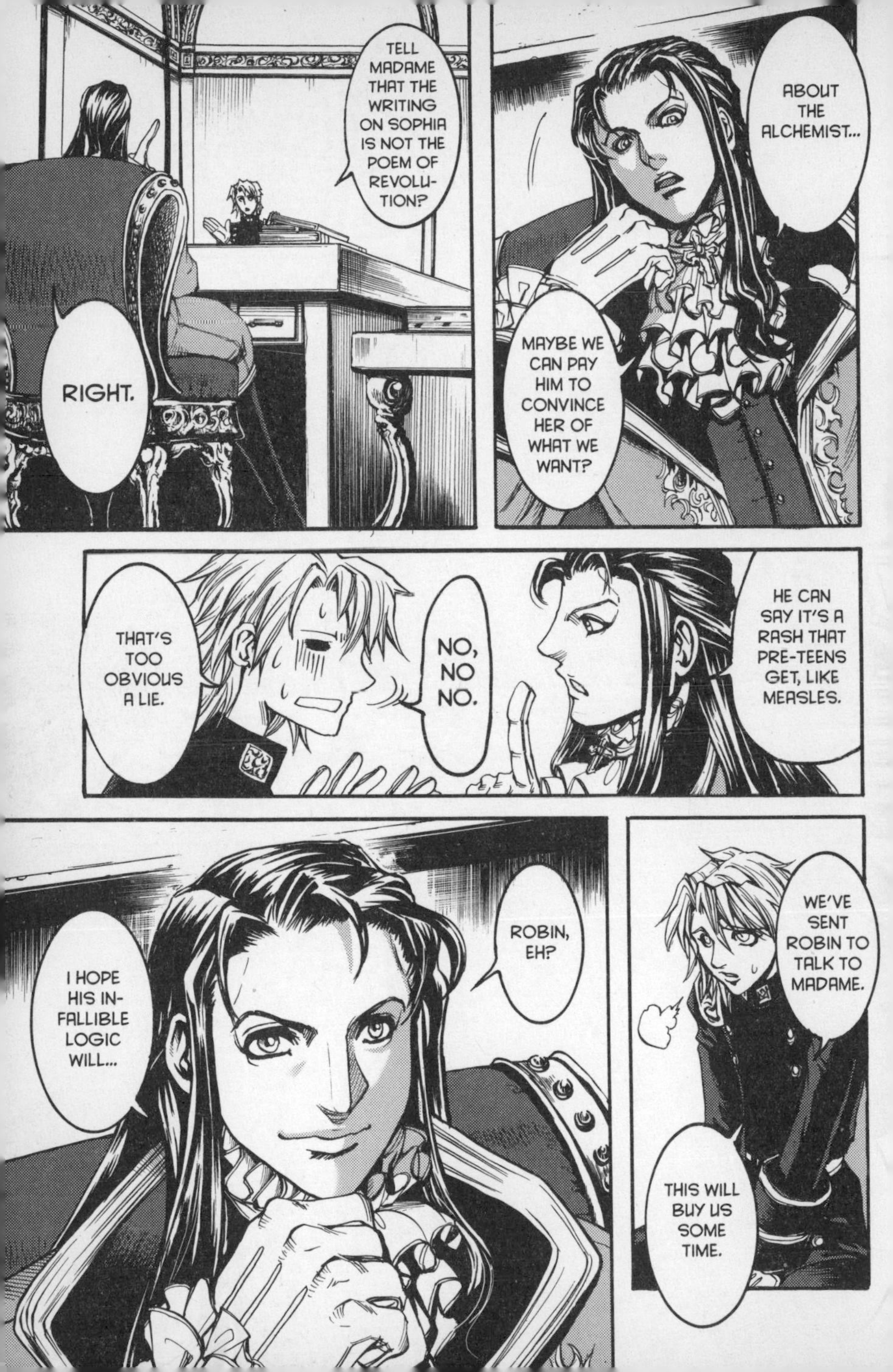
ABOUT THE ALCHEMIST...
MAYBE WE CAN PAY HIM TO CONVINCE HER OF WHAT WE WANT?
TELL MADAME THAT THE WRITING ON SOPHIA IS NOT THE POEM OF REVOLU-TION?
RIGHT.
HE CAN SAY IT'S A RASH THAT PRE-TEENS GET, LIKE MEASLES.
NO, NO NO.
THAT'S TOO OBVIOUS A LIE.
WE'VE SENT ROBIN TO TALK TO MADAME.
THIS WILL BUY US SOME TIME.
ROBIN, EH?
I HOPE HIS IN-FALLIBLE LOGIC WILL...

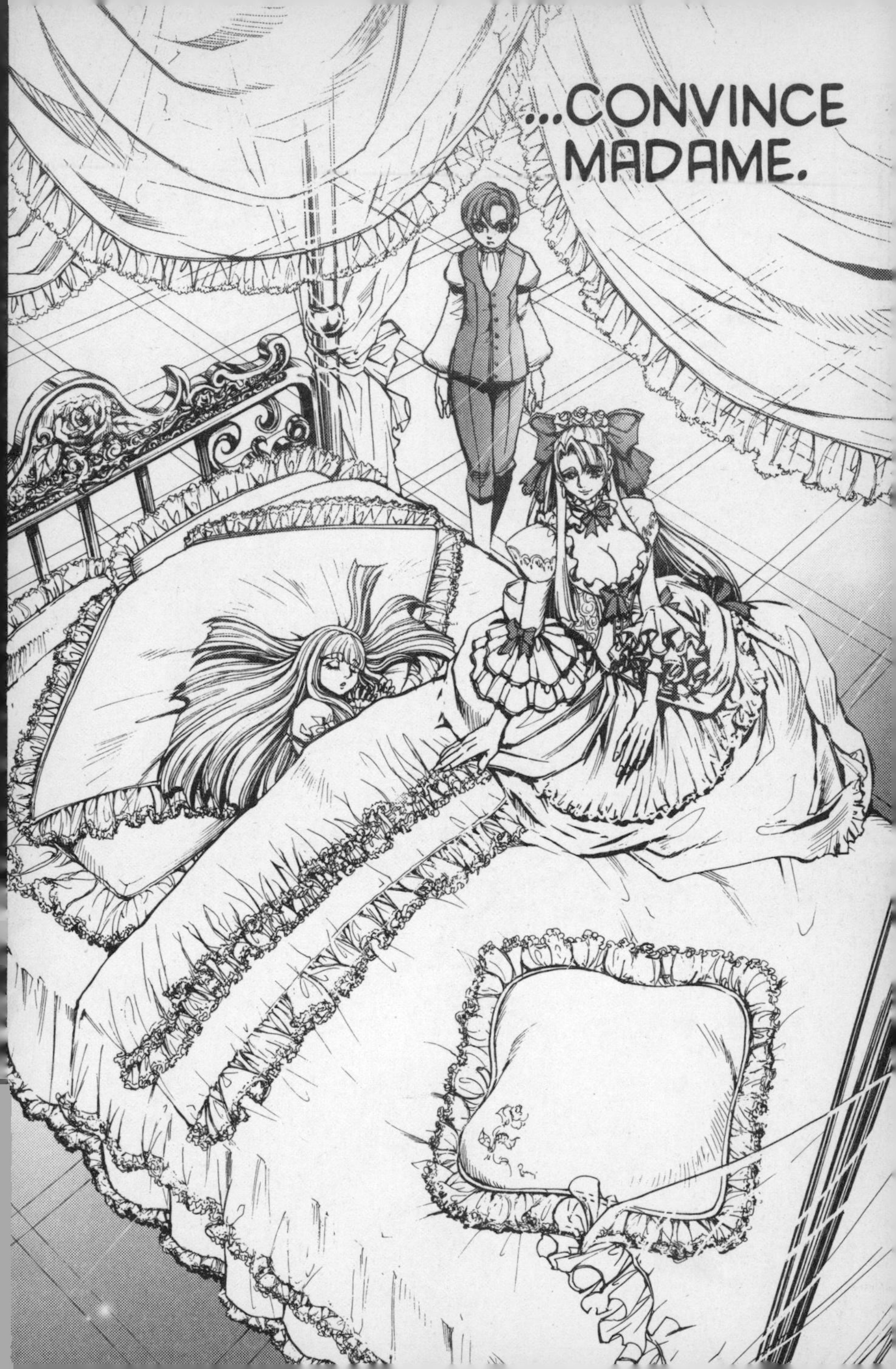
...CONVINCE MADAME.

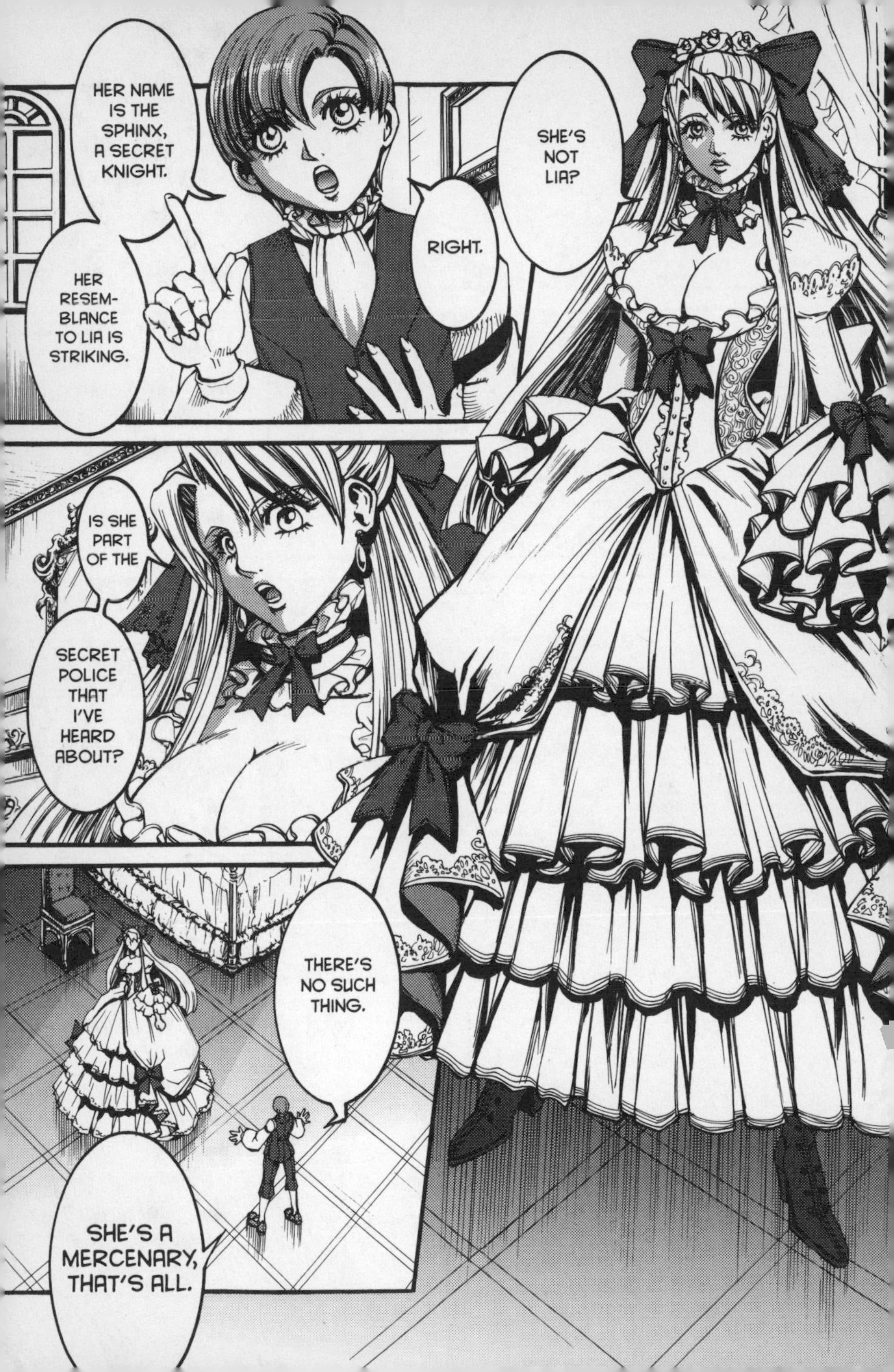
SHE'S NOT LIA?
RIGHT.
HER NAME IS THE SPHINX, A SECRET KNIGHT.
HER RESEMBLANCE TO LIA IS STRIKING.
IS SHE PART OF THE
SECRET POLICE THAT I'VE HEARD ABOUT?
THERE'S NO SUCH THING.
SHE'S A MERCENARY, THAT'S ALL.

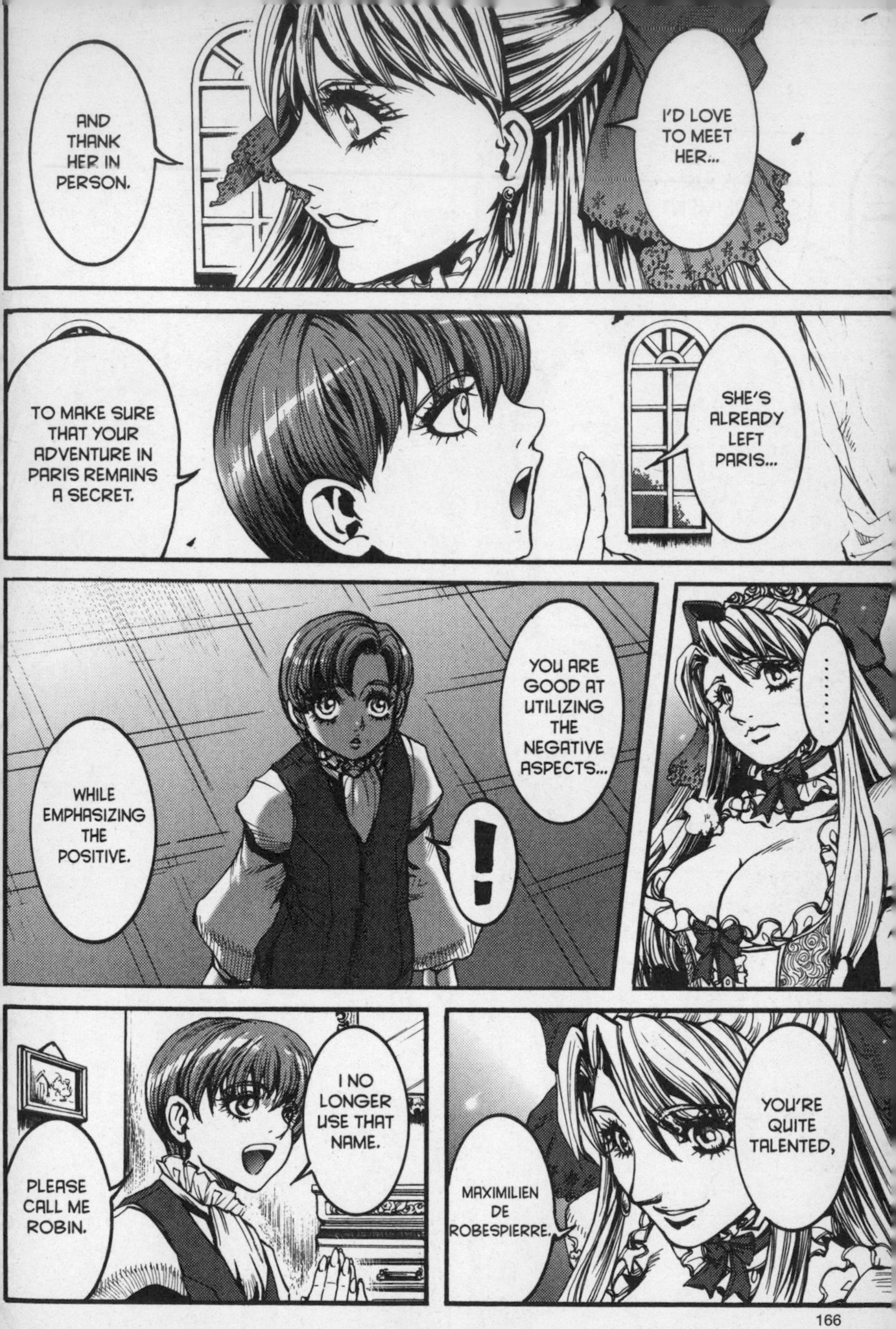
I'D LOVE TO MEET HER...
AND THANK HER IN PERSON.
SHE'S ALREADY LEFT PARIS...
TO MAKE SURE THAT YOUR ADVENTURE IN PARIS REMAINS A SECRET.
......
YOU ARE GOOD AT UTILIZING THE NEGATIVE ASPECTS...
!
WHILE EMPHASIZING THE POSITIVE.
YOU'RE QUITE TALENTED,
MAXIMILIEN DE ROBESPIERRE.
I NO LONGER USE THAT NAME.
PLEASE CALL ME ROBIN.

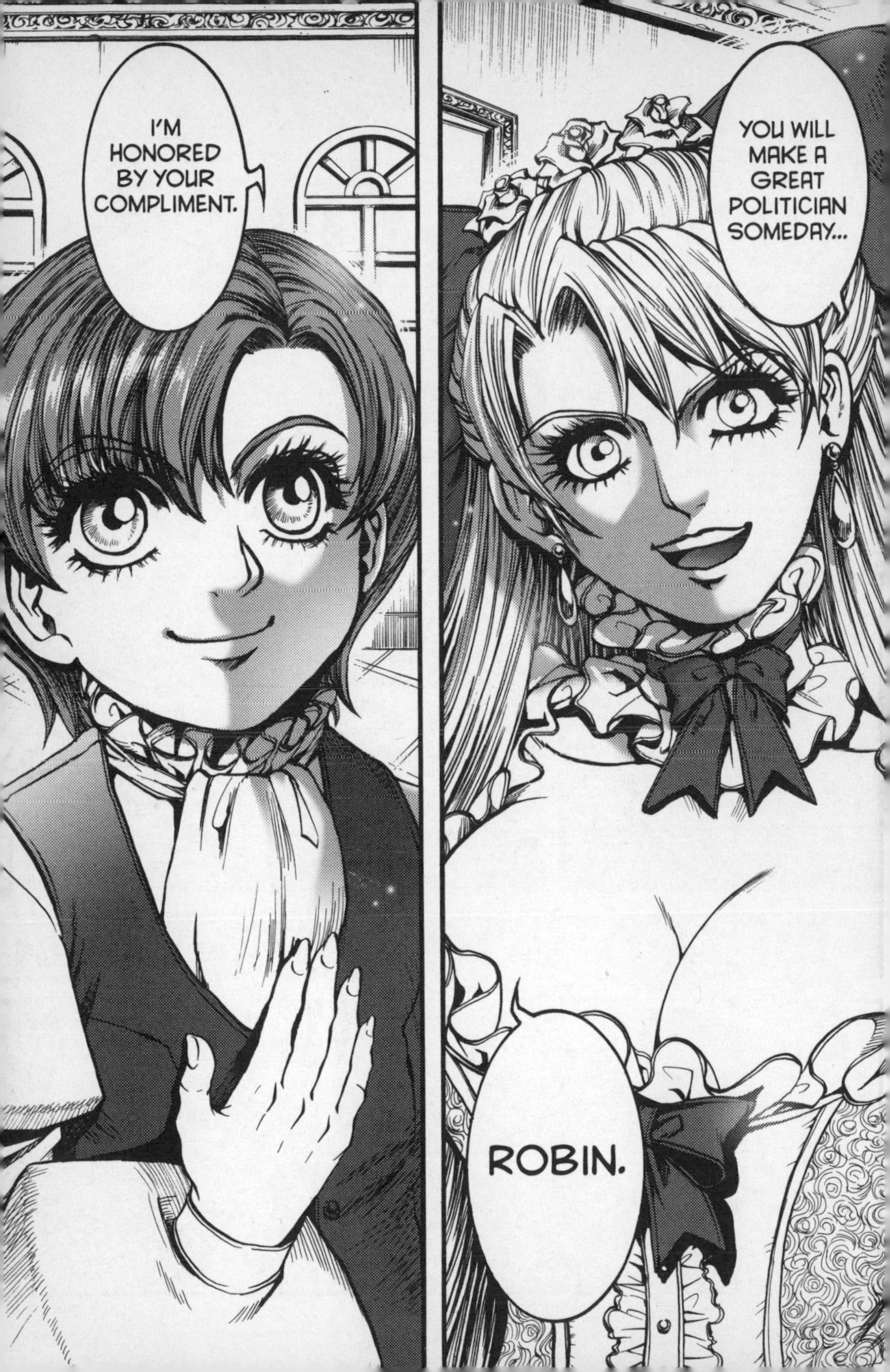
YOU WILL MAKE A GREAT POLITICIAN SOMEDAY...
ROBIN.
I'M HONORED BY YOUR COMPLIMENT.

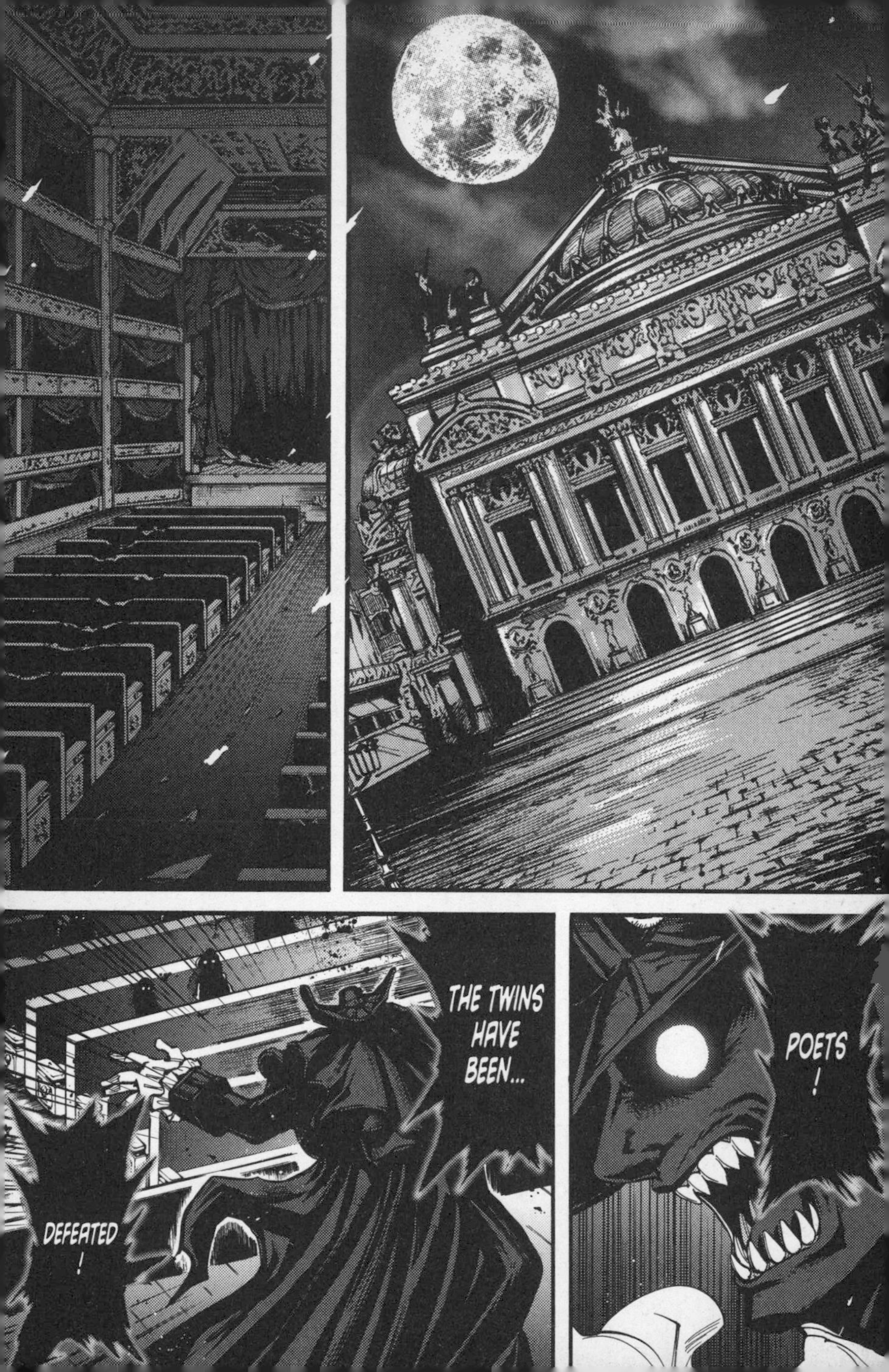
POETS !
THE TWINS HAVE BEEN...
DEFEATED !

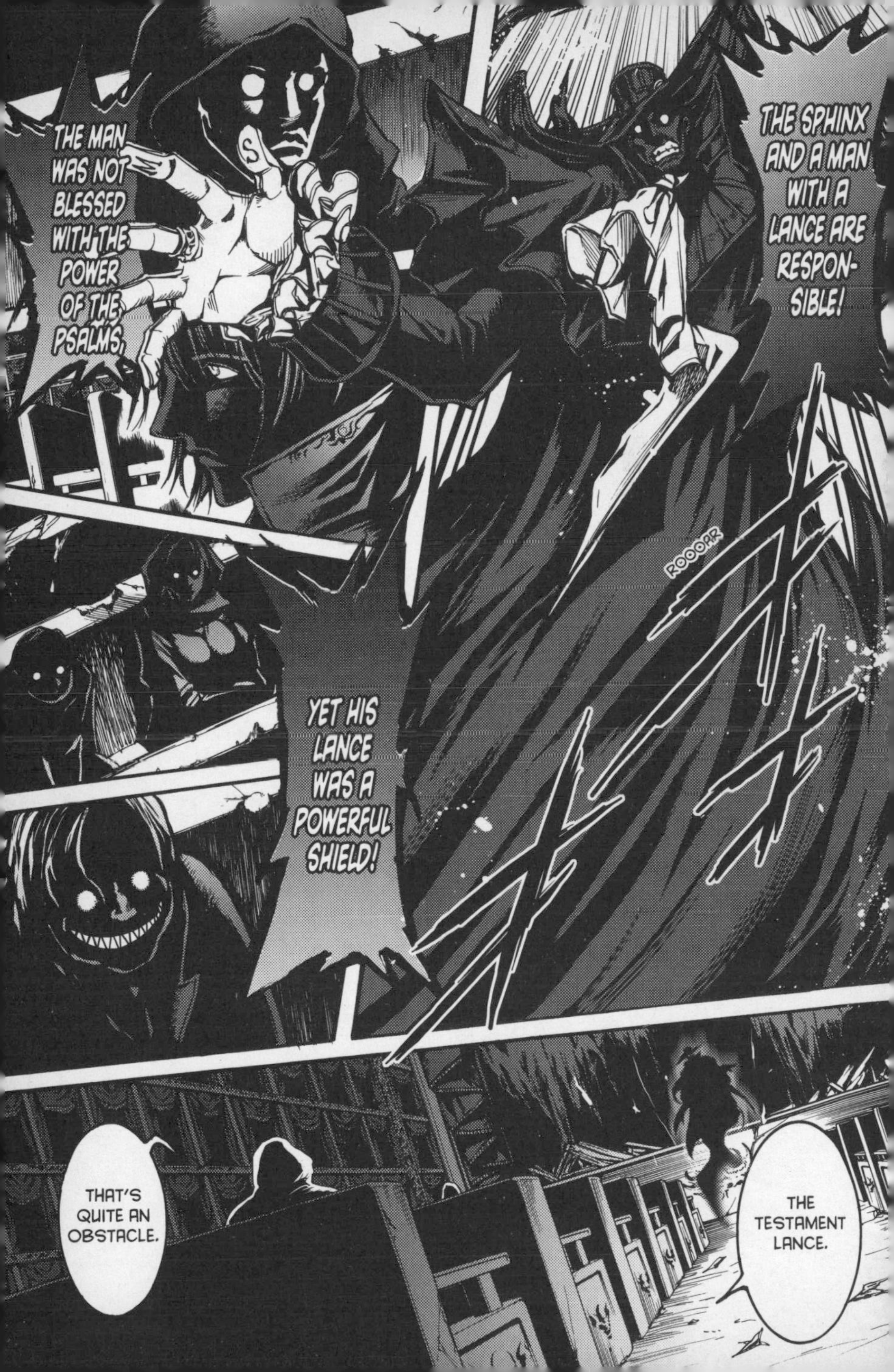
THE SPHINX AND A MAN WITH A LANCE ARE RESPONSIBLE!
THE MAN WAS NOT BLESSED WITH THE POWER OF THE PSALMS,
ROOOAR
YET HIS LANCE WAS A POWERFUL SHIELD!
THE TESTAMENT LANCE.
THAT'S QUITE AN OBSTACLE.

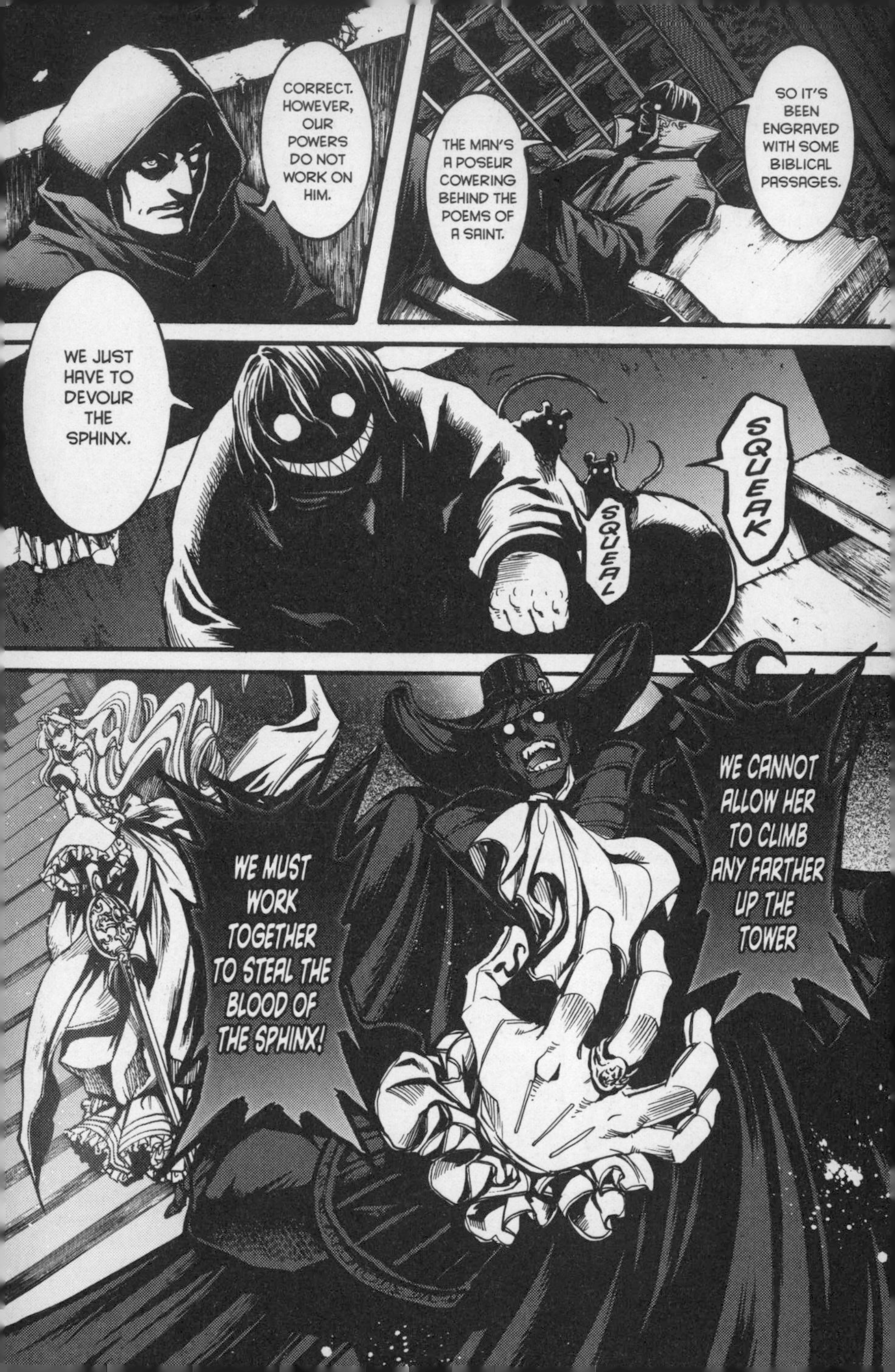
SO IT'S BEEN ENGRAVED WITH SOME BIBLICAL PASSAGES.
THE MAN'S A POSEUR COWERING BEHIND THE POEMS OF A SAINT.
CORRECT. HOWEVER, OUR POWERS DO NOT WORK ON HIM.
SQUEAK
SQUEAL
WE JUST HAVE TO DEVOUR THE SPHINX.
WE CANNOT ALLOW HER TO CLIMB ANY FARTHER UP THE TOWER
WE MUST WORK TOGETHER TO STEAL THE BLOOD OF THE SPHINX!

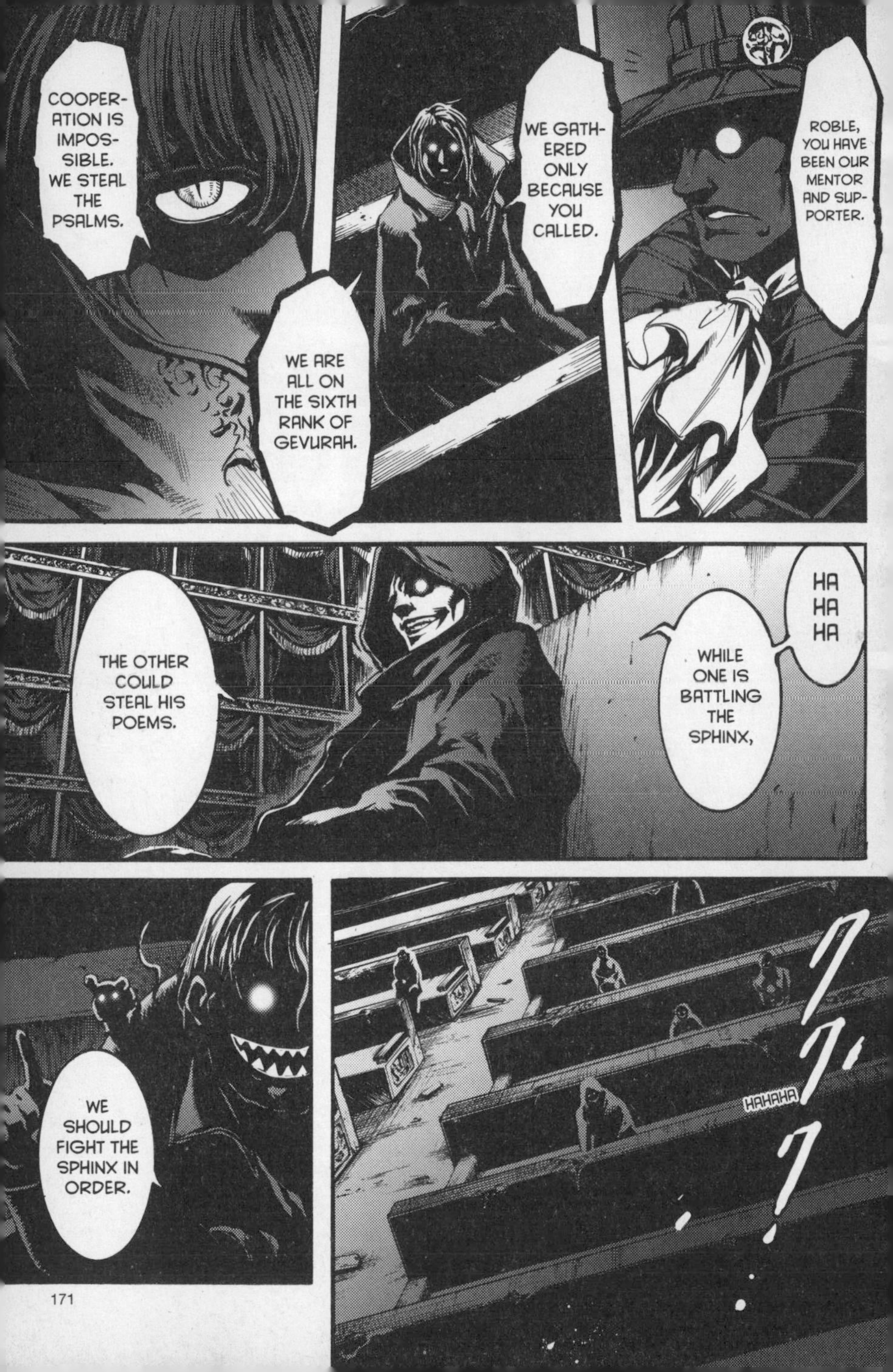
ROBLE, YOU HAVE BEEN OUR MENTOR AND SUPPORTER.
WE GATHERED ONLY BECAUSE YOU CALLED.
WE ARE ALL ON THE SIXTH RANK OF GEVURAH.
COOPERATION IS IMPOSSIBLE. WE STEAL THE PSALMS.
HA HA HA
WHILE ONE IS BATTLING THE SPHINX,
THE OTHER COULD STEAL HIS POEMS.
HAHAHA
WE SHOULD FIGHT THE SPHINX IN ORDER.

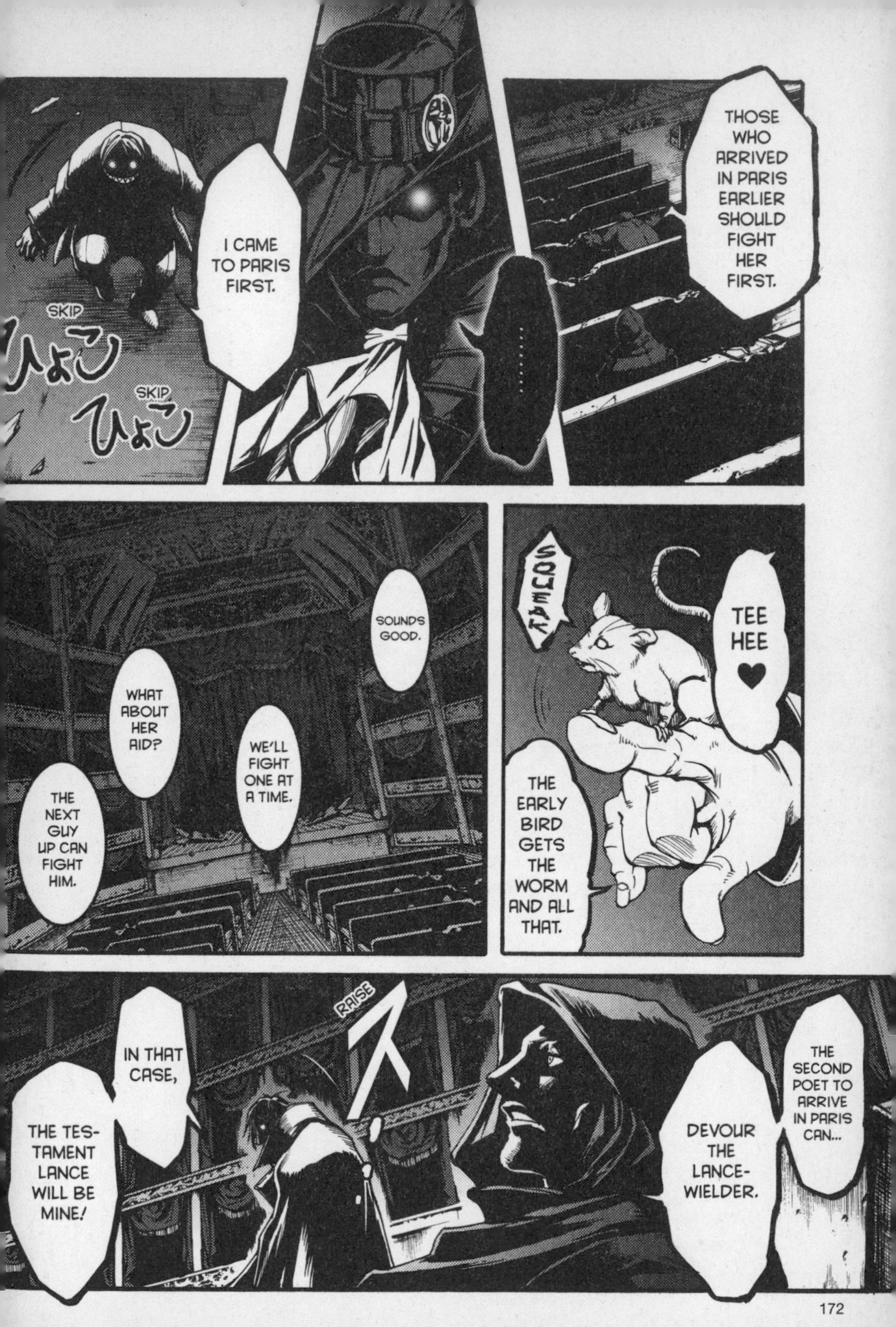
THOSE WHO ARRIVED IN PARIS EARLIER SHOULD FIGHT HER FIRST.
......
I CAME TO PARIS FIRST.
SKIP
ひょこ
SKIP
ひょこ
SQUEAK
TEE HEE ♥
THE EARLY BIRD GETS THE WORM AND ALL THAT.
SOUNDS GOOD.
WE'LL FIGHT ONE AT A TIME.
WHAT ABOUT HER AID?
THE NEXT GUY UP CAN FIGHT HIM.
THE SECOND POET TO ARRIVE IN PARIS CAN...
DEVOUR THE LANCE-WIELDER.
RAISE
ス
IN THAT CASE,
THE TES-TAMENT LANCE WILL BE MINE!

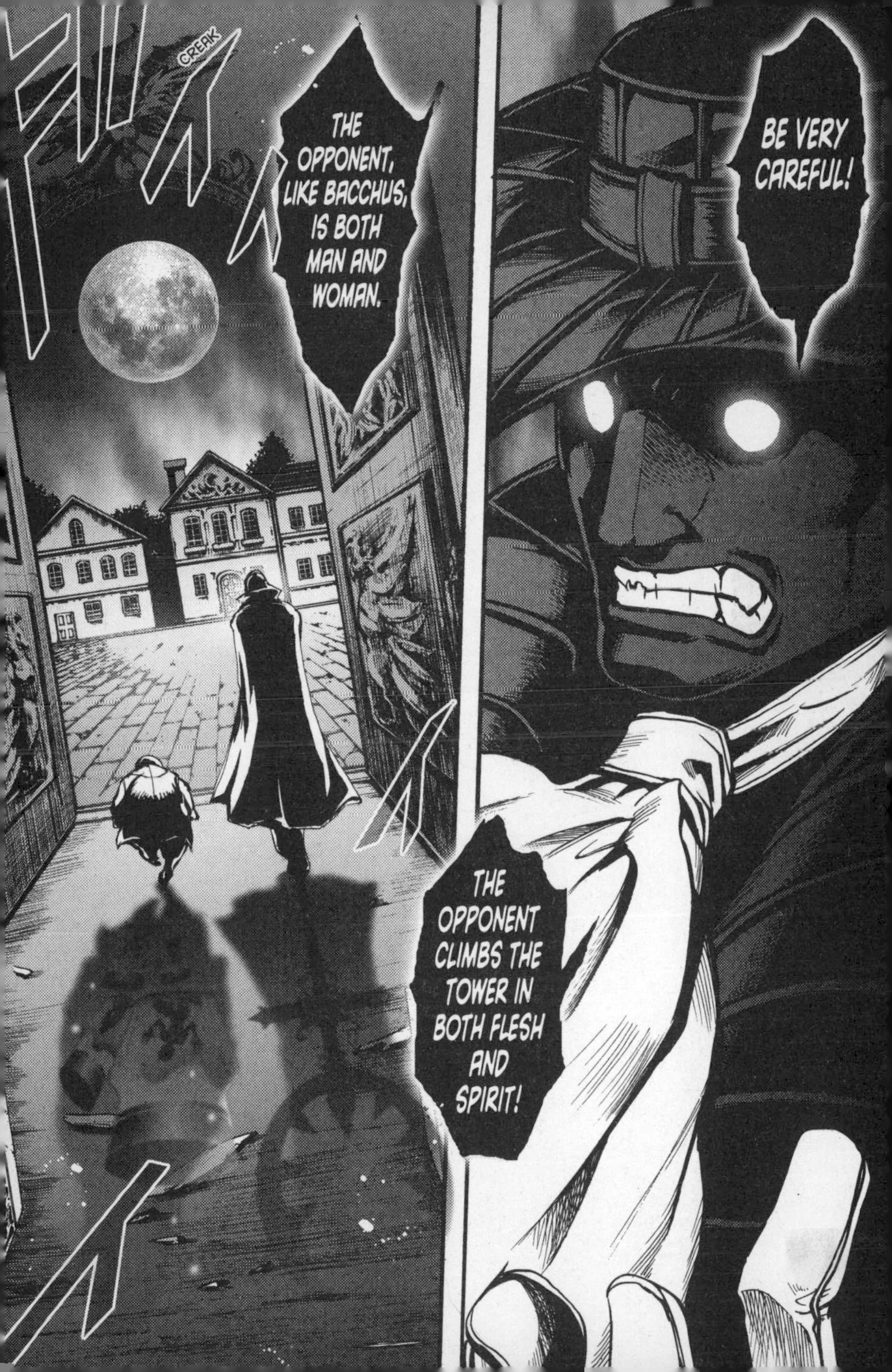
BE VERY CAREFUL!
THE OPPONENT CLIMBS THE TOWER IN BOTH FLESH AND SPIRIT!
CREAK
THE OPPONENT, LIKE BACCHUS, IS BOTH MAN AND WOMAN.

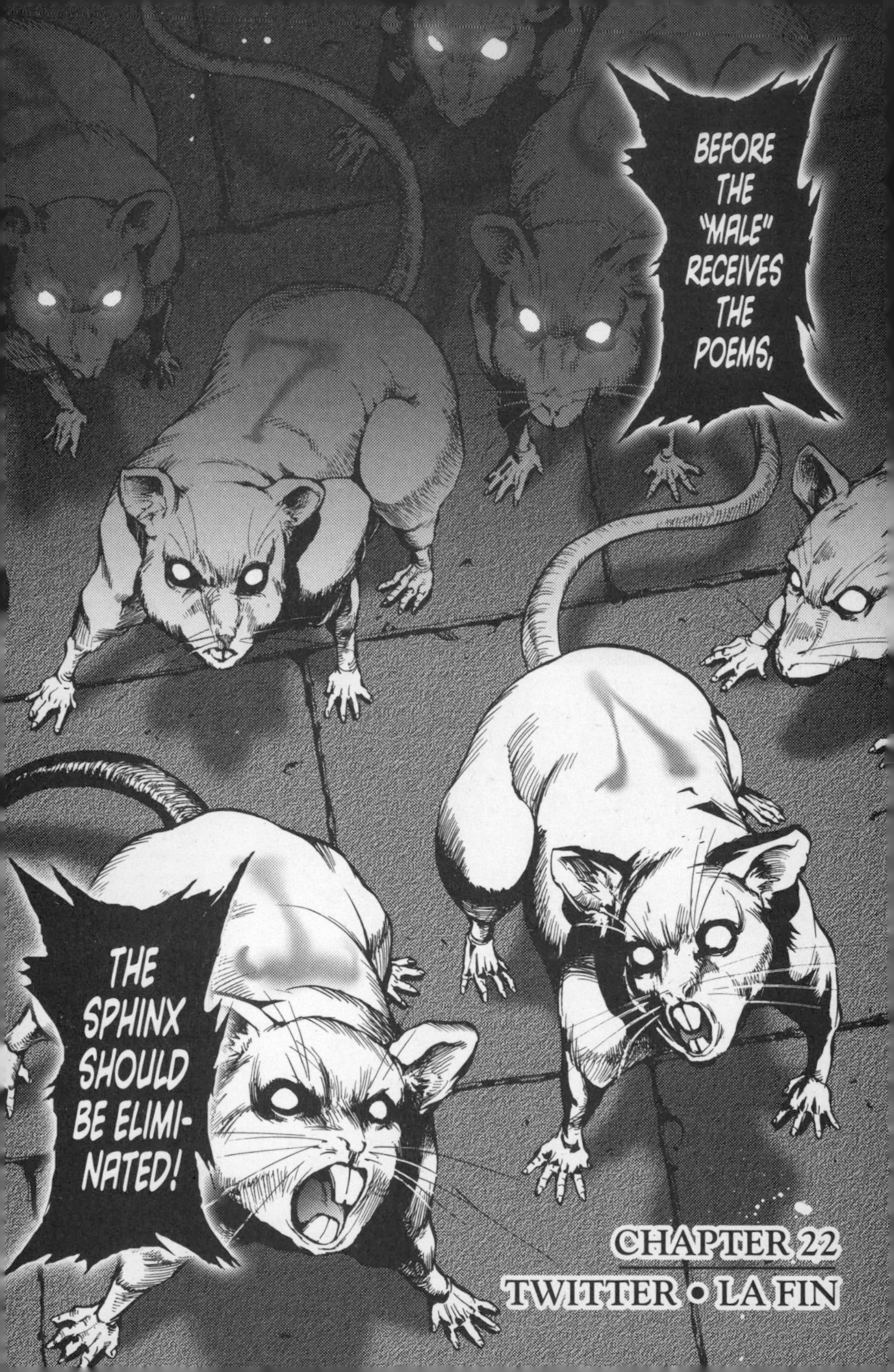
BEFORE THE "MALE" RECEIVES THE POEMS,
THE SPHINX SHOULD BE ELIMI-NATED!
CHAPTER 22
TWITTER • LA FIN

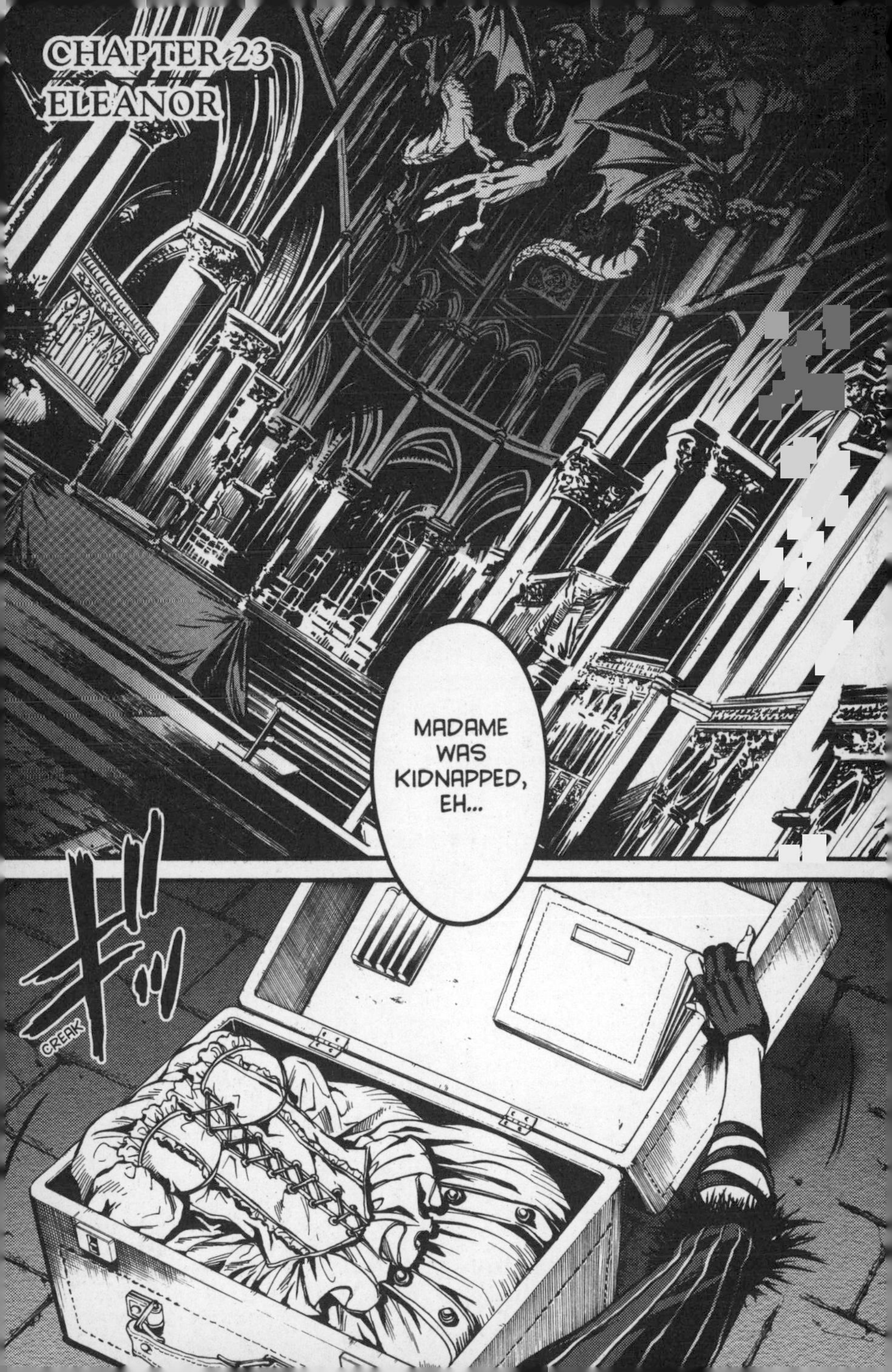

CHAPTER 23
ELEANOR
MADAME WAS KIDNAPPED, EH...
CREAK

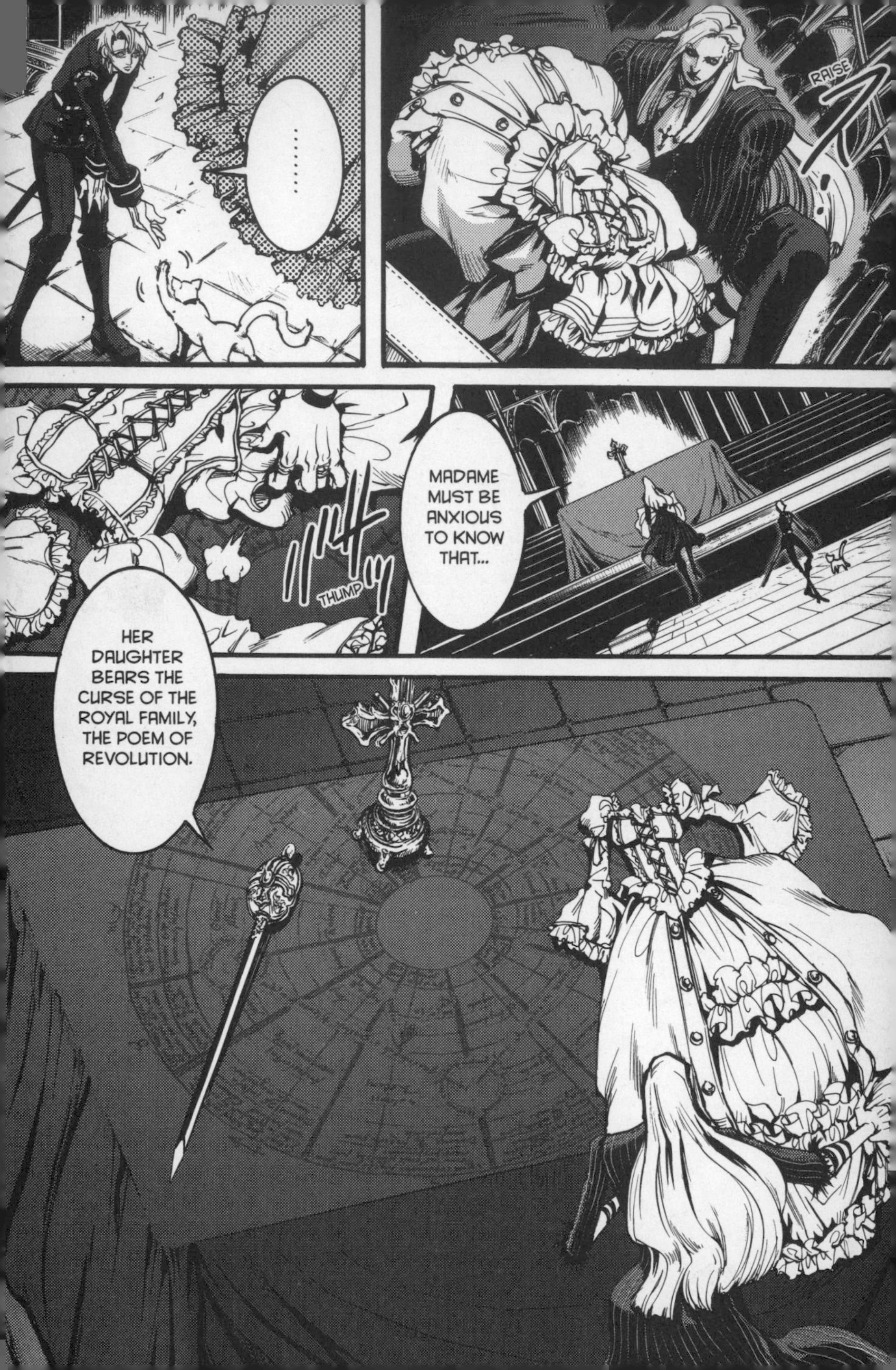
RAISE
......
MADAME MUST BE ANXIOUS TO KNOW THAT...
THUMP
HER DAUGHTER BEARS THE CURSE OF THE ROYAL FAMILY, THE POEM OF REVOLUTION.

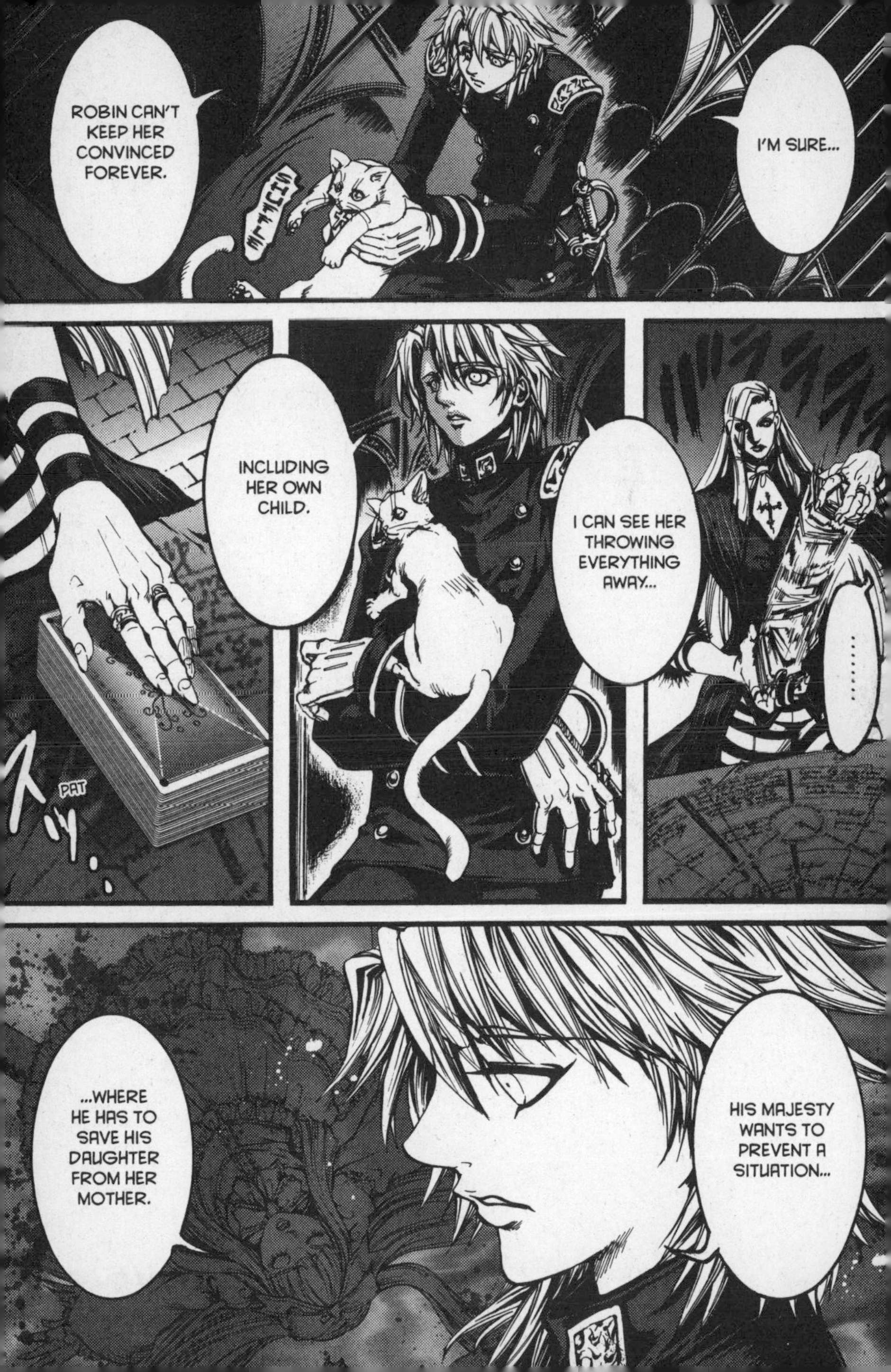
I'M SURE...
ROBIN CAN'T KEEP HER CONVINCED FOREVER.
SHUFFLE
......
I CAN SEE HER THROWING EVERYTHING AWAY...
INCLUDING HER OWN CHILD.
PAT
HIS MAJESTY WANTS TO PREVENT A SITUATION...
...WHERE HE HAS TO SAVE HIS DAUGHTER FROM HER MOTHER.

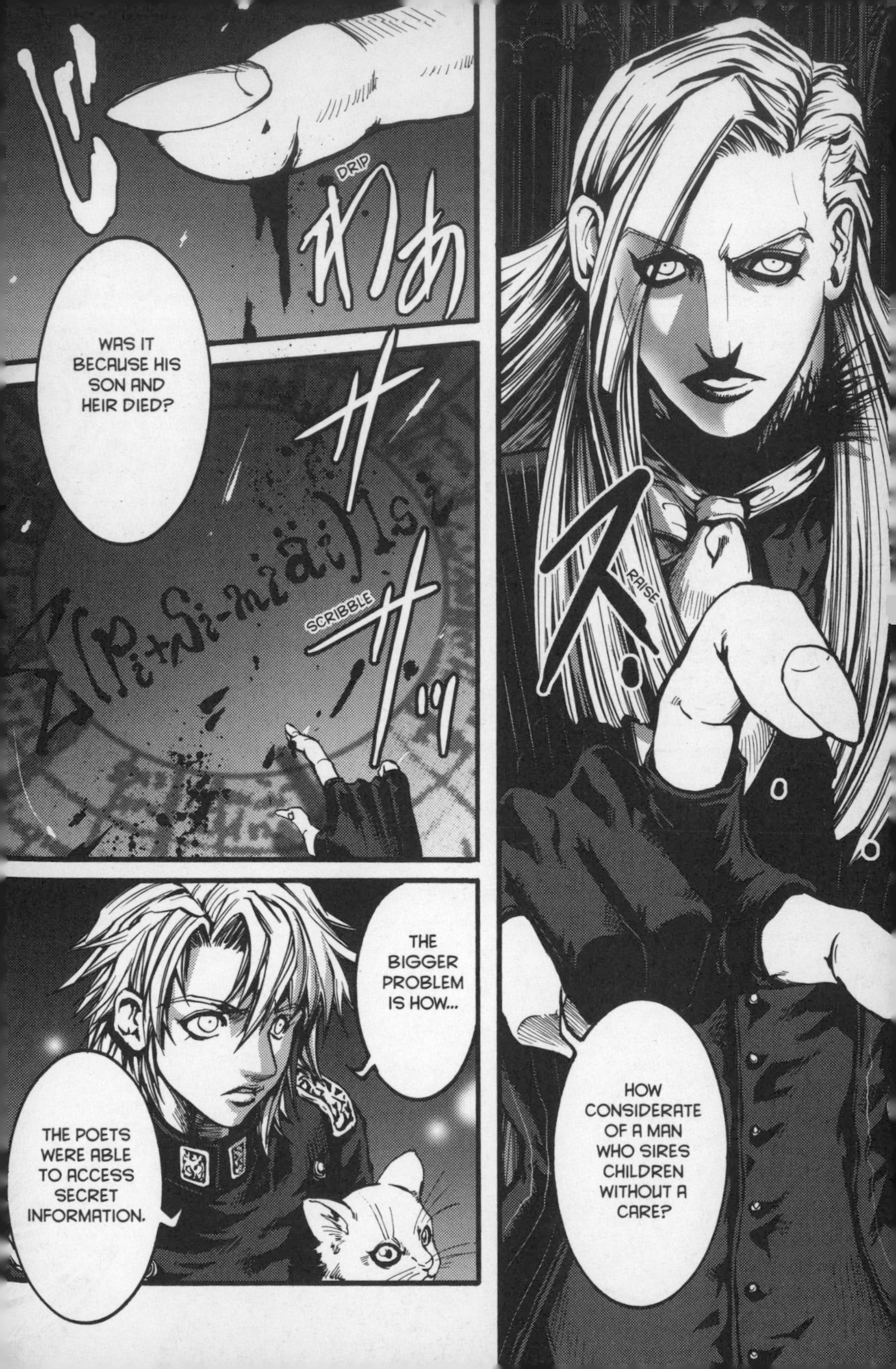
RAISE
HOW CONSIDERATE OF A MAN WHO SIRES CHILDREN WITHOUT A CARE?
DRIP
WAS IT BECAUSE HIS SON AND HEIR DIED?
SCRIBBLE
THE BIGGER PROBLEM IS HOW...
THE POETS WERE ABLE TO ACCESS SECRET INFORMATION.

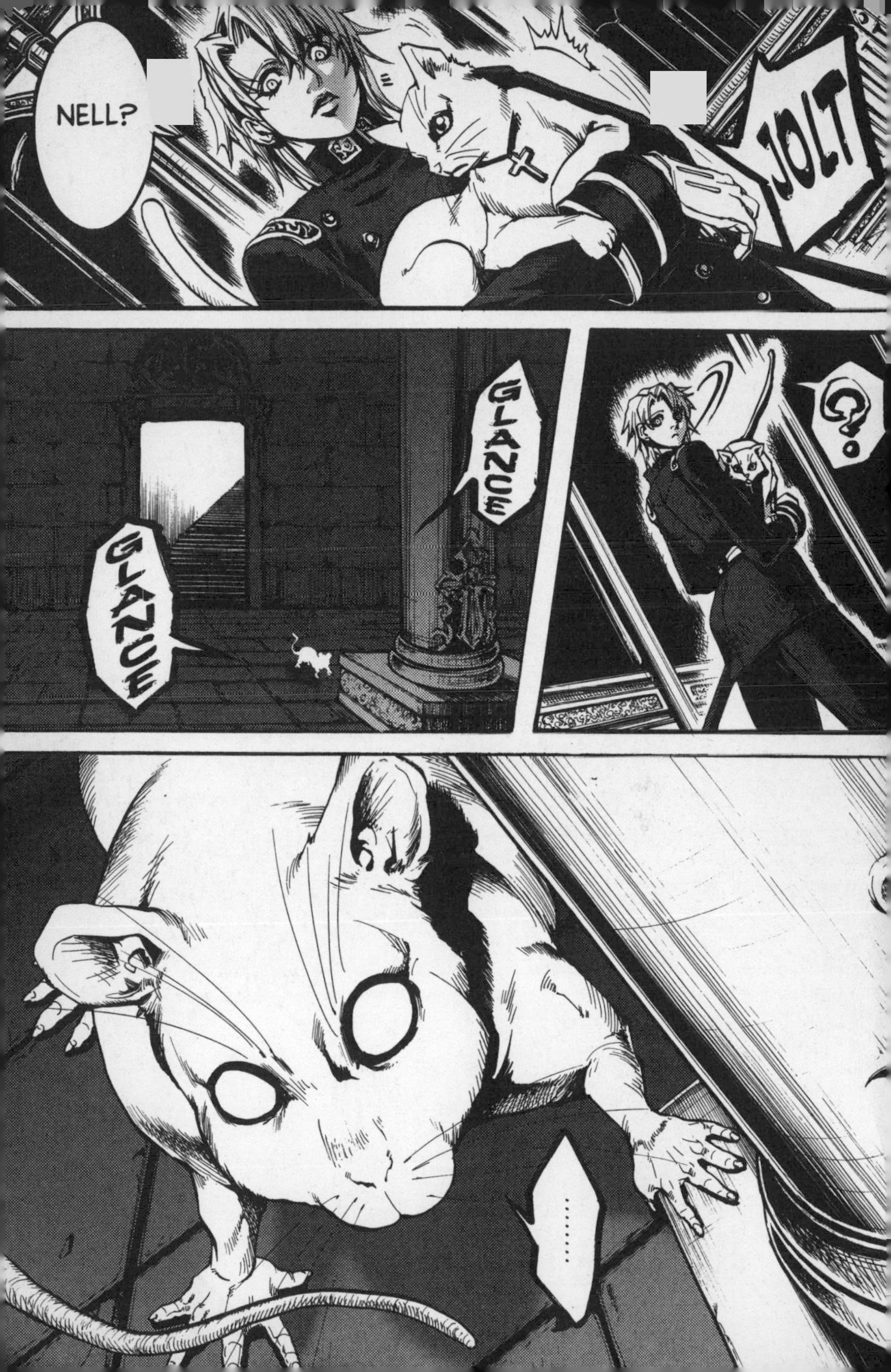
JOLT
NELL?
?
GLANCE
GLANCE
......

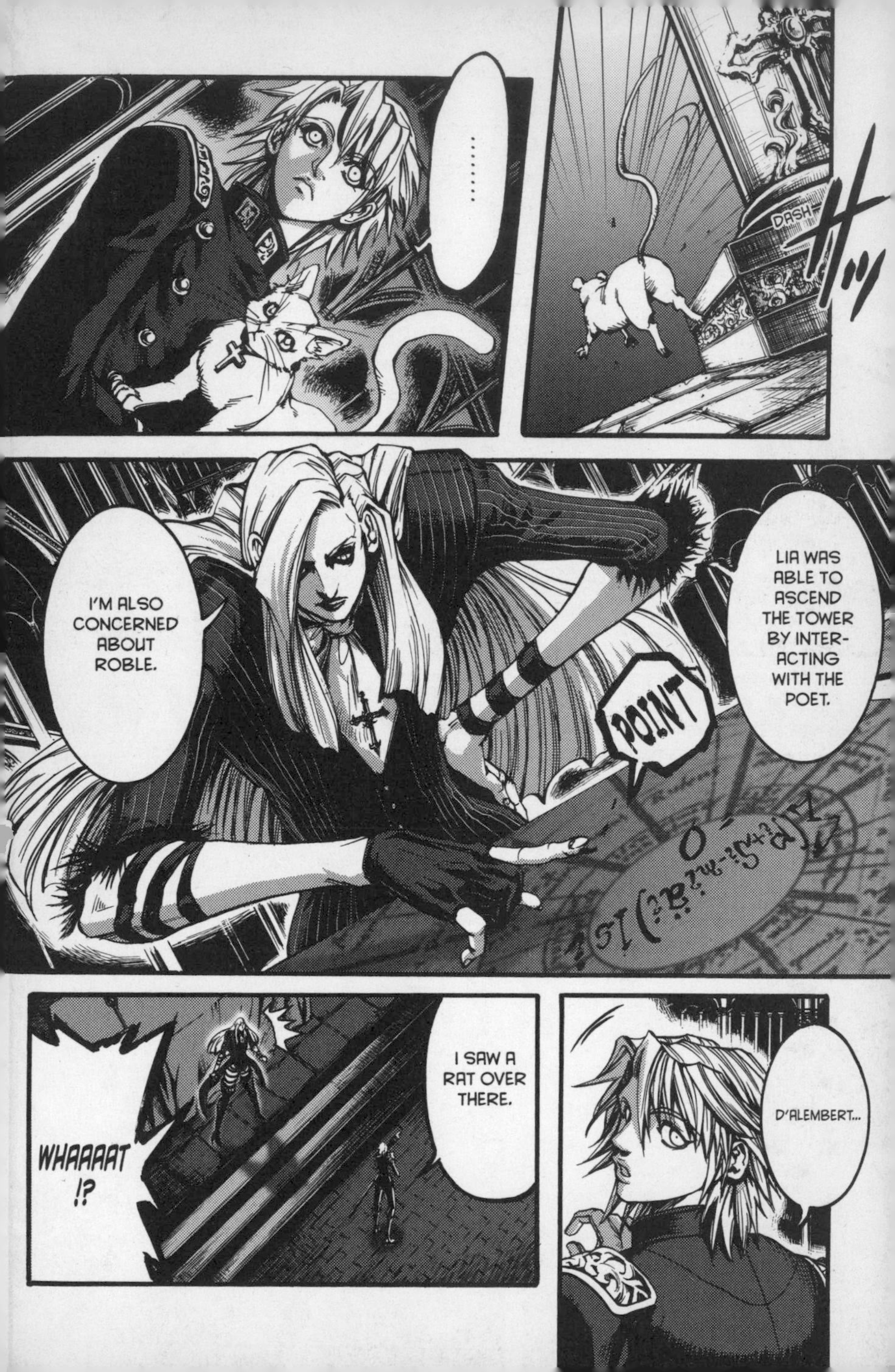
DASH
......
LIA WAS ABLE TO ASCEND THE TOWER BY INTER-ACTING WITH THE POET.
POINT
I'M ALSO CONCERNED ABOUT ROBLE.
D'ALEMBERT...
I SAW A RAT OVER THERE.
WHAAAAT !?

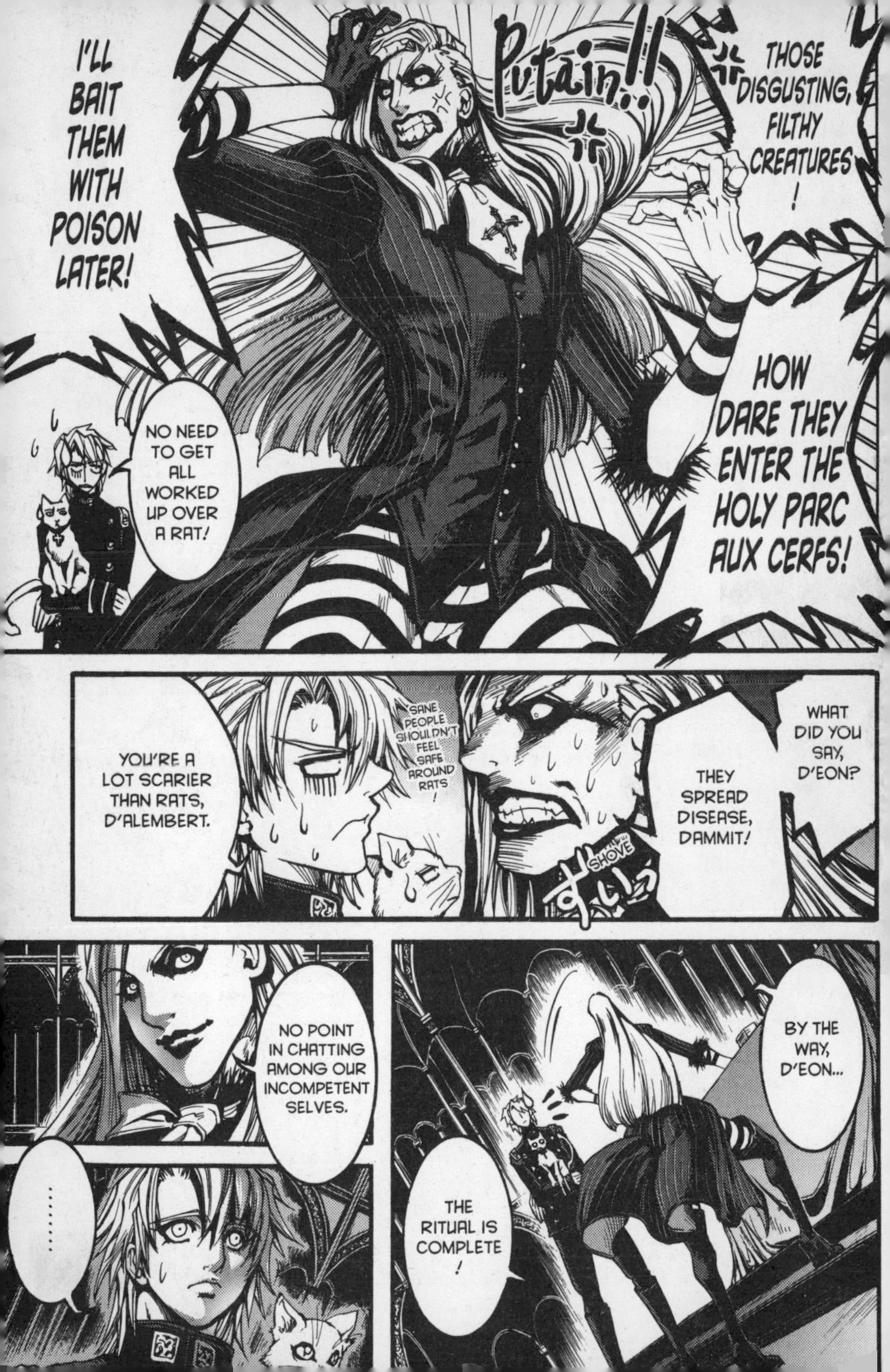
Putain!!
THOSE DISGUSTING, FILTHY CREATURES!
HOW DARE THEY ENTER THE HOLY PARC AUX CERFS!
I'LL BAIT THEM WITH POISON LATER!
NO NEED TO GET ALL WORKED UP OVER A RAT!
WHAT DID YOU SAY, D'EON?
THEY SPREAD DISEASE, DAMMIT!
SHOVE
すいっ
SANE PEOPLE SHOULDN'T FEEL SAFE AROUND RATS!
YOU'RE A LOT SCARIER THAN RATS, D'ALEMBERT.
BY THE WAY, D'EON...
THE RITUAL IS COMPLETE!
NO POINT IN CHATTING AMONG OUR INCOMPETENT SELVES.
......

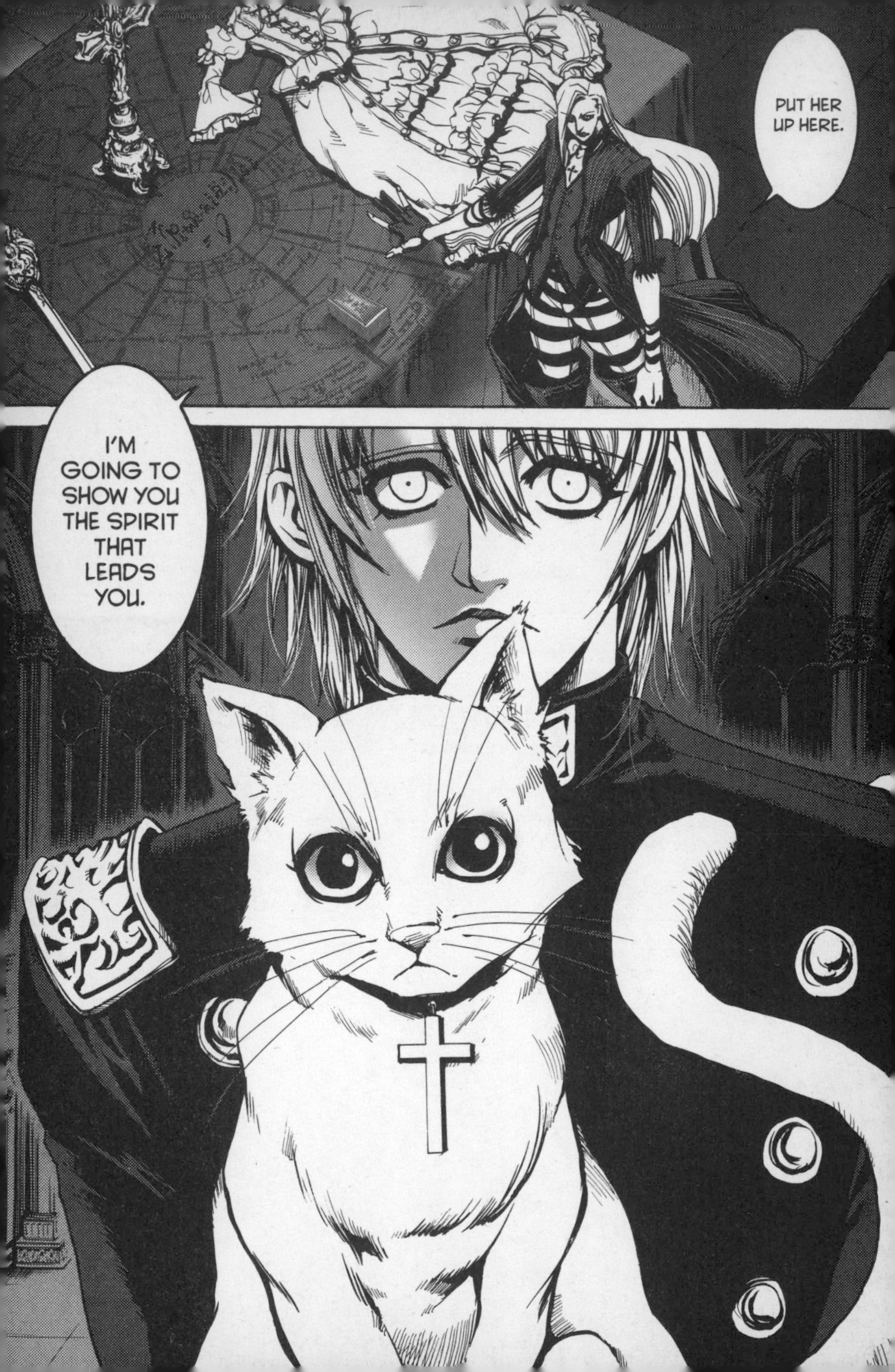
PUT HER UP HERE.
I'M GOING TO SHOW YOU THE SPIRIT THAT LEADS YOU.

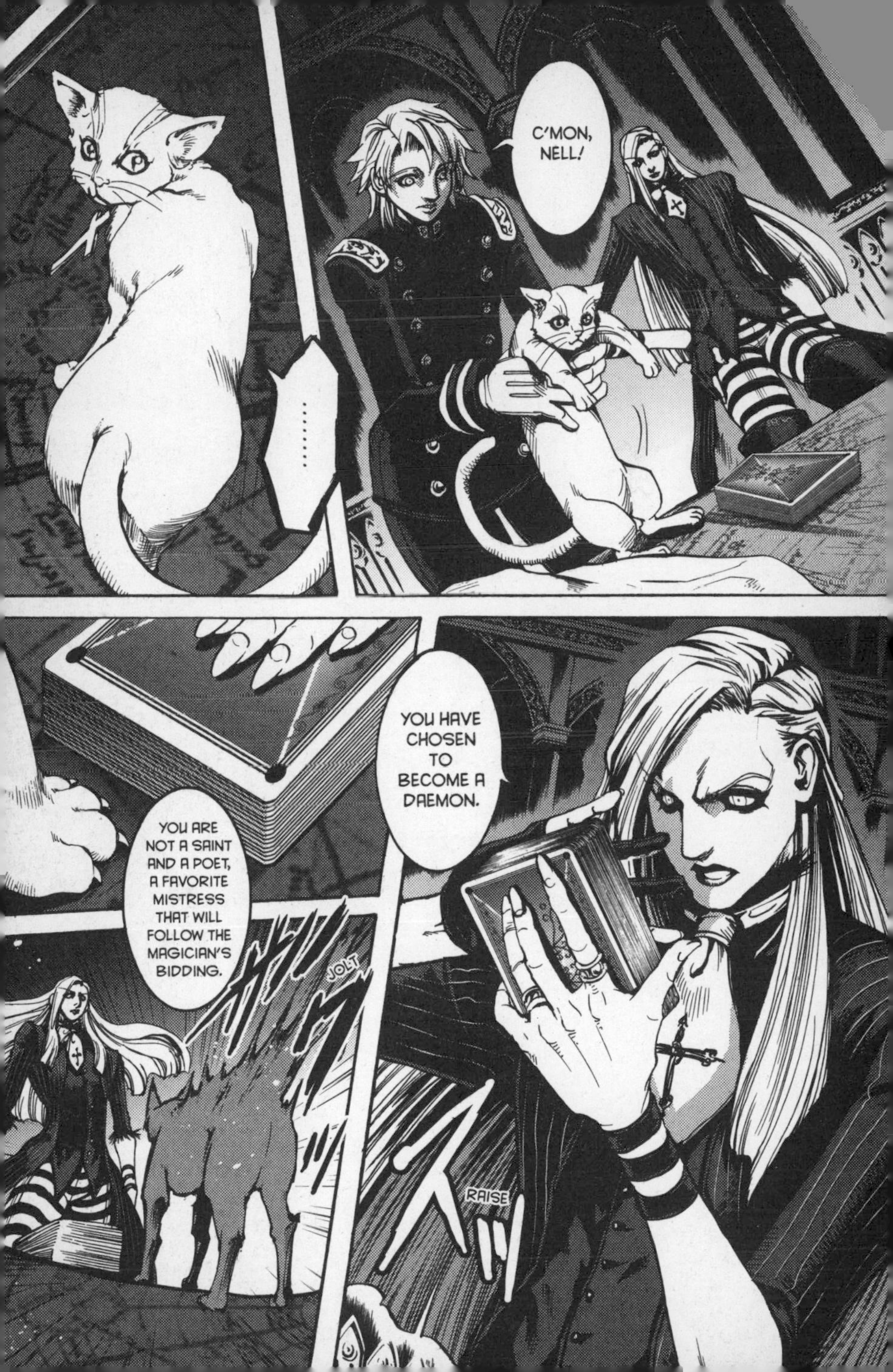
C'MON, NELL!
......
RAISE
YOU HAVE CHOSEN TO BECOME A DAEMON.
YOU ARE NOT A SAINT AND A POET, A FAVORITE MISTRESS THAT WILL FOLLOW THE MAGICIAN'S BIDDING.
JOLT

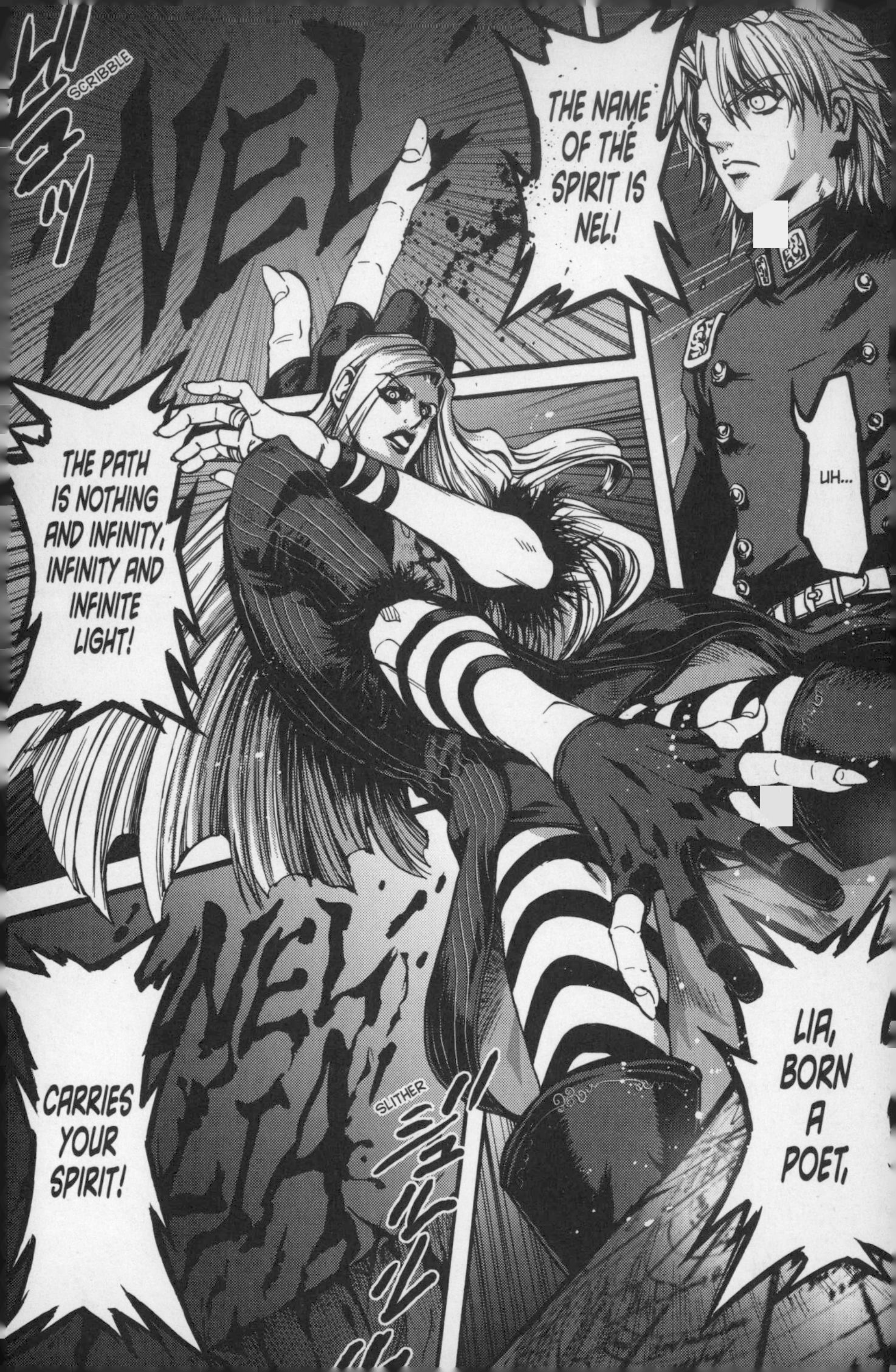
THE NAME OF THE SPIRIT IS NEL!
NEL!
SCRIBBLE
UH...
THE PATH IS NOTHING AND INFINITY, INFINITY AND INFINITE LIGHT!
LIA, BORN A POET,
SLITHER
NEL!
CARRIES YOUR SPIRIT!

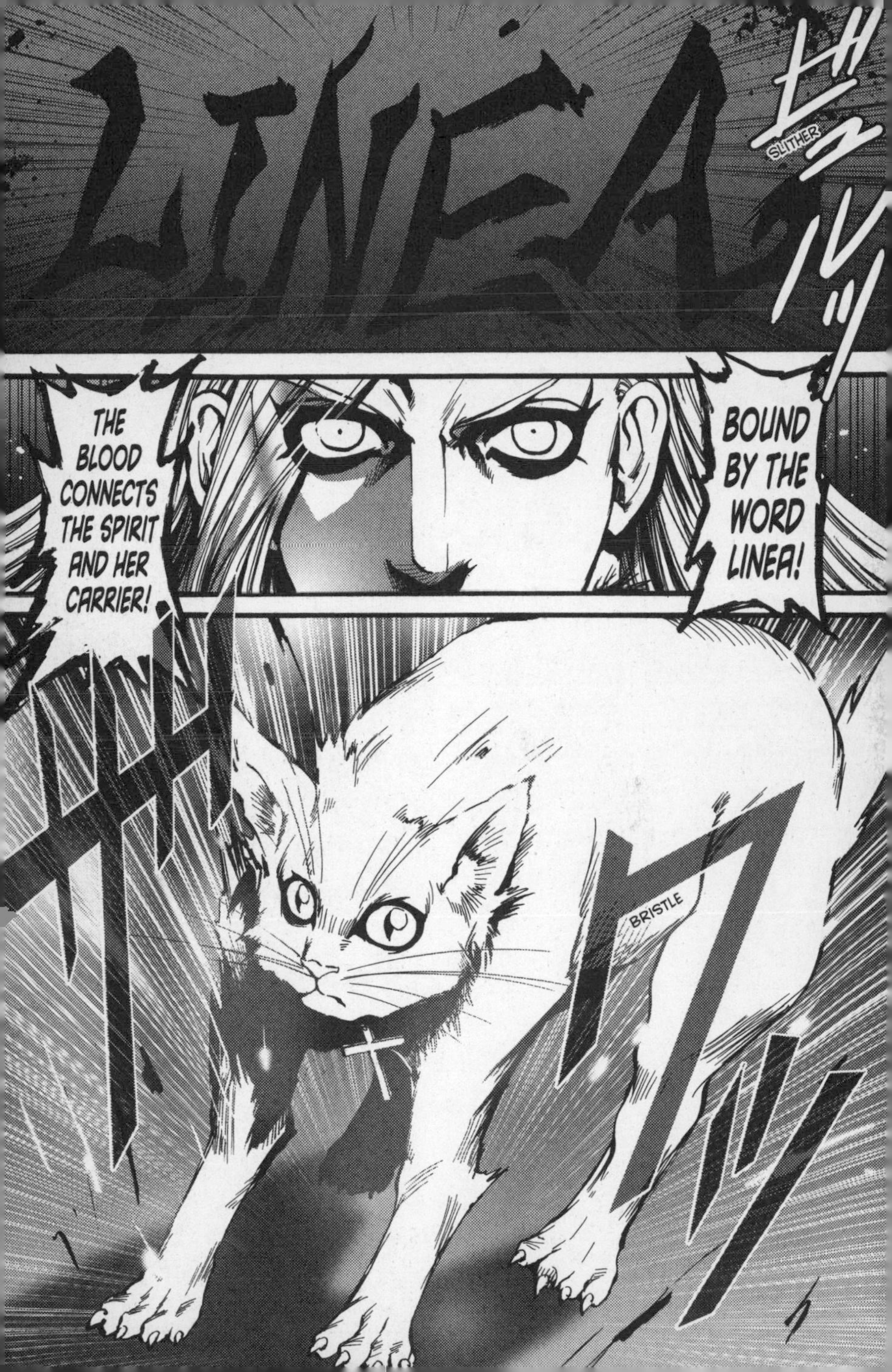
SLITHER
LINEA
BOUND BY THE WORD LINEA!
THE BLOOD CONNECTS THE SPIRIT AND HER CARRIER!
BRISTLE

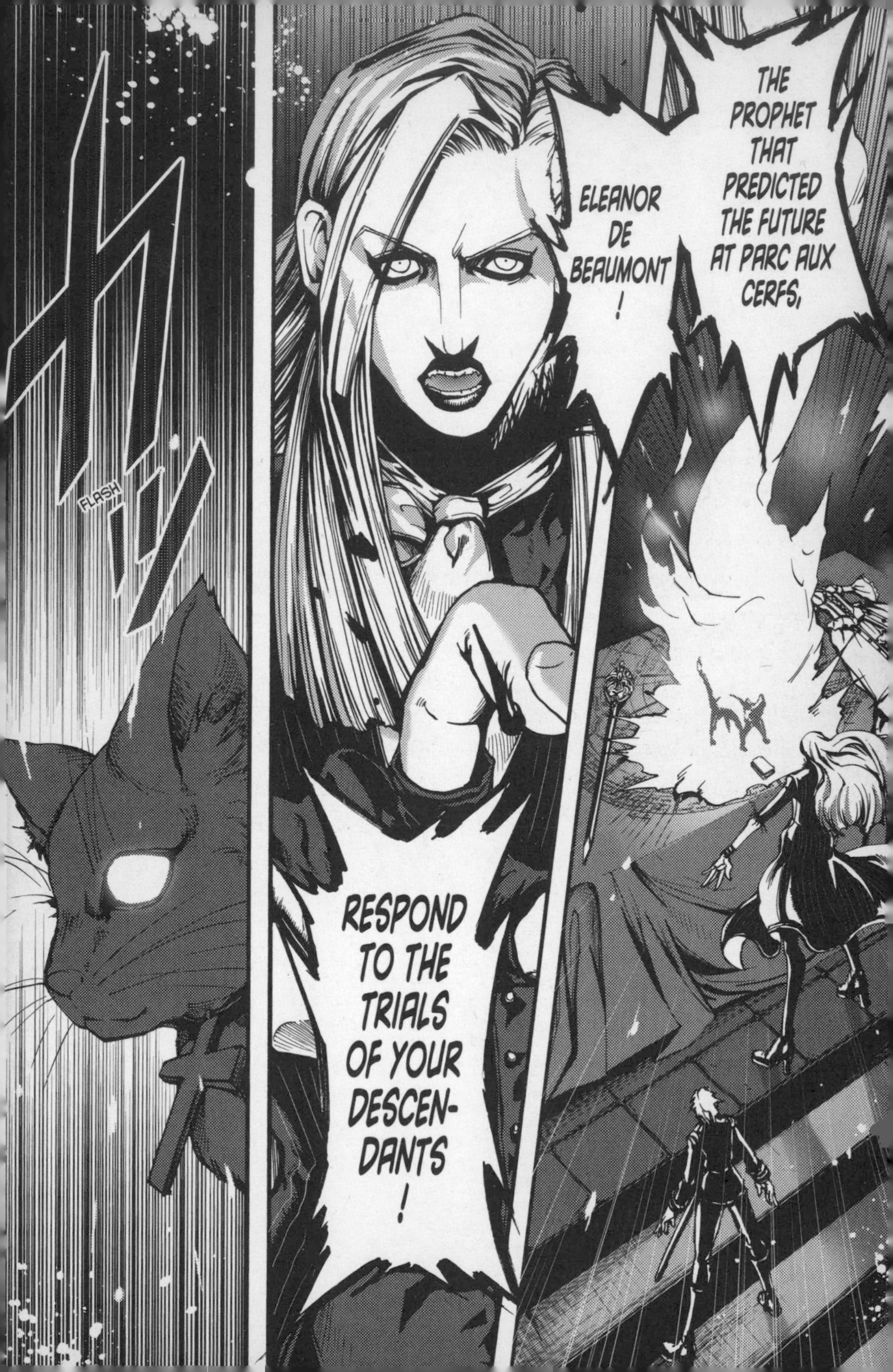
THE PROPHET THAT PREDICTED THE FUTURE AT PARC AUX CERFS,
ELEANOR DE BEAUMONT!
RESPOND TO THE TRIALS OF YOUR DESCEN-DANTS!
FLASH

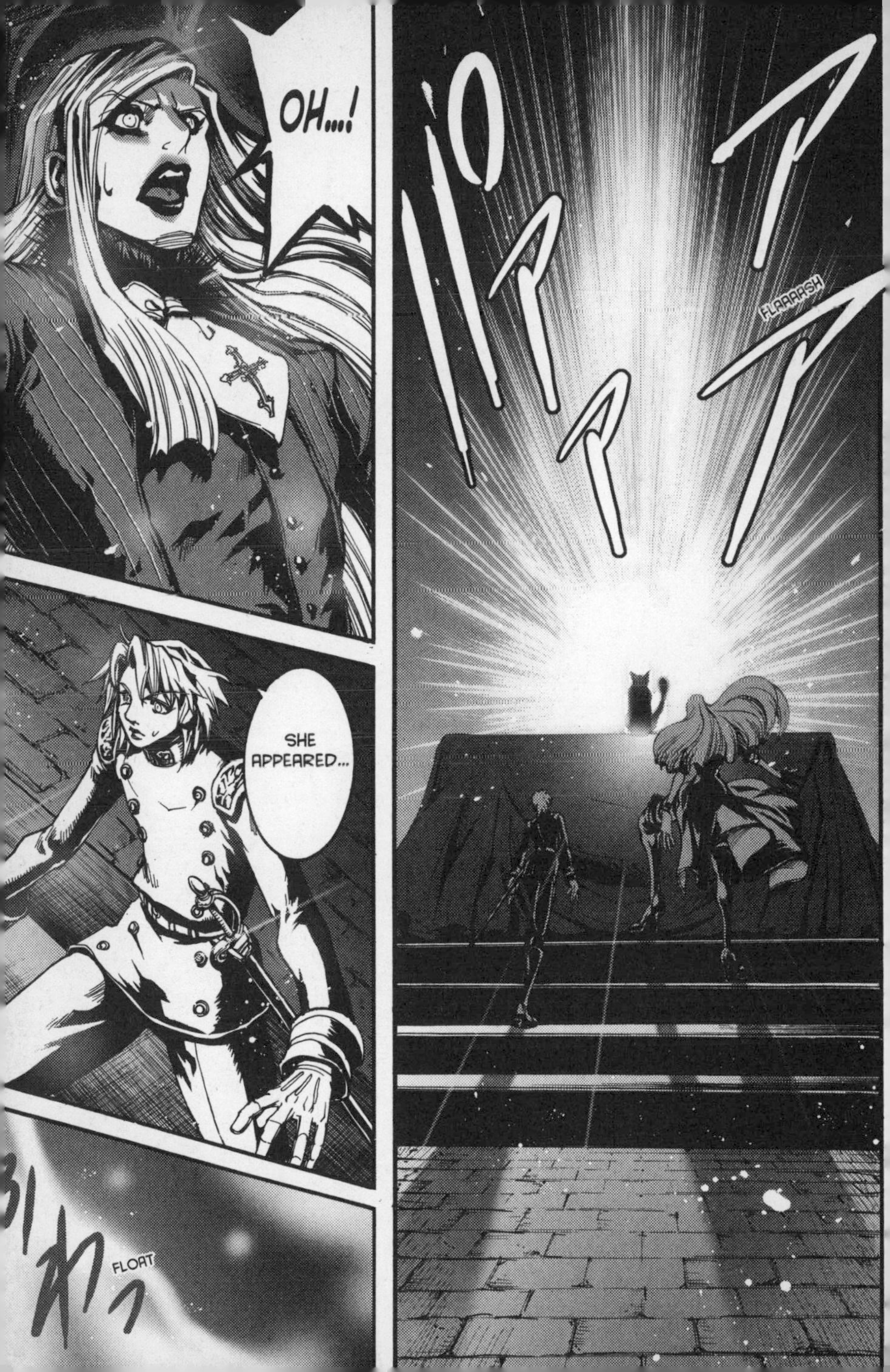
FLAAAASH
OH...!
SHE APPEARED...
FLOAT

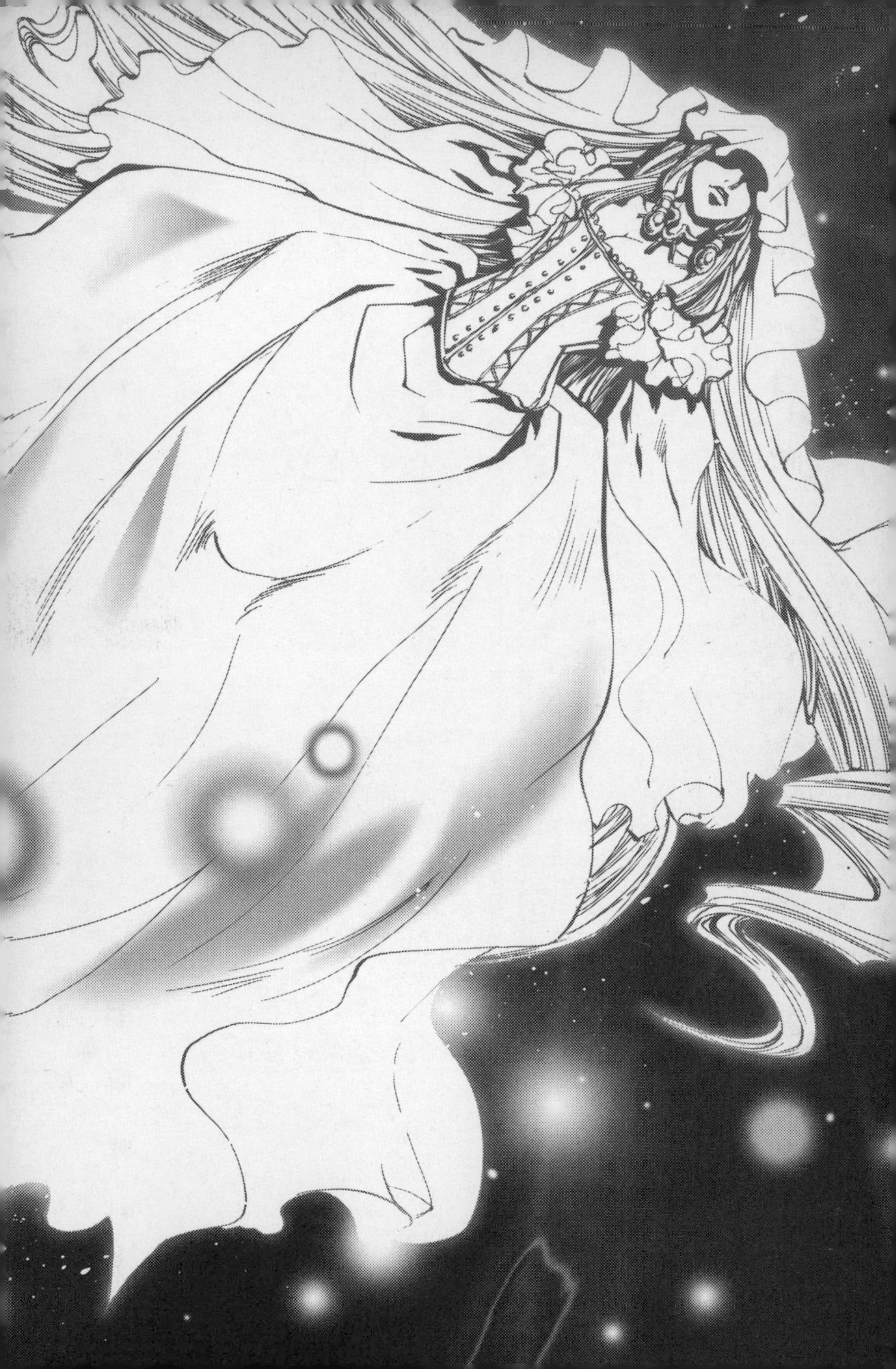

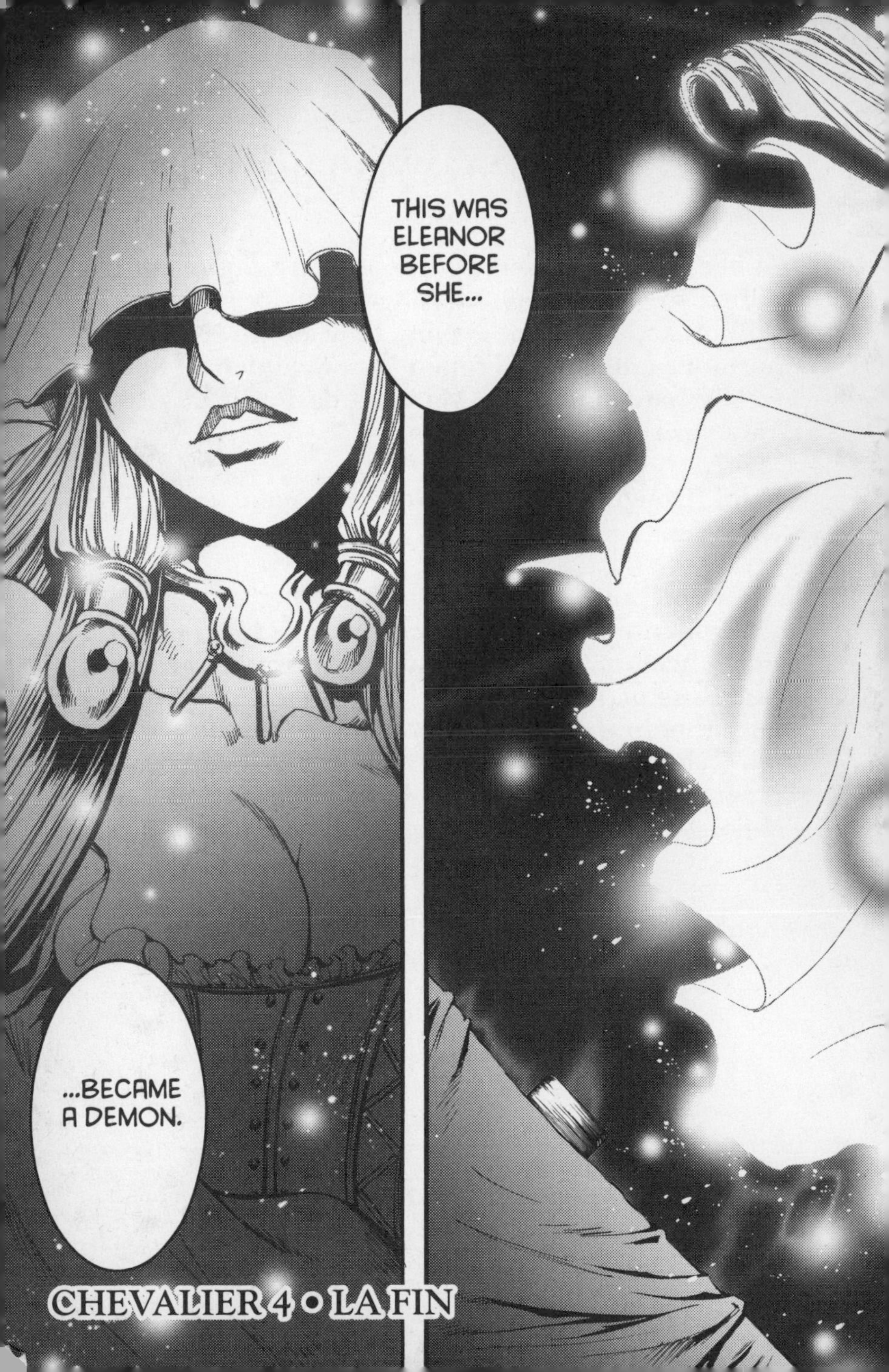
THIS WAS ELEANOR BEFORE SHE...
...BECAME A DEMON.

CHEVALIER 4 • LA FIN

IN THE BEGINNING WAS THE WORD...

It's been rather quick! We're already done with volume 4! We've been chasing the daily activities of d'Eon and Lia while having to wade through an enormous amount of French historical data. I had a really hard time with Madame de Pompadour's character.

I think Douglas and Saint-Germain make a pretty good team.

The anime and the novels are slowing down for the moment, but the manga version is just beginning to heat up! To me, the story's a cross between "The Rose of Versailles" and "Masked Rider." I'm really thankful that Ms. Yumeji accompanies my high-flying story with such detailed illustrations. I'd like to keep raising the bar for quality! It's a challenge, but I'd like to keep pushing forward!!

Thank you for your support!!

Tou Ubutaka

CHEVALIER MANGA PRODUCTION SITE

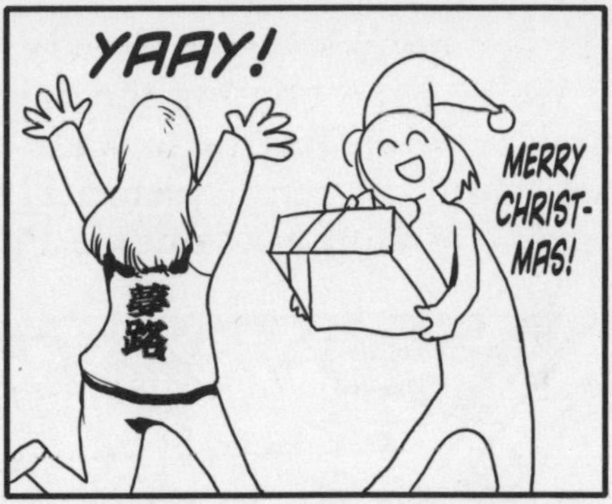
MERRY CHRIST-MAS!
YAAY!

MY CG ASSISTANT GAVE ME AN EARLY XMAS GIFT WHEN WE WERE REALLY BUSY. YAY! IT'S A BIG BOX! MERRY CHRISTMAS!!

WELL, I WAS EXCITED OVER NOTHING.

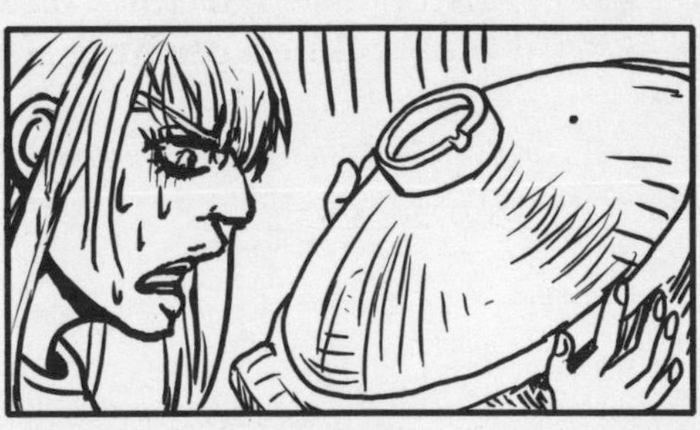

THE GIFT WAS A HUGE CLAY POT.
WHY?

SAYING THANK YOU SINCERELY WAS A GRIM AFFAIR.

KIRIKO YUMEJI

Translation Notes

Though *Le Chevalier d'Eon* was created by a Japanese artist and writer, it is set in eighteenth-century France, and its unique mythology is made up of various elements of Western languages, history, philosophy, and theology. Understanding these references will enrich your reading experience. Here are notes on some of the allusions to Western culture you'll find in *Le Chevalier d'Eon*.

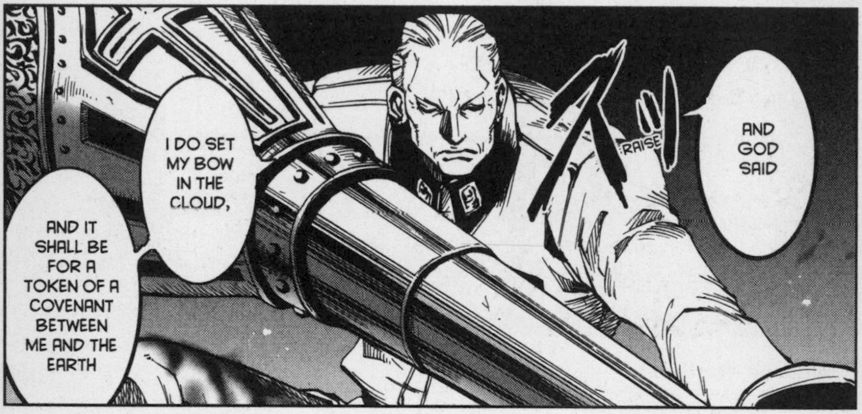
AND GOD SAID
RAISE
I DO SET MY BOW IN THE CLOUD,
AND IT SHALL BE FOR A TOKEN OF A COVENANT BETWEEN ME AND THE EARTH

And God said..., *page 18*

On the next two pages, Douglas is reciting Genesis 9:13–16, from the King James version. These lines are the words of God to Noah and his sons after the Great Flood.

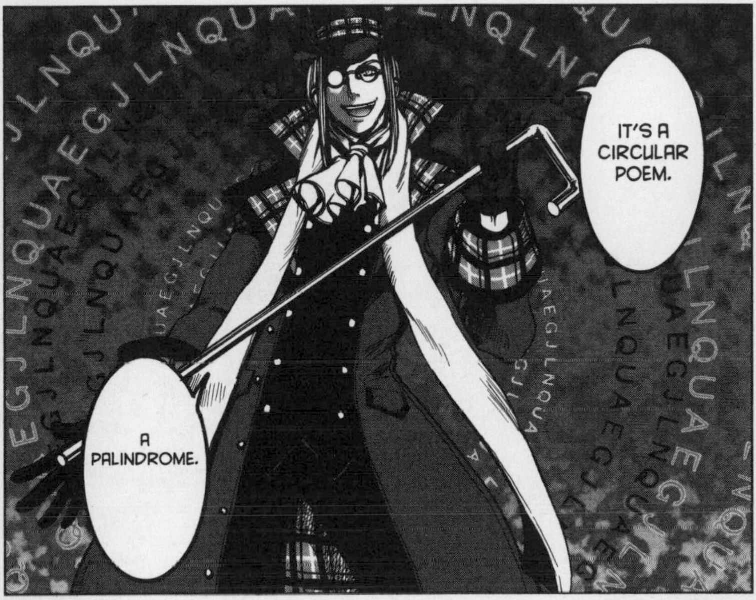
IT'S A CIRCULAR POEM.
A PALINDROME.

Palindromes, *page 59*

The twins sometimes refer to the magical palindromes they've created as "circular poems," and that's a good description of what a palindrome is: It's a word, phrase, or set of numbers that reads the same way forward as it does backward—though spacing and punctuation may be altered to make the phrase work both ways. Some well-known palindromes in English are "Was it a rat I saw?" and "A man, a plan, a canal: Panama!" The twins' palindromes are not original creations; they're all commonly known French palindromes.

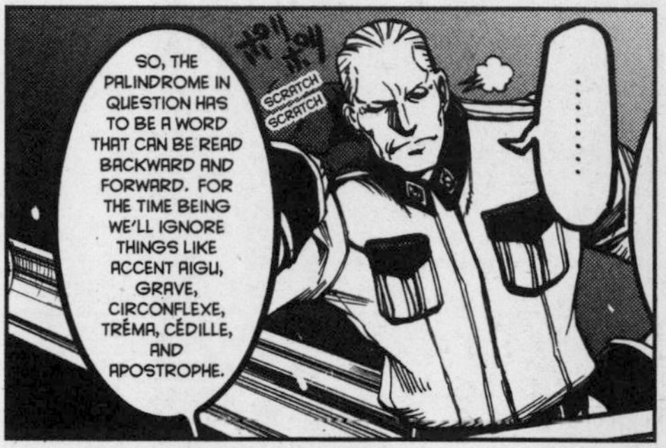
SO, THE PALINDROME IN QUESTION HAS TO BE A WORD THAT CAN BE READ BACKWARD AND FORWARD. FOR THE TIME BEING WE'LL IGNORE THINGS LIKE ACCENT AIGU, GRAVE, CIRCONFLEXE, TRÉMA, CÉDILLE, AND APOSTROPHE.
SCRATCH SCRATCH
....

Accents aigu, grave, etc., *page 62*

Comte Saint-Germain, in his lecture on palindromes, lists all the accents or diacritical marks commonly used in French to clarify pronunciation. In order to make the palindromes work, it's important to ignore the accent marks, since they would alter the pronunciation of the words and render the phrases unworkable in one direction.

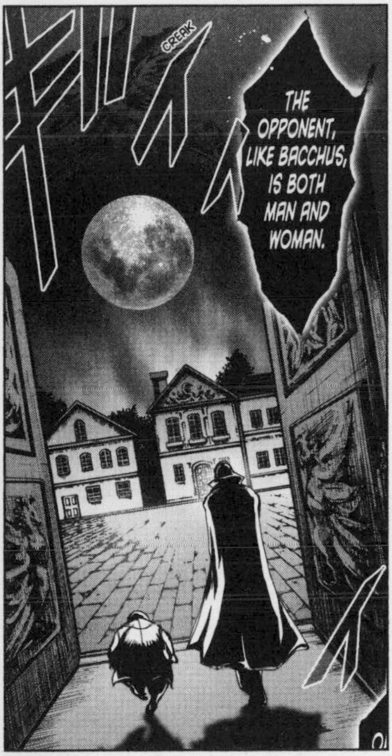
CREAK
THE OPPONENT, LIKE BACCHUS, IS BOTH MAN AND WOMAN.

Bacchus, *page 173*

Bacchus is the Roman name of the Greek god Dionysus. The god of wine and theater—also associated with the excesses, passion, and intoxication brought on by drink and art, and therefore a suitable hero for Roble—Bacchus was also often described as androgynous.

PREVIEW OF VOLUME 5 OF

Le Chevalier d'Eon

We are pleased to present you with a preview
of volume 5. Please check our website
(www.delreymanga.com) to see when this
volume will be available in English. For now
you'll have to make do with the Japanese!

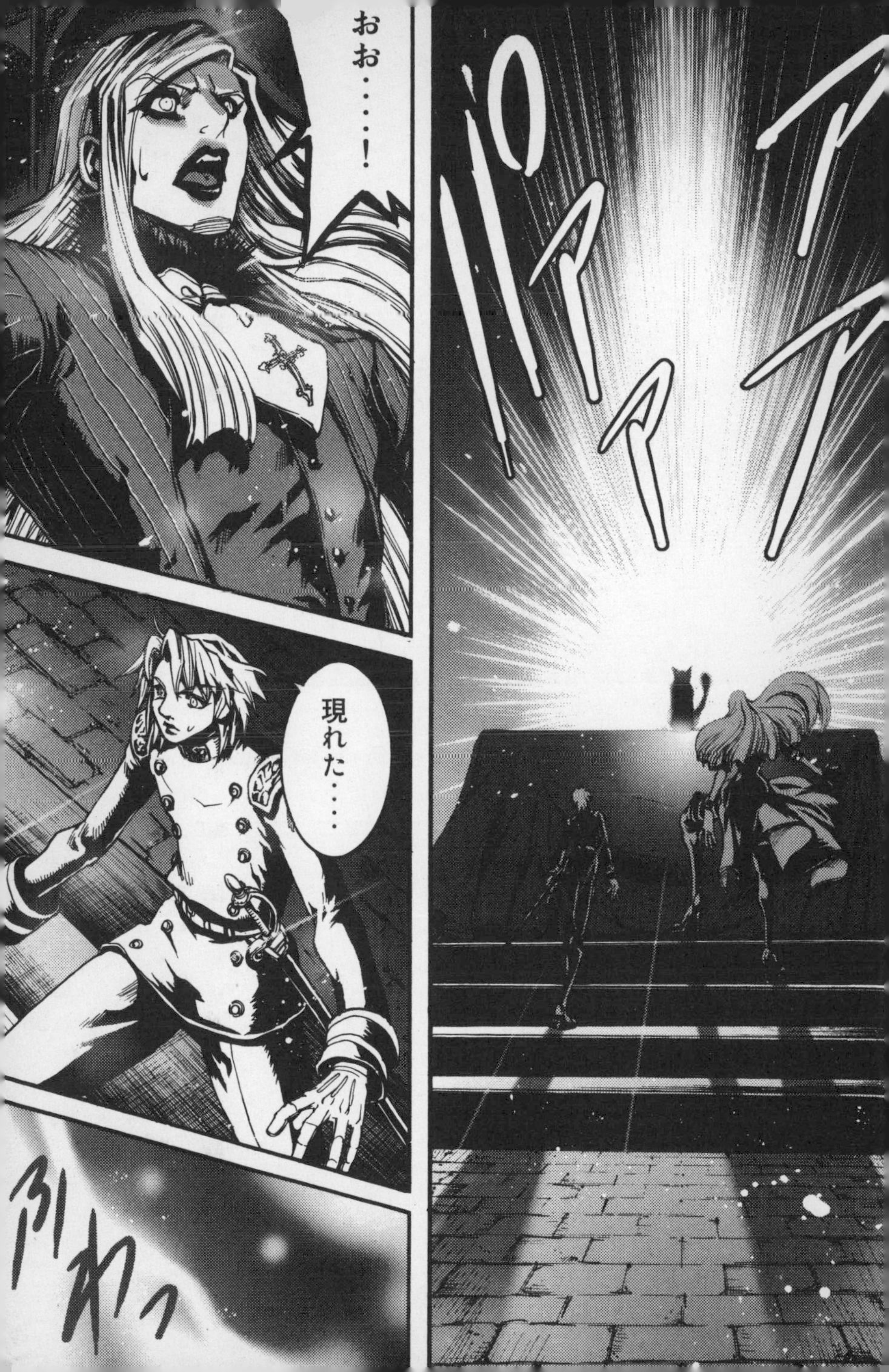
パアアアア
おお……!
現れた……
ふわっ

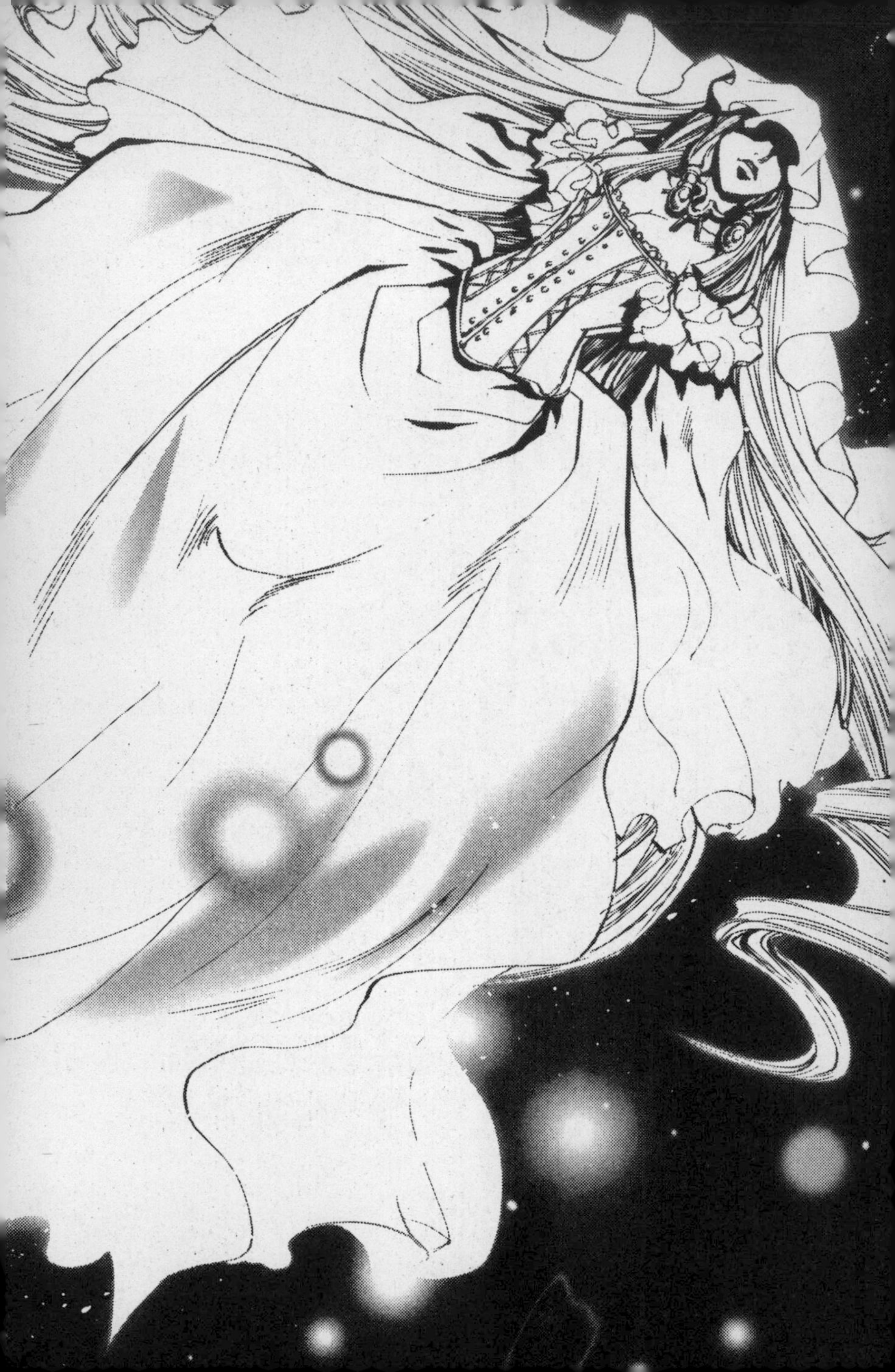

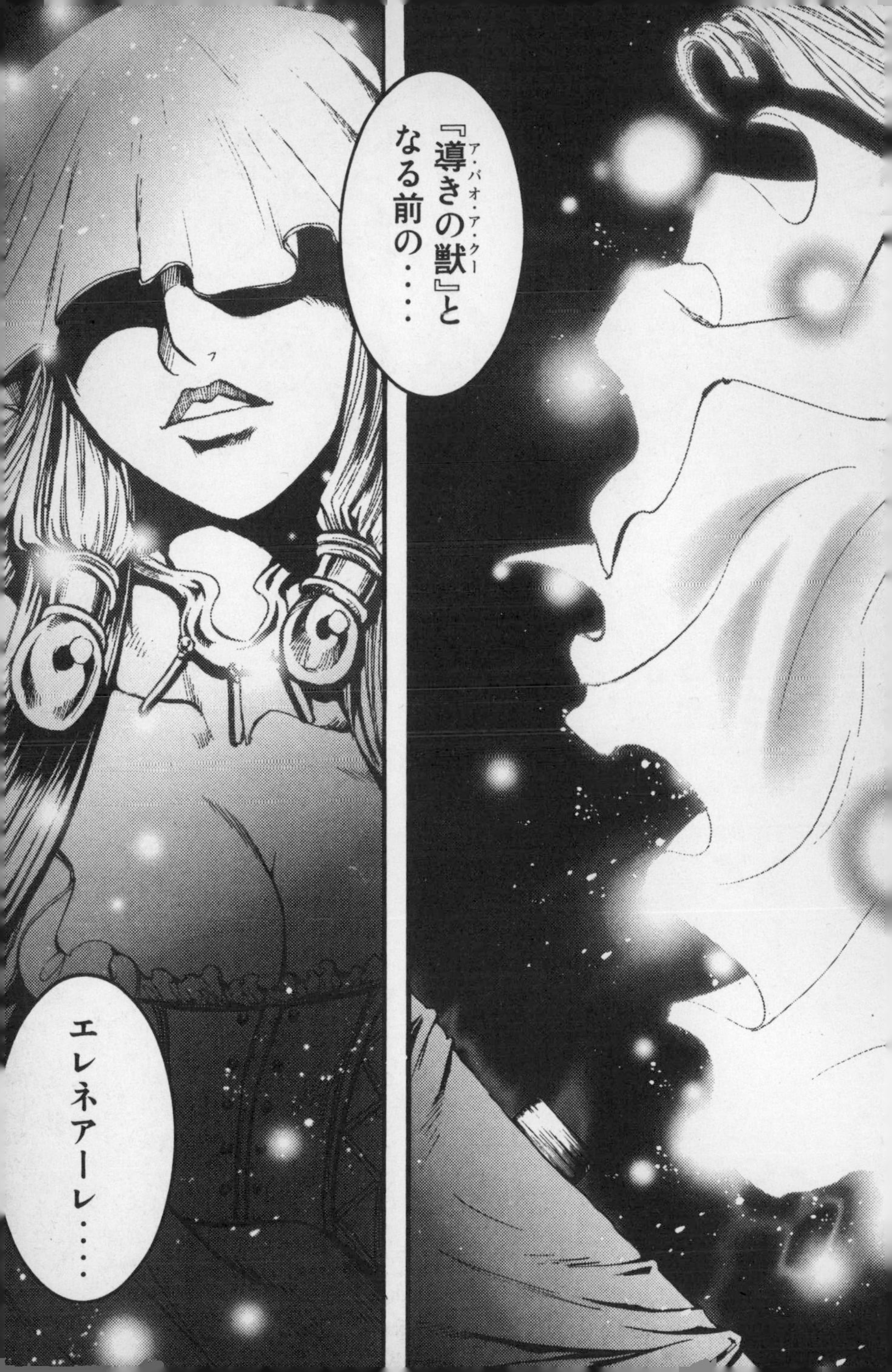
『導きの獣（ア・バオ・ア・クー）』となる前の‥‥
エレネアーレ‥‥

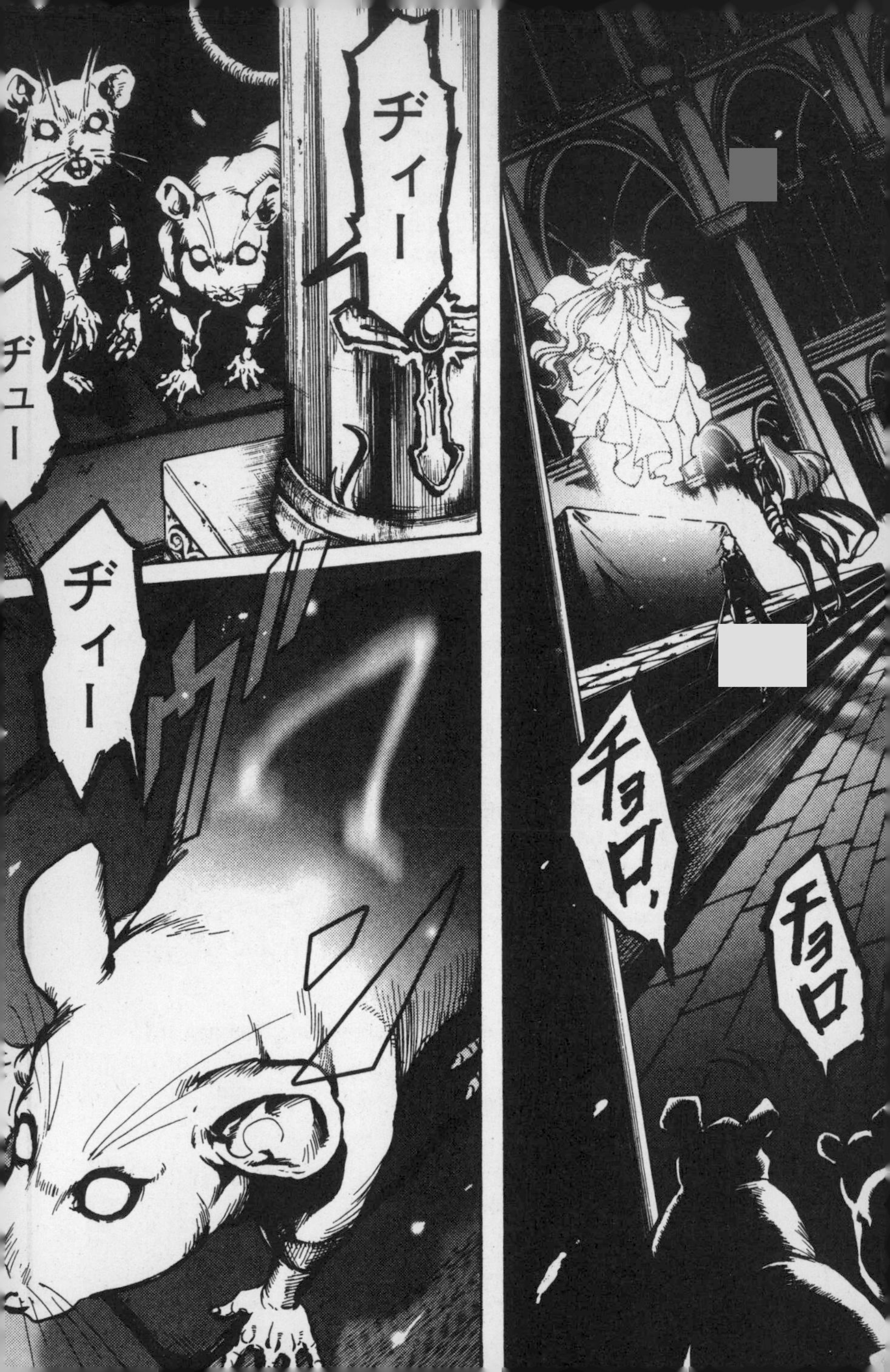
チョロ
チョロ、
ヂィー
ヂュー
ヂィー

Princess Resurrection

BY YASUNORI MITSUNAGA

HAVE A NICE AFTERLIFE!

Werewolves, demons, vampires, and monsters all thrive on fear, but now there's one new warrior who has them quaking in their supernatural boots: the beautiful Princess Hime, who fights the forces of evil with a chainsaw and a smile.

Not only does she look great in a tiara, she has magical powers that allow her to raise the dead. She's a girl on a mission, and with the help of her undead servant and a supercute robot, there's no creature of darkness she can't take down!

Special extras in each volume! Read them all!

BY HITOSHI IWAAKI

THEY DESCEND FROM THE SKIES.
THEY HAVE A HUNGER FOR HUMAN FLESH.

They are parasites and they are everywhere. They must take control of a human host to survive, and once they do, they can assume any deadly form they choose.

But they haven't taken over everyone! High school student Shin is resisting the invasion—battling for control of his own body against an alien parasite committed to thwart his plans to warn humanity of the horrors to come.

- *Now published in authentic right-to-left format!*

- *Featuring an all-new translation!*

Special extras in each volume! Read them all!

Tomare
STOP

YOU'RE GOING THE WRONG WAY!

MANGA IS A COMPLETELY DIFFERENT TYPE OF READING EXPERIENCE.

TO START AT THE *BEGINNING*, GO TO THE *END*!

That's Right!

AUTHENTIC MANGA IS READ THE TRADITIONAL JAPANESE WAY—FROM RIGHT TO LEFT, EXACTLY THE OPPOSITE OF HOW AMERICAN BOOKS ARE READ. IT'S EASY TO FOLLOW: JUST GO TO THE OTHER END OF THE BOOK, AND READ EACH PAGE —AND EACH PANEL—FROM RIGHT SIDE TO LEFT SIDE, STARTING AT THE TOP RIGHT. NOW YOU'RE EXPERIENCING MANGA AS IT WAS MEANT TO BE.